PARTICIPATING IN NATURE

THOMAS J. ELPEL'S FIELD GUIDE TO PRIMITIVE LIVING SKILLS

5th Edition

Dedicated to Grandma Josie. You taught me about edible and medicinal plants and brought me close to nature. You started me down the path I am on today.

HOPS Press
Hollowtop Outdoor Primitive School, LLC
12 Quartz Street
Pony, Montana 59747-0697
www.hollowtop.com

PARTICIPATING IN NATURE
THOMAS J. ELPEL'S FIELD GUIDE TO PRIMITIVE LIVING SKILLS
5TH EDITION

ISBN: 1-892784-12-2
Library of Congress Catalog Card Number: 99-60832

Participating in Nature: Thomas J. Elpel's Field Guide to Primitive Living Skills
Originally published as *Hollowtop Outdoor Primitive School Field Guide to Primitive Living Skills*.
Later published as *Thomas J. Elpel's Field Guide to Primitive Living Skills*

Copyright May 1992 by Thomas Elpel, HOPS (Comb Bound). 100 copies printed.
Revised and expanded Second Edition: February 1993 (Comb Bound). 200 copies printed.
Revised and expanded Third Edition: March 1995 (Comb Bound). 1,000 copies printed.
Revised Fourth Edition: February 1999. (First Paperback Edition). 3,000 copies printed.
Revised and expanded Fifth Edition: November 2002. 5,000 copies printed.

Photos were taken by the author or his family unless otherwise noted.
Illustrations of plants in this book were digitally adapted from these public domain sources:
-An Illustrated Flora of the Northern United States, Canada, and the British Possessions. Volumes I, II, III.
Nathaniel Lord Britton Ph.D. & Hon. Addison Brown. 1896, 1897, 1898.
-A Text-Book of Botany. John M. Coulter A.M. Ph.D. 1910.
-Flora of Montana Part II, W. E. Booth & J. C. Wright. Montana State University, Bozeman, Montana.
1959.

Legal Note: Life, including primitive living, is prone to occasional hazards. The author and publisher will
not be accountable for your accidents. Think safe.

All of the interior pages
of Participating in Nature are
printed with soy-based inks on
100% recyled paper, bleached
without chlorine. Remember to
recycle your papers!

HOPS Press
Hollowtop Outdoor Primitive School, LLC
12 Quartz Street
Pony, MT 59747-0697
www.hollowtop.com

The author on Hollowtop Peak.
Photo by Jack Fee.

Foreword

My high school art teacher, Ray Campeau, often told us that art is never finished. No matter how much you have worked on a piece you can always do something to make it better. You just have to choose a point to quit.

Writing is as much of an art as painting. Each time I sit down at the keyboard I write at my highest current skill level. I write using all the knowledge I have of my subject at the time, and I use the best of my present abilities to express my knowledge.

But the very next day my writing starts to become dated. Perhaps I learn some new skill, or I have a new insight on an old skill. Or maybe I just mature a little more and develop new skills for expressing myself.

This book is a painting that has been painted over many times. For continuity the chapters and skills are arranged in a sort of story form, as one day in a camping trip—from sunrise to sunset. Yet, the actual text has been written over and over again, with fragments of it dating back more than ten years. Each time I revise the book I add new skills and new dialogue.

Accuracy is important to me. I cannot print more copies of my old writing if I think I can do better than that today. Therefore, my writing is not finished until I am finished and underground. For economic reasons, I choose to publish before I am finished.

Thomas J. Elpel
Pony, Montana

$1.00 from every copy of this book sold is being donated to 3Rivers Park.

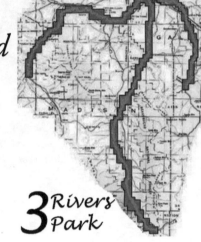

3Rivers Park

Canoeing, Rafting, Fishing, Hiking, Bicycling, Horseback Riding,
Hunting, Camping, Bird Watching, Wildlife Viewing
-A Place for People-

The scenic Three Rivers Watershed in southwest Montana consists of all land that drains into the Jefferson, Madison and Gallatin Rivers, forming the headwaters of the Missouri River. It is an exciting and beautiful place to live and work, naturally drawing in a steady stream of newcomers to the area. In fact, everyone seems to want a piece of this special place, as evidenced by the houses that pop up on every little hilltop with a view or in green meadows along the rivers. Unfortunately, there are also "No Trespassing" signs sprouting up across the landscap— blocking hunters, hikers and fishermen from tens of thousands of acres of private lands that used to be informally open to public use.

Our organization, 3Rivers Park, was **founded by author Thomas J. Elpel** to work with private land owners to increase public access along the rivers while preserving open space and productivity in the surrounding farms and ranches. The primary focus of our work is in finding creative ways to purchase recreational and open space easements from willing sellers. Recreational easements thus aquired are to be managed by 3Rivers Park for sustainable use by the public. For additional information about this undertaking, or to contribute towards the vision, please check out our website:

www.3riverspark.org

TABLE OF CONTENTS

SUNRISE

The sun is rising. Darkness is fading, star light diminishing. Light blue penetrating the eastern sky, a band along the horizon. Spreading westward. Birds starting to sing out, heralding the coming day. Last stars disappearing. The sky completely absorbed in blue. Stillness. Yesterday's noise pollution fallen in the night, stillness. The trilling sounds of a bird, backed with deeper bass as water falls, thumps, splatters, in between and around boulders in the stream, sounding out pure, clean, all of creation still, listening intently.

Silhouettes of the landscape once nearly hidden in night now becoming clearer. Mountains, trees, bushes. A faint glow on the horizon. Reddish orange. Spreading slowly, bigger. Now tingeing distant eastern clouds with red. Brighter. Objects taking on depth and color. My vision seeking farther into the darkness of the land, dim beneath a lighted sky. Horizon brighter. Clouds vibrant. Fire in the sky. More light. Deer grazing on the slope. Sun now touching the mountain peaks. Cold stone and banks of snow glowing reddish, Hollowtop peak standing rosy cheeked to the first rays of the morning sun. The deer moving through the sagebrush, calmly grazing. Clouds fading out. Light dropping off the mountains to the forests, tingeing the green with gold. Closer tree trunks becoming stained in red light, encompassed by golden green. The low light penetrates up the undersides of land and trees, pushing shadows from the normal points below to straight back and upward so they seem to entirely disappear, creating something of a shadowless land where light is everywhere, and nothing is hidden. The sun is rising. Now a bright fiery ball on the horizon. Clouds fading.

I wait, look, listen. The deer graze up the slope towards the forest. Red now fading completely. Bright, blue, wide open, the Big Sky.

This morning I am perched on a small hill, wrapped in my dusty wool blanket, sitting and leaning back against the trunk of Douglas fir tree. The breeze is cool and from the east. With the warming day the wind will soon switch and blow gently from the west. It feels good to be here.

The Tobacco Root Mountains with Hollowtop Peak on the right.

People are drawn to primitive living for many different reasons and to fulfill needs on many levels. On a physical level people often want to learn to become more proficient and self-sufficient in the wilderness. On an intellectual level people often come wanting to learn more about the ecosystem, or they want to learn about anthropology and primitive culture. Some come seeking a greater connection with the natural or supernatural world. Others come seeking something they can take home with them into contemporary life. For some that may be personal growth through challenge and accomplishment. For others it may be a philosophy about living to use in today's technological world. To me, *primitive living is a metaphor that teaches us about ourselves and the world we live in.*

1

The deer disappear into the forest. I remain still, sitting and watching the crisp morning. The sun washed away the cloak of night and unveiled a land of beauty. Except to my north, it unveiled something else, a road slicing across the hillside, winding back and forth, in and out of the trees. I trace along it with my eyes and follow it back in time.

I remember standing on another road, less than half a mile from here. I felt very attuned and sensitive to the land around me that day. I felt a unique connection with my surroundings, and although I often feel that I am given guidance and messages, the medium is usually through people or books that happen to be in the right place at the right time. This particular October day was the only time that I remember feeling almost spoken to. I could feel how the road cut into the "tissues" of the earth, and I noticed how the patches of grasses and trees on the hills seemed much like the patches of short hair and long wool on the buffalo. I could feel that this layer of trees and grass and life was a very thin, protective coat, like a skin. These thoughts and feelings moved me deeply and I felt compelled to express them in a communicable medium, which became a silk-screen print entitled, "*Earthskin*".

At the time of the experience I had been a year out of high school, and I was spending some time with my grandma here in Pony. It was another year and a half later before "*Earthskin*" reached its final form, and the print became a turning point in my life at that time. That is because, although I felt compelled to express the experience as artwork, I also felt that it was basically pointless. True, the print encompassed inspirational symbols and metaphors for me, and I hoped for others, about the need to change our ways and live more harmoniously with the environment. At the same time, I felt there were already plenty of other artists, writers, poets, and "spiritual leaders" conveying that message. There were plenty of people saying that we should live with the earth, but few were saying how. Those who did merely suggested organic gardening or suggested an outright retreat to nineteenth century homesteading. Returning to the past might be fine for a few people, but it is alien to most and therefore not realistic.

Earthskin

The skin of the earth is like that of the buffalo. The golden grasses are her short hair. The conifers are her wooly coat. The soil makes up the skin of the Mother Earth.

We cut into her flesh and butcher her the way we once butchered the buffalo to near extinction. We fenced across the open range and locked the buffalo away. Still we cut across the land and threaten to lock away the Earth Mother. Her wounds bleed freely. In the west the sun is setting on our ignorance.

Thomas J. Elpel

Now that I was out of high school, the question of how to live was especially relevant. I had to meet my own needs, and I wanted to do that in such a way that was environmentally sane. I felt that metaphors and symbols alone could not heal the earth nor keep me fed and sheltered. Metaphors, I knew, were valuable for the messages they conveyed—but, I came to realize that in order for the messages to have any real meaning they must be acted upon. *It does not matter how great the metaphor or the message; the meaning is lost when it is not used.*

How, I wondered, could I preach about the need to live in harmony with the earth, while using toxic paints as the medium for my message? How could I ever draw or paint or write about the need for all people to live sustainably when I had not yet done anything myself to achieve that? It seemed clear that if I wanted to teach people about living in harmony with the earth that I would first have to tangibly demonstrate it. Merely expressing it in art or writing was not good enough; in fact, it seemed hypocritical. "*Earthskin*" was my last piece of art before I committed myself towards a more practical path towards meeting my needs and helping the earth.

For the time, I abandoned the world of "messages through metaphors", and went in pursuit of more tangible results in the world and the environment. I was already well read on sustainable living ideas, and I was beginning to see that there were real solutions to our problems. Humankind could really live in harmony with the earth and prosper that way, not just in metaphors, but in every day physical existence. The solutions were out there, just not widely recognized. It was time to put those solutions to work in my own life.

Married in 1989 at the age of 21, Renee and I bought a property here in Pony and moved into a tent while we built our Dream home of stone and log. On a combined income of less than $15,000 a year, we paid for the building materials as we could afford them and built an energy- and resource-efficient home that was good for the environment and good for our pocketbooks.

I return to the present and to the road on the hill. The road was cut into the hill by the Chicago Mining Company, a small mining operation with little regard for laws or people. Like many mining projects in this area, this road was built without permits or bonding for reclamation. On the hill over-looking town, the company built a vat-leach facility for processing gold ore with cyanide. They built a five-acre pond lined with plastic to contain the toxic mining tailings "forever", then applied for permits halfway through the construction process.

We became part of the Concerned Citizens of Pony, a group of about thirty residents and property owners opposed to the project. The Northern Plains Resource Council provided assistance, coaching us on how to read the Operating Plans and Environmental Assessments, and how to clearly point out the flaws that needed amending. Our community was split between those who favored the project for jobs, and those of us who saw it as a disaster in the making.

The Pony Mill dumped mine tailings and cyanide in this five-acre pond within a few hundred feet of the town.

Any person who objectively looked at the situation could see that the "Pony Mill Site" was a bad idea just a quarter mile upstream from every spring and well in town, but of course the state approved the project over our objections. Our group did everything by the book, while the state agencies seemed to bend over backwards for the mining company, generating bad science in favor of a flawed plan. Furthermore, there was no reclamation bond, due to loopholes in the permitting process. All the laws of Montana were apparently meaningless to protect the people and the environment.

Century-old mining tailings have barely begun to heal. With modern machinery a mining company can move as much earth in a day as past miners moved in a year.

Thinking back, it was four years after I had the *Earthskin* experience before the impact of the moment hit home. My neighbor and I complained to the Forest Service that the mining company was illegally using a National Forest road. The Forest Service knew of the activity and apparently did not want to enforce the law, but had to because of our complaints. So a cease and desist order was sent to the company—with our names at the top of the page.

On the day the notice was sent out I came home to find that our house had been broken into and vandalized. I picked up the *Earthskin* print with damaged frame and shattered glass and hung it back on the wall. I stood there for a moment to look at the print, and for the first time I realized just how sensitive I was on that October day years earlier. When I felt the roads cutting into the flesh of the earth, it was not just a statement of being, it was I believe a foretelling of what would and did happen in Pony.

The Water Quality Bureau eventually revoked Chicago Mining's operating permit, because the company failed to monitor the ground water. It was the first time the agency had ever revoked such a permit. The company filed for bankruptcy in 1996, due to its own problems, not because of our efforts. The mill only operated once, just to be grand-fathered in before new legislation took effect—legislation that was written and passed because of the Pony situation.

The mill never went into full operation, but the impoundment still leaked small amounts of cyanide into the ground water. Lethal concentrations of cyanide spilled in and around the building, and cows died on the site. There was no fencing around the project, and children lived and played only a few hundred yards away. Nine years after this saga started the state finally cleaned up the cyanide spills and capped the impoundment to minimize the public health threat. But the mill site was still tied up in bankruptcy court, and the scarred hill became home to some of the worst invasive weeds ever brought into this country.

Two juncos land in the fir boughs overhead and flitter about in their business. I can hear the gurgling and rushing of the stream in the distance. I savor the feeling of the cool breeze on my cheeks. Seeing the mining road this morning makes me stop and think... I now realize that *we live in a culture that focuses on problems. Therefore we see them.*

It has become almost our human nature to seek out and battle problems—rather than to focus on and find solutions. We want to fight crime, rather than to promote peace. We seek to spray and kill invading weeds, rather than to nurture desired species. We work to combat diseases, but fail to promote health. In words this is a subtle distinction, but in actions, the results are worlds apart. I stopped seeking out all the world's problems, and instead focused—and acted on—it's solutions.

Building our own resource-efficient home helped us eliminate mortgage payments and high energy bills, giving us true freedom to do whatever we wanted with our lives. In the publishing business we discovered that we could print a book like this one with soy inks on 100% post-consumer recycled paper, proving that it is possible to make a good living without raping the world to get it. In the research for my book *Direct Pointing to Real Wealth*, I discovered that just about any enterprise could be converted to a green business that is good for the planet and more profitable than the same business run without regard for the environment.

A faraway plume of smoke rises slowly and steadily into the morning sky. It comes from the cement plant at Trident, about half way across the valley. This the Gallatin Valley, and from here I can see clear across it, some sixty miles or so, to the city of Bozeman and the Bridger Mountains. The plume of smoke reminds me about a fundamental law of nature...that *activity, that life in any form, requires energy and resources to exist.*

There are many who would suggest that we should practice only "no-impact" camping in the wilderness. I do not agree. You see, the person who carries in a lot of gear, from tents, to propane stoves, with the intent of living "no-impact", is, metaphorically speaking, living a lie. Such a person may claim to practice no-impact camping, but the truth is that the resources they pack in had to come from somewhere.

Our contemporary lives have become so removed from hand-to-mouth survival, that we sometimes delude ourselves into thinking our items of survival come from the store, rather than from nature. We think of ourselves as being somehow separate from nature. We think we can draw lines on the map and separate "wilderness" from "non-wilderness", but really, there is only one wilderness and only one ecosystem, and we are part of it. Like the deer eating grass, or the robin bringing materials back to build a nest, we all must use the resources of the earth to maintain

Ultimately there is only one wilderness, and we are part of it.

our own survival. This is true whether we live in an apartment building in the city, or in a wickiup in the woods. Our towns and cities are part of the wilderness ecosystem, another sort of successional change, much as there are successional changes in nature, where, for example, a grassland may be replaced by deciduous forest, which is later replaced by a conifer forest. Each succession brings in a whole new plant and animal biota and crowds the old species away. Our cities and towns are part of that successional process. As humankind moves in we bring with us our own flora and fauna, some intentionally and some by accident, which flourish within the niches of our own successional level. Thus, when I speak of "wilderness" I use the term in its broadest definition; to me all places are wilderness, and we are one of many species in the ecosystem.

In primitive living you learn about nature by using it.

Primitive living allows us to practice living on a model scale. By "living" I mean that process of procuring our needs for physical and mental well-being, including such things as shelter, fire or energy, water, and vegetable or animal resources. In primitive living we are faced with these needs as realities we must meet. We are faced with the realization that in order for our lives to go onward, we must take from the world around us; like the coyote stalking a mouse, we must kill and use to survive. It is too easy to forget that in the contemporary world. We think resources come from the store, and we forget that there are impacts and consequences throughout the ecosystem from our every purchase, our every decision. In primitive living we face those consequences directly. We can see the effect of our needing to eat causing the loss of life of a plant or an animal. We can sense that by picking the berries from the bushes we may be taking someone else's meal. Primitive living is a metaphor that gives us an awareness of the true costs of living, no matter where we are.

The metaphor of primitive living can also teach us that it may be okay to take from the earth; that perhaps we do not need to feel guilty about our actions, only aware of them. The deer takes from the ecosystem and causes surprising impacts; it's presence causes successional shifts throughout plant and animal communities, destroying habitat for some and creating it for others. Similarly, the presence of humankind living primitive, today or yesterday, creates all kinds of havoc in the ecosystem. Groups of primitive peoples rewrote the ecosystem daily as they hunted and gathered for their needs, or torched the brush to drive the game out. Even an individual person displaces habitat, competes for food, and forces the animals to take new trails, all influencing successional communities. Perhaps our contemporary cities are not so different. They are still wilderness; only different successional plant and animal communities are favored there. Primitive living, as a metaphor, can teach us that, like a bluebird eating a fly, perhaps it is okay to take from and alter the ecosystem. It is neither good nor bad, it is simply reality.

Of course, primitive living also reminds us that our link to the ecosystem goes both ways. We are participants in the ecosystem and therefore we have no choice but to take from it, and we will inevitably alter it, but we must also maintain it. Our actions affect successional communities of plants and animals in the ecosystem, and we are included in those communities. Succession will forever be in a state of flux, for as long as life exists. Nature will continue on, ever changing, destroying habitats and creating them. In the face of global climate change and ozone depletion, it is important that we consider what successional changes may mean for our own species.

Primitive living is a metaphor for living. It reminds us that no matter what technologies we have, we are still in integral component of the ecosystem. *Primitive living is a model for living that gives us the basic foundations, the very laws of nature, upon which all of our solutions, in primitive and contemporary living, must be built.*

Ⓞne of the reasons I teach both primitive and contemporary living skills is to help people become better stewards of this wilderness we live in. People need to be informed about this wilderness, and to become informed they need to use it.

In primitive living you learn about the wilderness as you create your niche in the ecosystem and gather the resources you need for living. For example, to harvest edible plants you have to learn about plants. You learn the

One of the reasons I teach is to help people learn to become better stewards of our world.

names and the habitats of plants. You learn about individual edible plants by eating them and by noticing the changes in the appearance and taste throughout the year. As you harvest plants you learn to recognize them throughout the year, as dead stalks, or seeds, or even by just the roots. As you seek out edible plants you begin to notice characteristics of the soil; you begin to notice that your desired herb grows better in one type of soil than another.

The knowledge that you learn in this way is not always "scientific", but you do develop an awareness of nature and natural resources. You will, for instance, learn the basics of geology as you look for different types of rock that are useful as tools in primitive living. You might look for quartz, quartzite, or chert rocks to use as "flint" in flint and steel fire starting. Or you might look for sandstone to use for sanding arrow shafts or bows, or to abrade a stone tool. You might look for a clay deposit for making pottery, or for various minerals for mineral paints. You will learn about geology as you spend hours searching along a river for just the right piece of round, symmetrical, fine-grained granite for a hammerstone. As you search for these many different geologic resources you develop a general awareness of them. You begin to notice if the rocks around you are igneous, or metamorphic, or sedimentary. Instead of merely hiking from point A to point B, the process of hunting and gathering for resources makes you investigate the land around you.

Likewise, the process of fishing or hunting without modern implements makes you stop and learn about the living beings you are after. Leave your fishing tackle and rifle at home then fish and hunt through observation and wit. Observe the fish, the squirrels, the rabbits, and the deer and learn their habits. Pit your wit against theirs as you improvise traps or spears or bow and arrow, or use your bare hands to catch your dinner. Without the aid of modern technology, fishing and hunting is not only an educational experience, but often a very humbling experience.

The process of primitive living is also a means to feel more attuned and in harmony with nature. Instead of being a tourist in the wilderness with a flashing neon tent and synthetic clothes, you can build shelters that blend into the environment. You can wear clothes made from quiet, soft, and lightweight brain-tanned buckskins, or out of wool from sheep or buffalo. Instead of depending solely on General Mills to provide your meals, you can supplement your diet from the world around you. These direct physical connections to the wilderness help you to become mentally attuned.

This book is especially about the primitive and simple knowledge and technologies that will help you to better connect with the world. Many of these skills were used by aboriginal or native peoples around the globe, while other skills have been newly developed by weekend aborigines or "abos" as we call ourselves.

Aboriginal skills are, of course, unique and different in every part of the world. The skills of the Inuit peoples of the Arctic Circle are inherently different from those of the Amazonian Indians. Some skills are very site specific, while others are universally applicable or adaptable. The skills in this book are skills that I know and use in my specific region, the northern Rocky Mountains, with a few added skills that I have used in other areas. I will not pretend to teach you skills I do not know or cannot use. In addition, there are many specific skills that have been thoroughly documented and published by others, such as flint-knapping or weaponry. I include only minimal descriptions and notes with these because each of these is worthy of a book on their own, and

The process of fishing or hunting without modern implements makes you stop and learn about the living beings you are after.

6

besides I would just be quoting the excellent work of others. Therefore I have included only brief discussions of those skills, with some notes on what I think is new information.

The juncos fly out of the tree and dart over my head as they race on their way. In my mind I say, "I agree. I should be on my way as well." I look around a moment more to the hills, the forests, granite peaks and sagebrush. It is amazing, that some people consider these mountains, the Tobacco Roots to be "sacrificial", because it is one of two ranges in the state with more mining claims than any others. To me, it is the ideal place for a school, a place to think about the processes and impacts of living; it is a place to search for more sound ways of living.

The reality is that 84% of all the gold mined from the earth is consumed for jewelry. People who purchase and wear gold are completely unaware of the damage they cause. A single gold necklace or ring may require more than a ton of earth to be ripped from the ground, pulverized, and sprayed with a cyanide solution to extract the yellow metal. Living habitats are destroyed, and native plants and animals are lost forever, often to be replaced by invasive weeds imported from other lands. Ducks, geese, and other wildlife sometimes die in the cyanide ponds. Mine sites are often left unreclaimed, and even those that are recontoured may require perpetual treatment of polluted water... a thousand or more years of damage just to inflate someone's ego with shiny metal.

The real jewels in this world are the intact mountains and meadows and trees and rivers of the natural world. Grinding these jewels up to make infinitely smaller, portable ones is hardly a worthwhile endeavor. But consumer choice is a powerful force. Consumer concern about cruelty to animals once put an end to the fur industry. Gold jewelry will fall out of favor too, as soon as people fully realize the impact of purchasing and wearing it.

Yes, I work on a computer with gold circuitry, and therefore I cannot be totally against mining. We do need gold for electronics, industrial purposes and dental work, but this is a small fraction of what is torn from the ground each year. There are a handful of reputable mining operations in the world that can easily produce the small amount of gold needed to meet essential needs.

I became chairman of the Concerned Citizens of Pony after the mill site was dead and the immediate threat of the cyanide was gone. All that was left was an ugly mess and weed patch on the hill. Our group steadily dissolved as our members went on about more pressing matters in their lives. But one thing I learned from the experience was that our laws were virtually meaningless, that it took politics to get things done. I wrote lots of letters to the editor like this one, blaming the state for fueling the noxious weed problem:

> To the editor:
>
> In 1998 the State of Montana spent $400,000 to clean up the cyanide hazard at the Pony Mill, including removal of the five-acre, plastic-lined tailings impoundment. This mess started ten years ago when a mining company sought permission to build a cyanide-vat leach facility on the hill above town. Many of us thought it was a bad idea, but the Water Quality Bureau (now the "Department of Environmental Quality") insisted it was a sound plan. The WQB/DEQ permitted this disaster to happen, and we are grateful that the department has taken the initial steps to clean up after itself. Unfortunately, the state quit its "reclamation" too soon, and the Pony Mill threatens the watershed in a whole new way: spotted knapweed.
>
> Knapweed establishes in disturbed, barren soils first, then spreads from there. Of the five large infestations in the watershed, three are the result of soil disturbance, and the worst is the Pony Mill Site. Knapweed seeds blow from the mill site to every other part of the watershed. Removing the tailings impoundment eliminated the cyanide hazard, but created five more acres of barren ground to fuel a knapweed explosion. The site has not been contoured, covered with topsoil, or seeded, but the DEQ seems to think it is good enough.
>
> Spotted knapweed already costs the Montana economy $42 million per year, and that figure is expected to rise to $155 million per year as knapweed continues to spread. The people of our community are working together to control the other knapweed infestations, and to rehabilitate the disturbed soils of those sites. But there is nothing we can do about the Pony Mill Site. The state must immediately finish its work there to rehabilitate the site. The up-front costs are petty compared to the costs of losing the entire watershed to knapweed.
>
> Thomas J. Elpel, Chairman
> The Concerned Citizens of Pony

The Department of Environmental Quality claimed that the weeds were not their responsibility, and by the letter of the law they were correct. But my letters to the paper made the department look bad and copies sent to the governor added pressure from that end.

The DEQ claimed that they could do nothing while the Chicago Mining Company was in bankruptcy court, and the bankruptcy trustee never returned their calls. It could have sat in bankruptcy court for the next ten or twenty years, but I called the trustee myself, got through on my first try, and he immediately agreed to "abandon the assets" so the state could move forward with reclamation. With the bankruptcy resolved, the state auctioned off the mining equipment on site, and a conservative legislature with a tight budget gleefully forked over another $290,000 to put the top soil back, contour the site and revegetate it—provided they would never hear about the Pony Mill Site again.

I still remember what the mill site was like before the Chicago Mining Company came to town. As a teenager staying with Grandma Josie, I used to hike up there at sunrise on summer mornings to sit and watch the deer as they grazed. The Pony Mill Site will never be the same place it was then, but the reclamation of it is certainly one of my proudest achievements.

Looking back, it is no surprise that after driving two thousand miles around the state looking for the ideal place for our home and school, that our search ended in the place where it began, right here in Pony. Our community is a place where we can make a difference, demonstrating through our personal lives and businesses that it is truly profitable to work towards creating a better world every day.

The ironic thing is that the most productive use of my time has always been on primitive journeys like this one. It is here in the heart of nature, when I cast off the contemporary world and walk the metaphor, that I find fresh resources and clear perspective to guide me through life. The morning is beautiful and alive, and I am glad to be here.

◊ ◊◊◊ ◊

MIND

The sun is rising slowly higher into the sky, but the morning is still cool. I stand up, drape the wool blanket around me and start walking. I can now clearly see the land, which was only recently cloaked in the darkness of night. It is a unique landscape and one of my favorite places. It is a landscape of miniature hills and valleys created by glacial forces. Granite boulders lay strewn throughout. The two-foot tall sagebrush is almost blue in color. There are patches of aspen trees scattered throughout the miniscape and an occasional older Douglas fir tree. A new generation of fir trees springs to life nearby, hundreds of young trees, most of them not much taller than myself. I feel like a giant among them. I do not have a particular destination this morning, but to savor the moment and to follow wherever my feet take me and my mind goes.

I strip a few leaves from the sagebrush, crush them in my hand and savor the rich smell. Dew clings to the sage and grass and soaks into my moccasins as I walk. A chickadee hops among the lower branches of a tree. Scattered clouds, thin yet puffy, float in the ocean of blue above. Mats of a spreading ground juniper feel soft and spongy under my feet. The deer graze among the fringes of the forest.

Nature, I have come to realize, exists as little more than wallpaper in most people's lives. In the modern world we are surrounded by pretty green foliage with a few flowers for splashes of color, plus birds chirping pleasantly nearby and manicured ponds with ducks looking for breadcrumbs. It is all very quaint, but who really pays much attention to wallpaper?

At best, we are sometimes so taken with the scene of a rainbow after a storm or a butterfly visiting a flower that we pause for a moment to admire the walls of our world, but that is about as far as it goes. Some inspired individuals appreciate the scenery enough to seek out narrow wilderness paths where they can get a completely unobstructed view of the walls. But very few people ever make it beyond the paper.

The real world, as people experience it, is the world of people and culture. It is a world that we have built and it has real substance and action—buildings, cars, movies, parties, song and dance, and an endless stream of newsworthy events. With so much going on, why would anyone ever stop to investigate mere wallpaper?

Nature remains a two-dimensional pretty picture in our lives, only rarely broken by the magnificent buck that unexpectedly comes crashing through the walls to stand in front of us. For a second the world takes on an undeniable three-dimensional aspect, hinting that there is more beyond the walls. But the moment passes as quickly as it came, and nature returns to its two-dimensional normality. We look at our watches and continue on, eager to keep our appointments in the real world. But what might happen if we stopped to investigate the wallpaper?

Nature exists as little more than wallpaper in most people's lives.

When you learn the names of a few wildflowers and birds and rocks, then you will simply pay more attention to them. You will recognize the flowers and trees when you pass on the street or in the woods. No longer will you be able to ignore them as mere splashes of color on the walls, but as something you are familiar with, like seeing an old friend. The natural world becomes a bit more interesting, if only because you know something about it.

It is when you stop to say "hello" to this old friend that you begin to notice more of the wallpaper. "Who is this?" you wonder, and "Who is that?" Soon you may find yourself making herbal tea from some of those wildflowers, or adding edible greens to your salad.

But there is so much more to explore. Try learning to start a fire-by-friction using wood from the local trees, or making pots from clay you have dug up by the side of the road. Go camping without a sleeping bag or tent and make a warm shelter from the available sticks and grasses and bark. Make your own moccasins from animal skins you have tanned, and walk quietly through the woods feeling the earth beneath your feet. Catch a fish with your bare hands, or run down a mountainside just for the fun of it. The more you discover the natural world, the more you become a part of it.

The gap that separates people from nature is both immense and imaginary. It can take decades to bridge the gap, to truly know and

The gap that separates people from nature is both immense and imaginary.

feel that you are one with the earth. But in due time you may just wander off the beaten path and right into the wallpaper, meeting friends and neighbors as you go, until you are immersed knee—deep in a swamp— catching bugs, following the birds to their hiding spots, and wondering what in the heck that unusual plant is just a little farther over there. Years later you may find yourself in a meadow of wildflowers and wildlife—even if it is just an vacant lot in the city—surrounded by friends you have seemingly always known, only to look back and realize how far you have come. There in the distance is what you once called the real world, the world of people and culture. But now it seems like a house of smoke and mirrors, a place with bright lights and loud sounds, full of self-importance but empty of substance. The real world, you have discovered, was in the wallpaper all along.

I stop and pick up a rounded granite stone from the ground. It is six or seven inches long, four wide, and maybe three inches thick. I run my hands over all its surfaces, turning it over and examining it's platforms. I step over to a granite boulder, practice swinging twice, then whack the smaller stone near its edge. A round disk of rock, thick at one edge and thin and sharp at the other, pops off the stone, flips in the air and lands on top of the larger

granite boulder. The granite is coarsely crystalloid, making a crude and very jagged edge. I check the edge with my finger; it is sharp enough. It is a simple blade, called a "discoidal" stone knife.

In that one simple movement I have replicated one of the earliest technologies of our species, a crude stone blade. It is from such simple beginnings that all our technological and cultural constructs have originated. Hundreds of thousands of years ago our ancestors made similar blades of stone and started our species down this path of tools and knowledge that would differentiate us from all other inhabitants of this world. From such simple stone blades we have constructed much.

The stone is still cold from the night. I put it into my pocket. It brings back memories...

In due time you may just wander off the beaten path and right into the wallpaper, meeting friends and neighbors as you go.

Discoidal Stone Knives

Many of the primitive skills I know I learned from my cousin Melvin Beattie. Mel is actually my mom's cousin, and my second cousin, but to me he is Cousin Mel. We have often worked on our primitive skills together.

One time we were out hunter-gathering in his pickup truck—we were hunting for anything that might be useful, and we were gathering it. We stopped along the Missouri River north of Helena, a few miles east of Wolf Creek, Montana. There we found and harvested a nice patch of dried dogbane stalks for making cordage as well as a few rocks with diverse potentialities, from hammer stones to bowdrill socket rocks. We also found a patch of mullein stalks, which offered us the irresistible opportunity to make some crude atlatl and dart sets. (The atlatl and dart is essentially a spear with a spear launcher.) We quickly made two sets and then hurled the darts around for a half hour or so.

A discoidal blade, made by striking the end of a rounded quartzite stone against another hard rock on the ground.

Walking along the dirt road we noticed a few rounded quartzite stones that had rolled down from the hill above. Immediately we noticed that they had each been broken in a particular and very unnatural way. Someone at sometime had been making discoidal stone knives. Discoidal knives are disc-shaped tools made by whacking one rock against another in a controlled manner.

We climbed up the slope to look for more evidence of stone working. There we found not just a few quartzite cobbles, but thousands, and nearly every one had one, two, three or more discoidal knives broken off them and taken away. The site may have been used as a Native American knife factory for hundreds, perhaps thousands of years.

I was surprised at how large the blades were. Most measured six to eight inches across and must have weighed several pounds apiece. I usually make much smaller ones, only two to five inches across. It is very likely that the big discoidal knives were used for skinning and fleshing buffalo. I had to admire the physical capabilities of a people who could regularly wield such a heavy knife.

Discoidal knives are very useful for skinning, fleshing, chopping, and a variety of other tasks. Quartzite cobbles are probably one of the most common rocks used to make them, although basalt and many other fine-grained rocks work well too. Quartzite is a dense, hard, semi-glassy rock found occasionally along many of the major rivers in Montana. Coarse-grained rocks, like the granite, do not work nearly as cleanly, but can be serviceable.

To make a discoidal knife, start by selecting a quartzite or other fine-grained stone, preferably one that is oval-shaped. Next find another hard stone to bash it against. Hold your good stone with both hands and practice swinging it a few times, then whack it, an inch or so from its edge, against the other rock. It is a good idea to wear glasses for this step, even though most of the debris flies away from you.

It may take a few tries, but with enough force applied to the right spot, you will cleanly shear off a disc-shaped piece of rock, thick at the point of impact, tapering to a fine and sharp edge along the other side.

The first knife is always the hardest to shear off of a stone. A round stone is structurally very stable; when you hit it the shock waves

Chopping with a discoidal blade.

11

are distributed and dispersed all around the rock. The next discoidal is much easier to make, even if it is on the opposite side of the rock, because the shock waves travel differently through the entire structure.

Discoidal stone knives are simple and fun to make. You can make as many as you want, and when they become dull, simply toss them aside and make some more; they're disposable.

◊　◊◊◊　◊

With my new stone knife in my pocket and the leaves of sage in hand, I walk, or wander on and add to my bouquet of smells; I pick some needles from the Douglas fir and the top from a horsemint plant. I savor the smells and rub the plants on my arms, neck, and face. They are stimulating to the body and mind.

I step onto the rutted trail leading to Hollowtop Lake. It is a recreational trail for hikers, bikers, horseback riders, and off-road vehicles. Some shards of broken glass from an old beer bottle momentarily grab my attention. A sparrow darts out of the sagebrush and flies away, and a jet passes overhead leaving a trail of steam across the sky. We have constructed much since the dawn of the Stone Age.

As a practitioner and teacher of primitive skills, I often meet people who go into backlash from "technological overdose". They blame technology for all the world's social and environmental problems and come asking, "What level of technology should we live by?"

I once thought similarly and for a short time in junior high I even advocated that we should all drop everything to go live as a hunter-gatherer society as a means to "save the world". Needless to say, I did not have many followers, and because of that—and because I knew I would not want to live under primitive circumstances full time either—I quickly grew beyond that way of thinking. Thus, it surprised me years later to hear professionals in the primitive skills business advocating hunter-gatherer life as a solution to the world's problems. I remember one extended conversation around the nighttime campfire that, in short, went something like this:

"To save the world we need to get away from technology and return to a hunter-gatherer society."

"But who would do it?"

"Ya, even if everyone did return to a hunter-gatherer society their kids would start producing technology and soon society would be just as it is now."

"I guess the world is shot to hell."

There was a time when I believed that we would have to give up our modern technology and live as hunter-gatherers in order to "save the world".

While the futility of convincing everyone to live as hunter-gatherers is obvious, there is similarity between this vision and the many other visions for "the right way to live" that may be unnoticed. One other vision supported by many people is that the right way to live is as organic five-acre farmers living with essentially a 19th century level of technology much like the Amish people. Another common vision is that we should create a society limited by the renewable energy captured from the sun through solar cells, wind energy, waterpower, and biomass. The similarity between each of these visions is that people create the visions first and then try to fit humanity into the picture afterwards.

I realized by the time I entered high school that if we are going to create a world around us that is socially and environmentally stable then people will have to want to. So instead of trying to pin any set vision of the world on society I started asking, "What is human nature?" and, "What sound ideas and technologies exist that appeal to human nature?"

I have found that to appeal to human nature ideas and technologies need to be socially acceptable and economically sound. That is, they must appeal to the quality of life people desire, and they must be practical. People tend to make the best choices they feel they have available to them. People will adopt technologies and techniques, which incidentally bring us towards a better world if those choices are the most favorable for directly enhancing their own quality of life and economic situation. In pursuit of ideas that meet these criteria, I have discovered an incredible and beautiful world of opportunity just waiting to be received. The reason people do not always take advantage of those opportunities is because they do not know all the choices and no one ever bothered to ask what choices exist.

To me, the means to creating a more sane world is to 1) give people knowledge of more and better choices and 2) get out of their way. They will do the rest. Good ideas do not need to be legislated or mandated, just shared. That is the basis of the contemporary living skills program through our school.

As for a philosophy about technology and society, remember that all technologies are relative, and that they are neither good nor bad, but it is how we use them that makes them that way. True, we might have the technology to annihilate ourselves, and that alone may seem to be sufficient grounds to say we have too much technology, but consider such a simple technology as fire.

People who did not know how to use fire may have been awed by the incredible technology of those first people who discovered fire as a tool. But fire as a technology gave people the ability to do many things both good and bad. Fire was a means to keep warm and cook food and

Fire is a technology that gives us the ability to do many things, both good and bad.

make tools, but it was also a technology that could be used to wage war and ravage ecosystems, both of which happened. With a wide range of simple knowledge and technologies humankind succeeded in ravaging the earth in ways which have left environmental scars for millennia.

Indeed, 73% of all large mammals in North America fell extinct upon the arrival of humankind at the end of the last ice age 11,500 years ago. The casualties included two species of peccary, the sloth, two types of llamas, the camel, the horse, the native moose, two species of deer, one species of antelope, two of musk oxen, the mastodon and mammoth, saber-toothed tigers, a giant beaver and a giant capybara, a tapir, the spectacled and short-faced bears, a cheetah and an armadillo. These animals survived many ice ages and interglacial cycles, but dropped dead immediately upon the arrival our own species. Similar waves of extinctions have followed humanity in every new land we have colonized.

Interestingly, the animals we call "native", such as the bison, elk, deer, moose, grizzly bear, black bear and caribou, were originally Eurasian species that were already adapted to humans. These species came across the Bering Land Bridge along with the first Americans.

Most of the big game animals we call "native" were originally Eurasian species that crossed the Bering Land Bridge along with the first Americans.

Along with the slaughter of native species, primitive peoples also waged war upon each other. In war and in peace the per capita rate of homicide and outright genocide of past cultures with simple technologies dwarfs the per capita homicide and genocide in the world today.

Regardless of what we think about technology, humanity is going to forge ahead anyway. We went from the horse and buggy to the moon in under a hundred years and the growth curve of technological development is going to continue. For us as individuals, to have a successful philosophy about technology today is to have a philosophy that allows us to feel integrated and not alienated as we grow older in a world that will soon be significantly different from the world we know now.

Primitive living in today's world is not a way of escaping the contemporary world; we cannot escape it. We are always in the contemporary world; and it is a place where we can no longer hunt the wild buffalo, because they are gone. It is the same wilderness, but a new reality that we have created. Primitive living is not a retreat to get away from today's world, but an integral part of contemporary life, a source of perspective and understanding.

I pause a moment to pick a dandelion blossom and to tie the laces on my footwear. The glint of an aluminum can shines out from the underbrush along the trail.

My footwear is a synthesis of the ancient and modern. The moccasins I sewed myself, from deerskin that I tanned. I wear the moccasins inside a "tire sandal". It is an exciting combination.

As a rule, people and cultures tend to use the best resources they have available in their environment to meet their needs. Footwear has long been a challenge to Stone Age cultures.

Native Americans often brought multiple pairs of moccasins along on journeys, then sat around the campfire every night to fix them. Buckskin does not last very long against the abrasive ground. For this reason especially, primitive peoples around the world walked barefoot most of the time.

Barefoot walking is a wonderful way to get directly in touch with the earth. However, it isn't that practical for the tender-footed modern weekend aboriginal. After about one full day of barefoot walking, I have enough cuts and splinters in my feet to force me to wear soles for the next three days while I heal. But barefoot walking is also slow and careful walking. If I need to move quickly over any distance, then it is time for soles.

I reach into the brush for the aluminum can. I place it on the trail, smash it, and put it in my pocket to haul it away. Animals I realize, do not judge their environment. From ants to mice to deer, the creatures accept their environment without questioning it. They do not look at the litter of humankind and frown at our negligence. They do not have beliefs about what is right or wrong. They only operate in terms of their own immediate security: Is this particular element safe or hostile? Is it useful?

A pile of refuse left behind by humans might provide food for one creature or shelter for another, or it may become just another part of the scenery to others, like any other rock or tree. Deer for example, have no fear of parked cars, as long as the cars remain parked and otherwise non-threatening.

Primitive cultures too tend not to judge their environment in terms of right or wrong, but only in terms of usefulness. The new resources and technologies that enter their environments are seldom judged by where they came from or how they were made, but by how economical they are for meeting their specific needs in the here and now.

Anthropologist Richard B. Lee learned that on his second day studying the Dobe !Kung bushmen in Africa. They talked him into driving them in his truck to their foraging grounds. He drove while they all rode in the back singing songs about sitting around getting fat while the truck did all the work. In two hours they harvested enough mongongo nuts to sustain themselves for five to ten days. Reflecting on the incident, Lee said it was an intelligent use of their resources—after all, he wrote, "Why hike in the hot sun for a small meal, when the bearded White man might take you in his truck for ten large ones?"

To survive and prosper in primitive living you have to harvest more calories of energy than you expend.

In primitive cultures the driving force of belief is and was economics. To survive and prosper, primitive peoples had to harvest more calories of energy than they expended. They had to adapt and make economical decisions to enable them to harvest more calories with less effort, just as we do today. They would not resist a glass bottle as a source of arrowhead material any more than you or I would pass up a twenty-dollar bill lying on the sidewalk.

Primitive living is not a matter of replicating the past. The past no longer exists. We cannot torch the forest to drive out game because we have to make shared management decisions with other users. Primitive living today has to reflect the realities of today's world, and maybe that is not so bad. Some old opportunities may be gone, but new opportunities abound.

Some things have changed, but many new opportunities abound.

The wild buffalo may be gone from the plains and forests, and the "White Man's buffalo" may be off limits, but other new opportunities for primitive living now exist. After all, wildlife management and hunting regulations have helped to build back the populations of deer and elk and other game animals. New game species thrive here today, like the Chinese pheasant. Likewise, many of our choicest wild edible plants are non-native species.

Certainly, we should do what is possible to preserve our native species and limit invasion and contamination from foreign plants and animals, but we also have to acknowledge that what was done was done, and we need to consider ways to successfully integrate native and nonnative species for long-term stability.

I walk, enjoying the adaptation of my footwear. I like wearing moccasins. My feet do not rot in them like they do in sweaty tennis shoes. There were many years when I had little choice. I chose to wear tennis shoes because it was better than spending all my time fixing moccasins. There were so many other exciting things to do with my time. I gaze a brief moment up at the dissipating vapor trail of the jet. Strictly speaking, the vapor trail is not natural. Yet, it came from nature, and it is an expression of nature, just as much as my moccasins are.

I twirl the dandelion blossom between my fingers, then stop and bury my nose in it, buttering up with the pollen. This dandelion is not a native to this land. It is an import from Europe. Nonetheless, it is still my friend.

The day is yet young, and I walk onward, enjoying the morning and the freshness of thoughts. A mouse sees or hears me moving and scurries away through the grass and sage. I stop to pick a cream-colored buckwheat blossom; I savor the smell and walk on my way. Like many other people, I walk to think about things or to find inspirations for writing. Walking provides a sort of rhythm, which is neurologically linked to that part of our brains which causes us to talk to ourselves. As I walk I engage in this on-going dialogue in the back of my mind while I also seek to tune into the landscape. Thus, when I am in the wilderness my conscious mind cycles back and forth from what is going on in the world inside my mind to what is happening in the world outside, much like the writing style in this book.

My feet have taken me down by the creek to a stand of willows. The sun has not yet reached in through the trees and brush here. The air is still very cool and damp. I select a long, slender willow twig that is straight, without any forks, or sharp bends in it. I pull the discoidal stone knife from my pocket and slice across it—once, twice—and it cuts through. I return the knife to my pocket and walk onward, with the willow in hand, towards a patch of sunlight in the meadow. The meadow I find is quiet, and the warming sunlight penetrates deep into my thoughts.

I run my hand along the willow's length to strip away the leaves. It seems that willows and ideas may have a lot in common. They weave well, integrating into new constructs, twining round and round each other into new wholes. Flexibility is the key to weaving something new and beautiful...

Willow and willow/cattail baskets.

Twined Baskets

Twined baskets can be made with many different types of materials, but two materials that work well in my area are willows and cattails. Twined baskets can be made with just the willows, or the willows may be used for the framework and interwoven with cattails. The process for either is largely the same. Other flexible twigs like red-osier dogwood can be used for basketry too.

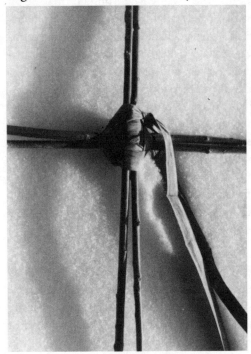

Step One.

You can make baskets any time of year, but winter is really the best time. In summer the willows and cattails are green and full of moisture. A basket made with really moist materials will shrink a lot while drying so that even a well-crafted basket becomes very loose. To prevent this you can cut the materials and let them dry partially or wholly before you make them into a basket. Materials that are completely dried need to be soaked in warm water before you use them.

You can pick through thickets of willows and cut the long, slender branches, or you can find an area that the highway department has trimmed in the last few years. The highway department mows down the bushes and trees along the roads on a regular basis. The willows quickly sprout up from the roots the next year, and all the twigs grow to a similar length and girth. In some places you can find miles of straight, slender willows growing along the road—a perfect crop of basketry materials grown by the highway department. Also along the highway you can often find cattail swamps for easy access to those materials as well. Gather a quantity of the materials you want to use, but harvest intermittently through a patch to minimize the visual impact.

With willow baskets you can work any place that is easy to clean up. But to make willow/cattail baskets I would recommend working in the bathroom, next to the bathtub. I fill the bathtub with hot water and soak the cattails in that. Then I sit on the edge of the tub while I work.

Step 1. To make a willow or a willow/cattail basket, start by selecting several willows of equal length and girth. These will become the framework, or spokes of the basket. Technically, these first pieces are called warps, but I call them spokes since it is more descriptive. The basket in the photos was started with four willows (eight spokes), but you could also start with six or eight.

Hold the willows together and cut all the big and little ends off. Save the middle sections of the willows, which are neither big nor little, but fairly even along their length. Lay these across each other as shown in the first photo, and make sure the tip and butt ends alternate all the way around, so that there are not two butt or tip ends next to each other.

Now you start with your weavers (which are also known as wefts). Pick up two willows or two cattails leaves, depending on the type of basket you would like to make. Make sure the weavers are the same length and girth. Tie a simple overhand knot at the tips of these weavers. Now, pick up the spokes and hold them together at the center with your left hand, and with your right hand, hang the weavers at the knot on the set of spokes coming out to the right. Twist the weavers together one time to secure them around those spokes. Then rotate around to the next set of spokes and bring the weavers in front and in back of those spokes, and again twist the weavers to secure them, and continue rotating around the basket. Continue rotating around the center until all the spokes are firmly lashed together. Your

Step Two.

basket should then look like the first photo, except that you may be using willow weavers instead of cattails.

Step 2. Now, gently bend and spread the spokes apart from each other as shown. The willows may not bend all at once, so just spread them apart a little to begin with and more as you work along. Then bring your weavers around each spoke and each time twist, or cross, the weavers before going around the next spoke. This process of working with two weavers and crossing them back and forth between the spokes is called twining.

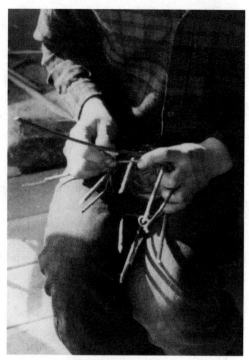

Step Three.

When you reach the ends of the weavers, tuck them in under the previous row to hold them, and select two more weavers, again equal in length and girth. Start the new weavers by tucking the tips in under the weavers of the previous row and continue twining. With willow weavers you may find that the butt ends are too thick to bend and flex around the spokes. Simply cut them off when they become unwieldy and start again with the tips of two new weavers. Keep twining around and around until your basket looks something like the one in the second photo.

At this point there are some very wide spaces between the spokes. You need to either add additional spokes or start shaping the sides of the basket. To add more spokes, simply poke an extra one in beside each of the existing spokes, and gradually spread them apart as you continue twining. In this case, I chose to start shaping the sides of the basket, and I switched from cattail weavers to willow weavers.

Step Four.

Step 3. Start the walls of the basket by gently bending the spokes as you continue twining. A good way to do this is to hold the basket in your lap with your left hand and put your fingers between the spokes. Use gentle pressure between your hand and your thighs to gradually curve the spokes to the position you want, while you continue twining with your right hand. Make the twining very tight to help pull the spokes inward, and use the fingers of your left hand to pull the twinings down tight between the spokes as shown in the third photo. Keep working with the basket in your lap and you will be able to move very quickly once the walls are started.

As you form the walls you will need to decide between either lengthening the spokes and making the sides higher, or finishing the basket with the existing spokes. To lengthen the spokes, simply slide a new spoke in next to each of the original spokes and continue working up the sides of the basket as far as you would like. The basket in the photos was finished without adding spokes.

Step 4. There are a couple ways you can finish the rim of your basket. To finish the basket in these photos I bent each spoke over and pushed it down alongside the spoke next to it. Step four shows this in progress, with the last spoke being bent over and inserted beside the adjoining spoke. I would especially recommend this method for finishing the rim when you are working with willow spokes and cattail weavers; it will help hold the cattails in place. If you are just working with willows then you can use this method, or alternately, you can bend each of the spokes over and use them as weavers, and twine them right into the rim.

When you have learned this basic technique then you will be able to make baskets of many sizes and shapes, and from many different materials. I've even made decorative planter baskets from rusty old barbwire.

◊　◊◊◊　◊

A sudden, momentary breeze sends a whisper of cool air up my back and a slight chill of excitement along my spine. We have constructed much since the dawn of the Stone Age and not all of our constructs are material in form. Besides mere tools and products, our species has constructed ideas and beliefs. We have created social and political organizations, and we have created definitions of our world. Our species has become unique among animals in the way we use our minds. We still have the need to eat and survive and reproduce, but also to worry and to ask "Why?"

"Why are we so disconnected from nature?" "Why are we destroying the planet?" "Why did our ancestors wipe out so many species when I thought of them as good stewards of nature?" "Why are we here?" "Why doesn't anyone seem to care?"

It is usually assumed that the modern brain evolved at least 100,000 years ago, and that we have been asking questions ever since. The database of mental facts about the world continues to change, but the basic wiring is the same now as in the first of our species. Or is it?

Certainly the gray goo we are born with is essentially the same gray goo our earliest sapient ancestors were born with, but that doesn't mean we are wired the same now as then. The human brain is in many ways a blank slate at birth. It is wired mostly through the processes of mimicry and accumulated experience.

For example, if your family did a lot of building when you were growing up, then you are probably pretty good with a hammer. First you mimicked your parents swinging a hammer. You were not building anything, just beating on things with sticks or toy hammers. But you kept mimicking your parents and soon graduated to hammering nails into a wooden block, and eventually learned to really use a hammer. The process of learning is not merely a matter of storing facts and figures, but of actually weaving neural circuitry. You wouldn't think it takes a lot of circuitry to pound in a nail, but you might be surprised when you watch someone who never learned to use a hammer. When you watch what they are doing wrong, then you realize that in your own hammering you are constantly adjusting the trajectory, speed and angle of impact as you drive in a nail. You never consciously thought about all the variables before. You just pounded a lot of nails while your brain subconsciously absorbed the feedback and wired itself to optimally perform the task.

Virtually all other skills and knowledge are acquired the same way, from the way we clean house to our language and religious beliefs. We mimic the people we are surrounded by and copy everything they do until we build a similar neural network.

If a person sees a mouse or spider and shrieks in obvious fear and terror, it is not because they have consciously thought about mice or spiders, but because they have simply mimicked others within the culture doing the same thing and therefore wired in a similar nonconscious response in their own brains.

In other words we assume that we are a sentient, thinking species, but most of our actions are driven by subconsciously programmed impulses. Just imagine sitting down to a nice meal of dog or cat or cockroaches. How would you react to it? In some cultures these foods are delicacies. If you react in disgust, it is only because you copied and wired our cultural reaction into your own neural network.

Our ancestors were incredibly attuned to the natural world, but not necessarily sentient. They were connected to the world like the jaguar, able to stalk and kill and live in great attunement with the natural world, but not exactly aware that they existed. They lived in harmony with nature only because they never realized they were separate from it. Like the jaguar they operated on animal instinct and programmed impulses handed down and adapted from generation to generation. When they hunted a species to extinction it was done like the jaguar, completely in harmony with nature, completely without awareness or guilt of the crime.

The human brain is an evolving neural network, capable of many different configurations. As human society evolved into the first small cities, our

Primitive living is a metaphor we participate in and act out.

ancestors were faced with increasingly complicated problems where mimicked behaviors of the past were ineffective at suggesting appropriate responses. Any problem with known solutions could be reacted to impulsively without thought, but the new problems favored new thinking, new strategies, a new consciousness. Bit-by-bit we have become sentient—aware that we exist—and aware of the consequences of our existence. This concept of self-awareness is an idea, a piece of neuro-circuitry that has been passed down from generation to generation, evolving and expanding through the millennia.

Many people today are drawn back to Stone Age living precisely because they are sentient. They are aware that we exist. They are aware that our species is destroying the natural world. They are aware that their peers live by nonconsciously mimicking the Jones' in the constant pursuit of meaningless material wealth without thought or guilt. They see that we are largely a society of nonconscious automatons, consuming the planet only because wealth and status is favored in our culture and mimicked from generation to generation. They are drawn to this life because they have glimpsed something beyond the wallpaper of nature. They feel disconnected from the earth, yet recognize our ancestral ties to the land. They seek to restore a lost relationship with the natural world, to become "one with nature". But they also come looking for something they can use in the contemporary world. They are searching to find a bit of wisdom, new personal strength, or a philosophy for living to take home with them. They want to fulfill something in their personal lives that is missing from the contemporary world.

I have come to realize that the role that primitive living plays in our contemporary society is much like a **metaphor**. In the conventional sense a metaphor is a story about life, which is simplified into characters and settings of stereotypes and symbols. We learn simple lessons about life from fanciful stories about princes and princesses or Old Man Coyote. We may not be able to describe exactly what those lessons are or how they affect us, but the stories do nonetheless make change in our lives. In today's complex world, primitive living is like a metaphor, but it is better. Primitive living is a metaphor we participate in and act out. Life is simplified down to the bare essentials like physical and mental well being, shelter, warmth, clothing, water, and food. We go on an expedition to meet those needs with little more than our bare hands. As we quest to meet those needs we learn to observe, to think, to reach inside ourselves for new resources for dealing with challenging and unfamiliar situations. We build up our personal strengths, and at the same time we interact with and learn about the world around us. In a story we can only join a quest in our imaginations. But in primitive living, we physically leave the contemporary world. We journey into the world of primitive stone-age skills, and we return with knowledge, wisdom and strength to enrich our lives in contemporary society.

We journey into the world of primitive stone-age skills, and we return with knowledge, wisdom, and strength to enrich our lives in contemporary society.

I experienced the power of this "experiential metaphor" when I was sixteen. I went on a twenty-six day expedition with **Boulder Outdoor Survival School**, where we hiked 250 miles through the desert canyons of southern Utah. We ate little and generally endured a lot. The personal strengths, the wisdom, and the ability to persevere that I brought back from that "quest" have helped me to be successful in contemporary life more than any other single thing I have done.

In a similar way, Renee and I went on a "quest" together, an adventure where we started in Pony and walked five hundred miles across Montana to Fort Union on the North Dakota border. That was a year before we were married. At the time we could not give a definitive answer as to why we were doing it. But looking back, I would say we were testing and building our relationship and our abilities to work together towards common goals, before formally committing ourselves to a long-term relationship. Thus, primitive living can be like a metaphor that we participate in: we quest and learn and grow.

Primitive living can be a metaphor in a more direct way as well. A metaphor is filled with characters and personalities, which connect with the needs and desires of our subconscious minds. In a story we mentally join those characters in a quest. In primitive living we become those characters. You can see many such personas expressed when you go to a primitive skills rendezvous. People act out such roles as the anthropologist, or the craftsman, or the entertainer, or the teacher.

We are all actors. At every moment, when we are just being ourselves, we are acting out a character that feels good to us. Each of us plays many roles, switching from one character to another every day depending on who we are with, or if we are working or playing. I myself play many roles, from businessman, to writer, to teacher.

The value in thinking about the roles we play is to give us a source of perspective. For example, today there are many people out crusading to "save the earth". That is okay. The point is, however, that many people who are involved in that kind of a mission are really acting more out of the need to satisfy a subconsciously driven ego as "crusader" than out of any genuine desire to make the world a better place.

Consciously thinking in terms of personas is a good way to determine what we are attracted to and also to ask ourselves why we are attracted to that. A person who genuinely wants to make the world a better place to be may make some markedly different choices than a person who's ego is caught up in the fantasy of being a crusader.

Goal setting is a matter of finding the fantasies you are totally consistent with, inside and out, and making them your reality.

Now there is nothing wrong with fantasy. Every one of us is caught up in them all the time. I personally have fantasized all my life about being like the native scout, able to travel light and invisible, like the wind, living with nature with only my bare hands. That is my personal quest in primitive living, and I select skills that help me move towards fulfilling that fantasy.

Consciously knowing your fantasy or fantasies is important, because you need to have clear outcomes in anything you do. In primitive living, especially, you can be pulled a thousand different directions; there are so many types of skills, and so many ways of doing them. It is easy to get caught up in other people's rules from their own fantasies, while losing track of what you really want for yourself. It is easy to end up with lots of fragments of information and beliefs, without any whole for you to fit them into.

I stop at a granite boulder. The area is littered with them, relics of an ice age long gone. This boulder is about the size of a car. At first glance one would think they are all a light gray in color, but in fact many of them are almost orange. They are covered with thousands of tiny lichens and some moss, representing several different species. I can sometimes lose track of time exploring the vast microscapes of these magnificent boulders.....but not this time. I climb up on the boulder and jump off the other side.

It is important when you go questing, to have some idea of what you are questing for. Success, in either primitive or contemporary living, is attained by having clearly defined goals. Defining the personas you are attracted to is a good way to help define your goals. Simply ask yourself what personas you find attractive. If you were to describe your wants and desires in the form of a person, or people with a title, what would that be? Are you the anthropologist? How about the prophet or the spiritual guide? Are you attracted to the idea of being the survivalist that endures against all odds? Or perhaps you are the survivalist who finds peace and harmony wherever you go. This list is of course endless. But once you identify the personas you are attracted to then you can better ask what it is you need to do and learn to achieve that experience.

You can also ask yourself why you are attracted to these types of characters and behaviors. This is important. At any moment an individual has all kinds of different drives in different directions. You might find yourself attracted to the ideal of being in harmony and at peace with the whole of nature, while at the same time fantasizing about surviving Armageddon, in a violent, charred black world. The two fantasies are not exactly compatible.

Often our fantasies are driven by temporary urges from some neglected part of our egos. We might indulge in that fantasy of surviving some harsh, war-torn world, and that might feel good in the imagination, but in the imagination only. The reality of physically living in such a world would be anything but pleasant. We must reflect on each of our fantasies and ask ourselves if that is what we really want to make of our world. It is okay to have those temporary urges. Just acknowledge them and let them go. Identify the fantasies that would be satisfying in your imagination and in reality.

This is the process of goal setting. It is a matter of finding the fantasies that you are totally consistent with, inside and out, and making them your reality. When you identify those fantasies then you keep them in mind every day, always testing them for accuracy, and always modifying them as you mature and understand them better. Keep your fantasies in mind every day and gradually modify your behaviors until your reality is exactly what you have fantasized. This is the path of success in both primitive and contemporary living.

𝕀 pause for a moment along the way and bury my nose in a wild rose blossom. Then I eat the petals. There is not much substance to them, but just the same, it is kind of fun to eat flowers. A small patch of stonecrop grows nearby. It is a short, succulent plant with yellow flowers. It grows only a few inches tall, sparsely colonizing the bare, grainy soil where little else will grow. I pick a sample and eat that too, then return to my thoughts.

Gatherings are the heart of the Primitive Information Age, where ideas are eagerly shared with all who come.

There are many who would say that we should return to a primitive way of life and abandon the high technologies we have today. Yet, oddly enough, the technologies they protest are the technologies that are responsible for the surging interest in primitive skills today. Primitive living as we know it today owes its existence to the Information Age.

Granted, in many ways the Information Age is a lot of overblown hype. Ninety-nine percent of what passes for information is just celebrity soap operas. We hear that 500 channels of television are coming, and we know that means we will have 500 camera angles on the same dumb story. Yet, even if 99% of all "information" is garbage, it is the remaining 1% that the Information Age is all about. That remaining one percent represents an explosion of ideas, knowledge, and philosophy. That one percent is the exchange of ideas that will propel our species forward. It is that one percent that helps us to become better educated, better people—both as individuals and as a collective. And somewhere, buried in that one percent of information is a frenzied whirlwind of activity. That frenzy is the networking of primitive living skills practitioners from around the country and around the world.

People with an interest in primitive skills are naturally information-oriented. After all, learning and discovering is what primitive living is all about. Primitive living is a way to consciously learn about ourselves and the world, and the people who are drawn toward it usually want to learn it ALL. They want to know all the plants and their edible, medicinal, and utilitarian uses. They want to know about geology and how the rocks were formed and how to make tools from them. They want to know about the animals, and their habits, and how to track them and stalk them, and how to make primitive weaponry, and how to hunt with it. They want to know how to tan hides and make their own clothing and thread, and how to weave, and how to dye, how to make shelters, and fire, and rattles and drums, and on and on and on. That is a lot of information. It amounts to many tens of thousands of bits of information.

Primitive peoples of the past were often called "hunter-gatherers", because of their nomadic lifestyle, where they hunted and gathered for their food and resources. Today's primitives are "information-gatherers". We hunt and gather for bytes of information, for any little morsels of knowledge from any source that will further enlighten us—from books, articles, schools, teachers, friends and complete strangers. We are the packrats of the Information Age, always on the lookout for someone who might happen to have even one new piece of information about a particular skill or even a particular plant.

The emergence of the primitive community onto the information super-highway was far from spectacular. For years hardly anyone had a modem, and many practicing primitives did not have computers. Some did not even have telephones. In relative terms we were the horses and buggies of the high-tech information highway. Yet, this lack of technology was made up for by the overwhelming enthusiasm within the primitive network.

A new idea originating in Virginia could be communicated by phone or by mail to a friend in California and tested out there within days of its original discovery thousands of miles away. Ideas and technologies were tossed around the country this way, quickly reaching individuals in every state and many nations. Soon this new knowledge emerged at gatherings where people shared their skills with one another, or it appeared in print in a magazine, newspaper, or book.

I remember well the time when I was the only person I knew who was interested in primitive living skills. I had a few books to guide me, but otherwise I was on my own. In those books I had read that "nature is a university", and from that I inferred that I could learn everything I ever wanted to know directly from nature. When I graduated from high school I determined that I would spend a year in the wilderness to learn all I wanted to know. I admit I had some doubts about this venture before I started, and indeed, I only lasted three or four days before I came dragging back, tired and hungry.

Our ancestors first used stone tools some two million years ago, yet the invention of the bow and arrow is barely a few thousand years old. Without teachers it took our species thousands of generations to advance from stone tools to making and using bows and arrows. My own rate of progress in the university of nature was not much faster. What I learned is that nature may be the university, but it is the campus only. I still needed professors to teach me and to show me how to use the library.

To me, the dawning of the Primitive Information Age occurred in 1988 at the Rabbitstick Rendezvous in Rexburg, Idaho. I had the opportunity to join a first time gathering of primitive skills specialists. Fifty people with interests like mine had come together at one place to exchange knowledge. Each person had something unique to contribute, and we all benefited from the accumulated experience of the group. In only four days I learned so much that it took me an entire year just to put the basics of it into practice.

Today the primitive community has fully embraced the information age with high-speed modems and a strong presence on the internet. There are hundreds of primitive skills sites on the world wide web and discussion groups where individuals can log on after work and share ideas about sticks and rocks and dead things with other interested people all over the world. Before 1988 a person who could start a bowdrill fire and knew one or two other tricks was virtually a "survival expert". Today the standards have changed. The exchange of information has propelled everyone so far ahead of where they were then that starting bowdrill fires is now "kindergarten stuff".

Most people, myself included, do not have loads of time available every day of the year to do primitive skills. I personally have many other interests and goals besides primitive living. I choose to be married and to live in a nice house and to raise a family. I choose to run a business, to write books, and to be involved in environmental causes. I do not want to leave mainstream culture behind or I may lose the ability to influence and change it. When I go "on vacation" I work hard to pack in as much primitive living experience and learning as I can in the time I allot. As in business, success in primitive living requires clearly defined long-range and short-range goals, with clear plans for achieving those goals.

As an instructor of primitive skills I need to make my classes apply to my students. I recognize that, like myself, most of the people I teach have other obligations and goals in the world besides primitive living. They too choose to discover primitive living on the weekends, weeknights, and on short vacations a couple times a year. The best way that I can teach people these skills is if I learn them that way myself.

It has been said that the amount of knowable information in the world is doubling about once every eleven months or so, perhaps faster by now. Today we are swimming in a world of information. To keep afloat in it—in primitive or contemporary living—a person has to sort through it, effectively picking out the specific pieces that apply, and pushing aside the rest. At every moment you need to keep your fantasies—your outcomes— in mind. Pick through the pieces of information, and grab onto those that help to propel you towards your specific goals.

I take a seat upon a rock in the sunlight, and begin to work with the willow twig. One willow, I realize, will not make a basket, but I can make a simple stick figure of a deer, once I split the willow down it's length.

I learned to make split-willow figures of deer from Jim Riggs of Wallowa, Oregon. According to Jim, archaeologists have found these willow figures all across the southwest, some of them dating back several thousand years. Archaeologists believe the figures may have first been used in hunting rituals; in later times they were likely used as kid's toys.

Split-Willow Figures

Step One. Select a slender, green willow twig at least 30 inches in length. It should not have any branches growing off of it. Run your fingers down the willow to strip the leaves off. Then cut an inch or so of the small end of the willow. Stick your fingernails into the end of the twig where you cut it, and split it apart. Split it down the length of the willow as shown in figure 1. If the split becomes uneven with one half of the twig bigger than the other, then bend the fatter side more sharply as you work; this will re-position the split back to the center of the twig. Split the length of the willow, but stop about 1 1/2 inches from the big end.

Step Two. Kink the willow twig 90 degrees about 1 1/2 inches from the end, right where your split ended in the willow. This first section forms the back leg of the deer; the next section becomes the backbone. Leave about 2 inches for the backbone, with both halves of the willow together. Then kink only the piece that is on top. Kink it 90 degrees to begin shaping the front leg. Make the front leg the same length as the back leg; then kink the willow back on itself, so that the bark is showing. The end of the willow will stick straight up, forming the neck.

Step One. Split the willow.

Step Two. Form the legs and backbone.

Step Three. Fill in body and make the neck.

Step Three. Now take the "bottom half" of the backbone, which is sticking straight out, and use this to fill in the body. Wrap it around the front and back legs again and again until you run out of twig. Then tuck the end of the twig back inside the body to hold it in place. Sometimes you will have more length than you can use. Just poke the excess up through the body cavity, along side of the neckpiece, and you can use it in a moment. Now, take the other half twig and kink it about 1 1/2 inches up from the body to form the neck. Kink it back on itself so that the bark is showing. Bring the end down and wrap it around the body to lock that in place. Bring the willow back up to the top of the neck.

Step Four. If you had any extra willow left over from wrapping the body, then you can use that now. Just wrap the other direction around the body cavity, until you run out of twig, and tuck the end under the other wraps. Now return to the neck piece and bend the remaining twig over the stub that forms the neck and shape the head to look like the number "4". The tricky part is to hold everything together as you work.

Then take the remaining willow and wrap it around the neck and back to the nose. Start at the nose and wrap around the head again and again until the whole head is wrapped. Wrap the neck with the remaining length of willow and tuck the end in under part of the wrap to lock it in place. The action of wrapping from the head around to the neck will cause

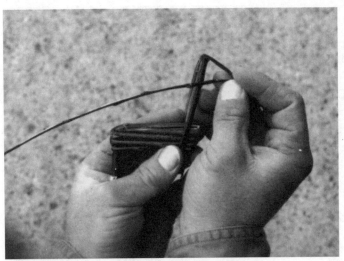

Step Four. Form and wrap the head.

the head to turn one way or another, depending on which direction you wrap it from. Jim said archaeologists found that roughly 75% of the split-willow figures they found had the head turned one way and the other 25% had the heads turned the other way. Archaeologists once thought there was some ritual significance to which direction the head was turned. But Riggs pointed out that the head turns automatically as you work, and suggested that each person just naturally works around the head from one side or the other. In our own test, Renee and I found that all of hers consistently turned one way and all of mine consistently turned the other.

At this point your split-willow figure is finished, and it should look like the examples in the photos. You may however have too much or not enough length of twig to finish the job. If there is extra then just cut it off. If it is short then it may look just fine with only part of the neck or head wrapped. The measurements suggested here for different parts of the body are only approximations. As you make more split-willow figures you will learn to adjust the proportions of the body for the length of the willow.

Split willow figures are quick to make. After you stumble though the first one or two the rest are easy.

◊   ◊◊◊   ◊

I take a moment to admire my handiwork. Willow bark always seems to have a glossy sheen to it. I like that. It is as if I am holding a toy deer which been polished, either by design or by time. It is almost as if it has been handled again and again through generations until it shone.

Funny it is—how a person can have so many thoughts and feelings about what is in essence, just a carefully mangled twig...

It occurs to me that no other species in the world would recognize this mangled twig as being "a deer". I recognize it as a deer only because of my cultural upbringing. My perception of reality is shaped by how I have been raised. Both perceptions of the deer are equally valid: the twig is mangled, and it is a deer. I have simply chosen to experience its reality as a deer.

I have noticed that in survival-type books, the first chapter is often about the mind, or about having a positive attitude. The reason-

The finished deer.

ing there is simple; the first element of survival is to be in your right mind. The mind that you choose to be in determines the reality of your situation. The difference between being optimistic or pessimistic can be the difference between life and death.

In both primitive and contemporary living the mind is the most powerful tool we have. It is in our minds that we will find both our limitations and our capabilities. It is through our minds that we can set free our abilities to prosper wherever we are.

Consider comfort. To a great extent, comfort is a process of the individual and collective mind. The Paiute Indians of the Great Basin Desert in Nevada and Idaho often wore only a breechcloth and sandals through much of the winter. The Australian aborigines are known for sleeping naked through the nights at temperatures in the forties and fifties. They can do this not because they are so much different or tougher than us, but because they define reality differently than we do.

In particle physics there is something called a wave-particle duality. Certain "particles" like electrons exhibit behaviors that are characteristic of both waves and particles. Basically, a wave can pass through multiple points at once, much like an ocean wave passing through a pier, while a particle, like a baseball can only pass through at one point. The subatomic particles of our universe have the ability to exhibit either behavior.

In the scientific laboratory physicists have conducted many tests to determine the speed and locations of these wave-particles. The startling result was that when they tested the speed they discovered a wave, but when they tested the location they discovered a particle. In the current realm of knowledge it is not possible to determine both speed and location at the same time.

A wave has an infinite number of points, while a particle exists at only one point. The wave, no matter how big or small, can always be divided in half, and then in half again and again and again. Like plotting points on a line, you can always divide the space in between any two points, and put another point in the middle. For a wave to become a particle it must collapse, out of an infinite number of points, into one particular particle point.

Scientists find this rather distressing because they like to run controlled tests where they have completely removed themselves from affecting the outcome. Yet in this case it is the scientist who causes the wave to collapse, while he or she is trying to determine a location. The popular analogy of this situation is of a cat in a box, where a random event such as the decay of a radioactive atom triggers the release of a deadly gas that kills the cat. Radioactive particles have a predictable rate of decay or "half life", but if there is only one particle left then there is only a 50-50 chance that it will decay and release the deadly gas. In the old view of physics something did or did not happen and we open the box to see the result. But in the new view of quantum or particle physics, nothing happens until we remove the lid. Until then there is a wave of quantum possibilities—the cat is in limbo with the possibility of being either alive or dead—and it is only when the observer removes the lid that the wave collapses into any particular reality. This is called the "observer effect". This concept of observer effect has altered the entire notion of reality.

Reality is ordered by our perception of it.

I remember watching a show on television where they were discussing brain surgery in some rural farm cultures in Africa. The farmers did not like the local village medical clinic, so they generally practiced their own medicine—including brain surgery. The video showed a clip of a young boy who had a serious head injury. He was sat down on a stump for exploratory surgery, to determine the extent of the wound. The tools were simple, unsterilized knives. No anesthetics were used, and the boy just sat there as the farm doctor further cut open the wound in his forehead to find out if more extensive surgery would be necessary. It may sound barbaric, yet these simple farming peoples were reported to have a surgery success rate of about 95%! The narrator went on to suggest that perhaps pain is a cultural phenomenon, something that is learned and passed down from generation to generation.

Most of us would have screamed or passed out if someone took a knife to our foreheads. Most of us would have died from gangrene had we been operated on with unsterilized tools. We have defined a world where such things are not possible, yet such things are possible where the world is defined differently.

As one modern doctor wrote, "A patient does not go to a physician with a disease. A negotiation takes place in which the vague, formless discontent of the patient is shaped into a disease almost as a sculptor shapes clay." The patient may have what seems like a random sample of symptoms, and together the doctor and patient examine them, inevitably focusing more on some symptoms and less on others, until ultimately the various ailments are pinned on the most likely definition—some specific disease defined by the collective mind, the culture. The patient comes in with the possibility of an illness and negotiates with the doctor until the possibilities collapse into a particular reality. There are even ethnic groups who contract certain ailments that only their own ethnic doctors can diagnose and treat.

In primitive living there is heat and cold and wet and mosquitoes. How we react to these elements of nature is a function of perception. Physically we may do the same actions—for instance, we may build the same shelter—

but our perception of our experience can range from being comfortable to being miserable.

People's perceptions of comfort, including my own, often change as they spend more and more time out camping. The cold becomes less cold, the hot less hot, and the mosquitoes less annoying. It is not a matter of being tough and taking it. Rather it seems as though reality gradually redefines itself until you are comfortable with less. Something happens and the mosquitoes seem to bite less. Those that do bite seem to sting less.

I stand up and place my completed split-willow figure on the rock I was sitting on. I prop it up so it is leaning against another, smaller rock. Perhaps someone will discover it. Perhaps not. I walk onward.

◊ ◊◊◊ ◊

SHELTER

The morning sun peels coolness from the land. A light breeze rustles the quaking aspen leaves. A yellow swallowtail butterfly flutters among the flowers of early summer. I pause and bury my nose in a serviceberry blossom. Then I walk around a bend in the stream and follow a trail a short jog to my camp. My camp is within a hundred yards of a main road, but people rarely wander off the road to explore the bushes.

Much of the wilderness goes unused. In the outback, people stay on a handful of well-defined trails leading to a few spectacular lakes and peaks. The smaller streams, trickles, springs, and ponds are usually unused and unknown, and these places are usually the most interesting. People rarely wander off the beaten path except in hunting season, so for the most part you can have the woods to yourself, just follow the trails that no one else is using.

Similarly, urban areas are largely under-used. All you really need to camp is a bottle of water from the kitchen tap and a bush to build a shelter in. There are always undeveloped lots and bushy parks to camp in, provided they are safe. As a teen-ager in a town of thirty-some thousand people, I built shelters in brushy, undeveloped fields near my home. It was always nice to go "camping" for the afternoon when school was out. Once in a great while I would camp overnight right in town. Today I still keep a campsite and swimming hole "retreat" close and accessible to our home in Pony.

Most everyone grows up building forts. Some of us, however, never quite grow out of it. In my case what was once child's play is now a profession; I just changed the name. Instead of building mere "forts", I now build "shelters".

We expect primitive shelters to look "house-like", but free-standing structures like this require much more work and may not perform as well as a natural shelter that has been improved upon.

Building good shelters is one of the most important primitive skills there are. If you are going camping in the cold and wet without any gear then you need to know how to stay alive and comfortable. Staying alive and comfortable requires some darn good fort building.

I combed through every outdoor-survival type book I could get my hands on when I was growing up, looking for shelter-building techniques that would keep me warm without any gear. The results of my searches were surprisingly disappointing.

It seemed that most "shelters" required at least a sleeping bag to be survivable. I wanted to be able to camp without carrying a tent or a sleeping bag. Other types of shelters had the potential to be comfortable, but required a week or more to construct. That would have been fine if I wanted to set up a tent next door through the construction phase, and if I wanted to stay a while, but I wanted to move and explore, and to stay in a new place every day or two. In all my reading I found very few shelters that could be built relatively quickly and still keep a person alive and comfortable. And those unfortunately, required materials that were not present in my area.

What I have learned about shelters since that time, I have learned largely on my own through trial and error. I slept in enough cold, wet shelters to figure out how to build some warm, dry ones. Learning to build good shelters completely transformed my experience of primitive camping. For years it seemed that I was miserable every time I went out, just too stubborn to give up. So it was a real thrill the first time I slept warm and cozy without even a blanket. The more that I learned to think for myself and design shelters to meet the conditions at hand, the better my camping experiences became. Sure, I've been cold and damp many times since—usually because I started my shelters too late in the evening—but it doesn't bother me any more, because I always know that tomorrow I can finish the job and sleep well. I've even learned to *enjoy* being uncomfortable from time to time, only because I know that I really have a choice in the matter.

A fallen tree can make a really nice <u>shingle</u>. A few slabs of bark were leaned against the back of this log to serve as additional shingling and <u>air-proofing</u>. The shelter is also built as a <u>fire reflector</u> to warm a person from both sides.

So here I will share with you my hard-earned knowledge about shelter building. But instead of merely giving you some various shelters for you to replicate, I want to teach you how to *think* shelter.

You see, every time and place is different, and at every time and place your own personal goals or objectives will also be different. For instance, there may be times and places so warm and dry that you can sleep right out in the open with no shelter of any kind, not even a blanket or a tarp. Yet, there will also be times and places where you will need to protect yourself from pouring-down, freezing-cold rain. For each time and place your objectives will likely be different too. One time you might be camping for recreation; another time you may be camping for survival. You may be on a weekend outing, or you may plan to be around for a month. You may come to the area only once, or you may be back on a regular basis. The type of shelter you build, and the location you choose for it, will vary tremendously depending on the **time**, the **place**, and your **goals**.

Therefore, *every primitive shelter you ever build will be completely unique*, and suited to the particular conditions at hand. Instead of teaching you solely "shelters", I want to teach you about the separate elements of shelter. Those elements are: **shingling, fire, insulation, and air-proofing**. In a nutshell, *shingles* help to keep you dry. *Fire* is used directly and indirectly in many different ways for heating. *Insulation* is used to trap the available heat inside, and *air-proofing* is like weather-stripping to stop cold drafts of air. Each of these elements come into consideration in every shelter you build, in both primitive and contemporary living. Once you understand each of these elements of shelter then you can assemble them into the appropriate shelters to meet the needs of your specific times, places, and goals. You will be able to predict how a new structure will perform, based on the elements of shelter, even though you've never built one quite like it before.

Debris on a lean-to serves as <u>shingling</u> and <u>air-proofing</u>.

This rock shelter serves as a <u>shingle</u> and a <u>fire reflector</u>.

28

The Elements of Shelter: Shingling

Shingles on a contemporary shelter like your house carry moisture from rain and snow away to keep the inside of the structure dry. The function of shingles or shingling on primitive dwellings is the same, only the materials used are often different. Instead of asphalt or steel roofing, for instance, you may use such materials as tree bark, logs, grass, leaves, dirt, rock overhangs, caves, or a tarp. Most of my shelters become combinations of several different methods of shingling.

By themselves, shingles will not make a warm shelter, but they will keep you dry, and they do block the cooling wind. Most often you will use some method of shingles in combination with other elements of shelter, such as insulation and/or a source of heat.

This wickiup has bark and debris to serve as <u>shingling</u>, but also as <u>insulation</u> and <u>air-proofing</u>. It has a <u>fire</u> inside for a a source of warmth. Overhead trees provide additional <u>shingling</u>.

The **wickiup** may be the most classic example of shingling. The wickiup is a tipi-shaped structure, generally made with a fairly close framework of vertical logs or poles. It may be open on most of one side, facing a fire, or it may be fully enclosed, with a fire in the middle. If the fire is inside then the smoke is allowed to rise up through gaps in the framework at the peak of the structure. All other holes around the sides are filled with smaller sticks, or stuffed with grass, or shingled over with bark and other debris. The outer layer of debris helps shingle the water away, but even without that layer, the vertical poles and logs catch the moisture and channel it to the ground. The water may sometimes run down the inside of the logs, but even then it rarely drips in the middle of the shelter. The wickiup shown here is not tight enough to keep out a driving rain, but the canopy of spruce trees overhead acts like another layer of shingling to catch and divert the rain. A heavy rainstorm is reduced to just a misty, dripping shower down below.

Cottonwood groves are especially good for building wickiup shelters. A pole framework can be covered with layers of bark shingles from dead trees. We built two such wickiups on a field trip with my daughter's seventh grade class and survived—damp, but comfortable—through 1.3 inches of rain that fell during that day and night. Cottonwoods are prone to breaking in storms, so be cautious in choosing a location.

I rarely build freestanding shelters like the wickiup. I use the same principles, but I prefer to begin by selecting a campsite that takes advantage of some **natural feature** of the environment. For example, in an area with sizable trees, I look for a **large tree** that has fallen over, leaving just enough space for me to crawl underneath. That can be improved upon by leaning slabs of bark against one or both sides of the tree to widen the dry space underneath. Slabs of bark are natural shingles and really easy to use. Simply start at the bottom of your shelter and layer the bark up to the top, so that the water will always fall from one bark shingle to another without ever being channeled inside. I like to shingle right over the top of the tree trunk, to prevent water from hitting the trunk and following it down around it's circumference to drip inside. Optionally, you can wedge slabs of bark up slightly under the log, such that water will hit the log, and follow it around its circumference to drip on the bark and away from the inside. That method is faster and takes far fewer materials.

If I am in an area with **boulders**, then I look for one that provides some form of shelter. Often you

A double lean-to <u>shingled</u> with bark provides heat for two people from one central <u>fire</u>.

Thatching is a lot of work, but makes a long-lasting <u>shingle</u>. We built this hut at home, using old baling twine to tie the rye grass and tansy in place. Chris Morasky and Vince Pinto, two interns at our school, completed the hut and lived in it for a summer.

can find a wall or two or part of a roof among large boulders. These partial shelters can be completed with other materials like logs or bark. Frame in a wall with full-length logs, then fill in the gaps with smaller sticks, always being sure to over-lap them as you go, so that water will drip from one stick to the next, and not inside. You must be especially careful when building a shelter beside or under a boulder, because moisture will often follow the contour of the rock and drip inside the shelter. You may be protected from direct rainfall, but you could still get soaking wet from a steady drip right in the middle of your home.

There are a number of ways you can avoid that problem. Ideally, you want to find rocks that do not have any surfaces that will direct water towards your future shelter. Just look at the patterns of moss under the rock. Moss will only grow where there is moisture. On the underside of a boulder the moss will generally grow along narrow lines where the water runs in. Ideally you want to find a site that does not have those pathways for the water leading into your shelter. That is difficult to do. Most often you will need to divert those little streams of water with other methods of shingling, or even little mud dams to redirect the flow.

Perhaps the most ideal shelter from the rain is a **rock overhang** or a **cave**. If you have that then all you have to do is move in. In my area there are no natural caves, and only a few rock overhangs, but there are a lot of mine shafts. Mine shafts can be extremely hazardous, since loose rock can fall from the ceiling. I usually avoid camping in or by them, but I have seen a few that were very stable and would be safe enough.

Grass also works extremely well for shingling a shelter. For most short-term shelters you can simply lay the grass on some form of framework with the tops pointing downward to wick water away. I seldom find enough grass in my area to cover an entire shelter, but I do like to stuff it in between the cracks of shelters built from logs. Alternately, if you are building a long-term shelter, and you have ample time to spend at it, then **grass thatching** can provide complete shelter from the rain and snow for years to come. Thatching generally refers to grass or other plants that have been tied on to a framework, either with the addition of cordage, or by simply tying the plants themselves around the stick framework and hanging them down.

Even small **leaves** can work well as a form of shingling. It would be impossible to layer tiny little leaves like shingles, but you can get a shingle-like effect by piling up enough leaves, a foot or two, on the sides and roof of your shelter. Likewise, **dirt** is not really shingle-like, but it can work extremely well for that purpose when it is sloped enough and packed down, so that moisture will run off quickly, without soaking in.

A **tarp** or **poncho** is an easy, one-piece shingle that can be arranged dozens of different ways to protect you from the wind and rain, assuming you brought one with you. My preferred way to use a tarp is to simply sit up and drape it over me, or to roll up in it at night if I have a bedroll. I tend to be a bit lazy, and I very seldom bother to tie a tarp up to anything. I just lay it over me. But you have to be especially careful that rainwater off the tarp will not roll down onto the layer below you and run inside. Most often I use a tarp or poncho as a shingle patch to cover gaps in unfinished shelters. No matter how good your shelter skills are, it is always handy to have at least a poncho to help keep you dry in a pinch.

◊   ◊◊◊   ◊

I toss my blanket into the shelter and pull out my water bottle. A robin lands in a willow, looks at me and flies on its way. A rock invites me to sit down. I do. I drink a quart of water and reflect on my campsite. Sitting here thinking, it seems that primitive living has a lot to teach us about contemporary living. Primitive shelters for example, have a lot to teach us about modern construction.

An insulated debris hut, bird style.

To me there is very little difference between primitive and contemporary structures except the level of complexity and longevity. The principles and objectives are largely the same; only the materials are different. Consider energy efficiency in shelters. A lack of insulation results in higher costs to replace the heat that is lost. In contemporary living this shows up as a monthly bill from the power company. In primitive living you pay the power bill more directly as you expend energy gathering quantities of firewood and staying up at night putting it on the fire. In the long run, insulation always conserves energy.

Primitive and contemporary shelters are alike in other ways as well. For example, in primitive living where you are directly exposed to the elements, it often makes the most sense to build your shelters facing southeast so the morning sun can quickly warm your campsite. It has been pretty instinctual knowledge for millions of years that when you are cold you can warm yourself by sitting in the sunshine. The sun is a source of tremendous warmth, and you can heat a home with it. I find it remarkable that anyone would consider building a contemporary structure that does not utilize the sun's free warmth. It is unfathomable that most contemporary homes and offices are built without any consideration of the sun at all. The plans are drawn on paper and placed on the land without any site consideration at all. But any shelter that is not integrated with the landscape is going to be a poor shelter.

People often expect that an energy-efficient home is going to cost a lot more than a house of standard construction, but that is not necessarily true. It does not cost any more to put all the windows on the south side instead of on the north. You might have the same amount of windows; it just takes a little bit more design work to make sure every part of the house is properly lighted. Likewise, for the thousands of dollars that a sophisticated heating system costs, you can insulate a house sufficiently so that it needs no heating system at all. Low-cost, high-efficiency homes are the subject of my book *Living Homes: Thomas J. Elpel's Field Guide to Integrated Design and Construction.*

Our own house looks expensive, but actually cost very little, roughly $10 per square foot in 1995 dollars. It looks good not because we used costly materials, but because we skillfully used some very low-cost resources. We put our minds to work to make up for a lack of money. What we got is an elegant, but inexpensive home that is remarkably energy efficient. See the ad for *Living Homes* in the back of this book, or our website for more details.

Gradually people are becoming more conscious of the earth and more aware of the advantages of working with nature. A shift is developing in architecture and construction. People are beginning to realize that it is economical to build houses that do not pollute. It is a trend that we want to encourage through our school. In either primitive or contemporary living, a shelter is only as good as it is energy-efficient. With that in mind, lets consider the element of insulation in shelter building:

The debris hut is built with insulation, which also functions as shingling and air-proofing. It is usually kept warm with body heat.

The Elements of Shelter: Insulation

Insulation is not a source of warmth. Rather it is a way of trapping warmth and keeping it in the shelter. In a contemporary shelter like your home, insulation is made up of lots of tiny air spaces. Dense materials, like stone, steel, or water conduct heat away very quickly, while lightweight materials with many air pockets trap heat in. Heat still conducts through such materials, but very slowly from one air pocket to another. If you have been dressed up in cold weather, then you have experienced the effects of insulation keeping you warm. If you have been drenched by a cold rain, then you have experienced heat being rapidly conducted away from your body. Insulation comes in many forms, *but most of them work on a similar principle of trapping air in little pockets, to interrupt the flow of warmth.* Insulation in contemporary shelters usually comes in the form of fiberglass, cellulose, or foam. In the wilderness, insulation comes in the form of leaves, grass, fluffy bark, just plain debris, and even snow.

Grasses, sedges, and cattails all contain air spaces within individual stalks, making them exceptional insulators. Leaves may not contain air spaces inside, but when heaped together they create air space between them, just as a down jacket is insulated by the spaces between the feathers. Any kind of debris that can be heaped up with lots of air space inside will make a good insulator. Logs are fairly dense but still have quite a bit of insulation value, since there are small air spaces inside the wood. Sawdust from the log is even better, since there is air space between the flakes. Even dirt has some insulation value, though it too is fairly dense. As you may see by now, insulation plays a big part in our day-to-day lives in the contemporary world, from the walls of the house, to the blankets on the beds and the clothes we wear. Insulation is just as vital in primitive living.

You can **boost the insulation value of your clothing**, if you are caught out in a sudden cold front by simply stuffing your clothes with dry, fluffy debris. The inner bark from some trees such as the cottonwood can work well, as can the dry grass tops sticking up out of the snow. Many dead flowers, such as from sagebrush or goldenrod, will stick up out of the snow all winter, with fluffy tops that dry out quickly after every storm. Cattail down makes one of the best, and

A grass blanket serves as <u>insulation</u> to trap in warmth. <u>Fire</u> was utilized as a source of warmth in the form of a hot coal bed in the sand beneath the bed.

certainly one of the softest, insulators. Just look around you to see what you can find that is light, soft, and dry, and you can stuff that inside your clothes for extra insulation.

On my winter camping trips I wear **sweatpants** over my jeans so that it is easy to stuff grass or other insulation material inside. I prefer sweatpants to thermal underwear for a number of other reasons too. First, I always thought thermal underwear was too restrictive, while sweatpants allow more freedom of movement. Another bonus is that sweatpants can be taken on or off without completely undressing—a valuable asset on a cold winter day. Sweatpants also act like "gaiters" to help keep jeans dry. Stuffing grass inside offers even more protection to block wet snow from seeping through the layers. Finally, I do not like to spend money on clothing or gear that I am just going to trash out in the wilds anyway, and sweatpants are easy to come by at the second-hand store, while thermals usually have to be purchased new.

Reportedly, the Inuit peoples along the arctic coast had a double-layered system of clothing that was so warm they could just lie down and fall asleep wherever they happened to be. That insulation was vital to them because of where they lived. Besides being in one of the coldest regions of the world, they also had almost no firewood, save for what occasionally washed up as driftwood along the seashore. In wintertime their small skin tipis were almost as cold inside as outside. They wore their real shelters on their bodies. Animals also wear their shelters. Their fur or feathers insulate them and keep them warm throughout the year. For added warmth many animals will burrow into the snow and be covered over by it.

Besides stuffing leaves and grasses into your clothes for insulation, you can also stuff them inside or on top of a shelter for added warmth. Stuffed inside a shelter, leaves insulate you as a sleeping bag would, and you simply crawl into the middle of the pile to sleep. On top of a shelter, leaves insulate the structure, much like a contemporary home. Then you can move around inside to work.

The most well known form of insulated primitive structure today may be the "**debris hut**" or the "**leaf hut**", which in it's modern form and name can be accredited to Tom Brown Jr. The leaf hut is an excellent shelter in areas where there is a lot of dead organic matter on the ground, such as deep layers of tree leaves. The inside is shaped like a sleeping bag, defined by sticks leaning against a horizontal ridgepole. This is typically covered over with two feet of leaves, serving the dual purposes of insulation and shingling. The inside is stuffed with more insulation, preferably very soft and dry grass, leaves, or moss. The debris hut has so much insulation in it that stays warm with only your body heat.

I rarely use the debris hut in its generic form since most of my area has very little leaf litter or other debris. Here, only by cattail patches, haystacks, and sometimes around cottonwood trees, is there a truly adequate supply of insulation for a conventional debris hut. Most places I camp at have about as much debris as a suburban lawn, making the leaf hut an impractical shelter much of the time, but I do take advantage of any insulation I can find. Some areas have at least enough insulation to stuff the inside of a shelter, and this can be adequate insulation throughout the summer, if the outside of the shelter is tightly shingled with other materials to keep out both air-flow and rainfall.

◊　◊◊◊　◊

I always try to adapt my shelters to take advantage of local features in the landscape. I built this shelter against an L-shaped granite boulder. The boulder provided two walls, and all I added was a sloping roof and wall of aspen logs from the top of the boulder down to the ground. Water shingles from one log to another down to the ground and keeps the inside dry. I bring along two wool blankets and a poncho to sleep in when I camp here. The shelter is designed to shed water and to enable me to blend quietly into the environment. It helps me to feel connected to the area.

Shelters, as they are illustrated in most outdoor books, are typically freestanding structures built on level ground. But building a shelter from scratch like that requires a lot of time and materials, and the

Taking advantage of natural features in the landscape can save time and help make your shelters blend into the environment. This shelter is designed for <u>shingling</u>. Blankets or a sleeping bag are used for <u>insulation</u> and <u>air-proofing</u>.

end product often stands out and is easy to see. By locating your site where you can take advantage of rocks or trees to use as ready-made walls or ceilings you can greatly reduce the amount of work necessary. The finished shelter becomes tied into the visual landscape, making it far more difficult to see.

For the same reasons, I strive to adapt contemporary structures to the local environment as well. I like to build with natural materials from the area, such as native stone or log; these blend into the landscape and aesthetically tie the structure to its environment. We also use natural colors for such things as the roofing, and for painting trim. I think that houses with the feel of nature can help people feel a greater connection with the earth, much more so than living in a structure with flat white walls.

Using local natural materials makes economic sense as well. In primitive living it makes more sense for me to adapt my shelters to the local resources such as dirt, logs, and stone, than to hike five or ten miles to bring back a huge quantity of cattails. Likewise, for our home we built with stone and log and bermed it into the earth. Thus our contemporary home is built of similar materials to my primitive shelters. This saves a great deal on cost, since much of our house was laying about in the form of rocks in the roads and fields. It was free for the picking.

I screw the cap back on the water bottle and set it inside the shelter. Looking back, I guess primitive skills have given me a very well grounded, practical approach to contemporary living. In primitive living, when the chores are all done and my physical needs are taken care of I can go exploring. Similarly, in contemporary living, with our physical needs largely taken care of (i.e.: no house payment and low energy bills), Renee and I can do almost anything we want for the rest of our lives.

The Elements of Shelter: Fire

As a rule, in either primitive or contemporary living, it is more economical over the long-term to invest in insulating your shelters, than to waste a lot of fuel. A drafty shelter in contemporary living costs you through your power bill. You pay a price in primitive living for leaky shelters too, because you burn a lot of wood, and you have to gather it. If you are like most people, then you will probably burn all the firewood that is closest to your shelter first, and then you will work outward in a circle, walking a little farther each time. If you are merely passing through then it may be economical to consume a lot of wood, especially if good insulating materials are scarce in the area. If you plan to stay a while then it will likely be economical to build a tighter, more insulated shelter that requires less fuel to keep warm.

A rock overhang serves as a natural shingle. The hot coal bed provides a source of "fire". Blankets are used for insulation, and a tarp is used for air-proofing.

Often, especially when you are moving everyday, a shelter that depends on fire can be the most comfortable shelter you can construct in the least amount of time. In this context I am using the word "shelter" to include any means that keeps you adequately warm through the night. Thus, on a very warm night when you are sure it will not rain, a shelter may consist of covering over your **cooking fire** and curling up on the warm earth without even a blanket.

On a slightly cooler, but still rainless night you might sleep on that warm earth and start a new fire next to you. Or you might build a trench fire. A **trench fire** is simply a fire built in a trench as long as your body, so it warms you from head to toe. Your internal thermostat wakes you at the appropriate times to add a little more fuel. Be sure you can reach the firewood without having to get up.

The next step up, to improve upon an open fire, is to build **reflectors** behind you and on the other side of the fire. A reflector is any object, like rocks, logs, or debris, stacked up to reflect heat back from the fire. It prevents the breeze from so easily channeling the warmth of the fire away. A reflector built behind you will warm the side of you that is away from the fire. A reflector built on the other side of the fire will channel more heat from the fire towards you, saving firewood. I like to utilize natural reflectors, particularly rock overhangs. I first start a fire in a trench near the rock to warm the ground and the rock, being careful to keep the fire far enough away from the rock to avoid turning it black, and small enough to avoid causing heat stress to any overhanging rocks that could be popped loose. Then I cover over the trench fire, and start a new trench fire a few feet away from the rock out cropping. I lie down with the fire on one side of me, the warm ground below me, and the warm rock reflector behind me. It is really amazing to sleep warm through a cold, cold night without any blankets or coverings at all!

The idea of burning a fire in a trench and covering it over to sleep on it is called a **hot coal bed**. The hot coal bed may be the most classic example of a shelter utilizing fire.   It is not often used with a second fire as I have described, but instead in conjunction with some type of a bedroll, like a wool blanket.

The hot coal bed is a true luxury in primitive living. When I sleep on a hot coal bed I imagine myself as a hot dog slowly baking over the coals, rolling over from time to time, baking evenly on all sides. I like to lay there in my humble bedroll and soak up the warmth, feeling it penetrate all through my body. I like to breathe the cool night air and gaze unfocussed at the galaxy above.

To make a hot coal bed, start by digging a trench. Next build a fire in the trench and let it burn very hot for a couple hours. When the fire dies down bury the coals with several inches of dirt and lay your bedroll on top of it.

Some people like a coal bed pit or trench which is roughly the width of the body and long enough to warm from the shoulders to the knees. I prefer a narrow, long trench, eight to twelve inches wide and the full length of my body to warm me from head to toe. The trench should be about eight inches deep. It needs the depth to accommodate the hot coals and several inches of dirt. Some people dig a deeper pit and line the bottom with rocks for thermal mass to hold the heat. I believe that only adds extra work. The existing dirt or sand will serve as thermal mass as long as it is not soggy wet. In most soils the pit can be dug very quickly, usually in five or ten minutes using a simple

Any stable rock out-cropping with a dry place to dig can be a good site for a hot coal bed, especially if it has southern exposure.

digging stick. If there is sod then dig it out first and set it aside for later reclamation.

The fire should burn in all parts of the trench. It is not the coals that ultimately keep you warm, but the hot thermal mass of the earth and rocks. Therefore, to work properly, the fire must heat the entire trench. After a couple hours let the fire die down. Remove any large chunks of wood, and transfer these to another fire pit or put them out. Cover the coals with dirt or sand and check for hot spots. Roll out your bed and periodically recheck for hot spots until the soil cover is thoroughly warm. Add more soil cover to any hot spots.

The soil you use to cover your hot coal bed with will contain some amount of moisture, and steam will rise from the soil almost as soon as you cover the coals. Without some type of vapor barrier you will get steamed all night long, and you will be soggy by morning. A rain poncho or a sheet of plastic works well to block the steam.

A co-instructor once tried to let his bed steam dry before he put his bedroll on it. However, the convection of the air over the soil quickly cooled off the hot coal bed. He was awake all night. Therefore, put your bedroll down right away to insulate and protect the warmth. It is helpful if the vapor barrier wraps all the way around your body, except your face. It will serve as a windbreaker and will give you at least some protection against rain, dew, frost, or snow in the night.

When the ground is frozen in winter one can often find a dry, sandy, moderately protected site with easy digging at the base of rock outcropping with southern exposure. A hot coal bed can also be dug in ground that is frozen by alternately thawing the ground with fire and digging down. However, the process is time consuming, messy, and hard to reclaim. A hot coal bed built like that will likely be an ugly scar by spring.

As you have seen, fire can be a form of shelter in it's own. Of course, in stormy weather you will usually want to combine your fire with other elements of shelter, especially shingling. One common combination of shingling and fire is the wickiup, as discussed previously. You can also use fire in combination with a insulation-based shelter, such as the debris hut. For a little extra heat, simply warm some good-sized rocks in the fire, then pull them out and let them cool until you are positive they will not ignite the insulation, and put the **hot rocks** inside the shelter. Optionally, you can build a **hot coal bed with a debris hut** over it. Start the hot coal bed first, then gather materials for the debris hut while the fire is burning. This combination will keep you warm in a place where you have no blanket for a hot coal bed, and not enough natural insulation for a full-blown debris hut. With adequate insulation you do not need to rebuild the hot coal bed each day because the insulation holds the heat in, and most importantly, the coal bed neutralizes the cold emanating from the ground, so that even after the coal bed dies you at least are not sleeping over cold ground.

One of the fastest and warmest shelters you can build in dry weather is a **hot coal bed with a debris blanket**. Dig a trench and start a fire, then collect as much dry, fluffy insulation as you can while the ground is warming. After the trench is filled in, simply place a log along each side of the coal bed and fill the bed with insulation. The ground warms you from below, while the insulation traps the heat in from above. A poncho or tarp is helpful when available, to block ground moisture and air infiltration. Put the tarp on the ground below you then wrap it up over the insulation.

Digging a trench for a hot coal bed.

Another way to heat a shelter from below is with a **chimney draft bed**. The chimney draft bed has a fire in a low spot or a hole below the shelter with a chimney running in a trench below the shelter and rising on the other side. The trench is often lined and topped with rocks, then covered with dirt, with a bed on top of that. Stoke the fire and put a rock lid on it to channel the heat and smoke through the chimney under the shelter. The chimney draft bed requires some extra thought and work, and I have not yet built one. But in the classic book, *Outdoor Survival Skills*, author Larry Olsen writes, "[the chimney draft bed] is unequaled for comfort in cold weather."

Another type of shelter is heated with red hot rocks. That shelter is called the **sweatlodge**. Usually used for ceremonial purposes, the sweatlodge is a virtually airtight shelter, or at least as much as can be achieved in primitive circumstances. Red-hot rocks are placed in a pit inside to radiate heat. In the conventional sweatlodge water is poured on those rocks, generating profuse amounts of hot steam for a primitive sauna. For a habitable shelter however, do not pour any water on the rocks, and they can keep you and the shelter warm all night.

◊　◊◊◊　◊

A wasp flies by. It buzzes once around my face, becoming the focus of my attention. It checks me out from all sides then descends to land on my pack, taking my thoughts with it.

It seems that I have a lot of gear with me on this trip, but I suppose that is one of the trade-offs in primitive living. In primitive living you can either bring the gear you need for your physical needs or you can improvise on the trail to meet those needs. By not bringing gear you can have more freedom to explore, to run, and to play without the burden of a pack. But when you do not bring gear it takes a great deal of time to improvise to meet your needs directly from the ecosystem. With shelters, for example, one can bring a tent and sleeping bag or blankets, be burdened on the trail, get to camp late and then have little to do to prepare for sleep. Without a tent, one can bring blankets or a sleeping bag and build a rain shelter if necessary, thus having less weight, but more work. Or it is possible to bring no tent, and no blankets, and no sleeping bag, but to build an effective and appropriate shelter at camp. It may take a long time to build a shelter, but without the burden of a backpack one can skip and play and crawl through the bushes all day long and still arrive in the same camp very early, with time to build a quality shelter.

One thing for certain, is that shelter can be a major expense in both primitive and contemporary living. In contemporary culture you can spend hours every day at a job working to pay off a shelter. In primitive living it is possible to spend hours each day constructing a shelter. You can recoup some of that investment in your primitive shelters by staying several nights. If you stay in a shelter for three nights, and it took you three hours to build the shelter, then you have an investment of just one hour per day, rather than three. Stay for a week, and it only costs you a half hour per day. If you are moving every day then you about have to stick to some very simple improvisations on nature for your shelters; you have to create shelters that take only an hour or so to build.

In contemporary society it is no wonder that we spend so much time paying for our shelters, when you consider how elaborate they are, compared to primitive dwellings. Many people spend their entire lives working to pay for their shelter, and never do pay it off. Looking back, I think even our own home was expensive. It cost us several years of wages to pay for it, and several years to build it. In fact, we are still finishing old projects *and* adding on new ones. We could conceivably spend much of the next ten years working on our place. Life is short, and you have to decide how you are going to spend it.

I would like to see the cost of contemporary shelters come down for all people, so that people can apply themselves towards more fulfilling ventures. One way that this might happen would be by adapting some types of primitive shelters to modern living. Specifically, I would like to do a low-income housing project some day, adapting Mandan earthlodge-type structures for modern living. I think it would be possible to get an elegant, energy-efficient, dome-shaped home at a price quite competitive with trailer houses. It should be an interesting project.

A slight breeze passes through, rustling the aspen leaves. I can feel a subtle, but refreshing coolness on my cheek. I tune into it, savoring the aliveness. I listen as the breeze passes away... Always, everywhere, the air moves endlessly. The breeze feels good now, but I can still remember my early shelters. They were drafty. The ceaseless flow of air always found me.

The Elements of Shelter: Air-proofing

Air-proofing barely qualifies as a separate element of shelter since slowing air-infiltration is a crucial part of nearly every shelter any way. Even a simple reflector helps block the major air movement, the wind. A shingled structure, such as a wickiup also stays warmer when air flow is minimized. More so, the very essence of an insulated shelter, such as the debris hut, is to be completely draft-free. It might seem that air-proofing should be included with insulation, since insulation plugs up drafts, but there is a slight difference. Air-proofing a primitive structure is the

equivalent of caulking and weather-stripping a contemporary building. Weather-stripping materials may have no insulating air spaces at all; even dense materials are commonly used, such as caulk. The purpose of these materials is only to stop direct drafts of cold air.

Perhaps, however, the real reason air-proofing is considered here as a separate element of shelters is because it was always my nemesis when I started building primitive shelters. Living in an area that is poor in insulating materials, I always built drafty shelters and suffered for it. I tried for years to build warm wickiups and debris huts, and usually ended up cold because I could not stop the flow of air.

Eventually I realized that neither the wickiup nor the debris hut were appropriate for most places I camped. I had to adapt to the two materials I did have in abundance. Those two materials were dirt and logs. Granted, dirt is not a great insulator, and you would freeze if you merely dug a hole and laid against it.

The scout pit is built in the ground for maximum <u>air-proofing</u>. It often has a hot coal bed underneath it for a source of <u>fire</u>. The dirt covering functions as a <u>shingle</u>. Bark or other debris can be added for better shingling.

However, dirt is really effective at blocking air-flow. Remember, in the previous section I wrote about the sweatlodge as being a virtually airtight shelter. Well, that air-tightness is generally achieved with a covering of dirt.

Likewise, a debris hut with a shortage of insulation can be aided by a covering of dirt to seal it good and tight. In our area, however, with almost no insulating debris, I realized that I would have to depend almost exclusively on dirt. I wanted a shelter that would be truly warm and comfortable where I could sleep soundly with no

blanket of any kind, and without having to put wood on the fire all night. I had to design a shelter that worked well in my area. The shelter I came up with is a combination of several elements of shelter construction. I call it the scout pit. (Since developing the scout pit I have heard that a somewhat similar shelter, by the same name, is used as a camouflage shelter in some classes at Tom Brown's Tracker school in New Jersey. From what I have heard, it is typically deeper, and filled with leaves, rather than having a hot coal bed in it.)

The **scout pit** is an underground shelter, which may be lined with grass, leaves, or other soft dry materials to serve as an insulating blanket, or it may have a hot coal bed beneath the pit.

To begin with, choose a site where the impacts will not be readily noticeable. Avoid digging in an open meadow. The dark soil will stand out as a blotch in the green grass. Your shelter will be hard to camouflage, difficult to reclaim, and it will look suspiciously like a gravesite.

It is better to dig in the forest where there is scanty undergrowth, or in a gravel bar where there is nothing growing. Choose a site where little or nothing is growing, and it will be easy to make your shelter blend right in. One time while finishing a pit shelter I walked twenty feet away and was shocked to turn around and see that my shelter had "disappeared".

Digging a scout pit.

Constructing the roof.

Look for a site that is fairly easy to dig in, and look for a site in reasonably dry ground. As always, be alert to possible dangers, such as flooding, and do not build your shelter in the middle of an animal trail. In some locations you might stack up logs and other obstacles to discourage both stock and wildlife from walking on your roof. Also check your location for fire hazards, especially if you plan to use a hot coal bed. Rotten roots and dry, fluffy forest soils are capable of holding a smoldering coal for weeks. A fire can burn underground for weeks before it breaks out into a raging forest fire. People who start forest fires, no matter how accidentally, do receive the bills for extinguishing the fires, often for many millions of dollars.

To build a scout pit, start by digging a trench big enough to lie in, with room to roll over comfortably. Use a digging stick to break up the soil; and use your hands, a can, or a flat piece of wood to scoop the loose soil out of the pit. Two flat pieces of wood together can work especially well.

If the ground is dry and warm, and especially if there is a significant fire danger, then I would advise just stuffing the shelter with insulating leaves and grass for warmth. If the ground is cold and damp, and if the fire danger is low, then I would recommend making a hot coal bed beneath your shelter.

To make a hot coal bed under your scout pit, start by digging down an additional eight inches or so into the floor of your shelter. Kindle a fire and make sure it burns along the entire length of the pit. Burn a hot fire in the pit for one to two hours, depending on how damp the soil is. Let the fire burn down to coals and use a stick to spread them out evenly across the pit. A hot coal bed built on the surface of the ground almost always requires a vapor barrier because the soil put over the coal bed is usually damp. But a hot coal bed in a scout pit dries the dirt in the walls all the way up. Scrape this dry, warm dirt off the walls to cover the pit; then there will be no moisture on the coal bed, and you will not get steamed as you sleep in there. Spread a few inches of dirt over the coals.

You can choose to fill your shelter with insulating leaves, but I personally prefer sleeping in the scout pit with no insulation. The insulation can be a little bit restrictive when you want to roll over. I like sleeping right on the ground, without insulation, in an envelope of warm air from the coal bed. If you have no coal bed then stuff the pit with dry grasses or leaves to use as an insulating blanket. Also, if you have a hot coal bed you may choose to stuff the shelter with insulation the next night, rather than tear the shelter apart to rebuild the coal bed. I find that I am perfectly comfortable with just the heat of the coal bed the first night, and that next day I have the additional time I need for the more tedious task of finding bits and pieces of insulation.

With or without insulation, next lay sticks and logs across the pit at ground level and leave a small opening to crawl in and out of. Place grass or bark over the cracks between the logs, then cover the logs with the soil excavated from the pit. The soil cover makes the shelter tight against air infiltration. Scatter debris over the top for camouflage. The finished shelter will be like an underground cocoon, a sort of underground sleeping bag.

I normally leave the doorway open, and my shelters stay warm, even as heat is rushing out through the opening all night. The pit itself blocks all air infiltration from the bottom and sides, and the dirt on the roof does the same. By then the hatch is pretty negligible. However, on particularly cold nights, or if my coal bed seems a little weak, then I cover the doorway with a coat, or slabs of bark or other insulation to limit the flow of air.

The scout pit is a primitive luxury!

Two scout pits. One has a tarp for a roof that can be easily removed to rekindle the coal bed. The other was built wide enough so that a row of hot rocks could be pulled inside each night for warmth.

I build most of my pit shelters in level ground with the doorway directly upward, which has the potential to be a liability in wet weather. We live in a dry area, so that is seldom a problem. Nevertheless, it is important to know how to weatherproof a pit shelter.

In wet weather a simple wickiup shelter can be built of brush over the top of the scout pit to protect the pit from the elements and to give you a dry space to work and cook during the rain. Essentially, you can have your kitchen and living room upstairs, while your bedroom is in the basement. Alternately, if you have a tarp you can lay this out flat over your shelter and anchor it in place with rocks. It will shed the water off of your underground shelter.

I have also built scout pits that were not entirely underground, and had the doorway to the side. When trees fall over they often pull up a big plug of earth, kind of like a ready-made scout pit. The roots are still right there, and they can be a fire hazard, but in wet weather it can be safe to start a fire and make the hot coal bed, after you have finished digging the pit out to fit your body. That much done, I have leaned sticks up against the wall of dirt attached to the tree roots, thus giving me a sloped roof, and the opportunity to put a door out the side. Just be careful to monitor the fire conditions. It is possible for the fire from your coal bed to burn underground through the dead tree roots. The smoldering coals may surface a few weeks or months later to ignite a forest fire.

Another way to put a door out the side where rain cannot fall into it is to build a scout pit on a riverbank, with the door facing out towards the river, provided you are sure you are above any possible flood line. Such a shelter also has excellent potential for nature observation, since so much wildlife walks right along the riverbanks during the nights. Dug into a riverbank it would also be easy to install a chimney draft bed under the shelter for long-term comfort. That may be my next shelter. The fire would be down below the shelter, with the chimney going under the length of it, and rising at the other end.

The scout pit with a hot coal bed under it is really quite a comfort in the wilderness. You can lay there, with no blankets, but perfectly warm, with an open view of the stars straight above your head. Or you can sit in the doorway of your pit, with the pit as a backrest, and the roof as a desk-top for writing in your journal. On a frosty morning you can be warm and toasty as you sit up in your shelter to watch the wildlife, with only your head sticking out above ground level. The scout pit with a hot coal bed is more than a shelter; it is a luxury.

◊   ◊◊◊   ◊

I stand and follow a path to a nearby spot where I have camped in the past. A small tan-colored bird darts out of a rose bush beside the trail. I did not see what it was, but I pause and peek into the rose. A small nest and three delicate eggs are hidden there. I leave the nest alone and continue my way to the old campsite. It is a site which, we have used for hot coal beds in the past. The hot coal bed is a bed of hot coals in a trench covered with soil. The coals warm the soil, and you place your bedroll on the hot ground.

The environmental impacts of the hot coal beds vary with the environment and the weather. The Pony area typically has a long wet spring followed by a dry, brittle summer. I have built hot coal beds during the moist spring and could hardly find them when I returned at the end of the summer. I dug out the sod and set it aside until I finish using the site, then I replanted the sod. In the rainy season the sod reroots and reclamation is quick. However, the same technique fails during the drier summer season, because the soil dries out and the plants do not reroot. With several beds near each other the scars can lend the impression of being some sort of cult gravesite.

The beds at this site were built two and three years ago and the long, narrow scars are still visible; there are weedy plants, including pennycress and shepherd's purse from the mustard family, growing in the beds. It could be another year or two before the beds disappear.

The Earth Lodge
A Mandan Indian-style dwelling

The earthlodge shown in these photos was built for our school by Chris Morasky and Vince Pinto when they came and stayed with us for a summer as interns. The earthlodge was Chris's suggestion, to build a long-term shelter that would be comfortable and habitable in summer and winter. He researched earthlodge designs and then undertook the construction project. The basic design consists of 4 upright poles connected by beams at the top to make a center square, plus 12 upright poles, also connected by beams, to make the outer circle. The original earthlodges were built without nails, so the upright poles had forked branches to support the crossbeams. For convenience, we used big nails instead.

Small poles were leaned against the outer circle to make walls. Additional poles were placed on top to cover the area between the inner square and the outer circle. A smoke hole was left open in the center. Historical designs called for a layer of brush to spread the load laterally among the poles, then a foot-thick layer of dry grass, topped with about a foot of dirt. We made some improvisations, using scraps of plywood instead of brush to spread the load, plus old carpet to hold the straw in place until we could get it covered. We bought a big round bale of straw, rather than collecting it by hand. A backhoe took care of the dirt work in about two hours.

The earthlodge was an incredible shelter for many years, though it had it's problems. The smoke hole should have been larger and the doorway should have been longer and shorter to help draft smoke out of the shelter. If the fire produced any smoke at all, then it quickly accumulated in the top of the structure and slowly filled the shelter from top-to-bottom, until we had to put our heads by the floor to get any air. Another problem was that we didn't have quite enough straw and dirt, so water gradually wicked through the roof and rotted the poles. (Plastic should not be used because it traps moisture in and accelerates decay.) Eventually we had to tear the shelter down.

The earthlodge had a layer of straw to hold up the dirt and to provide _insulation_. A central _fire_ heated the dwelling. The dirt served as _shingling_ and _air-proofing_.

The earthlodge was a nice cool place to hang out on hot summer days. A fire made it warm and cozy for winter camping. But eventually the roof timbers rotted and we had to tear it down.

40

Mandan-Style Earth Lodge

Historically, earthlodges were built about 40 feet in diameter and housed five or six families. The lodges were about 6 feet high at the outer ring and 12-15 high in the middle. Ours was a little under 6 feet at the outer ring, and about 10 feet high and 23 feet in diameter.

Mandan earthlodges had a smoke hole about 4 feet across. The smokehole and doorway were the only light sources from the outside, but if you have a skylight in your house, then you know how effective that is. Our smokehole was only about 2 feet across. It should have been bigger & higher to improve draft.

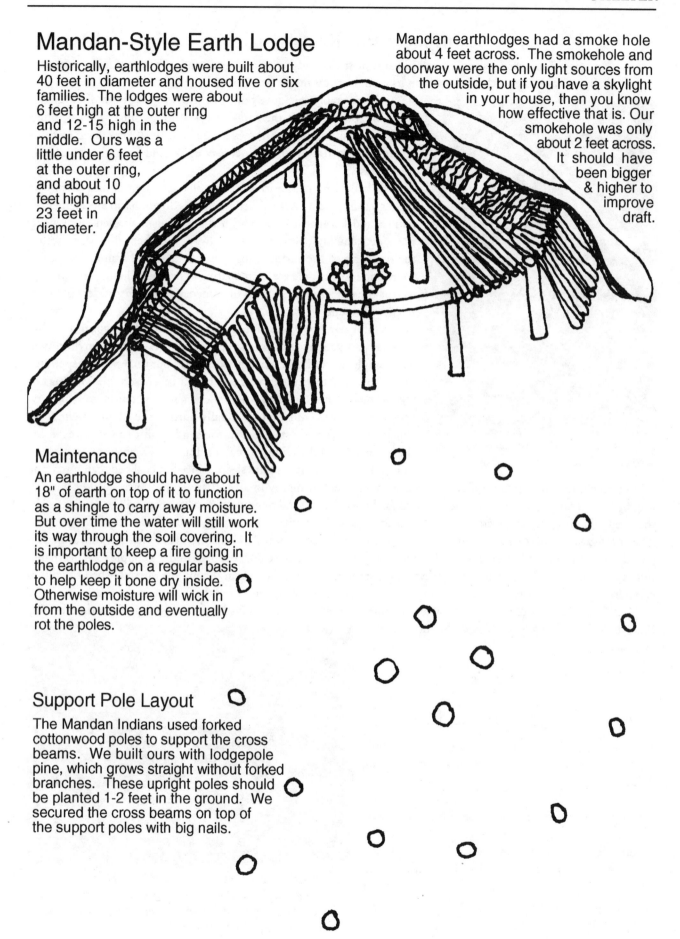

Maintenance

An earthlodge should have about 18" of earth on top of it to function as a shingle to carry away moisture. But over time the water will still work its way through the soil covering. It is important to keep a fire going in the earthlodge on a regular basis to help keep it bone dry inside. Otherwise moisture will wick in from the outside and eventually rot the poles.

Support Pole Layout

The Mandan Indians used forked cottonwood poles to support the cross beams. We built ours with lodgepole pine, which grows straight without forked branches. These upright poles should be planted 1-2 feet in the ground. We secured the cross beams on top of the support poles with big nails.

Impacts and Reclamation

You may think that a simple fort built out of sticks and brush and grass and dirt would leave very little impact at all, and would quickly disappear on its own, but you might be surprised.

A hot coal bed built at the wrong place and time can leave a scar for many years.

Remarkably, wickiups built *110 years ago* have been discovered at a site in Colorado with their framework still standing. That is longer than many contemporary homes have lasted. It is something to think about the next time you consider leaving behind a simple structure in the woods.

I make it a practice to dismantle all the shelters I build when I am through using them. Actually, stick shelters do not harm any element of nature, and I sometimes wonder if the animals may even enjoy using them occasionally. Nevertheless, I always tear them down and return the materials to the earth. Mostly it is a matter of human aesthetics. More and more people are participating in primitive living, and we have to tear the old structures down or someday the countryside will be littered with them.

Similarly, hot coal beds may not really hurt the environment, but they can easily leave visible scars. A hot coal bed in grassy environment will completely heal over in a few weeks to about three years, depending on the area and the time of year it is built. In a desert area you may be able to make a hot coal bed where there is no vegetation growing anyway, in which case you are not actually hurting the environment at all. But from an aesthetic standpoint, the sand or dirt can shift, exposing the bed of coals and leaving a visual scar for many, many years to come—quite an impact for one night's sleep. Since hot coal beds can impact an area so much, I try to minimize their use, constructing them primarily in areas that will heal over quickly, without leaving long-term environmental or aesthetic scars. I dig them in sand or gravel bars where they will be rearranged by the spring flooding, or I dig them in stands of cheat grass, where I am not disrupting established stands of vegetation. The cheat grass comes up from seed each year and favors disturbed soils, so I disturb areas where the cheat grass is already growing, rather than creating additional habitat for it. I also have hot coal beds under a couple rock overhangs in the area, and these I use on a regular basis. I have even made hot coal beds in the middle of established fire pits at campgrounds! I always reconstruct the fire pit when I leave, and you cannot tell that I slept in the fire.

Consideration of environmental and aesthetic impacts should always be part of your goals in determining the type of shelter you build, and the location you choose for it.

◊   ◊◊◊   ◊

I've used this area for quite a few years now. It is a favorite spot of mine. I have my swimming hole here, and it is one of my favorite places for observing wildlife.

I remember one early morning when I was returning to camp from my perch on the hill under the fir tree. I wore my moccasins so I could walk very quietly. But the grass was wet with morning dew, and wet moccasins are *slick* moccasins. I slipped, landing flat on my butt. It was not too bad of a place to sit though; so I stayed there a moment to tune into my surroundings.

A grass "sleeping bag" on hot ground. The grass bedding served as <u>insulation</u>. <u>Fire</u> was used as a hot coal bed beneath us. The logs walls and bark roof functioned as <u>air-proofing</u>, and minimally as <u>shingles</u>. From the video "3 Days at the River".

Then, in the complete absence of sound, there was a movement along the animal trail just down hill from me. I focused in on it. It looked like a coyote—but it was too big, and so light in color. It seemed to have just one distinct marking, a multi-colored, reddish-brownish-grayish streak on its face. Soundlessly it moved along the path, coming perhaps within fifty yards of me. I sat there in total awe.

The cool, slight morning breeze blew my scent right across the trail. It did not pause and look around. There was no curiosity; it had no interest in gathering more information. Scent was all it needed. In one smooth, flowing movement it went up over some vegetation and disappeared into brush. There was no sound. There was hardly a blade of grass disturbed.

For the briefest second, I sat there stunned. It was like nothing I had ever seen. Then it repeated itself... There was a movement on the trail, and a second animal flowed silently along the path. It seemed as though the first scene replayed itself, as if every footstep was identical. It came along the path, intercepted my scent at exactly the same point, and disappeared into the brush precisely as the first had. Their every move was made with total precision.

Here I am making a pile of spruce needles to block the doorway to a two person "debris hut". The canopy of spruce trees overhead functioned as <u>shingles</u>. The pine needle debris served as <u>insulation</u> and <u>air-proofing</u>. <u>Fire</u> was used for heating in the form of hot rocks brought inside the shelter. (From the video "Mountain Meadows".)

Were they coyotes? Were they wolves? I had heard that there are some exceptionally large and light-colored coyotes in Montana. But these animals did not look anything like other coyotes I had ever seen. Could they have been wolves? It all happened so fast. I still have no definite answer to that question. But that is okay. It was only an instant, yet the whole experience was so mystical; I would rather not pin a name on it. My body must have known what my conscious mind did not. Was it an accident that I slipped and landed on my butt? I doubt it. I leave the hot-coal bed site, and walk back to my shelter at the L-shaped boulders.

Fallen trees provide excellent scout pit sites, but you must monitor your fire carefully. The roots may hold a fire underground for weeks or months before erupting into a forest fire.

It is important to seriously consider where we locate our shelters. Our every action affects the lives of the plants and animals around us. In primitive living those effects are often temporary, lasting only the few days or a week that we use a particular site. But in contemporary living our shelters are much more permanent. In Montana people are throwing houses up willy-nilly all over the place, breaking up wildlife habitat as well as the scenery that brings people here to begin with. Everybody wants a house with a view, and as a result everyone is getting a view of houses.

Montana is often called the "Last Best Place", but instead of saving the last of its kind, we seem determined to develop this place to extinction before anyone else can, and we are succeeding. The popularity of this state is destroying the very thing that made it popular to begin with. Eighty thousand acres of biologically rich riverbanks and productive agricultural lands were lost to development in Montana between 1982 and 1992. The pace of development then accelerated, consuming another 123,000 acres in just the next five years.

One of the main reasons I've been so interested in the construction industry is to influence where houses are built. By writing about house building I can influence other people's decisions about where to build. And if I build the houses myself then I can choose where to put them. Everyone can enjoy Montana if we keep our houses in communities, rather than peppering them over the landscape. But I digress....

Choosing A Location

I have made location the last section of shelter building, because you must consider all of your goals, you must know about shelter construction, and you should consider environmental and aesthetic impacts—all before you decide where would be the most appropriate place to camp. Really, it all goes hand-in-hand, because you need to build shelters that are appropriate to the resources you have at hand, and you need to locate by sites that are rich in the resources you need.

I often spend more time choosing where I want my shelter and deciding what sort of shelter would be best for the site, than I spend actually building the shelter. This is especially true when my goal is to build a long-term shelter in an area that I want to come back to again and again. I may spend hours searching the general area and deliberating over each of the possible sites. I do make quicker decisions when I am merely passing through and staying only one night, but in either case, since I happen to be particularly lazy, I choose locations that provide some form of natural shelter that can be improved upon. In most places it is simply too much work to build a complete shelter from scratch. Instead I look for partial shelters—rock outcroppings, boulders, fallen trees, tree roots— anything that will provide part of a roof or a wall, or a reflector for a shelter. Taking advantage of such features saves work and helps me tie my shelters into the landscape so they blend in and disappear.

As you locate your shelters, there is one rule to always follow, and that is think *safety*. Build your shelters only in places that you are certain will be safe for the duration of time that you will be there. Do not locate in a flood plain if there is any chance of a flood while you are there. Do not build in an area that has the potential for an avalanche of rocks, mud, or snow. Look out for dead branches or trees that may fall down and avoid unstable rock outcroppings. Avoid building where there is evidence of regular and recent bear use, rattlesnake dens, or heavy insect populations. Also watch out for poisonous plants like stinging nettles or poison ivy.

Safety therefore, should always be one criteria for choosing a campsite location. There are some other guidelines you should consider as well. For instance, ideally you should build on dry ground, avoiding low spots, and far enough away from creeks, rivers, or lakes to avoid the heavy dew that usually falls at night. Ideally, you should locate in an open area where the sun will quickly dry out your campsite after storms and where it will warm you early on cold mornings. Ideally, you should locate where there are plenty of shelter materials available, where there is an abundance of firewood, with a source of water close by, and with sources of food and other resources nearby. Some of these guidelines are my own, and some are borrowed from other authors, but they are all pretty much common sense. I should emphasize, however, that safety is the only rule. The rest are merely guidelines. If they were rules, then they were meant to be broken. I have never yet built a shelter that complied with every guideline.

I have seldom built shelters where the sun could reach them in the morning, and I have often built them where the sun could not reach them at all, only because I had other objectives, other goals, that were more important to me. For the same reason, I have sometimes built shelters where there were very few resources at all. What is most important is not the guidelines, but your basic goals.

For instance, in a real survival situation you would want to camp in the open where you could be easily seen and found. You would want that spot in the sunlight for the warmth, etc. etc.

On the other hand, if you are camping for recreation as I do, then you may make different choices. I choose campsites that allow me to blend in to the environment where I can leave my shelters without people stumbling into them. I choose locations that are near my favorite swimming or fishing holes, stalking grounds, or resource areas. Many of my campsites are dark, damp, and cool, but that is okay. A good recreational campsite does not have to be the ideal survival campsite. The important thing is to build your shelter in a location that is safe and best fits all of your goals.

◊ ◊◊◊ ◊

I leave the hot coal bed site and return to my camp. My friend the rock invites me to sit once again. I do. A flash of movement inside the shelter catches my attention. A mouse crawls around my backpack, claims a flake of dry oatmeal on the ground, and disappears into a gap between the rocks. A good idea, I think, as my stomach growls. I nibble on some dried apples to tide me over for now. It is time to start my fire and cook lunch.

FIRE

The sun shines warmly, almost hotly on the land. It is almost noon. I reach into my pack and pull out my bowdrill set and a supply of tinder material. The tinder consists of dry, fibrous strips from the inner bark of a dead

Starting a fire with a bowdrill set.

cottonwood tree. I fluff up the fibers, shape them into a sort of "bird nest", and set it aside. With the point of my knife I start a new hole in the fireboard, cut a notch to the hole, and check the tension of the string on the bow. I wrap the bowstring once around the spindle, place my left foot halfway across the fireboard to hold it down, and place the tip of the spindle in the hole I started with my knife. I place my socket rock on top of the spindle, and hold it securely with my left hand anchored against my left shin. With my right hand I pull the bow back and forth, straight and level, thus rotating the spindle and creating friction and heat between the two surfaces.

Starting a bowdrill fire is a magical process. As I work the bow back and forth I remember the analogy that the bowdrill is like the union between male and female. The spindle is the male and the hole in the fireboard that receives the spindle is the female. Friction between the spindle and fireboard grinds wood punk from both surfaces which then spills into a notch in the fireboard. With enough friction, the punk heats up, begins to glow, and takes on a life of its own. The joining of the male spindle and the female fireboard results in the birth of a glowing baby coal. The process of creating that coal, which seems to be almost living, by merely rubbing two sticks together, is very much a magical process.

I pull the bow back and forth and apply downward pressure on the socket rock. Smoke is quickly pouring out of the notch and in fifteen seconds I have a large coal. I carefully remove the spindle, set it, the bow, and the socket rock aside in a safe place and tap the fireboard gently to jar the coal loose from the notch. I had placed a strip of dry bark under the notch before I started. I pick up the bark and gently drop the baby coal in the hole at the center of my fabricated bird nest, the tinder bundle. I gently blow.

The coal is indeed a baby and it should be treated that way. I cradle the bundle in my hands, gently closing in the front to wrap the coal inside. I am careful not to smother it, but only to blanket it. With steady, even breaths I blow in between my hands and let the smoke spill out the backside. In one minute I have a flaming bundle, a ball of fire.

Blowing a tinder bundle into flame.

Bowdrill Fire-Starting

Erosion beneath this cottonwood will one day tip the tree into the water. Cottonwood roots for bowdrill sets can be found in abundance in riverside driftwood piles.

There are many different woody materials all over North America that work well for making bowdrill **spindles and fireboards**. Most good woods are soft enough that you can easily dent them with a fingernail. Soft woods are better insulators to trap heat in the fireboard, while hardwoods tend to conduct more heat away. But the wood must not be too soft or rotten, or the drilling action will wear down the spindle and fireboard without ever warming the punk up enough to ignite.

The critical temperature for ignition is between 700 and 800°F, depending on the size of the particles in the punk, according to Dick Baugh in the *Bulletin of Primitive Technology*. Using a temperature-controlled iron, Baugh found that the finer punk ignited at the lower temperature, while coarser punk ignited at the higher temperature.

My favorite bowdrill sets are made from **cottonwood roots**. When you cut into a cottonwood root you will notice what looks like hollow tubes in the grain, presumably designed to transport water up into the trunk. When dried, these tubes hold minute amounts of air, which makes the wood a really good insulator. I also wonder if the air in the tubes helps to nurture the wood punk into a glowing ember.

Fortunately you do not need a shovel to get to the roots. Cottonwood trees grow most abundantly in the flood plains along rivers and streams, as they are virtually dependent on flooding for successful seedling germination. The same floods also cut away at stream banks, eroding the soil out from under the trees until they finally tip and plunge into the water. Their dried roots can be found in abundance in the driftwood piles along the rivers. Just look for the curvy lengths of wood. Pick a piece up and you will notice how light-weight it is compared to the branch wood, almost like balsa wood. Good roots are easy to carve, but still firm. Older roots become too soft and the spindles drill right through them. Roots can also be found where a tree has fallen in the forest, lifting it's roots right up out of the ground. Where cottonwood roots are not available, the roots of just about any other kind of wood seem to work really well too.

I have successfully used bowdrill sets made from the roots of **willows, aspens, junipers, mesquite**, and even **pine**. Although the branch wood of many of these woods are commonly used for bowdrill sets, the roots usually work better, or at least more consistently. Resinous woods like pine, spruce, and fir usually make poor bowdrill sets, because the tip of the spindle and the notch in the fireboard develop a polished glaze. The set squeals loudly, but neither surface is ground into wood powder. However, pine roots, at least those that appear open and porous like cottonwood roots, sometimes work for bowdrill sets. So keep an eye out for tree roots of any kind, and you will likely find good materials for making bowdrill sets.

It is also good to practice with the common branch woods in your area, since roots are not always available. Good bowdrill woods are available across the continent. Most, but not all, are soft woods which you can dent with a fingernail.

All members of the Willow Family usually make good bowdrill sets, including willow, cottonwood, aspen and poplar. Willows vary tremendously. Some people really like willow sets, but I often have trouble with them. The straight and slender shoots that sprout up beside cottonwood and poplar trees usually work exceptionally well.

The ribs of a dead saguaro cactus make workable fireboards and spindles.

Most members of the Cypress Family, including the western red cedar (and cedar shingles), incense cedar, and some junipers make very good bowdrill sets. The cypress and other members of the family should be experimented with as well. (See *Botany in a Day* for additional details on plant families.)

At least two species of the Maple Family—the box elder and big leaf maple—work well for bowdrill fireboards and spindles. Other maples may be worth experimenting with too.

Good bowdrill woods from other assorted families include buckeye, elderberry, seep willow, sage brush, alder, birch, hackberry, ash, basswood, redwood, silverberry, sycamore, sassafras, tulip poplar, trumpet vine, balsam fir, flower stalks of the yucca plant, and

Bowdrill set (top to bottom): socket, bow, spindle, fireboard.

even the ribs of the dead saguaro cactus. No doubt there are many more. You just have to experiment and find out.

The fireboard and spindle should ideally be of similar hardness, so that both surfaces are ground equally into powder. Otherwise, if the spindle is too hard then it will drill right through the softer fireboard without creating black punk. The opposite is also true—a soft spindle doesn't work well on a hard fireboard. For this reason, the fireboard and spindle are usually made of the same materials, unless the wood isn't suitable for both. For example, yucca works great for spindles, but the diameter of the stalk may be too small to make into fireboards. Therefore, I often use a yucca spindle on a cottonwood or cottonwood root fireboard.

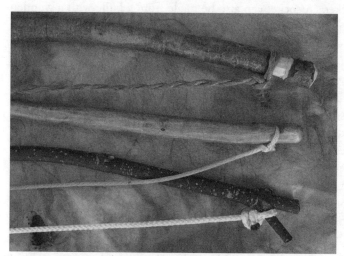

Here are three bows with different styles of notches.

The **spindle** should be 1/2" to 3/4" in diameter and at least 8 to 10 inches long. The bowdrill **fireboard** should be 1/2" to 3/4" thick, wider than the spindle and long enough so you can hold it down with your foot. I make the cottonwood root spindles and fireboards a bit thicker.

The **bow** should be a curved branch 20 to 30 inches long. I prefer a stiff bow while many other people like a flexible bow. The type of wood doesn't matter, as long as it is strong enough to do the job.

Nylon cord, braided rawhide, or cordage from plant fibers can be used for the **bowstring**. I mostly use nylon cord because I do a lot of demonstration fires, and I do not have the time to make all my bowstrings. Bowstrings can also be made of braided or corded rawhide. (See the section on cordage in the next chapter.) Rawhide strings can be made wet and either used immediately, or stretched and allowed to dry first. Plant fiber cordage usually must be doubled back on itself and corded a second time to make it durable enough for use with the bowdrill. I find it discouraging to work with plant fiber bowdrill cords because it typically takes a lot longer to make the string than it does to break it. If you do work with plant fiber cordage, then be sure to use a flexible bow. The nylon cords that I usually work with can handle the stretch of wrapping the cord around the spindle. But the plant fiber cordage doesn't stretch like nylon, so the bow should flex to relieve some of the tension on the cordage.

If you don't have any of these materials on hand, then you will need to improvise suitable cordage from whatever you can find. Shoelaces are an easy choice, so make sure your laces are in good condition before you go out. I've also made bowdrill strings from plastic baling twine. It has to be made into cordage before use, and still it has a surprisingly short lifespan.

The **socket** can be made from a piece of stone, bone, or wood with a hole in it. Rock hand sockets are the best, yet also the most difficult to find or make. Once in awhile you will get lucky and find a natural socket rock ready to use. But more likely you will have to use a sharp rock to peck out a suitable socket in a comfortable stone.

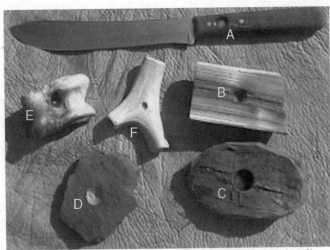

Bowdrill Sockets: A—Knife with socket drilled in handle against steel plate.   B—Hardwood socket. C—Cottonwood bark socket.   D—Stone socket. E—Deer "knee" bone socket. F—Antler socket.

Just keep pecking away at the center, and you will have a decent socket in an hour or so. I pecked a hole all the way through the stone flywheel of my pumpdrill (shown later in this chapter) in about four hours. When mass-producing bowdrill sets, which I sometimes do for group use, I use a masonry bit in a drill, which makes a good socket in less than a minute.

If you are really lucky you may find a rock soft enough to carve or drill into with a "beater" knife, one that you carry along just for these brutal jobs you wouldn't ever use a good knife for. I've used a flat-slot screwdriver for scraping out socket holes too. You might be surprised how many soft rocks there are in the world. Looks can be deceiving. Some talc rocks are so soft that the spindles drill right through them.

Sockets from dead wood need lubrication such as oil or chapstick to reduce friction at the top of the spindle. But a pitchy piece of wood provides it's own lubrication, as the pitch heats melts and glazes the socket. A socket can also be made from a knife with a wooden handle riveted to a steel blade. Drill the spindle through the wood to the metal and you will have a low friction socket that will not wear out.

The **tinder bundle** is made from any light, dry, fibrous materials like dead grass, sagebrush bark, or the inner bark of the cottonwood. If the grass is too coarse, then you can pound it with sticks or rocks to make it softer and more "fluffy". Another excellent tinder bundle material is the non-native annual cheat grass, which thrives in desertifying western rangelands. The grass favors fire, which creates more bare ground to grow more cheat grass. Please avoid spreading the seeds to pristine environments. The shredded bark of redwoods, cedars and at least one species of juniper also make excellent tinder. Dry cattail leaves can also be shredded to make good tinder.

Higher in the mountains you can use "pine fluff", the dried flower parts of the pines which often accumulate in

The shredded bark of the Utah juniper is an excellent source of tinder, but other related species have thin, scaly bark.

small piles around logs and boulders. Note that any plants that produce usable fiber for cordage can also be used for tinder, but you would be wasting perfectly good fiber material by burning it up. As a curiosity, even very fine steel wool can also be used. The steel fibers are so fine that they catch fire and burn, one of those things you almost have to see to believe.

If you have a large group to work with, and you would rather buy tinder than harvest it yourself, then try "oakum". Oakum is simply fiber from the jute plant (*Corchorus*). Oakum was used by plumbers to

A pile of very dry pine needles can work as a tinder bundle. Grind some dry pine needles and charcoal into powder to use as a coal extender in the middle.

Close-up of the bowdrill set.

A bowdrill coal on a scrap of cottonwood bark fiber.

pack joints around steel pipe fittings. Oakum from plumbing shops may come saturated with grease. For tinder bundles you will need the fiber without grease, called "dry oakum". The jute plant belongs to the Basswood Family. The inner bark of the basswood tree also makes good tinder. As you can see, there are many, many sources of fibrous, dry material for tinder bundles. Just look around. You can always find *something*.

To make a good tinder bundle, wrap the fibrous materials around two fingers of one hand, then poke the tail into the center as you pull your fingers out. Tying the tinder into an overhand knot can work well too, or just fluff the materials to make a ball, and press it down in the center to make it look like a birds nest with a small center. It should be tight enough that the coal will not fall out the backside and strong enough to toss around without falling apart, yet also loose enough that you can blow right through it to give the growing coal plenty of oxygen. With non-fibrous tinder like pine fluff, just make a mound in the center of your fire pit and poke a hole in the middle.

This basic bird's nest will be all you need for any high-quality tinder, and you can proceed with fire starting. However, tinder bundles made of coarse fibers should be improved by adding a **coal extender**. A coal extender is powdery, punky material, much like the coal itself. For example, if the tinder bundle is made of shredded cedar bark, you can rub a bit of the bark between your palms to reduce it to powder, and place this powder in the center of the bundle. The powder helps the coal to grow in size and heat, until it is large enough to ignite the nest itself and create flame.

The inner bark of the cottonwood makes an especially good coal extender. In fact, sometimes it is frustrating to blow it into flame, because the entire tinder bundle becomes one great hot coal, but won't flame. When I have access to this material, I pack my fire pouch full of it, then conserve it to make as many fires as possible. Most often I make a bundle of dry grasses found on site, then add a wad of cottonwood bark to the center. In my fire pouch there is always a layer of bark dust at the bottom, so I add a pinch of that to the very center of the bundle. Without this preparation, a coal placed in bundle of coarse grasses could just fall apart and spill through the back of the tinder bundle.

Teaming up makes it easier for kids to start a fire.

Other good coal extenders include dry powder from rotten logs or fungi, crushed insect galls from trees, or even the dry fluff of a cattail head. If there is no good source of tinder bundle material at hand, then you can get by with the aid of coal extenders to make a big enough ember to ignite pine needles or other fuel.

Proper attention to making a quality tinder bundle cannot be over-emphasized. It is a real shame to work hard to create a glowing coal, only to lose it in a poorly made tinder bundle—especially in adverse conditions, when you really need that fire.

Starting a Bowdrill Fire

A hunched position with a bent left arm (right) requires more forearm strength to push down on the socket. An upright position (below) allows you to lock your arm straight to better lean your weight onto the socket.

The notch should go all the way to the center of the spindle hole. Some of mine are square inside, but that is not necessary.

bent arm

The notch can face towards you or away.

straight arm

6-anchor your hand and socket against your shin.

5-hold the socket on the spindle with the left hand.

3-kneel down so that your right knee is behind your left foot.

2-place left foot halfway across fireboard, 1" to the left of the hole.

7-keep the bow level, and pull it back and forth with your right hand.

8-apply your fingers above and below the string to adjust tension on the spindle.

4-wrap the spindle one time into the bowstring.

1-place bark under notch to catch coal.

9-keep drilling until the smoke comes 'through' the wood punk.

10-fan the coal gently and transfer it carefully to the tinder bundle to blow it into flame.

Wood punk is ground off of the spindle and the fireboard. It spills into the notch to make a small pile. With continued drilling the punk turns black and ignites. Success!

Wrap the cord around the spindle one time. If it ends up 'between' the cord and the bow, then take it out and wrap it again so it is 'outside' the cord, as shown here.

The cord may loosen and slip around the spindle as you drill. To tighten it without stopping, just push down on the cord with your thumb and up with your fingers.

Bowdrill Technique

Starting a fire by rubbing sticks together may seem like magic, but like any good trick, it is just a matter of learning and practicing the technique. Success at starting a fire with the bowdrill is dependent on three things: the quality of the parent materials, the quality of your finished set, and the quality of your technique. Once you have gathered the right materials then shape them like art work. The fireboard should sit flat on the ground. The spindle must be arrow straight. Here then, is the proper technique for right-handed people (opposite for left):

1. Place a piece of bark or other material **under the notch** to catch the coal before you start drilling.
2. Place your **left foot** halfway across the fireboard and **one inch** to the left of the hole in the fireboard.
3. Kneel with your **right knee** almost directly behind your left foot.
4. **Wrap the spindle** one time into the bow string and place the spindle in the hole in the fireboard. The bow should be positioned so that you can pull it back and forth beside you and not across in front of you.
5. Place the **socket** on top of the spindle and hold it with your left hand.
6. Since your left foot is half way across the fireboard the spindle will stand up right alongside your shin. Your hand with the socket should be held firmly against your shin, with the spindle straight up and down. The movement of the bow being pulled back and forth puts a lot of sideways force against the spindle. You need to **anchor** it against your shin to be able to control it. I literally "pinch" my hand in between my shin and the socket so it cannot move.

Most people place their shoulder directly on their knee and apply pressure to the socket with the forearm, as shown in the upper right picture. However, you may find it easier to use an upright position with a locked arm, to better transfer your body weight onto the socket, as shown in the main picture.

7. With your right hand pull the bow back and forth, **turning the spindle**. Keep the bow level and take full strokes. Speed is not as important as good steady technique and downward pressure on the socket.
8. If the bowstring slips around the spindle use the fingers of your right hand to **adjust the tension** of the cord, as illustrated.
9. The first wisp of smoke can come surprisingly quickly, but keep drilling until the notch is packed full of wood punk and the set is smoking profusely. The pile of punk may be brown on the outside, but near the spindle it should be black. When you see smoke coming out through the wood punk, and not just around the spindle, then you know for certain you have an ember. Sometimes I blow gently on the wood punk while drilling. That seems to help just a little bit.
10. When you get that precious ember, the next thing to do is calm down. People get excited about their first coal, and they yank the bowdrill set away, scattering a hard earned coal several feet in every direction. You have time. A coal will smolder for several minutes before consuming the punk. Carefully pull the spindle out of the hole and set it aside. Place your set in a safe, dry spot. Carefully take your foot off the fireboard and **fan the hot coal** in the notch by gently waving your hand. Tap the fireboard and pull it away from the glowing ember.

The wood punk welds itself together as it glows, forming a durable ember. Pick up the bark and gently drop the coal into the center of your tinder bundle. Hold the sides of the bundle and blow long, steady breaths into it. Allow the smoke to pass out the back. Cradle the tinder closely around the coal. Blanket it to keep it warm, but not so tight that you smother it. Blow long steady breaths and it will grow and spread, smoke, and then flame.

Trouble Shooting

If the Spindle Flips Out of the Cord: •Your left hand and socket may not be anchored properly against your shin. •The tip of the spindle may be worn too flat. •The socket may not be deep enough. •The hole in the fireboard may not be deep enough, or too close to edge. •You may be running the bow at too much of an angle.

If the Spindle Wobbles: •The spindle may not be straight enough. •The hole in the board may be too wide.

If you have more Smoke from the Socket than the Fireboard: •Try lubricating the socket or top of spindle with Vaseline™, chapstick, grease, pitch, wax, or oils from your hair.

If you have Smoke but No Coal: •The notch may not be cut deep enough or wide enough into the hole. •The wood or base may be too damp. •Too much pressure may be creating flake or thread-like particles that are too big to ignite. Try easing up on the socket. •Try harder. •Try different materials.

If you are Exhausted, Frustrated, Mad and Swearing up a Storm: •You are really close! Just take a break and come back to it a little later with a cool head.

Starting Bowdrill Fires with Damp Materials

Like any good scout you should always be prepared with a quality bowdrill set and dry tinder and kindling *before* the weather turns wet. Assuming you have also found or built some sort of shelter, then it is not too hard to make fire, even in damp weather. But even good scouts fall in the water sometimes, or get their gear soaked in the rain. So then what do you do? Do you drill harder and faster and longer to create fire from damp wood? Not necessarily.

Conducting tests with bowdrill sets soaked for 30 minutes in a bucket of water, Dick Baugh of Palo Alto, California, noted that fast and furious bowdrilling just ground away the wood before it could dry out and warm up enough to ignite. The secret to driving moisture out of the set, Baugh reported in the *Bulletin of Primitive Technology*, is to drill lightly until the set started to smoke, then stop and rest. After several cycles of light drilling and resting, the bowdrill set is dry enough to start fires with normal speed and pressure.

Always look for tinder or pine needles up off the wet ground, in the protective shelter of the trees. Even in a heavy rainstorm there are usually dry twigs and branches on the lee side of tree trunks. Dead cottonwood trees may be soaked on the outside, but just peel the bark back and at least some of the fibrous tinder will be dry. If all else fails, then find the best wood you can, and whittle away the outer layers to get to the drier wood inside. Use shavings of the dry wood as tinder and kindling to get a fire big enough to start drying out wet wood. With or without matches, starting fires in wet conditions will quickly test and hone your wilderness skills.

Survival Bowdrills: Fire From Nothing

You may be wondering how to create a bowdrill fire from scratch in the wilderness if you do not have any string for the bow, or even a knife to make the fireboard and spindle. When you have mastered basic bowdrilling then you will be ready for these increasingly primitive techniques.

Spindles and fireboards are the easiest parts to make without tools. The spindle can be cut by abrading the branch or stalk back and forth across the edge of a sharp rock. Find a large rock, so it will stay still when you lean into your work. Cut all the way through the spindle this way then taper the ends by abrading them on a flat, but coarse rock. Again, a big rock is helpful so that you can lean into your work without the rock moving around.

Primitive fireboards can be improvised in many ways. A crude, but "conventional" fireboard can be made if you split a branch down the middle, creating two flattened pieces. Breaking a branch will often cause it to start splitting, so you can continue the split by pulling it apart with your hands, or by wedging another branch into it. After you rip the branch in half, then you can cut it to the desired length by abrading it, as described for spindles. Also use the abrasion technique to cut a notch for the coal. It is important to find a rock with a narrow cutting edge, or the notch will be too wide to hold the spindle. Next, use a sharp-pointed rock as a drill bit to start the pilot hole for the spindle. Other variations of the "knifeless" fireboard were popularized by Mors Kochanski, author of *Bushcraft*:

Forked Stick Fireboard—A forked stick is used as a ready-made and notched fireboard. Just whittle a small pilot hole to keep the spindle from kicking out.

Two Stick Fireboard—Two sticks are tied together to make a fireboard. The coal drops into the crack between the sticks. This trick helps when working with flower stalk spindles that are not wide enough to make a fireboard. You could also tie two small branches together if you don't have tools to carve a flat fireboard.

"Notchless" Fireboard—A pilot hole is drilled into the fireboard and used as the notch to catch the coal from the second hole. Notching between the holes is exceptionally easy, because you are cutting with the grain, instead of across it. After use, each hole becomes the notch for the next new hole. This technique also keeps the coal up off the damp ground.

A "notchless" fireboard. It is easier to cut a notch with the grain from hole to hole, than to cut across the grain from the side of the fireboard.

Crack-in-a-Log Fireboard—Find a log with a crack in it and start drilling into the crack. The punk collects and forms the coal right in the crack.

Thick chunks of cottonwood bark or other types of tree bark are often used for **sockets** in survival bowdrills because they are the easiest to find. To make a primitive **bow**, simply abrade part way through a green branch, then pull down on the branch a little to split the end. Then finish cutting through the branch. The purpose of the split is to hold the bowdrill string. Make the other end of the bow the same way.

The challenging part of the survival bowdrill is to create a serviceable bowstring if you do not have quality cordage materials on hand. Barry Keegan of New York has done essential research in this topic, as documented in *Wilderness Way* magazine. Keegan uses outlandishly thick "cordage" for the bowdrill, rarely smaller in diameter than a pinkie, and often as big as a thumb. With minimal modification he has shown that it is possible to make functional bowdrill strings with tree bark, tree roots, even whole, pounded twigs. I will enjoy testing out his methods too.

◊ ◊◊◊ ◊

I place the flaming tinder bundle in my fire pit and stack a few small twigs on it, tipi style. The flame flickers and fades. I blow and the flame revives and grabs at the tiny twigs. It catches and grows. I nurture the flame into a fire and add larger wood. The wood sizzles and pops; a small coal lands outside the fire pit and dies. Orange flames dance about the fire. A stick burns through and collapses to glowing embers. A wisp of smoke curls up through the trees. I gaze at the coals as my thoughts return to the process of making fire.

The bowdrill is the most used, most written about method of primitive fire starting by modern abos. It also reflects our Yankee fascination with gadgetry. With our wimpy civilized bodies we can use the technology of the bow and string to greatly accelerate the spindle, and the socket on top makes it easy to apply downward pressure. Yet, there are surprisingly few records of native peoples ever using the bowdrill in North America. The method of choice for starting fires was the more basic **handdrill** set.

The handdrill lacks a bow and socket of the bowdrill. Instead, the spindle is simply twirled with the hands to create friction with the fireboard. I remember the time when I told myself I did not need to bother learning how to start fires by this method. After all, I had a nice bowdrill set and a good flint and steel set. I thought, "How many fires do I really need?"

On the other hand, the handdrill does have the quality of requiring less time to construct; an asset when you need to start a fire from scratch in a hurry. "But then again," I thought, "I am not interested in survival skills. My interest is in being comfortable in primitive living." Primitive peoples certainly did not throw away every fire set only to make a new one at each campsite. More likely, they took pride in their work and made sets they used over and over. Likely their fire sets had sentimental values. I can understand. I have carried the same

How many fires does a person need?

socket rock since I was a student in 1984, and I still remember the Russian olive tree in 1988 that provided the bowdrill bow I carry today. I prefer to carry a set that I know rather than fine tune a new one at each camp. Hours can be wasted re-making a good set, hours that could otherwise be expended exploring and learning about my environment. It seemed to me that learning the handdrill was not the best investment of my time to help me reach my goals in primitive living.

I have since discovered that I was both right and wrong. I had the opportunity to learn the handdrill technique from two experts, so I tried it, and I was quite amazed. I always expected it to be so hard to do. But with the right materials it is surprisingly easy. I still prefer to carry a well-tuned fire kit with me when I go camping, but the handdrill is a real thrill. It is quite an experience to pick up two sticks and start a fire with them, after only the most minimal modifications.

Handdrill Fire-Starting

The handdrill.

Handrill spindles are typically a lot thinner and longer than bowdrill spindles. The fireboards are a bit thinner too. Since there are few plants or trees that provide long, skinny spindles *and* flat wide fireboards, you will often have to find a combination of two different materials that work well together. This becomes a challenge when learning on a set that doesn't work, because you have to wonder, "Is it the combination of materials, or is it my technique?"

Fairly soft woods are employed for handdrill sets. Good materials for **handdrill spindles** include the dead stalks of the yucca, sotol, mullein, teasel, sunflower, cattail and seep willow. If you already have a fire and you just want a good set, then you can straighten crooked stalks over the fire (see arrow-making for details), otherwise you will need to hunt for the straightest stalks you can find.

If you have time to cure them, then you might try green woods with pithy centers like oceanspray, mock orange, elderberry, willow, and the sucker shoots of maples, boxelder, cottonwood and buckeye. The slender sucker shoots can often be found at the base of mature trees or sprouting from stumps of trees cut down a year or two before along highways. The sucker shoots should be peeled, straightened over heat, and several of them tied in bundles help keep them straight as they dry. Handdrill spindles should be 16 to 30 inches long and as slender as possible, from about 1/4" to 1/2" in diameter.

Good materials for **handdrill fireboards** include yucca, sotol, cottonwood or cottonwood roots and the roots of other trees, plus red cedar, incense cedar, redwood, sagebrush, buckeye, elderberry, saguaro ribs, seep willow, clematis vines and many more. Pawpaw is a favorite in the southeastern states. Fireboards for the handdrill should be between 1/4" and 5/8" thick, wider than the spindle and long enough so you can hold it down with your foot. Thinner is usually better, so the punk doesn't have so far to fall and cool as it spills into the notch. However, if the board is too thin, then you may drill all the way through before getting a coal.

The best handdrill sets I have ever tried were made by Chris Morasky, consisting of a sotol fireboard from the desert southwest combined with a spindle made from the sucker shoots at the base of a big-leaf maple, a tree native to the cool, moist northwestern states and provinces, but sometimes planted domestically in other northern states. The danger in working with such an easy set like that is that you may not work hard enough when you are faced with a more challenging set of different materials.

The dead flower stalks of the **yucca** are a favorite for many people. Yuccas in the desert southwest often grow flower stalks tall enough that the skinny top can be used as the spindle, while the thicker base can be used as the fireboard. Yuccas grow wild as far north as Montana, but usually with small, crooked flower stalks. Yuccas are also planted as ornamentals from coast-to-coast, so your best bet may be a hike downtown. Once when passing through Portland, Oregon, I collected a bundle of fifty nice long yucca stalks in front of an auto supply store... I imagine the owners were quite surprised to see their landscaping cleaned up when they arrived at work that day. I've used yucca spindles with favorable results on cottonwood, cottonwood root or juniper root fireboards. Lacking better materials, I'll use a mullein stalk spindle on a sagebrush fireboard. Clematis, a vine growing along the major rivers, can be used if a short length is cut from the vine and attached to the tip of a straight, stout spindle such as a mullein stalk.

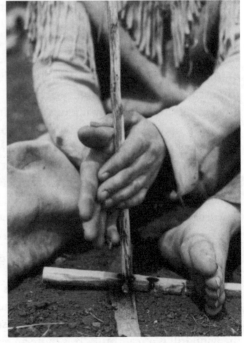

Handdrill close-up.

Handdrill Technique

To use the handdrill start a **hole and notch** in the same fashion as for the bowdrill. Position yourself as shown in the picture on the previous page, with your butt on the ground and one foot out to hold the fireboard down. Optionally, you can kneel down with one foot forward on the fireboard, as shown in the group photo below. Take off any rings and put them in a safe place.

Place your hands together at the top, and start twirling the spindle. Use as much of the **length of your hands** as you can to get the most revolutions each way. Make sure you are moving both hands, instead of holding one still and moving the other. Apply **downward pressure** as you work and your hands will move down the spindle. Take your time and learn the technique before working for speed. Keep the spindle as straight up-and-down as possible as you work. At the bottom, **hold the spindle** with one hand then move the other hand to the top and hold the top. Move the other hand up and start spinning. Make the move quickly because the spindle cools off fast.

Warm up the set gradually and save your strength. Practice and rest first, before going for fire. Try to **stay relaxed**, except for the muscles in use, and be sure to **breathe**. This may be the greatest challenge in doing the handdrill fire!

Try **different parts of your palms**. Sometimes I use my hands flat against the spindle, but I can get more pressure by tilting my hands out, so that the edge of my palm and pinky are the only parts in contact with the wood. You can also **spit on your hands** to get a better grip on the spindle, but keep in mind that too much moisture will quickly lead to blistering.

If the spindle squeaks or simply twirls without creating any punk or color, then **add a pinch of grit** in the hole to break up the polish and create friction. As the set warms up then increase the speed and downward pressure and start it smoking. When it is smoking heavily then apply your best burst of speed and downward pressure to boost the temperature to the ignition point. When you see smoke coming out *through* the mass of punk, then you know you have a coal, but a few more passes down the spindle will still help, if you have the energy left to do so.

Starting a fire with a handdrill is a good group project.

I must emphasize the importance of having the right materials. I have seen people with very good hand techniques being frustrated by a bad set, and I have seen other people start fires easily, even with marginal techniques. I have experienced both good and bad sets, and frequently they were of identical materials! Sometimes just switching to a larger or smaller diameter spindle will make all the difference.

I often work with difficult materials like mullein on sagebrush that require lots of brute force downward pressure to generate a coal. With good quality materials like seep willow on sotol, I tend to apply too much downward pressure and drill right through the fireboard so fast that the punk never warms up to ignition temperature. I try not to apply so much downward pressure, but sometimes it is easier to just grab a fatter spindle, that won't drill through the fireboard so quickly.

Whether you are just beginning or quite experienced, you might get a fire very easily, or you may have to work hard, going beyond your perceived limits of physical endurance. I have learned to hope for the former and plan on the latter.

An alternate method of working the handdrill, called **floating**, was popularized by Scott Kuipers of New Mexico. Scott became known in primitive skills circles for starting handdrill fires by working from the bottom to the top of the spindle. To do this, just "waddle" or "walk" your hands up the spindle as you twirl. Moving your hands up is the spindle is surprisingly easy, and it is good to experiment with it when you are warming up the set. It is much more difficult to achieve the downward pressure while you are moving up the spindle, but each time you practice it will get easier. Initially, the technique will allow you to get from the bottom to the top without stopping the spindle. You also have the option of keeping your hands in one spot on the spindle and using a short spindle. Many people have become proficient with this method since Scott first demonstrated it.

One thing I especially like about the handdrill is that it is a good tool for bringing groups together. Two or more people can take turns on the spindle, working together to create a fire. It provides an external focus for people to work with. It demands and an intensive level of physical, mental, and emotional energy that quickly breaks down all barriers between people. Everyone becomes wrapped up in the energy and excitement of cooperating towards the common goal of generating an ember.

◊   ◊◊◊   ◊

My small fire has dwindled in my moment of distraction. I add more tinder and firewood to rekindle it. The fire in the sky above burns hot, seeming to grow more intense with the day. Amazing it is. Day after day after day—there it is, burning its supply of hydrogen and helium fuel. For some four billion years it has burned away, with billions of years of fuel left to go. It is our fusion campfire, warming our little bubble and fueling all life on our world.

We live in a universe of energy. We are surrounded by hundreds of billions of galaxies, each comprising hundreds of billions of stars like our own. Our own planet is made from the debris of some former star blown apart in a supernova. Fusion welds together the lighter elements like hydrogen into heavier and heavier elements like iron and uranium that gravitate to the center of the star. In a large star the core builds up heavier and heavier until the force of gravity collapses the star in a sudden implosion and subsequent explosion. Fresh nuclear and other materials are blown across galactic space. The early days of our own planet were much more radioactive, and there were likely many spontaneous nuclear blasts from the rich supplies of uranium. I put another stick on my own campfire, appreciating the magic.

There are many ways to create fire, besides with the bowdrill, the handdrill, fusion or fission. For starters there are seemingly dozens of variations on the basic concept of the spindle and fireboard.

For "trainers" on your handdrill, you can add "thumb straps" using cordage or a buckskin thong. Tie the midpoint of the thong to the top of the spindle, and tie a loop at each end of the thong. Put your thumbs in these loops and pull downward as you spin the shaft. You can apply a lot of downward pressure without your hands riding down the spindle. This could be called the **thongdrill**.

Somewhat similarly, I have been told of an Egyptian handdrill or "**spooldrill**" in the Louvre Museum of Paris, where a sort of "spool" had been mounted to the top of the spindle. The spool flared out from the spindle to support the hands, so downward pressure could be applied without one's hands riding down the shaft.

Another variation of the handdrill is to add a socket, like you use for the bowdrill. The difference is that this socket is held in your mouth, so your hands are free to spin the shaft. This technique is called the **mouthdrill**. I consider this to be potentially dangerous, because you could slip and poke your eye on the spindle.

A safer version of this is to use a big log for the socket. Make an indentation near the end of the log to serve as a socket then prop the log up such that it is bearing down on the shaft. This could be called the **logdrill.** The log will provide the downward pressure while you keep the spindle moving.

Yet another variation of the spindle and fireboard concept is the **pumpdrill**. Cordage is attached to the top of the spindle and to a handle that rides up and down the shaft. Wind the cordage around the spindle to pull the handle to the top. Then put it in the fireboard and push down on the handle. The cordage pulls out straight, causing the spindle to turn. A heavy flywheel is attached and balanced on the spindle with enough mass to keep the spindle turning when the string is unwound. The spinning shaft winds the cordage back around it, and pulls the handle back to the top, ready for you to push it down again.

The pumpdrill in the photo is equipped with a stone bit for drilling holes through thin materials like wood, bone or shell. A much larger flywheel would be required for starting fires, since it must carry enough momentum to overtake the friction with the fireboard so the

A pumpdrill for boring holes.

spindle can wind up the cordage again.

The spindle and fireboard combination used in each of these fire-starting methods is very common because it is so efficient. The two surfaces of friction are very small, concentrated, and constantly in contact. Other methods of primitive fire starting exist, but some are less efficient because more surface area is used and then repeatedly exposed and momentarily cooled. This lack of efficiency is compensated for by their fundamental simplicity.

One such method is called the **fire plow**. It consists of literally rubbing two sticks together. Bart Blankenship, author of *Earth Knack: Stone Age Skills for the 21st Century*, has developed proficiency with this technique. Bart uses cottonwood on cottonwood for this. He picks up a dead branch with a reasonably sharp point and starts rubbing it back and forth along a log to create a groove. Once a groove is started he increases his speed and pressure and generates a punk through the friction. This punk is pushed to one end with every stroke and eventually ignites. But sometimes it requires half a dozen guys with strong arms to take turns until they get it!

You will probably have a lot more success with the fire plow if you live in the desert southwest where the sotol plant grows. Vince Pinto of Raven's Way Traditional School made it look easy working with a sotol set. But even with good wood like that, it still takes a bit of work to develop the technique.

Similar to the fire plow is the **fire saw**. The fire saw is made with hollow materials such as bamboo, rivercane, or elderberry. A half round of this is placed on the ground, with a groove cut in across its width. The sharp edge of another piece is sawed back and forth in this groove (it looks like a cross), and the punk falls through the groove onto the ground below the hollow stalk.

Vince Pinto (Raven's Way Traditional School) demonstrates the fire plow with a board and plow made of sotol stalks from the desert southwest. Start by rubbing the plow stick back and forth to wear a six-inch long groove into the board. Pick up speed as you go and the coal will form at the end of the groove. Good materials and good technique make the fire plow look easy.

A totally different method of primitive fire making is called the **fire piston**. Originally from the south Pacific, it works similarly to the modern diesel engine. A plunger is made to fit a hollow bamboo stalk exactly. A small wad of dry moss tinder is attached to the end of the plunger. With a single whack it is plunged into the bamboo cylinder, causing compression and friction of the air inside, which ignites the tinder. The plunger is removed and the glowing tinder is transferred to a tinder bundle. All the fire pistons I have ever seen or tried were made on a modern lathe from tropical hardwoods, water buffalo horn, or Plexiglas™, but it should be possible to make one in the field. It would be interesting to experiment with rivercane or elderberry as substitutes for bamboo.

You should realize that ultimately a person could spend an entire lifetime just learning primitive friction fires. You know you cannot do everything, so you would be wise to **consider your goals** and learn the methods that seem most appropriate for your objectives. I recommend mastering the bowdrill as a good standby method for making fires. From there you can go anywhere.

However, there is one other method of semi-primitive fire making that is worth knowing. It is called flint and steel. I think that starting a fire with flint and steel kit is easier than using matches, and I often take my kit with me when I want to focus on new skills besides the bowdrill or handdrill.

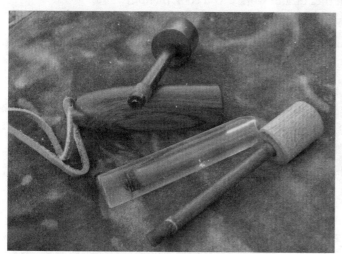

Here are two modern fire pistons. The acrylic piston was made by Steve Leung to make it possible to see the spark inside the chamber. The hardwood piston was made by Jeff Wagner.

Flint & Steel Fire-Starting

With flint and steel, a steel is struck against a flint or flint-like rock. The rock shears off tiny flakes of metal. The shearing, ripping action heats up the flecks of metal so much that they catch fire. The sparks are literally pieces of flying, molten metal. The **metal match** sold at many camping supply stores works on a similar principle, except that it consists of magnesium and steel and the sparks come from the magnesium.

To nurture a single tiny flint and steel spark into a fire, the spark is first caught on a material called **char cloth**. Char cloth is usually made from 100% cotton material that has been previously charred in the fire and smothered. This partially burned material is easily re-ignited by the tiny spark. The cloth is then transferred to the tinder bundle and blown into flame.

It is surprisingly easy to come up with the materials to make your own flint and steel set. Any stone with a somewhat glassy appearance will work for a "flint" rock, except glass which is too brittle. **Flint, chert, quartz, and quartzite** are some of the most common flint rocks used. It is the silica in the rock that works so well for flint and steel. Just pick up rocks with sharp edges, or break some rocks so they have sharp edges, and see what works.

For a striker, I have used a **carbon steel pocketknife** for most of my fires since I was first a student in 1984. With the repeated strikings I have worn all the way past the finger hold on the main blade, more than an eighth inch of metal, making it difficult to get the blade out. Use pocketknives only with the blades closed. Another striker that works even better is the common

From left to right: a mountainman style "C" striker, a file and a carbon steel pocketknife. They all work well as strikers.

steel file. Just knock off a three or four-inch piece with a hammer and you will have a first-rate striker. Use the edge of the file to strike the rock. The files work best if the ribs have been ground off so that the edge is smooth. This way the rock shears off tiny strips of metal, rather than skipping along the ribs. Files are easy to come by in quantity, and for this reason they are excellent for teaching. I have taught as many as sixty kids in one day to start flint and steel fires with used files. Local ski shops donated their used ski files and each kid went home with a complete flint and steel set.

The striker has to be carbon steel. Stainless steel, like a Swiss Army Knife, does not work. Some say it is because the metal is too hard; others say it is because it is too soft. Many carbon steels, such as horseshoes, also do not work, depending on how they are tempered. Even files do not work if you cook them in a fire.

A small tin works good to make and store char cloth. Or you can make the char in a folded tin can lid and store it in a watertight film canister.

For **char cloth**, any 100% cotton, untreated material will work, including cotton handkerchiefs, Levi's, canvas, burlap sacks, and cotton belts. I prefer the thicker materials like the canvas and cotton belts too hold a better coal. The material must not have any synthetic materials in it, or the char cloth will be brittle and shiny and will not catch a spark. Some dyes and treatments can be more deceptive, because the finished product looks and feels right, but will not catch a spark. But Levi's usually work, even with the dyes. Alternately, besides cotton cloth, you can char the white pith found inside plants such as sunflower and mullein stalks. This charred pith can work well, but it is difficult to hold on the stone without crushing it.

An obvious problem with flint & steel is that you need to have a fire to make the charcloth before you can use the flint & steel to make fires. That's okay.

It is just a matter of being prepared and bringing along your kit. The one exception I know of is in the northern forests where the true tinder fungus (*Inonotus obliquus*) can often be found growing on birch trees. The dry, powdery core will catch a spark just as it is. If you find the fungus, a workable piece of scrap metal, and a flint rock, then you would be able to start a flint & steel fire completely from found materials. But I wouldn't bet my life on being able to find all three at the same time!

To make the char, burn the material thoroughly so it is not brown, but not so much that it turns to ash. The most direct way to make charcloth is to burn the material in the open fire then smother it in dry dirt. The problem is that the cloth tends to burn from the edges, so the edges turn to ash even while the middle of the cloth is still not charred enough. A better approach is to fold the materials and stuff them inside a tin can lid "taco" as pictured. Place the char cloth in a hot part of the fire for a minute or two then bury it in dry dirt to deprive it of oxygen. Leave it a few minutes, then dig it out and test a piece. If it works properly then you may store it in a tight, dry canister like a film container or a birch bark canister.

You can make bigger batches of char in bigger containers. Band-Aid cans are especially popular for making char, although the metal cans are quickly disappearing in the age of plastics. Sometimes I use a coffee can and char an entire pair of jeans at once. It helps to have a lid on the can with only a small hole so the material will smolder without being consumed in flame. Even a flat rock placed on top of the can will work.

One important note here: bigger batches of char cloth require significantly longer burn and bury times. A full coffee can of cloth may take twenty to thirty minutes to char properly, and it will have to be buried for at least half an hour to completely smother the coals.

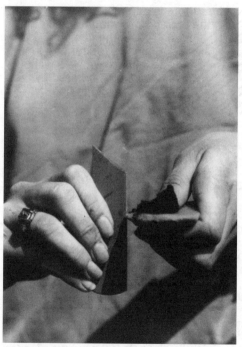

Swing the striker straight down along the sharp edge of the rock to make sparks. Hold the charcloth on the rock to catch the sparks.

To make a flint and steel fire, first prepare a tinder bundle and set it aside. Then practice making sparks. Hold the spark rock in your left hand so that a sharp edge is laying horizontally and facing your right hand. Hold the striker vertically by the tips of your fingers on the right hand. Avoid holding it in any way that will bring your knuckles near the edge of the rock (!).

Practice taking one good deliberate stroke at a time. Bring the file nearly straight down so that the sharp edge of the stone shaves the file edge and shears off the metal. Following through in a long stroke seems to help. When you get good sparks then you are ready for the char cloth.

To catch the sparks you can hold the cloth on top of the rock with your thumb or below it with your fingers. You can also place the cloth directly in your bundle and strike into it, or you can do all of the above. I use just one postage stamp-sized piece of cloth on top of the rock and hold it as close as possible to the edge without interfering with the striker. Alternately, if you have a carbon steel sheath knife you can stick it at an angle into a log with the blade down and char cloth at the tip of the knife on the log. Then you strike the back of the knife with a large flint-like rock.

When a spark catches on the cloth and glows cherry red, blow gently to help it spread. Next, place it in the tinder bundle and blow it into flame as you would for a bowdrill coal. Be sure and put your flint and steel kit in a safe place as soon as you have your spark.

◊ ◊◊◊ ◊

My fire is burning well. I place the end of a long stick into the fire and fetch an orange out of my pack. There is no need to chop firewood in the wilderness. Just put the end of a stick or even a long log into the fire and it will not burn past the edge of the pit. The fire cannot follow the log unless another piece is placed next to it. Two logs side-by-side will shelter the heat between them and allow the fire to spread, but one log is safe, as long as it is not rotten and full of air passages. Knowing how to correctly start a campfire and manage it safely and efficiently is a crucial wilderness skill for any camper.

Principles of Fire-Starting

I grew up around fires. Grandma Josie cooked on a wood stove, so we lit that fire at least twice a day. We also went on a lot of picnics in the mountains, where we started fires to cook our hot dogs, tea, and marshmallows. I simply don't remember a time when I didn't know how to start a fire, and I don't remember anyone giving me lessons. So it is surprising to meet people who really don't know how to start a fire. It is a lot like learning a language. If you grow up with it then you absorb it subconsciously, without ever thinking about it. But if you learn it as an adult, or from a book, then you have to study the mechanics behind it and consciously focus on doing the skill correctly until you learn it.

With our children, we never really gave them the opportunity to start a campfire with matches. I reasoned that if we brought matches on our camping trips that they would just take the easy way out and never develop any real proficiency with flint & steel or bowdrill. If they could start a fire by these methods, I figured, then matches or a lighter would be a snap. Well, just before my daughter's 13th birthday we went on a horse-packing trip in the backcountry. One morning I asked her to hop up and start the fire while I went out for a short walk. She couldn't find the flint & steel, so she grabbed the lighter out of the first aid kit. When I came in a half-hour later she was quite aggravated, asking me "Dad! Where's the flint and steel kit?" She was unable to start a fire with a lighter and tinder-dry needles, only because she was placing the flame too close to the fuel and smothering it. She also had the needles spaced too far apart to create a chain reaction. So, with that in mind, here are some basic principles of starting a fire with matches:

Principles of Fire-Starting

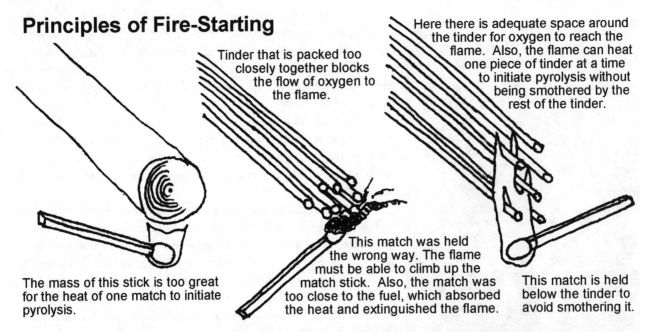

Tinder that is packed too closely together blocks the flow of oxygen to the flame.

Here there is adequate space around the tinder for oxygen to reach the flame. Also, the flame can heat one piece of tinder at a time to initiate pyrolysis without being smothered by the rest of the tinder.

The mass of this stick is too great for the heat of one match to initiate pyrolysis.

This match was held the wrong way. The flame must be able to climb up the match stick. Also, the match was too close to the fuel, which absorbed the heat and extinguished the flame.

This match is held below the tinder to avoid smothering it.

1) Heat rises, so that when you light a match you have to hold the tip downward to let the flame burn up the matchstick towards your fingers. That helps it grow large enough to light something else before it goes out. 2) Heat causes the fuel to undergo "pyrolysis" which breaks the organic matter down into a volatile, combustible gas. It is the gas that burns, not the wood or tinder itself. You have to start with fine tinder of little mass (such as the dry grass illustrated above), so that the heat from a match will warm the mass enough to cause pyrolysis. 3) Heat from the burning gas initiates more pyrolysis to release more combustible gasses, creating a sustainable reaction as long as there is dry fuel on the fire. 4) Damp woods must dry before pyrolysis can take place, so place them on or near the fire to dry *before* you need them for fuel. 5) A fire must have oxygen to burn. Separating the fuel a little bit may be all it takes to invigorate a sluggish fire. 6) When hot air rises, it draws in cool air and fresh oxygen from below, helping to sustain the fire. A fire placed on a mound will be more effective at drawing in fresh oxygen than one in a pit.

Keep in mind that there is less oxygen available at higher elevations, so it can be more difficult to start a fire or to keep it going. That makes attention to detail even more important to successfully stay warm.

◊   ◊◊◊   ◊

Camp Fire Logistics and Safety

Fire safety, according to Smokey Bear or the Boy Scouts, is plain and simple. Always clear away any organic matter within a wide circle around your campfire. Always carry a bucket and a shovel. Always drench the fire so it is cool to the touch before you leave, even if you are just going for a walk. These kinds of rules are simple and easy to remember, and that's important when you have masses of inexperienced tourists or kids camping in the woods. If every fire is drenched then there is little chance of anyone accidentally starting a fire.

But primitive living is a different kind of game. It would be senseless to put your fire out every time you leave camp when there is no guarantee that you will be able to start another when you return. Primitive living is inherently fire-intensive. Fire is used to keep warm inside brushy, tinderbox shelters, and bon fires are used to dry out the ground for pit shelters or hot coal beds. In just about any primitive encampment you will find something flammable precariously close to the fire, but it is not carelessness. On the contrary, the use of fire in primitive living requires that you think and plan very carefully. You must learn to observe and run mental simulations of what could potentially happen in any situation, so that you can always be safe with fire. Smokey's rules work great for people who have little experience with fire, and you should always err to the side of caution. But when you become more comfortable with fire and how it behaves, then you can start becoming more creative in how you use it.

The circumstances of every fire you make are going to be somewhat unique. You may be stopping in the middle of the day to cook a quick meal. The weather may be fair or stormy. You may be setting up a campfire for a long-term camp or for an overnight camp. You might be building a fire near your shelter or in it. The techniques by which you set up and manage your fire should always be unique and appropriate to the circumstances at hand.

As a rule, always **think ahead** to how you can restore a site when you leave. Think through a reclamation plan before you dig in to make a campsite. Especially try to select sites where little or nothing is growing. Then you won't have the problem of killing something and leaving a fire scar. Build your fire on the flat ground. You can scatter the ashes when you are done and kick dirt across the blackened ground to reclaim it.

If you have to build a fire where there is vegetation, then consider digging a shallow pit. Always dig up the sod, if there is any, so you can replant it on leaving. I often water the sod after replanting it, and sometimes I gather nearby seeds and plant them to reclaim my campsites and campfires. Urinating on the fire pit can aid with both putting the fire out and reclaiming the site.

Also be careful not to blacken boulders with your fires. Build your fires far enough away from the rocks to keep them clean. Besides, it is frequently to your advantage to make your fire a few feet away from big boulders. Then you can sit between the fire and the boulder. The rock face will function as a reflector to warm your backside.

Be especially careful to avoid making fires in organic matter. Many forest soils are made up of partially decomposed leaves or needles that look a lot like dirt, but which are quite flammable. A coal can smolder underground for weeks before erupting into a full-scale forest fire. Also be careful with tree roots, particularly rotting tree roots, which can create a similar situation.

You should always be safe with fire, yet you do not need to be paranoid about it except in especially dry times. If it is raining, snowing, or just plain damp or green out, then you would have a hard time starting a forest or range fire even if you wanted too. During such times you can be pretty carefree with your fire. You can leave it smolder when you are away for a few hours or when you are asleep. You can allow a few sparks or hot coals to fall on the ground while you are making a hot coal-burned bowl or preparing a hot coal bed for the night. You can start a small fire inside your flammable little shelter and sleep warm beside it. You can kick a little bit of dirt over the pit and assume that the fire will be completely out soon.

In drier times, however, you should be paranoid about handling fire. Paranoia can be a resourceful state at certain times; managing fires in a risky fire season is one of those times. In primitive times people were typically very careless with fires, and fires raged on all the time. For the most part it did not matter. Once in a while, during particularly extreme conditions there were surely fast moving fires that trapped and incinerated unfortunate animals and people, but that was a rarity. Moreover, it would not have been an issue, since there was no media to report it.

Today's world is different, however, and people who accidentally or intentionally start wild fires will receive the bill to put them out—often for millions of dollars. Moreover, you could potentially be negligent for homicide if someone was killed by the fire. Your campfire may be peacefully smoldering as you leave camp, but what if the wind kicks up once you've been out hiking for twenty minutes? In extreme fire conditions you should put your fire out every time you leave camp. If it is that dry then it will be easy to crank out another coal when you return.

If a fire does get out of control, then do everything you can to contain it without endangering yourself or others. Water is best, but seldom readily available, and you may not have any containers to put it in. Dirt is also very effective to extinguish a fire. Use whatever pans, rocks, or sticks you can to fling dirt on the fire. Blankets can be used to beat out a grass fire, especially if dipped in water first. But perhaps the most important way to stop a fire is to remove the fuel source. A fire spreads easily between many sticks, but hardly at all on a single stick. Separate all the burning members and it will be much easier to put them out. On the other hand, you may have to clear a firebreak around a fire to keep it from spreading.

There are many ways to design the layout of your fire pit. A mound is the most ideal from the standpoint of drawing oxygen into the flame, but I most often prefer the flat ground or sometimes a shallow pit, which contains the fire and makes reclamation easy.

You rarely need a rock ring around the fire, unless to help contain it during particularly hazardous conditions. Otherwise, rock rings usually get in the way of most campfire activities. The rocks block some of the heat from reaching you, and make cooking more difficult. Also, you may be burning long pieces of wood that stick several feet out of the fire pit. It is easier and safer to push the wood into the fire if there are no rocks in the way.

The one way I like to use rocks is to build a **shingle** over my fire during damp weather, or at a permanent camp. I like to have one or two rocks on each side, supporting a large, semi-flat rock over the fire. I keep it wide open in the front, with a smaller opening out the back to carry away the smoke. This setup does several things. Most importantly it protects the fire from rain. Secondly, it reflects most of the heat my direction, so I can keep warm by a very small fire. Third, it creates an oven to help to keep the coals hot all night, so the fire can be rekindled in the morning. Last, a flat rock over the fire can be a useful cooking or warming surface.

Building the fire is pretty simple and straightforward. Just blow your tinder bundle into flame and place it in the fire pit, then start adding small twigs **tipi-style**. If the ground is damp then put something down under the tinder bundle, like a piece of dry bark, or more tinder. The tipi shape is the best form for starting a fire, because the individual smaller flames of the fire come together and intensify into one bigger flame. Put your kindling on slowly. The fire needs lots of oxygen, and too much kindling will smother it. I often start constructing a small tipi, then add a little more loose tinder at the peak, to pull the flame up through the kindling. Then I add more kindling.

You only need to maintain your tipi fire until a strong flame and a few coals are established. Then add the fuel on pretty much any way you want, gradually adding bigger and bigger sticks.

Dry **pine needles** are like gasoline. You can really shortcut the process with them, eliminating the need for building a tipi of kindling. Still, put the needles on one small branch at a time or you will smother your fledgling fire. Dry fir and spruce needles seem to ignite even easier than pine needles.

With an established fire you can put on large branches or even whole trees. Just put the ends in, and push them forward a few inches at a time as they burn. Keep each branch or log a few inches apart from each other where they stick out of the pit, and the fire will not be able to follow along them. In **wet weather**, especially if your fire is unprotected

Set the flaming tinder bundle down, then place small twigs on it one-at-a-time tipi-style.

in the rain, then you will need a bigger fire to dry out the wood. On one overnight outing in wickiups with my daughter's seventh grade class we received more than an inch of rain in the night. We had a big fire out on a gravel bar in the rain, and I knew we would not be able to restart it in the morning, so I went out several times in the night and dragged long logs to the fire to keep it alive. It was nice to be able dry out by that fire in the morning.

Please, always reclaim your campfire sites when you leave and clean up other people's past messes as well. As you travel you will find many fire rings that were put together years ago, and used only once or twice. Dismantle any that seem unnecessary and restore the area. Always try to leave your environment better than you found it.

◊   ◊◊◊   ◊

I dig my fingernail into the orange to peel it. Immediately I catch the acid-sweet orange smell. It is stimulating. I finish peeling the orange and toss the peels into the fire. I save out one peel and fold it, outside out, and squeeze it towards the fire; there is a small flash of flame. A student in one of our classes showed me that. The volatile oils in the **orange peels** are like organic lighter fluid.

While we all may be pyromaniacs at heart, I think it is important to keep caution in mind when handling fire. Even a little **butane lighter** can kill. Some lighters have an explosive power equivalent to several sticks of dynamite. At least two people have died in welding accidents when sparks penetrated their pockets and ignited the lighters. So if you bring a lighter camping with you, be careful with it around the fire.

Another fire technique I had fun with as a kid was **splitting cardboard matches** into multiple matches. I read about it in a book called *Bushcraft* by Richard Graves (Note: Another great book called *Bushcraft* was written by Mors Kochanski.). According to Graves, the technique was used by prisoners of war to conserve their matches. One match can easily be split into two matches just by peeling the cardboard apart from the tail to the match head. Each of these can be split again into two or three matches with a sharp knife and a careful hand. Making a total of four matches from one original is pretty easy. Making six is quite a challenge.

You can also make your own **waterproof matches**, simply by dipping wooden match heads into melted paraffin wax. Just be sure to test them afterwards, since the wax coating can sometimes interfere with lighting the matches. You don't want to be stuck with waterproof matches that are fireproof too!

I eat the orange one slice at a time and enjoy every bit of it. The fire burns quietly in the pit. Several ants crawl out of a hole in an aspen branch on the fire. They run in circles looking for a route off the burning wood. Three of them follow the length of the branch beyond the fire's edge. One gets caught by a flame, shrivels, and falls into the ashes.

Sitting here thinking, it seems that the one thing that marks the evolution of human culture more than any other is the technology of fire. The use of fire is woven into the very fabric of our lives. In primitive living it cooks our food, warms our shelters, helps us to straighten arrow shafts, and fires our pottery, among other things. In contemporary life we are even more dependent on fire as a tool. One would be hard pressed to find an item that did not involve fire in some part of its processing, packaging, or shipping. We put fire in our cars to move us. We put fire in tiny copper wires which run through our homes so we can turn on a light bulb here or run a toaster there or to power a computer where we type while the fire arranges our words in patterns of light on a screen. There is so much we can do with fire as a tool, and so little we can do without it.

Our dependence on "fire", meaning all types of energy, is also at or near the center of many of the world's environmental problems. Because of this, and for other similar reasons, there are many people who think that we should revert to a simpler type of civilization. Of course this type of thinking is useless because the idea of retreating to the past is counter to the tendencies of the human behavior. Very few people will listen.

However, there is one conservation organization with a more progressive approach. Rocky Mountain Institute (RMI) in Snowmass, Colorado was established in the early 1980's by Amory and Hunter Lovins as an energy policy "think tank". Amory was once described as the "top five" of the top ten energy experts in the world. In the mid 1970's other experts projected skyrocketing energy demand in the decades to come. We would have had to build power plants at an exponential rate to meet projected demand. Amory Lovins called that the "hard path". He proposed an alternative, "soft path" using energy-efficient technologies to meet future demand.

Lovins invented the concept of "negawatts", so that utilities and governments could compare the cost of conservation measures against the cost of increasing power production. Negawatts represent power saved from one application that is made available to another application. For example, a compact fluorescent light bulb uses about 1/4 as much energy as a standard incandescent bulb to put out a similar amount of light. Replacing one 100-watt bulb with one 25-watt compact fluorescent therefore "generates" 75 negawatts of saved energy to use somewhere else. Rocky Mountain Institute provides information to utilities and governments then they let market forces do the rest.

Time has proved Amory more than right. Energy production grew very little over a twenty year period because conservation measures allowed the existing energy supply to meet the needs of many more people and businesses. Amory and Hunter's ideas have changed the way power companies around the world do business. Between them they have saved enough energy to power a modest-sized country.

Their work reflects an understanding of the human nature. To be accepted by society, environmentally sound living must be attractive to peoples' quality of life and the ideas must be financially sound. Because the research and the ideas at RMI reflect this understanding, their ideas are being accepted and used. Among other things, they determined that we could save approximately three-fourths of the electricity we are using today cheaper than we can produce it in existing power plants. And we could reduce our emissions of greenhouse gasses by more than half—at a profit. The work from RMI is accelerating a shift towards energy conservation. If you are connected to the grid in any way then you have undoubtedly been affected by their work.

By brother Nick and I work together on a handdrill coal.

I push the branch further into the fire and pick up a small granite stone from the ground. I notice the partially formed crystals in the rock. Most are white but some are black. A rock may seem quite lifeless, yet it is a mass of whirling electrons and phenomenal power. At any moment we are surrounded by a supply of energy quite beyond belief...

A thought comes to mind, and I smile as I remember one of the most enlightening acquaintances I have met in Montana. That person was Father John Kirsch of the Catholic Church. He was still taking people out on nature hikes high into the mountains when he was more than 80 years old. He called himself a mystic, and he would proudly announce to you, "I talk to rocks." Father Kirsch did the wedding ceremony for Renee and I in the Pony park. I did not notice it, but someone else later said he wore his hiking boots with his ceremonial robe during our wedding. We were sorry to hear of his passing in 2002. He will be missed.

I return my rock friend gently to ground. The orange I ate certainly stimulated my appetite. Perhaps I will put something on the fire to cook for lunch.

◊　◊◊◊　◊

WATER

The noonday summer sun shines on the land. It is warm. Heat waves rise above the land. A bead of sweat runs down my forehead. I pour some brown rice into my tin can, add water and chicken bouillon, and place it on the fire. I stoke the fire, but only a little to avoid causing my lunch to boil over. While my lunch is heating up I will be cooling off. I pick up my water bottle and follow a narrow path fifty yards through the bushes to the creek.

I discovered this spot as a teenager. I was walking on the nearby road and I heard the sound of the rushing, pounding water. I knew that there must be a small waterfall in the stream to produce that much noise. I followed the sound and literally fought my way through the dense thickets of willows, currents, and stinging nettles. What I discovered was a small, beautiful, secluded sanctuary like none I had ever seen.

Today I sit upon a small boulder in the middle of the stream. On my left is a moss-covered boulder ten feet tall. On my right stands a boulder almost as high and another that is two feet higher. Upstream, a random pile of smaller boulders divides the flow of the water into three separate falls. The most powerful of the falls pounds white over stair-stepped boulders and gushes into the pool behind the bigger boulders. Bright green moss on the granite stones highlights the pure, virgin white.

Waterfall swimming hole. Painting by Thomas J. Elpel

On the left a short, but still powerful, white waterfall spills down a few feet and pounds on a smaller boulder, sending an alluvial spray of white water around the rock and into the pool. The weakest of the falls is a little to the left of center between the other two. It starts behind a boulder and then free-falls to the pool.

In the middle of the pool lies another good-sized rock, covered with moss. In the shade of the rocks and close to the water, the moss is dark green. On top it is bright fluorescent green, with three or four small clumps of equally bright grass growing from the moss base. The pool itself is one and a half feet deep and ten feet across between the big boulders. Most of this streambed is lined with rocks, but this one pool has a sandy yellow bottom. It was because of this sanctuary that I decided to make my campsite nearby and visit this place often.

I dip my hand into the water flowing beside the rock and feel the coolness moving around my fingers. I take a moment to relax and breathe. I gaze into the water, then up at a birch tree growing beside the stream, near the exit to the pool. This water birch is quite different from other birches. Instead of one large tree trunk, it has numerous smaller trunks, seldom larger than four inches in diameter here in the mountains. There are usually a mix of live and dead trunks on any given birch tree. The birches are very useful trees, and there is much that can be made from the bark.

Birch Bark Canisters

Primitive peoples used birch bark to produce many diverse elements of their culture, ranging from cooking pots to canoes. The birch most commonly used for this was the **paper birch**, *Betula papyrifera*. It is a big, showy tree with white bark. Big sheets of this bark can be soaked in hot water, then creased and folded, much like origami paper, to make containers and other useful implements. Unfortunately, paper birch does not grow wild in southwest Montana. (A closely related species, the **weeping birch**, *Betula pendula*, has been planted in many towns, and can be used similarly.) Our own water birch *(Betula occidentalis)* is not nearly as big nor as stately as the paper or weeping birches, but it is delightful to find, and it is useful for many projects, including small canisters.

The **water birch**, as the common name implies, can be found in moist places, usually near creeks or rivers. It is a reddish or brownish, many-trunked tree that seldom grows taller than 25 feet. Its distribution is patchy in southwest Montana; it grows abundantly by some rivers and streams and not at all by many others. Most water birches have a number of live and dead trunks, which are typically no larger than four to six inches in diameter.

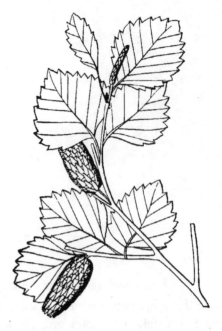

Betula occidentalis: the water birch.

The birches are unique trees, especially because of their resinous bark. The **resins** seem similar to those found in some modern plastics, and like plastics, birch bark is slow to decay. I often find small sections of dead trunks where the inside has completely rotted away, but the bark is still intact. Once, along a creek in southern Utah I found what at first appeared to be a piece of semi-transparent vinyl, photodegrading in the sun. Closer inspection revealed that it was a piece of birch bark. All the cellulose had rotted out of the bark, leaving only the resins. Given the near synthetic properties of the birch, it would not surprise me if a sharp chemist-turned-primitive could produce vinyl or something like it on a camping trip. For most of us, however, the resinous bark is useful as a **fire-starter** because it burns (with a thick, black smoke) even when wet. Primitive peoples made torches with the bark.

But the focus here is on **birch bark canisters**. The water birch is too small for traditional folded and stitched bark work, but there is one type of canister that is fun and easy to make with the water birch. The finished canister is essentially a hollow section of branch with corks at both ends.

I learned how to make these canisters from my cousin Melvin Beattie. Mel learned how to make birch bark canisters after seeing one in a museum, which an Indian trapper had used for storing beaver castor. Mel examined the museum artifact, then decided to collect some birch and replicate the artifact. The method I describe is what I learned from him.

First, start by **selecting a branch** from a live tree. Pick only from an area where there is an abundance of the trees. Select a branch that is just big enough that you can grasp the entire circumference of the branch with one hand. Examine the branch carefully and look for a straight section at least five or six inches long that is completely free of knots, bumps, or cuts. Birches have a great deal of character, so you may have to look around a little to find one that will work. Ideally you should find one with two or three workable sections so that you are not wasting so much live tree for your project. Examine the potential branch very carefully before you cut it. Make sure you have the piece you want before you kill it.

Next, **mark each end** of the section(s) where you want to make a container. Typically, the length of your container will be determined by the length of a straight, blemish-free branch you can find, which is

Birch bark canisters.

rarely more than seven or eight inches. Now, saw through the branch at the mark that will become the smaller end of your container. In other words, cut off the top part of the branch, and leave the other end, of larger diameter, to serve as a handle while you work. I use the saw on my Swiss Army knife for this task.

That done, use a sharp blade and **score a line deeply** all the way around the branch at the other mark you made. You must cut all the way through the inner and outer bark for this to work. Then use another blemish-free stick and gently, but firmly rap the bark of your container-to-be. This process only works in the early summer when the sap is up. The bark almost "floats" on the wood and you need only rap it to loosen the bond. **Rap** all over the section you want to remove for a container. Then grasp the circumference of the stick and try to twist the bark off the branch. This should be like opening an extremely tight jar lid. Grunt and give it all you've got, and it may come loose. If it does not come off, then rap on it some more and repeat the process until it does come loose. Then **slide the hollow tube** of bark right off the end of the branch. The reason you cut the smaller end of the branch was so that the bigger end could slide off, as opposed to vice-versa, sliding the smaller diameter bark off of the larger end of the branch.

Set the hollow tube of bark aside and **cut a cork** from the now debarked branch. Simply cut a one-inch-long piece from the branch, and push it into the end of the bark tube where it came from. Next, cut a cork for the other end, again using the original wood to get an exact fit. I use about an inch of the debarked wood for the cork, and I leave that attached to an additional inch or so of the branch that still has the bark on it. This serves as an easy-to-grip handle. When the cork is in place, the canister looks like a simple stick, and few people would guess it was hollow.

Birch bark canisters have a variety of uses besides for storing beaver castor. You may use your canister as a small canteen, or you may use it to store many small items, such as matches or fishing tackle.

Drying and shrinking can cause the corks to loosen up, so you may want to save a piece of branch to make a bigger cork if necessary. Sometimes, however, the corks become tighter fitting when dry.

◊ ◊◊◊ ◊

I break my gaze away from the birch tree and tune in for a moment to the sounds of the waterfalls. This place always makes me thirsty. It is not so much that I need water, but that I need to drink in the beauty of this place. I reach for the drinking cup on my belt. The cup is copper, including a copper handle. On the opposite side from the handle is a mountain lion cast in silver with a gold head. I panned the gold in junior high and made the cup in a high school jewelry class. I loosen my belt, remove the cup, and dip it into the stream to bring up the cold, clear water.

Copper drinking cup.

I drink, but then remember an incident from a mile or so upstream from here. I was camping with some friends and they taught me something very interesting about water and people. On that occasion I dipped my cup into the stream as now, and I savored the cool creek water. My reverie was broken though as one of the guys noticed me drinking the water and hollered, "You actually drink that stuff?!" He was horrified at the thought.

"It is some of the best water I've ever had." I answered, surprised that he was surprised. I have gotten by on some pretty murky stuff in the past; I have literally drunk from cow tracks in the mud where everything was coated with a heavy white crust of alkaline. No, this mountain water was just plain good.

About a half hour later it was my turn for shock. This same individual opened up his fly and urinated two feet from the edge of the stream and twenty feet upstream from where I had previously been drinking.

Since that time I have noticed that people who do not drink the water are more likely to not respect the water. I have also noticed that people who are fearful of the water may also be less comfortable in the wilderness as a whole. For these reasons, and because the water tastes so good, I usually encourage people to leave their filters and tablets at home and savor the water. But ultimately that is a decision you have to make for yourself.

Giardia & Water Purification

When I say I encourage people to drink the water I have to admit that I am a little biased. Roughly 30% of people have no symptoms from giardia, and after ten years or so of drinking assorted muck I would say that I am included in that 30%. Someone who has been affected by giardia will likely give you different advice.

The one thing I can say for certain about the effects of giardia is that those who have had it talk about it years afterward, long after medication has killed the critters. I will never forget the immortal words a fellow student on a 26-day trip in 1984. We were all getting together and sharing our individual stories after three days of solo. Several people "got hit" with giardia, and one man told us, "I could shoot farther out the back than I could the front."

Clean, safe water is a rarity in the modern world.

Giardia is a one-celled protozoan that attaches itself to the lining of the small intestine and multiplies rapidly in the nutrient-rich environment. The organism can pass through the digestive tract as a cyst with a protective, thick wall. It may remain viable in cold water for more than two months, and an infected host is capable of expelling millions of cysts each day.

Symptoms include severe diarrhea, stomach cramps, and sulfurous belching. Symptoms typically occur one to four weeks after ingestion. Antacid and diarrhea medications can both mask the diagnosis and hinder treatment. The commonly prescribed drugs are quinacine hydrocloride and metronidazole. **Treatment** takes ten days or more. According to a Montana Department of Health and Environmental Sciences pamphlet on giardia, "Fatalities directly attributed to giardiasis are rare." How comforting.

The problem of giardia has dramatically increased in the past thirty years or so. It is unclear whether the giardia is a newcomer to the backcountry or if people are simply more educated about the disease now than before. It is also possible that by drinking sterilized city water people's immune systems have weakened so that they are more susceptible now to the effects of giardia, as well as other water borne bacteria.

Most people in the country grew up drinking creek water all of their lives, and never thought twice about it. But younger generations have been taught to think of all water as contaminated and full of bacteria.

In a rural town like Pony, many of the springs are easily contaminated and the wells are little more than glorified creek water "filtered" through a few feet of dirt. More than once I've seen tiny creatures swimming about in a fresh glass of water. My great aunt once had her water tested, and she was told that it was contaminated with high levels of coliform bacteria. When the state suggested that she should treat the water she replied, "Well, we've been fine for the last twenty years; I don't see why we need to start treating it now." I bet that at least half the springs and wells in our community are similarly contaminated, yet they've worked well for generations. Susceptibility to water borne bacteria undoubtedly has a lot to do with how strong your immune system is. In any case, giardia and other water borne bacteria are in our streams and lakes to stay. It is your choice whether or not to treat your water. If you choose to treat your water there are many ways to do so, including filtering, halazone tablets, iodine, boiling, or with super-oxygenated water.

Water filters are usually bulky, expensive and sometimes tediously slow. Be sure to shop for the filter that purifies the most water in the least time. A good quality water filter is a real pleasure to use, especially for water that is clearly contaminated. It gives you the secure feeling that you are being safe and not playing Russian roulette with your guts. I finally bought a water filter because my guests on wilderness expeditions were usually uncomfortable drinking untreated water. Unfortunately, the first trip I used the filter was the first time I got sick from the water!

Realistically, I don't think the filter caused the problem. More likely the problem came when we were trying to read the directions by moonlight, filtering water on a 20°F night when the water froze solid in the tubing. That's when I dropped the bag of trail mix in the creek and soaked half the bag. We were just down stream from a ranch with lots of cows near the creek, but we ate our trail mix anyway. My friend Jeff got sick four days later, on the last day of the expedition. I got the same symptoms the following day at home. There was a lot of belching with a peculiar flavor I don't know how to describe, accompanied by a yellowish diarrhea that completely emptied my bowels. But after a thorough purging on the toilet one day, I felt fine the next. I knew the filter didn't make me sick, but I mentally associated the two, and I couldn't stand to even look at the filter for more than a year after that!

Halazone tablets (p-dichlorosulfamoryl benzoic acid) were used by soldiers during World War II, before other forms of water purification became available. It works well in neutral or acidic water, but not in alkaline water or in the presence of nitrates, a common pollutant. It has a shelf life of about five months when stored below 89°F, but loses up to 75% of its potency when exposed to air for just 48 hours. It is also questionable whether or not halazone tablets really work in cold water. In short, this is an older form of water purification that isn't worth bothering with today.

Iodine can be used in several different forms for water purification: as tablets, liquid, or crystals. **Iodine tablets** are available at most camping supply stores, and they are very effective at killing anything in the water, but they have a short shelf life even when new, and rapidly lose potency after opening. The tablets also give the water a nauseous taste and can be harmful if used over an extended time period. Renee and I only used tablets once. We brought some iodine tablets on our walk across Montana. The one time we used them was to flavor the water at Two Dot, Montana because the alkaline town water tasted worse than the iodine tablets!

A 2% tincture of liquid iodine from the drug store, like that used in a first aid kit, can be used as a less expensive alternative to tablets. Just add 8 drops to one quart of water and let it sit for about fifteen minutes before drinking. But make sure it is fresh iodine, since it too has a short shelf life.

The best form of iodine for water purification seems to be **USP-grade resublimed iodine crystals**. The crystals "sublime" from a solid to a gaseous state without passing through a liquid phase in between. A small pinch of iodine crystals (4-8 grams) can be re-used almost indefinitely for water purification. Just put the crystals in a one-ounce bottle with water and hold it in your hand to warm it up to body temperature for a few minutes until the water is saturated with iodine from the crystals. Then add 10 millimeters of this saturated water (*but not the crystals*) to your canteen for every quart or liter of volume. The temperature of the water in the canteen doesn't matter; it can be very warm or ice cold. But wait a good fifteen minutes for the iodine to kill everything before you have a drink.

Iodine crystals sound almost like alchemy or a great placebo at first, since the crystals can be re-used indefinitely. But I finally bought a water purification kit and tried it myself, and the treated water certainly had the smell and flavor of water treated with tablets, although it was not nearly as strong. Apparently there is enough iodine in the water to do the job. The difference in taste may be simply that the iodine sublimes into a gaseous state, rather than dissolving into a liquid form. I've also noticed that the iodine flavor becomes less and less noticeable the longer the water sits, suggesting that the iodine slowly escapes from the water.

Iodine crystals are nearly inert, but they will evaporate (sublime) into the air if the cap is left off the bottle. They will also completely sublime into water if placed in a large enough volume.

The purpose for warming the water in the one ounce bottle is because the warmer water holds more iodine before reaching a state of saturation or "dynamic equilibrium" at which point the crystals stop dissolving. After pouring the saturated solution into your water bottle, then you can replace the water in the one ounce bottle so that you will have saturated iodine water ready when you need it to treat the next batch of drinking water.

So, you may be wondering, if iodine crystals are so good for water purification, then how come you cannot buy them at the camping supply store downtown? The reason is simply that the crystals are toxic if accidentally ingested, so there is a potential liability issue there. Fortunately, you need only 4 to 8 grams of crystals for water purification, while the lethal dose is considered to be above 15 grams. Still, you want to be careful to avoid accidentally ingesting any of them. Due to the liability issue, you may have to look around a bit to find a source for iodine crystals. Be sure to check at our website at **www.hollowtop.com** for possible leads.

Another method of water purification treatment uses **super-oxygenated water**, notably a product called "Aerobic 07". The product is a concentration of stabilized oxygen in water with approximately 1,000 times the normal oxygen content of water. A few drops in your water will kill all anaerobic bacteria. The word "anaerobic" means not-oxygen, because these bacteria require an environment without oxygen to survive. The bacteria in your gut and those that would make you sick in the gut, are anaerobic bacteria.

Aerobic O7 is made by a company called "Good for you Canada". It may be good for you too, and it is available in many camping supply stores. The two concerns about the product are that: 1) it might also kill off the good micro flora in your gut, and 2) it may increase the number of free radicals bouncing around in your body damaging your DNA. With these side effects, Aerobic 07 is probably no better or worse than using iodine tablets.

At least the super-oxygenated water has no noticeable flavor.

Boiling is another way to purify water for drinking, although it too has it's drawbacks. The biggest obstacle to boiling batch after batch of water is that it is time consuming and you can easily spend most of your camping trip just tending to pots of water on the fire. But one trick I discovered is that you can very quickly boil water in those discarded **beer bottles** that seem to be found throughout the wilderness. The slender shape exposes lots of surface area to the fire, while the dense glass conducts the heat easily, and the narrow top acts like a lid to better trap the heat inside.

Bottles found on the beach of a reservoir work great for boiling water to drink. Here I am also cooking in a primitive clay pot with a lid, both made from clay found nearby.

Let it boil for a few minutes then take it off with an improvised potholder to cool. You can even lift a bottle off with a straight stick. Just push the stick down into the bottle and tip the bottle until there is enough friction to keep it from sliding off the stick.

You might be surprised that you can boil water in a bottle without breaking it, but as long as the bottle is completely full to start with, then the glass will stay the same temperature as the water inside. Even ice water can be placed right on the fire and brought to a rolling boil in a matter of a few minutes without cracking the glass. I find it takes at least two bottles per person to stay properly hydrated. That way you can boil water in one bottle while another one is cooling off to drink. The narrow neck of the bottles also helps keep out the ashes, so that the boiled water tastes a lot better. Still, boiled water typically tastes flat because the air has been boiled out of it.

Giving the water a good shake will help to restore some of the air and improve the flavor. I usually just add some good flavored herbs like mint leaves or berries like rose hips to make a delicious tea.

One last method of water purification I recommend is simply **eating aromatic leaves or seeds** each time you drink untreated water. Aromatic plants, like those from the Mint family or Parsley family, have potent volatile oils with anti-bacterial properties. Juniper berries are another good antibacterial plant. Some Native American medicine men chewed juniper berries while treating sick patients. This helped to kill airborne pathogens that they might be inhaling. A few species of plants with strong concentrations of volatile oils, like "wormwood" (*Artemisia absinthium*) of the Aster family are used specifically to kill parasites in the intestinal tract. Plants like that are too potent to use on a regular basis, but you can safely eat the aromatic

I never liked the taste of beer, but rose hip tea boiled in a beer bottle is pretty hard to beat! The label doesn't burn off easily, because it is cooled by the water in the bottle.

mints and parsleys—provided you can identify them properly. Be sure to read *Botany in a Day: Thomas J. Elpel's Herbal Field Guide to Plant Families* for more information. Just eat a few anti-bacterial leaves each time you drink and you will treat the water right in your stomach. This is far from a foolproof method, but it is something. Soaking a few crushed leaves in a pot of cold water will have some benefit too.

◊   ◊◊◊   ◊

I sip at my cup of water; it is cold and almost sweet. As I sip at the water I also sip at my thoughts. I realize that I am very fortunate to live in a place that has such good water, although even here there is some contamination. Most of it is from century-old mining tailings, which leach heavy metals into the water. But the streams support many trout, and trout are good indicators of water quality. The fish did disappear for a short time on one nearby stream when a small mining company spilled sulfuric acid in the creek, however, the creek recovered quickly. The mining company was fined $20,000 for the incident, but they left instead of paying the fine.

It is amazing to me that we are not more foresighted in this country about how we take care of our water resources. In much of the Silicon Valley, where I lived as a child, the ground water is irreversibly contaminated with chemicals. Friends from eastern states have described how there are limits to the number of certain types of fish that you can eat, due to heavy metal concentrations in the flesh.

Our own town of Pony is just a tiny community in a rural area with miles and miles of undeveloped lands around us. You would expect that we would have crystal clear, drinkable water, and for the most part we do. Yet, even here the assaults on the water are endless from mining tailings and various spills. One flooded mine shaft beneath an old cyanide pond on a nearby mountain pass finally gave way a few years back and sent a flood of orange mud water down the creek right through a neighboring town. But that didn't even make the news around here.

Downstream the waters become increasingly contaminated from individual septic systems and city sewers, plus herbicide residues and nitrates from farming operations. I have seen thousands of freshwater mussel shells buried in the banks of old river channels, but almost no living mussels left in the rivers today, and it is illegal to harvest them because they have become so rare. I know what the water is like in so many parts of the world. I know what our asset is worth here in the mountains. Our water tastes good, and it is good. That is a rarity in the modern world.

It is unfortunate that we, *Homo Sapiens*, take water so much for granted. Industries and governments often take water for granted, as we have learned in Pony with the mining industry and the lax state and federal regulations. We as individuals also take water for granted. It is easy to do. The water is there when we turn on the faucet and we rarely think about where it comes from or how it gets to us. Most of us, however, would be shocked and probably angry if we turned on the faucet and nothing happened.

Here in America, few of us have ever had that experience, and few of us will. Yet water shortages and water rationing is becoming more and more common throughout America, especially in the West. However, shortages are unnecessary, because more efficient water use can leave more water to go around. This is much like the idea used with energy for "increasing supply" through greater efficiency. It is often cheaper for cities to increase their water supply through efficiency rather than developing new sources. Projects such as fixing leaky pipes, installing low-flush toilets, and installing low-flow showerheads can be cheaper than building dams or buying water rights. Communities can even reap a net profit from such conservation projects because some water conserving devices like showerheads conserve hot water, and that saves energy.

In the previous chapter I introduced Rocky Mountain Institute and their concept of "negawatts" for conserving energy. The institute has broadened its horizons over the years to deal with many other resource issues, including water. The concept of negawatts evolved into "negagallons" to give city utilities a new way of evaluating water supply and demand. They demonstrated that it was more economical for one Colorado city to retrofit homes with water efficient toilets, showerheads, and other conservation measures, than to build a new dam. The city's proposal for a dam was dropped, largely due to their work.

Through water conservation we can meet the needs of many more people without needing to take any more water from the resources of nature. Some communities even require contractors to improve the water efficiency in existing buildings to free up enough supply for the new buildings they construct. This way new buildings effectively use no new water. It also saves taxpayers a fortune.

Eventually though, water efficiency reaches its peak and people have to look elsewhere for water. A likely source is through *recycling*. A variety of biological methods exist which purify sewage water so that it is cleaner than many municipal water supplies. The city of San Diego is already recycling a million gallons of water a day by using water hyacinths for purifying wastewater. Recycling will allow cities to achieve greater and greater efficiency until someday we will only need our water supplies for the purpose of replacing water lost to irrigation and evaporation.

I drink my water and dip up another cupful. I gaze at the reflecting patterns of light on the water and drink it in. Again I remember my companion urinating in the water. It really seems a shame to have to think about human waste and sanitation while savoring the fresh, clean water, but then again, having that clean water in nature is dependent, among other things, on how we dispose of human waste.

Crapping in the Woods

For more than 99% of human history our species had neither toilets nor toilet paper, so you would think that we might instinctively know how to crap in the woods, but the truth is that most people are exceedingly uncomfortable with the whole idea. Some people simply refuse to crap or even urinate without a real toilet, and many of those who actually do crap in the woods leave behind little brown monuments with "snow-capped" peaks of toilet paper. The unfortunate reality is that we need some potty training for adults in the wilderness, so here it is:

The standard "technique" is to dig and use a cat hole fifty yards or more from any water source and away from any trails. Look for some soft ground, such as the barren leaf or pine needle litter under many trees. You can carry a digging stick with you, or find any sturdy stick nearby to dig a hole. For lack of a digging stick, or in frozen ground, you can cover your stuff with a rock or a cow pie, etc. Our ancestors most likely just dropped it and left it without covering it up at all, but there were a lot less people then. Today it is important to show good courtesy to your fellow campers by burying it out of sight and smell. Besides, burying it eliminates the problem of flies getting into it and subsequently visiting your dinner back at camp.

I discourage you from using **toilet paper** at all when you camp. There are plenty of natural alternatives, and we have not evolved in the last 100 years to become genetically dependent on toilet paper. If you feel that you have, then at least bring toilet paper back to your campfire to dispose of it, or burn it on site with a lighter, especially in the desert. In desert areas both stools and toilet paper can dry out and more or less "petrify" or mummify. With some slight shifting of the sands these will surface and serve as landmarks for years to come. A good desert technique to prevent these landmarks is to take a stick and "mush it all up" into the soil until it looks like soil. It works. But, remember, if you use toilet paper, then be sure to haul it out or burn it.

For **toilet paper alternatives** you may use leaves from non-poisonous plants, or try smooth rocks, snowballs, or "ranger wipe". The thought of using a snowball may send shivers to your most private parts. But it is not that bad and it works well. Ranger wipe is when you wipe twice; first you wipe with your finger and then you wipe your finger on something else. Ranger wipe is widely used around the world and it is the reason that people in many cultures only eat with one hand, the other one.

Forest rangers on the leading edge of environmental ethics have attempted to make these kinds of suggestions to forest visitors in the past, but it didn't go over very well. People in our culture are very sensitive to the subject of wiping, and many people stop listening after words "toilet paper alternatives". Those well-intentioned individuals who did listen couldn't always handle the complexities of determining the best procedure in each new environment. Among other incidents, forest fires were started by people attempting to burn their toilet paper with a lighter.

The forest service personnel I know have since simplified their advice, suggesting visitors just dig a cat hole well away from the water and bury it. They don't even try to mention toilet paper alternatives. The fact that you are reading this book suggests that you probably use your head more than most. You can evaluate each situation and determine the best techniques for answering "nature's call".

No matter which methods you use, I recommend you search around for some **aromatic plants** to clean your hands with. Aromatic plants, like sagebrush, mints, or pine needles, have potent volatile oils with disinfectant properties. Rubbing your hands vigorously with these plants is much better than cleaning your hands in a creek and possibly contaminating the water.

There are some people who believe that you should not even swim or bathe in the water. Instead you should bucket water away from the source for bathing and washing, even if you are not using soap. I think that is going a bit too far. We are part of the ecosystem, just like any other creature that walks into the water, and we need to fully participate in nature to better appreciate our place within it.

Ultimately, you will have to set your own standards for taking care of the water. But here is a good rule of thumb to go by: when you use the water for any task, *ask yourself if you would drink a few feet downstream from where you are using it. If you think twice about drinking the water, then think again about what you are putting in it.*

◊ ◊◊◊ ◊

These thoughts aside, I take a moment to savor my cup of creek water, and to tune in to the roaring of the creek over the falls. A fish swims by my perch. I follow it with my eyes as it makes a circle around the pool and returns to the protective cover underneath the boulder to the right side of the pool. Two more fish are hiding in there. If they were in a more accessible spot I might be tempted to practice my hand at fishing.

Fishing by Hand

With these thoughts of fishing I remember a favorite quote from author Tom Brown Jr. in *The Search* where he said, "Nature provides everything. All you have to do is look and take it." It is an appealing concept, and it is largely true. Nature is a banquet and all we have to do is harvest the bounty. The challenge is figuring out *how* to harvest it.

Harvesting is often very simple, but without knowledge of how to do it, the banquet is always out there, close enough to see, but out of grasp. One of my greatest thrills in primitive living was learning how to literally reach in and pluck the bounty from the streams.

The first time I caught a fish by hand was when I was working in Arizona along the Verde River in the Mazatzal Wilderness. The big carp, considered "trash fish" by most anglers, are nonetheless a delicacy in primitive living and they are often fairly easy to catch. The carp frequently feed in shallow water and sometimes in places so shallow that they stick halfway out of the water.

Fishing a small stream. Reaching under an obstacle will not scare the fish as long as they cannot see that your arm is attached to the rest of your body.

I made my first catch when I saw a group of about seven or eight carp feeding along the shore, almost out of the water. There was a thicket of reed grass between me and them. I knew that I would scare them if I tried coming through the reeds, so instead I grabbed an overhead tree branch and vaulted myself over the reeds and directly on to the group of fish. I caught two of them and threw them on the bank.

After learning that I could catch carp by hand, or by foot as the case may be, I caught them consistently throughout the rest of my stay, mostly by trapping them in small pools, or catching them in shallows along the river. Returning home to Montana though, I watched the little eight to ten inch trout swim by in our mountain streams and once again the wild bounty was in sight but out of grasp. It was another year before I learned that all I had to do to catch them was to reach in and pick them up.

A group of us went camping in the mountains late one June. We saw numerous trout and small mountain suckers milling in the shallows of the lake near the spillway. Without much knowledge of what we were doing three of us made some crude forked spears and waded into the water. We did catch fish, some by hand and some with the aid of the spear, but our results were inconsistent. The spear seemed to work well. The fish were seldom scared of the forked stick slowly moving closer to them and it was fairly easy to pin them to the mud where we could reach in and pull them out by hand. After a couple hours we had gathered a small mess of fish.

Then the rest of our group, including my sister, a cousin, and Renee came over to try fishing too. They waded into the water and without any more knowledge than we had, they reached under a floating log and started pulling fish out left and right. In short order we had a total of seven trout and ten suckers. We added these to a pile of spring beauty tubers and glacier lily corms. We cooked our "fish casserole" in a pan we found.

It was a thrill to catch those first fish by hand, and the mystery of why our results were so inconsistent drove me to practice my fishing techniques the rest of the year, all the way into December. My

Mountain suckers, wild onions, puffball mushrooms, and a can of unopened beer, all found in the wilds.

grandmother's place was about two blocks from our home and we crossed a small creek on the way there. The brown trout and the brook trout swim up small streams like that one in the fall. Rainbow and cutthroat trout spawn in the spring. While fishing small streams is legally closed during those times of the year, I was not so much interested in keeping the fish that year as merely understanding how to catch them. Every time I walked to Grandma's house I stopped to play in the creek and chase fish, and each time I walked into the house with my coat sleeve sopping wet and my arm totally numb.

I learned that the fish are not scared of hands mingling among them as long as you move calmly. Most importantly, you need to be in a place where the fish cannot see what the hand is attached to. Having cover between you and the fish is important for hand

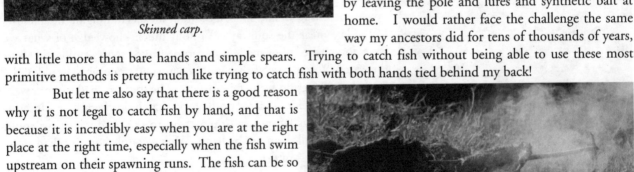

This carp was caught by hand in a marshy area along the Jefferson River in southwestern Montana... I sat on it until I could work my fingers into its gills.

fishing, and you could probably create cover and habitat in many places that lack it by tossing sticks and leaves in the water where they will stay without washing away. Incidentally, this organic material helps feed the fish since some ninety percent of fish food in small headwater streams comes from insects that live directly or indirectly on the organic litter that falls in the water.

Fishing by hand and spear, by the way, is illegal in Montana, and probably in many other states as well. I had to ask a game warden before I believed it. Our fishing laws are set up such that the only legal methods of fishing are those that are specifically included in the law. Anything not written down is simply not legal.

This creates a bit of a problem for people like me, because the idea of fishing with modern tackle seems like cheating, and I consider myself handicapped by leaving the pole and lures and synthetic bait at home. I would rather face the challenge the same way my ancestors did for tens of thousands of years,

Skinned carp.

with little more than bare hands and simple spears. Trying to catch fish without being able to use these most primitive methods is pretty much like trying to catch fish with both hands tied behind my back!

But let me also say that there is a good reason why it is not legal to catch fish by hand, and that is because it is incredibly easy when you are at the right place at the right time, especially when the fish swim upstream on their spawning runs. The fish can be so thick in the streams, and in such shallow water, that it is almost impossible Not to catch them. It would be pretty easy to abuse the resource.

Indeed, when the Lewis & Clark expedition paddled up the nearby Beaverhead River in 1805 they stopped for a few days to do some fishing using primitive means. On August 18th they used a net, and on the 19th they used a seine of willow brush. Then on August 22nd they made a "brush drag" and swept it along the river, catching "528 very good trout". I don't

Smoking carp by a campfire.

74

Crayfish can be caught by hand in many streams and rivers. Closely related to the lobster, they are a real delicacy in primitive living. Drop them into boiling water to kill and cook them.

Important: Do not transport live crayfish from one waterway to another. Crayfish that were originally native to Louisiana (like this one I caught in Utah) have wiped out many pristine ecosystems in the West, consuming every scrap of vegetation, every snail, insect, and tadpole—even fish, turtles and garter snakes.

believe they were abusing any ethical limit back then, because the streams were much healthier, and the human population was so sparse that they spent the previous four months paddling across Montana without seeing a single human being. But the world is a much different place now.

The way I see it you need to seek a reasonable balance. Always buy a fishing license, because much of the money goes towards improving fish habitat. Observe the positive intentions of the laws by staying within the daily limits to avoid over-fishing. Better yet, voluntarily set your limits lower than the legally allowable limits for game fish like trout, and rely on trash fish like carp and suckers for most of your food. Then you won't be competing with anyone else and you can take all you want. Many of our carp and suckers were introduced from other parts of the world and some have become nuisance fish here, so you would be helping out by removing a few of them.

Of course you will need to research the fishing laws of your own state so you know what is and is not legal, and only you can decide how you want to approach this legal and ethical issue.

◊ ◊◊◊ ◊

A flash of movement downstream catches my attention, and I sit still to watch for a moment. A slate gray bird, a little smaller than a robin, stands upon a rock, bobbing quickly up and down. It is the American dipper. It calls twice *zeet, zeet*, then runs upstream through the water. In and out. In and out. Constantly bobbing up and down. These peculiar birds live here all summer and winter, feeding on aquatic insects in the stream, oblivious to the freezing-cold water. They can swim under water by paddling with their feet, and sometimes they even use their stout little wings as flippers. This one races upstream past me, hopping in and out of the water and

The barrel cactus of the desert southwest has naturally hook-shaped spines. You can carefully remove a few spines with a knife without harming or disfiguring the plant.

seemingly bouncing from boulder to boulder. It flies right up over the waterfall and out of sight, and I turn my attention to other things.

On the bank beside my swimming hole is a small patch of stinging nettles. I frequently get stung by them when I come through them to get to the water. I set my drinking cup upside-down on the rock beside me, making sure it is in a secure location. Then I leave the rock momentarily, and collect a few dead stinging nettle stalks. These are leftovers from last year's crop. Carefully I pick out the dead stalks and avoid touching the live ones. Live nettles have formic acid in the little white hypodermic-style needles, or hairs, on the underside of the leaves. These deliver a potent sting early in the spring to protect the succulent plants from grazing animals. Later the formic acid becomes weaker as the plants become coarse, and the dead stalks are entirely free of it.

I return with the nettle stalks to my perch in the stream and set them aside, except for one. The fish linger in the shadows beneath the boulder, close but out of reach. I run my hand along it to strip away the remaining stubs of the leaf stalks. Then I flatten the stalk, starting at the base and working my way up. I use the tips of my fingers to apply pressure, crushing the stalk. Nettle fibers can be used to make cordage, and cordage can be used for just about anything—including fish line.

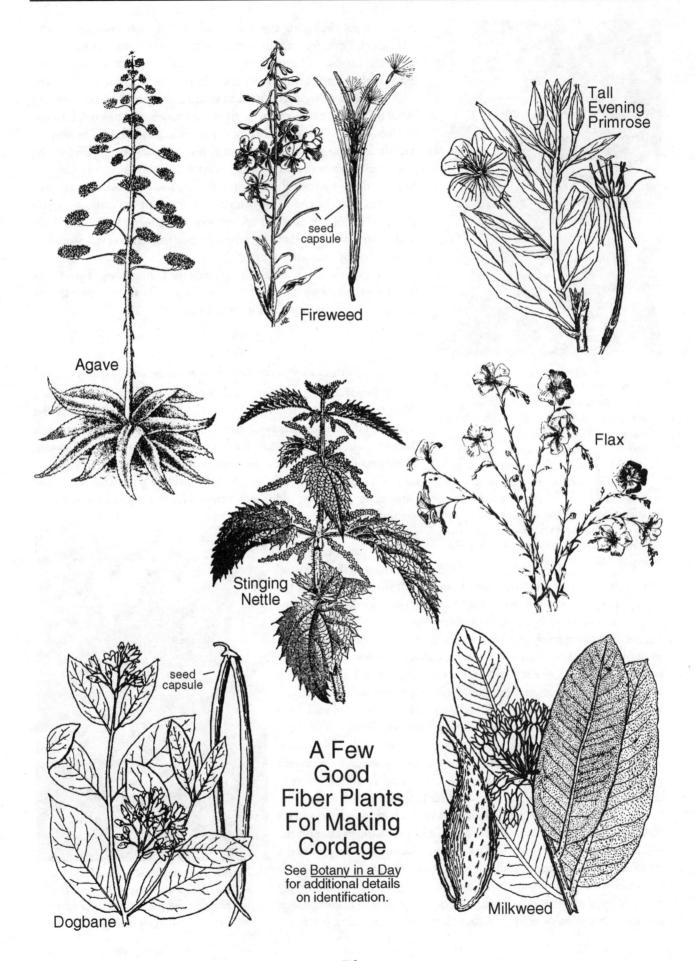

Agave

Fireweed

seed
capsule

Tall
Evening
Primrose

Flax

Stinging
Nettle

Dogbane

seed
capsule

A Few
Good
Fiber Plants
For Making
Cordage

See <u>Botany in a Day</u>
for additional details
on identification.

Milkweed

Making Cordage From Natural Fibers

Cordage, or string, is one of those simple little things which we seldom think about but use every day and take for granted. It is only when we need a piece of cordage and do not have any that we begin to notice just how handy it is. In primitive living cordage is an integral part of many other skills. Primitive peoples used cordage for such diverse projects as fish nets and fishing line, rabbit nets, hammocks, bow and bowdrill strings, woven bags, trap strings and snares, lashing, sewing, and for just tying things up.

Today natural fiber for cordage is produced on an industrial scale, with plantations of agave for sisal fiber in Brazil and Africa. Another agave grown in Mexico provides henequen fiber. Hemp fiber comes from nonpsychoactive varieties of the marijuana plant, grown legally outside the states. Abaca, or manila hemp is made from the leafstalk fibers of a species of banana plant, *Musa textilis*. The palmetto, a native of the southeastern states, produces fibers used in brushes. Jute fiber is grown in India and Bangladesh, used especially for twine and burlap. Kenaf, a hibiscus grown mainly in India, is used for canvas and cordage. Coir is a rough-textured fiber from coconut husks, often spun into a thick twine for weaving into doormats.

In more primitive circumstances when you need a piece of cordage you can often improvise and use a supple willow or willow bark, or find a scrap of baling twine—or if you have a buckskin shirt, you can cut off a piece of fringe. If you do not have any of these, or if these do not meet your needs, then you may want to make your own cordage. Across North America there are many sources of high-quality plant fibers for cordage including: dogbane, milkweed, stinging nettle, fireweed, tall evening primrose, domestic hollyhocks, flax, wild licorice, yucca, agave, sotol, cattail, bulrush, and the basswood tree. Other fibrous plants which are often used as tinder for fire starting, such as grass, sagebrush bark, juniper bark, cedar bark, or the inner bark of the cottonwood or aspen can also be used to make a weak, but thick cordage. Cordage can also be made from sinew fibers from animal tendons, plus rawhide, hair, fur, and wool. There are several different ways of preparing the cordage material, depending on the source:

Fireweed, tall evening primrose, flax, and wild licorice: The thin, stringy bark needs to be loosened from the stalks through a process called retting, basically a mild rotting or at least a thorough soaking of the stems. Retting can occur naturally when the dead stalks are constantly wet from rain or snow. In winter the standing dead stalks are often nicely retted at the base, beneath the snow. If you can wait for your cordage, then you can do your own retting, soaking the stalks for a few days up to several weeks, to loosen the fibers. Fireweed, tall evening primrose, and wild licorice separate fairly easily from the stalks, just by peeling off the bark when properly retted. Flax fibers take a bit more work.

Several varieties of the annual flax, *Linum usitatissimum* are cultivated for linen fibers and linseed oil. In the wild or in flowerbeds you are more likely to encounter *Linum lewisii*, or another species of flax. Any species can be used for cordage, but most will have short stems with lots of little branches, and therefore shorter fibers for cordage making. The green stems can be gently scraped with a dull knife or even a fingernail to peel back the fibers, as can the retted dead stems. Start at the base and work your way up, scraping the fibers back a little bit at time into a curly mass until you reach the tip. Then straighten the fibers out to dry and discard the stems. For mass production the stalks are retted up to six weeks, then dried, beaten and scraped to remove the fibers, and finally combed to separate the waste.

Dogbane, milkweed, stinging nettle, hollyhock: These are my favorite cordage materials. To separate the fibrous bark from the stem, start by using your fingers to flatten the stalk from one end to the other. Crush stubborn spots by biting them or by flattening them gently with a rock. Flattening the stalk splits it lengthwise into four pieces. It splits the stalk top and bottom (where your fingers were) and along the sides. By running a finger down one split you can open the stalk so you have the four lengths laid out flat. Place these across the palm of your left hand and start the next step at the butt end.

Bring your right hand down across the stalks to break them, and peel up the broken sections with

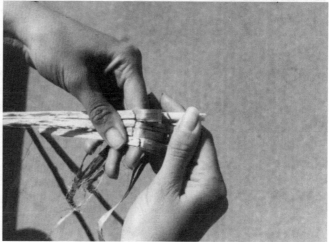

Separating the fibers from a dogbane stalk.

77

your thumb as shown with dogbane in the photo, thus leaving the fibers behind. Break off no more than two inches at a time. Be careful as you pull these pieces away, as they will cling to fibers at the end and pull them out. To disconnect the fibers from the chunks of stalk, use the extra fingers on you left hand to grasp the fibers and secure them as you pull the broken pieces of stalk back in the opposite direction. Do this full step repeatedly until you have cleaned the length of the stalk. It takes some practice, but you will soon become proficient at it. Hollyhocks are processed the same way, but they require retting first, as described in the previous section. Hollyhocks are also very mucilaginous (slimy) to work with.

Yucca, agave, sotol: These are all members of the Agave Subfamily of the Lily Family (see *Botany in a Day*). All occur in the wild of the southwest, with the range of the yucca running north all the way to Montana. Each of these plants are grown domestically as well.

If you need cordage material right away, then look for partially rotted leaves with strong fibers intact at the base of the plants. A properly aged leaf can be beaten up with a wooden mallet on a log to help separate the fibers. You can also scrape away the green matter with the edge of a knife from a live leaf to expose the thread-like fibers. With the yucca you can leave the sharp point on the tip to serve as a natural needle.

If you have a little more time, and a source of green leaves or a whole plant (preferably one culled from a landscaping project rather than harvested wild) then you can steam pit the leaves to help break down the green matter. Read more about steam pits in the chapter on cooking. Once the leaves have been steam pitted, then it is easy to scrape away the green matter to free the good strong fibers.

Twisting Fibers into Cordage

After you have removed the fibers from the plants, take and twirl them between the palms of your hands to clean away any extra material and debris. Most types of fibers need a small amount of this type of cleaning. Then the fibers are ready to be made into cordage.

Cordage can be made any thickness and for any purpose from thread to rope. Start with a bundle of fibers roughly the thickness that you want your finished product. Tie these together at one end with a simple overhand knot. Next divide the fibers into two equal bundles and hang them on your left index finger so that the knot is on your finger and the strands hang down both sides (photo #1). For clarity in the photos, half the strands were dyed black. Hold it securely with your left hand and use your right hand to twist the fibers. Twist the fibers of one strand (photo #2) and then the other (photo #3) both in the same direction, and

78

5

6

7

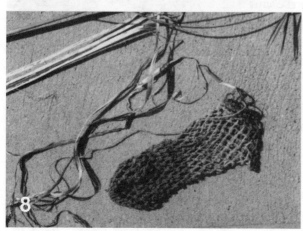

8

hold each strand securely. The energy pent up in the fibers wants to unravel, but if you hold the strands tight and remove your left hand, pulling your finger out, then that end, at the knot will twist around itself, thus using the energy to bind itself. It will only twist this way a little bit on its own (photo #4). You will have to help it along to twist it tight (photo #5). Next, put your left index finger between the strands again and repeat the process (photo #6), gaining a quarter to half an inch with each pass, and make the cordage as long as you want (photo #7).

Separating the fibers with your index finger isn't necessary, but it is easier to learn it that way. Your hands will subconsciously adapt to more efficient techniques over time.

Please note that everyone has s different system for fingering the cordage, so expect that this process will sound quite different in another book. There are many pathways to the same end.

The process of making the cordage makes the fibers many times stronger than they were before. With fibers that are already strong, like dogbane, a piece of well-made cordage the size of coarse fishing line can be too strong to break by hand. To get that strength the cordage must be very uniform along its length. If one strand becomes smaller than the other then the big strand will run straight with the smaller one wrapping around it. This makes very weak cordage. To correct this problem, simply move some fibers from one strand to the other to even out the sizes, and keep cording.

When you are near the end of the fibers and you want to make a longer cord, simply lay more fibers on the others and twist them right in. It is important to stagger the splices to avoid having two joints in one spot, which weakens the cord. The cordage in the net bag (photo #8) was spliced on a little at a time as I netted the bag. It was made of dogbane, stinging nettle and evening primrose fibers.

If you need extra durability, such as for a bowdrill cord, you can make a small cord more than twice the desired length, fold it in half and cord it again. Some commercial ropes are corded that way for extra strength.

Alternately, you can work with three strands at a time by simply holding the strands over both the index finger and the middle of your left hand, and cording as you would for two strands. I notice a big difference in between 2-ply cattail cordage (i.e.: 3 strands) and 3-ply cattail cordage. The 3-ply seems a lot stronger, even when it has no more material than the 2-ply cordage.

Mastering this skill of cordage-making will help you with all your other wilderness skills, from fire-making to setting traps, making bows and arrows, and simply keeping your clothes from falling off.

◊   ◊ ◊ ◊   ◊

Primitive Fishing Tackle

Our ancestors likely fished with nets, traps, spears or their bare hands more often than with a hook and line. It is simply a matter of survival economics—why waste time on a technology that catches just one fish at a time, when there are other ways to catch fish by the hundreds? Nevertheless, there were also many times and places, especially in deeper water, when a hand-made hook and line were the only way to effectively pull fish out of the water. Hand-made fishing tackle is especially relevant to practicing abos today, since it is about the only primitive technology that is still legal to use.

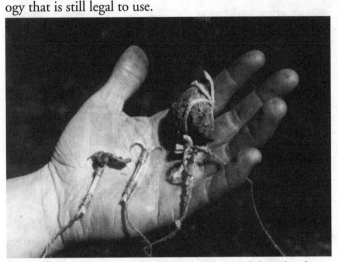

Barrel cactus fish hooks with dogbane cordage made by Nils Behn.

Commercially manufactured fishing tackle is both compact and lightweight, so it is easy to bring along on a camping trip. You only need to bring along the hooks, sinkers and line, since you can make a pole from a willow any time you want one. But if you are like me, then you would probably rather figure out how to catch a fish on a hook and line you've made yourself. Unfortunately, the primitive fishing tackle shown in many survival books doesn't always work

One of the most common "hooks" illustrated in wilderness survival guides is called the **gorge hook**, basically a short piece of bone or hard wood sharpened on both ends, with the fishing line tied in the middle. Bait is put on the hook such that the fishing line is flattened against it to make a skinny hook that is easy to swallow. When the fish bites and you pull on the line, then the hook turns 90° to the line, theoretically wedging itself sideways in the fish's mouth. In my limited experimentation, I found that it was an effective way to feed the trout. At best, I once had a trout part way out of the water. That was the closest I ever came with a gorge hook.

Reports from other practicing primitives are similar. In one class on primitive fishing, twelve students made gorge hooks and surrounded a small pond stocked with foot-long bass. The bass took the bait, but not the hooks, even though the hooks were theoretically sized properly for the fish. The class used up all their worms, then switched to crawdads for bait, but never did catch a fish.

On the other hand, I have heard of gorge hooks being used successfully for catfish, so apparently the key is simply to select the proper type of hook for the fish you are after. It is a simple and obvious concept, but not one that is mentioned in most survival manuals. One thing I have learned about fishing is that when an author includes an illustration of primitive fishing tackle, it does not necessarily quantify that they have actually caught any fish with it!

One style of primitive hook that I know really works is made from the spines of the barrel cactus. The spines are naturally hook-shaped and just need to be tied onto a line. Of course the barrel cactus only grows in the desert Southwest—but then, we modern primitives do get around!

Over all it seems that fishing with primitive tackle may be the least desirable of the available methods. But there are certain circumstances where no other fishing techniques are applicable, and that makes the primitive hook and line the best alternative at those times. More research needs to be done in this area, and I am newly excited about working with primitive tackle after making a "J"-shaped bone hook in a class with Paul Campbell at Rabbitstick Rendezvous. I think it has real potential for trout. Now I just have to try it out...

◊   ◊◊◊   ◊

Nils casts his line into a pool along the Snake River in Idaho. He caught five big suckers in one evening at this spot.

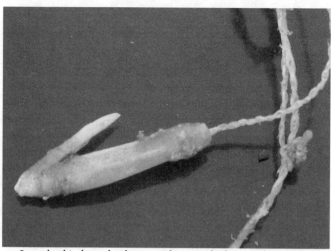

I made this bone hook in a class taught by Paul Campbell (author of Survival Skills of Native California) at Rabbitstick Rendezvous in Rexburg, Idaho.

I finish stripping out the fibers from the nettle stalk in my hands, and then pick up another. I process each of them, saving the fibers and dropping the broken pieces of stalk into the water. The individual pieces are like miniature canoes, each being tossed around in the stream and quickly being swept away. Soon they will be rotting food for bugs in the stream. Then fish food. Perhaps someday they will even be my food, as I continue honing my fishing skills.

The pile of stalks beside me has been reduced to a coil of fibers, which I save to cord later. The process is so automatic now, I do not even think about it. My hands just work away, while my mind wanders.

I dip up another cup of water, drink it and again place my cup on the rock. I remove my clothes and leave these on the rock also. I hop into the pool and quickly drench myself under the waterfall. The water is icy and numbing. Seconds later I sit on the moss covered boulder in the middle of the pool, soaking up the warm sunshine.

There is something exhilarating about going naked into the wilderness. Stripping down bare to the elements is like opening all your pores and soaking in a bath of nature. The sun, the air, the water, the soil, the rocks... every element of nature seems to come alive, fresh and sensuous. Striping down is possibly the quickest way to open up your senses and attune yourself to the nature around you.

Being naked is natural, and I think our society would be better if we humans were more casual about our bodies. Through the entire existence of our species, it has only been in the last few hundred years that we have learned to be ashamed of our bodies.

While I value nudity, I also believe strongly in not pushing it on other people. Nudity may seem very simple and "logical" to those who are used to it, but other people may be intimidated at the thought of exposing themselves, or offended at the sight of someone else. I can understand this, and I am not always comfortable with it myself. I have heard of instructors

A ten-second bath in a lake still partly covered with ice.

who will lead their group to a lake and will then strip down and dive in without a word. With the right group this can be a good way to quickly break through people's intimidations. Everyone else will usually follow the lead.

In regards to the law, it is my understanding that there are no federal laws against nudity. Nudity is supposedly legal on federal properties outside city limits, including Forest Service or Bureau of Land Management (BLM) lands. And while it is useful to know the legal standing of nudity, I nevertheless advise that you avoid creating a situation where someone else would like to call in the law.

A robin lands in the alder tree beside the pool. It speaks and I listen. What is it saying? As I listen, I remember. I once read in *Smithsonian* magazine about an ornithologist who was hired by Conservation International as part of the Rapid Assessment Program, a program essentially for the purpose of finding out what is in the American tropics before they are bulldozed over once and for all. In the article it said that this ornithologist, Ted Parker, could identify by songs alone, most of the 4,000 bird species that inhabit the tropics of the New World. According to the article, Parker could distinguish differences between the songs of hundreds of different varieties of closely related birds, songs that would sound identical to most of us. Parker's skill is an inspiration. I listen closer.

It is one thing to be able to identify birds by their calls. It is quite another to know what they are talking about. As it turns out, it is not as difficult as you might think to learn bird language, thanks to the work of Jon Young, an early student of Tom Brown Jr.

It was Jon Young's tapes, *Seeing Through Native Eyes* and especially tape number six of the series, *Learning the Language of the Birds* that really turned me on to birding. On that tape, Jon Young describes the process of deciphering bird songs to discover if there are other animals or people nearby that are beyond the limited range of your own five senses. It isn't a matter of translating any particular bird call into English, but rather of being able to interpret alarm calls based on the intensity of the alarm and the preferred habit of the bird sounding the alarm. For example, a ground-feeding bird like a robin is going to squawk about threats on the ground—such as a cat—while a tree-top feeding bird like a tanager is going to squawk about threats from the air—such as a hawk. You might have some experience with this process already, for instance, if you know who or what is coming up the road just by the tone of your dog's bark or the wag of it's tail.

In *Learning the Language of the Birds*, Jon Young out-lines a systematic process for distinguishing between normal or "baseline" bird songs versus their alarm calls. In theory at least, it isn't necessary to be able to identify which species of bird is making the call, as long as you know it's preferred habitat (low, middle, or high) in the tree cover. In practice, however, you have to learn at least the most common songbirds in your area to develop your skills then you can extrapolate that information to other species you are not so familiar with.

The robin sings; I whistle back, mimicking its call as best as I can. It squawks and flies away. Oh well. Warmed by the sun, I hop back into the pool to continue my bath. Gradually, I adapt to the icy water and stay in longer.

I feel much cleaner and more alive when I bathe in a cold mountain stream than when I take a hot shower at home. Hot water makes a haven for bacteria that live on the skin surface. An icy bath followed by sun-drying leaves me felling more refreshed than anything else I know.

Interestingly, a nice freezing bath is also a good **cardiovascular exercise**. Your blood vessels relax and dilate when you are warm and very quickly constrict when you leap into the icy water. I like to hike fast, or run until I am sweaty hot before I get in. Or, if I am at home and short of time, then I bicycle the 1.5 miles uphill as fast as I can, and jump in my swimming hole at the end of the ride. Afterwards, I sit on my rock and relax, soaking in the sounds and sunshine.

For now, I finish my bath. I splash about, stand under the waterfall, and then sit back on the rock to dry again. It is beautiful here, and now I must return to my fire to check on dinner.

◊   ◊◊◊   ◊

COOKING

The sun shines with the intensity of the noon summer day that it is, but the heat seems diminished now that I have cooled myself in the stream. I feel refreshed, relaxed and attuned. I drink another cup of water, fill up my water bottle and walk back to camp.

My pot of rice is nearly ready, and the fire is almost out. I add a little water to my dinner and put some wood on the fire. I find my rock to sit on.

When I am on the trail I often like the convenience of a **tin can**. I like cooking in a tin can because it is quick and easy to use, lightweight to carry, and it sits flat on the ground. I usually set it on the fire and come back when my dinner is done, and most of the water has cooked out. A meal like rice can take most of an hour to cook, but I only spend a few minutes with it. It is a miracle that I very seldom burn anything this way.

If you use a tin can for cooking then you should burn off the varnish coating inside the can. Otherwise it will burn and flake off above the water level in the can while you cook. Also, tin does react with many types of food. I always wondered why my can of lentils boiled up a deep purple color. Now I realize that it comes from the food reacting with the tin can. Rusty tin cans are sometimes used as a mordant for making dyes set. The minerals in tin interact readily with just about anything you put in the can. Tin gives plain boiled water a characteristic "tin taste".

But I find that as I grow older I am developing a finer culinary taste, and I am not always satisfied with food that has a tin flavor. Also, I am becoming more and more conscientious of what I put in my body. Sure, a little tin might not hurt, but I do quite a lot of camping, and I wonder what the health effects are from long-term consumption of tin. Fortunately, I also have **stainless steel can** that is as lightweight as any tin can, but it does not react as much with the foods. Recent research has shown that nickel does leach out of the stainless steel, but it is better than a tin can. This can originally had a handle on it. It was a product for use at mountain man rendezvous. But the handle came off, so now it is just a simple can.

Of course, there are other methods of cooking stews besides in a tin or stainless steel can. You can make pots from clay, or you could drape a piece of hide or stomach in a hole or hang it on a tripod and cook in it with hot rocks. You could make a birch-bark container if you have birch trees in the area, and there are other types of tree bark that can be made into pots as well. Often however, the best kind of cooking container you can make is a wooden cup or bowl. Wooden dishes are easy to create, just by hollowing out a piece of wood with hot coals from a fire. Then you can cook in them with hot rocks.

You may also be surprised to learn that some of the best wilderness meals can be cooked without any dishes at all.

Rock slab cooking. The ground squirrel easily stuck to the preheated rock. The hot rock cooked the back side while the fire cooked the belly. From the video "Mountain Meadows."

Cooking without a Pan

There are many, many techniques to cook a meal without depending on any pots or pans, some of which are demonstrated through the pages of this chapter. One simple and logical idea for cooking meat is to improvise, using a thin rock slab for a pan.

Rock Slab Cooking: Large flat rocks can be propped up on two or three smaller rocks, so that you can move the fire underneath it while you cook on top. Thinner rocks are obviously better than thick ones.

In the photos here I have used a very thin rock and placed it directly on the fire like a pan to cook my fish. It can be difficult to cook the thick backbone of a fish, but that problem can be easily solved by splitting it down the back instead of the belly, so the meat is of a more even thickness throughout. Use some sticks and quick fingers to flip the meat over to cook the other side. With a thin rock slab like this, it is easy to drag it carefully off of the fire with a stick, or you can grab a corner with a potholder like a folded piece of bark.

Vertical Rock Slab Cooking: Another innovative way to cook on a rock slab is to tilt the rock up vertically beside the fire and stick your meat to it, as illustrated on the previous page. The hot rock cooks one side of the meat while the fire cooks the other. I learned this trick from my cousin Melvin Beattie while we were shooting the second movie in the *Art of Nothing Wilderness Survival Video Series* called *Mountain Meadows: camping with almost nothing but the dog.*

The rock has to be heated first so that the meat will stick to it when applied. It may seem like a thick rock would work just fine for this trick, since the meat is applied to the hot side anyway, but the cold mass on the outside of a thick rock keeps sucking away the heat so the meat doesn't stick very well. So look for a thin slab that will heat easily by the fire. Something about an inch thick would be ideal. If you have nothing but thick rocks, then place one in the middle of the fire to heat it all the way through, then use a stick to flip it out and upright against another rock beside the fire.

Cooking on Hot Coals: While it looks really cool to cook on a rock slab, either flat like a pan or upright, it is not necessary to do so. In fact, my preferred way to cook small fish is to gut them and cook them directly on the coals, as shown below. It doesn't look like much, but it is very easy and very effective. Cook both sides then use a stick or some fast fingers to flip the fish on to a suitable rock or a slab of bark for a plate. Avoid getting too many ashes inside the belly. The skin protects the fish in the fire and the ashes and coals can be easily swept off, so that you can still eat the skin if you so desire.

Mud Bake: Larger fish or other thick meats may not cook evenly on the coals or on a rock slab, so consider wrapping them in a layer of clay or mud (or a layer of edible leaves and then clay). Then place the whole package on a bed of hot coals, with more hot coals on top to slowly and evenly bake it all the way through.

A nice mess of rainbow trout. I think there is no greater food in the world!

This one was split down the backbone instead of the belly to more evenly cook the meat.

Here is the same fish turned over to cook the other side. It was as delicious as it looks!

Although less glamorous, my favorite method is to cook the fish right on the hot coals.

Coal-Burned Containers

You can use just about any piece of dry wood to make a wooden cup or bowl, but I prefer working with **tree roots**, which I find along the rivers. Tree roots, such as cottonwood, willow, or sometimes pine, are very light and porous. The roots are made of tiny hollow tubes, which once transported water and minerals up to the main body of the tree. These tubes provide air spaces through the dead wood and make it easier to burn out the inside. But more important, the porosity of the roots makes them less brittle. This is important when you are abusing a piece of wood, first with scorching dry heat during the burning process, and later with the repeated cycles of wet and dry that come with use. Denser woods do not have the sponginess that roots do, so they often split open from the stresses of heat or moisture.

With tree roots it is best to make cup-like containers and burn them out from one end as shown in the pictures. This makes it easier to seal up the pores when the cup is done. With other woods it is usually best to burn in from the **side**, such as in the side of a log. The wood is less likely to split that way.

To burn out a container, first place the ends of two or more sticks into the fire to start them burning until there are good hot coals at the tips. The sticks serve as handles so you can hold the hot coals on the surface you want to burn, without burning yourself. Alternately, you can scoop some hot coals out of the fire and hold them in place with a flattened stick or a knife blade. Knives can work well for this, but do not use a good knife because the heat can ruin the temper of the blade. Hold the coals close together and gently blow. Gradually the coals will spread from the sticks to the surface of your container-to-be. Tree roots catch fire easily because of the air space in the wood. The roots will also sustain a coal on their own, so that you do not need to add hot coals through the process. Other woods take longer to start and you usually have to keep adding coals to keep the wood burning. It typically takes an hour or more of blowing and hyperventilating to make a coal-burned container, but there are some ways to make the job a little easier. First, you can blow through a straw, either the commercial variety, or a hollow, non-poisonous plant stem; this allows you to concentrate your breath on any one spot, and it gets your face farther away from the smoke and flame as you work. The laziest way to burn out a container, however, is to do it on a windy day so the wind can do the work for you. You can let the wind blow across the container as you work, or you can swing the container in "figure-eights" for additional wind. Just be sure to work only in damp weather when there is no danger of starting a fire.

As you work, periodically stop and **cut out the bigger chunks of charcoal**; then resume burning. Be sure to **watch the edges and sides** to make sure they do not burn too thin. **Drip water** on any thin areas to keep them from burning more. When your container is deep enough then douse the remaining coals with water and chop out the rest of the charcoal. Finally, **scrape the container** smooth with the edge of your knife and polish it by rubbing it with sand.

You can use your container at this point, or you can **water-proof it**. Containers burned into the side of a log are often water-proofed with a coating of pitch or grease. This helps keep water from penetrating and splitting the wood, but do not use pitch if you plan to cook in the container or the pitch will become part of your meal. With tree roots however, you can use pitch without it getting into your meal.

Coal-burning a cup.

Gentle, steady blowing keeps the hot coals glowing and spreading in the cup.

85

A finished cup.

Just mix a little bit of crushed, black charcoal into the pitch to stabilize it and drip the hot mixture on the bottom of the container (outside) to seal the tubes running through the wood. It helps if you heat the base of your container over the fire, before adding the pitch. You do not need to waterproof the inner surface since the moisture rarely splits root containers.

To **boil water** in your container simply heat some non-crumbly rocks in the fire until they are hot. Then, using two sticks for tongs, pull the stones out of the fire, blow the ashes off and gently drop the stones into your container of water. The water will boil almost instantly if the rocks are hot enough. *Do not gather rocks from a creek or any other perennially moist area. Rocks can explode when water is trapped inside them before they are placed in the fire. The moisture boils, expands, and suddenly blasts the rock apart.*

Making Hollow-Log Drums

Another fun use of the coal-burning technique is to make hollow-log drums. I've made several drums of aspen wood, when I found logs that were already rotten inside and hollow all the way through. To thin the walls, just take a few burning sticks from a campfire and put them in the hollow log. It is best to do this project on a breezy day during damp or cold weather when there is no chance of starting a wild fire. The heat is concentrated inside the log, and the air flowing through it will shoot a flame out the downwind side. It doesn't take long at this rate to burn all the way through the walls. But you can remove the burning sticks and the reflected heat inside the log will keep it going, so all you have to do is drip water or snow on the parts that are getting too thin. When the whole log is burned down evenly to three-quarters of an inch or less, then you can scrape out the inside with a knife and sand it down (Okay, so I cheated and used a disc grinder...).

Illustrated here are three different methods of tying the drum skin on. In the smallest drum (the walls are about one-fourth inch thick), I've put a drum skin on both ends and laced them together. In the middle-sized drum I drilled holes and inserted short dowels with ridges that were sold at the hardware store for doweling broken furniture back together. I simply draped the skin over the drum and cut holes where the dowels were to secure it in place. I also used the furniture dowels on the taller drum, but then laced the skin in place around the dowels. Note that the wider the diameter of the drum the deeper the sound.

◊   ◊◊◊   ◊

A hollow log burns like a blow torch when ignited. Once started, you can pull the firewood out and use the reflected heat inside to keep it burning. Here are three drums made this way.

Ⓐ plume of smoke curls up from my fire. The fresh wood is smoldering, getting hotter, but it is not quite ready to flame yet. I could blow and blow on it to get it started, but what's the rush? I wait a few more minutes until the embers have spread on their own, then give it a single full breath of air, and the wood bursts into flame. I sit back on my rock, and my mind returns to the art of cooking over a campfire.

As my culinary tastes have matured, I have begun exploring new cooking methods, besides merely boiling everything. A new utensil I like to bring along is a common **gold pan**. Instead of using it for panning gold, however, I use it for stir-frying, steaming and sautéing food, as well as for winnowing wild grains.

I started bringing the gold pan on my camping trips when I discovered that some strong-tasting wild plant foods could be made more palatable by stir-frying. It is helpful to bring a small amount of vegetable oil to aid in the process. The gold pan also works as a tool for winnowing wild grains. Plant seeds can be winnowed by the handful, without a pan, but it is hardly an economical use of energy. Primitive peoples often made special baskets for winnowing, but those took a tremendous amount of skill to make. The gold pan is a lightweight and very versatile alternative. Soon after I started with the stir-frying, my friend Jack Fee showed me how to do steaming and sautéing. Sautéing is basically steam cooking with the moisture already present in the food.

Sautéing fish and wild onions in a gold pan, with grass underneath and bluebell leaves for a lid.

Most of the time, when **sautéing over the campfire**, you will have to add extra water to have enough moisture to cook the food without drying and burning it. The basic methodology for steaming or sautéing is this: First, put a layer of non-poisonous green material in the bottom of the pan, like green grass. Onions, or something else with a good flavor is definitely better than grass, but grass will suffice. The greens prevent your food from burning in the pan and provide a source of moisture for steam. It also keeps your food from contacting and reacting with any tin in the pan. Then layer your food on top of the green matter, first the meats, then the mushrooms, roots, and greens, or whatever you happen to have. Then put a layer of non-poisonous broad leaves over the top for a lid to hold the steam in. In the mountains we like using bluebell leaves (*Mertensia spp.*) for that task. Then put the pan on the fire or hot coals and cook until done. Watch carefully to see if and when you need to add water.

Learning to stir-fry in a gold pan led to such an improvement in my culinary skills that it eventually led to the question "How could I cook a stir-fry if I didn't have my gold pan?" The question almost immediately answered itself. It was simply a matter of turning the process inside-out. Slabs of cottonwood bark work great for a pan, and hot rocks work great for stir-frying. Just dice the meat and greens and mushrooms right in the bark pan, then add hot rocks and pour on water as needed to produce steam. Keep the food and hot rocks moving until all the food is thoroughly cooked. Then remove the rocks and dig in! My mouth salivates just thinking about it.

But for the moment, I have some time yet before my rice is done. It is a good opportunity to make some ashcakes. Ashcakes are a simple bread made from a dough of flour and water that has been baked on hot coals. Usually I mix the dough in my cooking can, but I will use my copper cup since my rice is in the can. I pour a quantity of flour into my cup, add a pinch of baking soda, and stir the dry ingredients together with a clean stick.

A slab of cottonwood bark makes a great stir-fry pan. Hot rocks are stirred around with the food to do the cooking.

Ashcakes: Bread of the Modern Abo

Ashcakes. The very name never fails to raise an eyebrow. After more than a decade of cooking and eating ashcakes, I take the word for granted, so I routinely forget what it sounds like to people hearing it for the first time.

Ashcakes and rice cooking on the coals.

I forgot once again as I hastily packed for an overnight camping trip with my cousins. Food was an afterthought to my packing, and only at the last minute, almost as I was walking out the door, I poured myself a large bag of flour, and rushed to meet my cousins at the trailhead.

"What did you pack for food?" Ed asked as we walked.
"Flour." I answered without thinking twice about it.
"Mmm. Sounds Good." He joked.
"Yes it is; I'm going to make some ashcakes."
"Oh?" He queried, with a questioning glance.

Ashcake basics: Ashcakes are a simple bread made from a dough of flour and water that has been baked on hot coals. The trick to making good ashcakes is to keep the dough *dry*. Dough that is wet will stick to your hands first and then to the coals when you cook it. I add water a little at a time and stir with the stick until the dough is wet enough to work by hand, but still dry enough not to stick to my fingers. Then I knead the dough thoroughly and shape it into patties. The patties can be tortilla-thin or quite thick. Thin ones cook all the way through while thicker ones tend to stay doughy in the middle. To cook them, toss the patties on some medium hot coals. Cook both sides to your taste. You can turn them and take them out with quick, careful fingers, or—if you are sitting just out of reach—you can flip them with a stick and spear them to pull them out.

Blow the ashes off both sides and enjoy. Ashcakes are quite tasty hot off the fire. They make okay trail food the next day, but you must eat them soon. In a few days ashcakes dry into hardtack. I first learned about ashcakes as a student on a twenty-six day expedition in 1984. I had two ashcakes left over at the end of that trip, which quickly hardened, so I put them on a shelf and kept them as mementos for the next ten years!

Ashcakes can be leavened with a little baking soda. Baking soda helps the dough to rise a little, and it helps it to cook more thoroughly. Alternately, you can use any commercial biscuit or pancake mix with high-powered leavenings for some exotic ashcakes. One other way to leaven the dough is by culturing sourdough yeast.

Sourdough Ashcakes: Wild yeast floats everywhere through the air, and making sourdough is simply a matter of using this yeast. You will inevitably capture small amounts of yeast from the air as you mix standard ashcake dough. To turn it into sourdough, just leave it in a warm place for three or four days. You can store it in a plastic bag and open it to smell the progress each day. The dough must be warm to work, although it is fairly hardy. It will store fine in a backpack even on cold winter days, just so you sleep with it to keep it warm each night. When your dough is ready it will have a distinct sourdough aroma, and your previously firm, dry dough will now be sticky and more fluid. Pinch off enough for an ashcake and dust it with dry flour, then cook it. Be careful not to work the air out of the patty. Alternately, you can mix the sourdough starter with fresh dough and shape it into individual patties, allowing them to rise before cooking. You must use all of your sourdough or all except a pinch of starter to quicken your next batch. Wild sourdough without new material to feed on will quickly turn *very* sour.

Unbeatable wild strawberry ashcake pie.

Ash Bagels: Another type of ashcake is the "ash bagel". To make an ash bagel, first mix up regular ashcake dough, with or without leavening. Then shape the dough like a bagel. Bring a pot of water to a rolling boil. Drop the ash bagel in the pot and boil it for five or ten minutes. Then remove it from the water and finish cooking it on the coals like an ashcake to brown the crust.

Gourmet Ashcakes: Ashcakes that are already delicious can be transformed into gourmet ashcakes with the addition of just about any ingredients you happen to have. Butter on a hot ashcake is scrumptious, and butter and honey together is even more so.

For dinner try ashcakes as tortillas with refried beans. Or to make a cheese melt, fold a flat ashcake over a piece of cheese, pinch the edges together and bake. To make a pig-in-a-blanket first cook your hot dog on a stick and then wrap it with ashcake dough and toss it in the coals to bake the dough. For dessert, try raisins, cinnamon, and marshmallows baked inside an ashcake. Or try it with wild berries and sugar. The possibilities are as limitless as your imagination.

Pies are fun to make when you can find a patch of wild berries. Just cook the berries first with a little bit of sugar for sweetener and a pinch of flour for thickener. Make a bowl with the ashcake dough then pour in the hot, cooked berry filling. Pat some dough out flat for a lid,

Chowing down!

and pinch that together with the walls of the pie shell. Make the pie small enough so you can carefully pick the whole thing up, and place it in the hot coals of the fire. Cover the whole pie with hot coals to cook the top and sides. In five or ten minutes the pie is cooked and ready to eat.

Of course, few of our aboriginal ancestors had access to either wheat flour or sugar, so this is more of a modern skill. Ashcakes are especially helpful to tame an otherwise wild diet, since few people are adapted to the taste of truly wild foods. As for our camping trip, I shared my ashcakes with my cousins and they shared their supplies to make some gourmet ashcakes. We all agreed that ashcakes tasted a whole lot better than the name implies.

◊　◊◊◊　◊

Tin can and bamboo spoon/fork.

I work my dough to approximately the right consistency and pinch some off for an ashcake patty. I roll it into my bag of flour to make it less sticky, then pat it flat and toss it onto the coals.

I take the rice and bouillon off the fire to let it cool for a few minutes. Then I spear my ashcakes from the fire. I have a simple utensil, which I use both for eating and for flipping ashcakes. It is a piece of bamboo, and one end serves as a **spoon** while the other serves as a **fork**. The spoon end is made with one long diagonal cut through the bamboo. This forms a long, narrow scoop, since the bamboo is hollow. It is unconventional in design, but I like it better than any other wilderness spoon I have had. The fork end is made with two angled cuts to the center called a dovetail cut, except that the hollow stalk leaves two distinct points for a fork. I use this end for flipping ashcakes, and when they are done I spear them with the fork and lift them out of the coals without having to stand up from my sitting position.

On the other hand, it is sometimes a problem to thoroughly clean my utensil. As I become more and more lazy, I've started using **chopsticks** to eat with. I never learned to use chopsticks the conventional way, but just holding two twigs together makes a reasonable scoop to eat with. I break dead twigs from a tree and use them for one meal, and burn them afterwards. Less work is usually better.

Stone Ovens & Steam Pits

There are many, many methods of applying heat to food to cook it, and my own repertoire of techniques is still limited. But the more you learn about such methods the more you will become a primitive gourmet.

A **stone oven** is one good technique for baking, and is typically used for cooking breads. Now bread-making is not strictly a primitive skill, and most primitive societies made much less use of breads than we do in our culture. But for most of us modern abos to enjoy primitive living, we need to consume a diet that at least minimally resembles what we are accustomed too. Bringing along wheat flour for ashcakes, pies and breads is an easy and fun way to provide that kind of familiarity in the diet.

It is easy to construct a simple stone oven, assuming you have some large, semi-flat rocks to work with. Just stack up the rocks to create a chamber for baking in. Leave the front wide open so you can build a fire inside. Also leave a space near the top of the back for the smoke to escape. Then build a fire inside and heat all the rocks for about an hour.

When the rocks are sufficiently hot, pull out the firewood and scrape out the coals. Place your bread, or whatever you are baking, on a thin slab of rock, or on some green willow twigs, and place it inside the oven. You do not want the food directly in contact with the bottom rock, or it will burn.

Burning a hot fire in a small stone oven prior to baking.

Next, seal up the front and back of the oven with more rocks to hold the heat inside. You may want to seal up the remaining small holes between the stones by covering the oven with ashes or even dirt. Just be careful that no ashes or dirt gets into the food. Be sure to leave one small rock accessible, so you can periodically pull it out to peek inside at your meal. Bread usually takes a little longer to cook in a stone oven than in a conventional oven, but it is always worth the wait.

A similar type of oven called the horno can be sculpted with **clay**, using tinder material to block out a space for the oven and a short chimney. I have not yet constructed one of that style.

The **steam pit** is similar to the stone oven, in that hot thermal mass is used to cook the food. The technique, however, is quite a bit different.

Start by digging a pit three or four times as large as the amount of food you will be cooking in it. For one chicken-sized creature with some vegetables, the hole might be a foot deep and eighteen inches in diameter. For larger meals you might dig down only one foot, but then make a much wider pit.

Next, line the floor and walls of the pit with flat stones to hold the heat. Burn a good, hot fire over the entire pit for at least an hour, but longer for bigger pits. While that is burning, gather lots of green, non-poisonous plant matter to use in the pit. Green grass is commonly used, although it is not the most desirable flavor to steam into the food. Something with a gourmet flavor, like goosefoot greens (*Chenopodium spp.*) is ideal for use in the steam pit. Gather a big pile. It takes more than you think.

When the pit is very hot remove the remaining wood, and scrape out the coals. A shovel is ideal for this task, but a flat piece of wood or bark will also work. Next put a thick layer of greens down on the hot rocks. Make a nest with the greens and place your meal in the middle. When you are cooking a creature chicken-sized or larger, then you might want to put a hot rock inside the carcass for extra heat. Cover your meal with

A rounded loaf of bread fresh out of the stone oven.

Preparing a steam pit.

a thick layer of greens, then some kind of a lid, like bark, and finally dirt. Put on several inches of dirt to effectively hold the heat in.

The trickiest part of doing a steam pit is getting all the dirt off of the pit without it trickling down through the grass into your food. The key is to lay down lots of bark before you put the dirt on. To uncover the pit, first carefully brush aside as much dirt as you can, then carefully and surgically lift off each piece of bark with its load of dirt.

In some areas you may be able to find a flat rock large enough to cover the pit, which would eliminate the need for the dirt. For a finicky dinner crowd, you might want to put the food in a non-toxic canvas bag or cotton pillowcase to help keep it clean.

Some authors suggest that you should leave your meal in the pit to cook for two to three hours. Mine usually take longer, and I've had several undercooked steam-pitted chicken dinners, which quickly became shish kebab dinners when everyone grabbed willow sticks to finish the job. So I prefer to let my steam pits cook all day, or even overnight, if I happen to start the project in the evening. One nice feature about the steam pit is that it is difficult to overcook or burn your food. You may want to add a little water if the green matter is not very moist, but otherwise, just cover the pit and leave.

If you think the pit might be on the cool side, then you can also start a fire on top of the ground for extra heat. Just be sure you have a good covering of dirt on top of the dinner to keep it from burning.

All in all, the steam pit is an ideal cooking method for primitive living. You can prepare gourmet meals without the need to make any dishes at all. Steam cooking keeps most nutrients in the food, and it tenderizes even the toughest wild game until the meat nearly falls off the bone.

◊   ◊◊◊   ◊

I use the bamboo spoon to pile rice onto my ashcake tortilla. The ashcake becomes my plate and my meal. I savor its simplicity. There is something immensely satisfying about **simple foods**, and especially after the barrage of flavors that we typically encounter in contemporary life. When I go camping I usually bring some leftovers from the fridge to eat on my first day out, but otherwise I bring such things as oatmeal, rice, beans, instant potatoes, powdered milk, raisins, and flour, along with bouillon, baking soda, and sometimes salt, pepper, and cinnamon, or other spices. I supplement this with limited hunting and gathering, plus occasionally a little fresh carrion! For example, on one camping trip I cooked a pelican that had been electrocuted by a power line.

There are many advantages to carrying a simple diet on camping excursions. Initially, it is compact and lightweight compared to many conventional foods. Basic foods are easy to cook with, and they lack the strong odors of many conventional greasy foods. When you are in bear country you are wise to be mindful of the odors you make around your campsite and wipe onto your clothes. You want to avoid covering yourself with "bait perfume"; eating simple grains and so forth will help keep you smelling clean.

With a simple diet, especially one with little meat in it, it is helpful to consider your menu choices. Meals are best for your body if grains such as rice or wheat, etc. are eaten with legumes such as beans, lentils or peas. Grains and legumes each contain separate and essential amino acids. When eaten together the body can combine these amino acids into a **complete protein,** which effectively replaces protein from meat sources. Much of the world's population cannot afford the luxury of meat, so they gain the bulk of their protein from this combination of foods. When grains and legumes are eaten separately the body is not able to use them as effectively and much of the food value is lost.

To get complete proteins, rice and beans can be cooked together, or refried beans can be eaten with ashcakes. I usually bring an ample supply of food however, so I do not always worry about whether I am getting complete proteins at every meal and out of every ounce of food. I often have rice and ashcakes, but no beans. This does not provide a complete protein, but it is one of my favorite meals. Cooking my dinner in a clay pot made by my own hands makes it taste even better...

Primitive Pottery

I liked working with clay as a kid, and in high school I took a pottery class where we made pots with and without a potter's wheel. But there is a big difference between working with these commercially prepared clays in a classroom versus going out and collecting your own wild clay. It is a real thrill to scoop up the earth with your own two hands, make a pot, and fire it in a campfire. The greatest moment of satisfaction comes when you put the pot to use, cooking your dinner in it on the fire.

The first time I worked with wild clay I was a student on a 26-day expedition in southern Utah. We collected a few hard clay tablets and ground them into a fine powder with rocks. We didn't grind up enough clay to make pots, as I recall, but I did make some beads and some dice to play with.

Back home in Montana a few weeks later, I was exploring a new road put in by the power company. There was hardly any clay in the soil at all, but the water running down the road collected in a muddy puddle and stratified, leaving all the heavy sand at the bottom and a half-inch thick layer of clay on the surface. I scraped off the clay and brought it home and used it to make several pots and some more beads. When my pottery was thoroughly dry, I put it in my mother's Blaze King wood stove and loaded it full of dry cow manure. Fortunately, I did not burn the house down, and my pots and beads came out mostly intact. That, I later realized, was beginner's luck, since my subsequent, but intermittent, experiences with wild clay over the next ten years were utter failures. Finally I decided to stop and focus on the problem until I figured it out.

Harvesting Wild Clay

Soil scientists divide soil particles into three different types based on size: sand, silt, and clay. Clay consists of very small, very flat particles that tend to float in water almost like a feather in the air. In a mud puddle the sand sinks to the bottom first, then the silt, and finally—very slowly—the clay. The flat quality of the clay particles is also what makes clay work so well for making pots. There is a lot of surface contact between the flat surfaces, so the clay sticks together better than silt or sand would. Given its natural tendency to stratify into layers, you will often find clay in neat bands along the side of a hill.

Wet Processing: Sometimes you can find a cut along a road or a natural slope where you can simply scoop up good clay with few impurities. If it is moist, then you can roll it into a long "snake" between your palms. The more that it holds together, the better the clay.

If there seems to be a lot of impurities in the clay, then you can stratify it to clean it up. Many potters stratify the clay in a bucket, or in a large glass jar if they want to show the layers. The problem is that the water cannot drain out of the bucket, so you end up with four layers: sand, silt, clay and water. When the bucket has set overnight to stratify, you pour off the water, then pour the soupy clay into a canvas bag to drain, but this all takes extra time and equipment.

I found a thin layer of good clay in a bank along a local reservoir.

Large clumps are broken up, then the bucket is stirred until the clay is suspended in water.

The clay water is poured into a pit and allowed to drain and stratify into layers.

During my research I remembered the mud puddle by the road from years ago. I reasoned that if I poured a bucket of clay water into a hole in the ground, it would stratify and the water would quickly drain out, leaving behind clay that was just right. I tried it, and it worked! I've used the technique dozens of times since.

I use a five-gallon bucket at least two-thirds full of clay, then add water and stir vigorously with a stick, until all the clay is suspended in the water and the stick doesn't hit anything in the bucket. Any roots or other organic matter will float to the top so it is easy to scoop them out. Then I pour the soup into a small pit in the ground, preferably in sandy soil that will drain quickly. On a hot, dry summer day, the soup will stratify into layers and drain out in just a few hours, so that the clay is ready to scoop up by hand. The process can take several days in cold, damp weather.

If you don't have a bucket, you can improvise with a poncho or plastic bag in a pit. Stir the clay water in the poncho, then lift the poncho and pour the mix into the hole.

If you don't have a five-gallon bucket, then you can simply lay a poncho or sturdy plastic bag in a pit and use that for the bucket. When the clay and water are all stirred up, just lift the poncho carefully and pour the muddy soup out into the hole.

Some clay deposits I've found contained more impurities than clay, but the pit technique easily separates the good from the bad. A whole bucket of mixed raw material may produce just enough clay to make one pot, but if that is all that is available to work with, then it is a real thrill to get any at all. Other clay deposits with few impurities seem to provide nearly unlimited material to work with. Also be sure to watch for those natural mud puddles where the clay has already stratified out of the surrounding debris, so that it is ready to collect and use.

Dry Processing: Depending on when and where you are, you might find deposits of dry clay powder, hardened clods, or even slate tablets, where layers of clay have been compressed in the earth to make a soft rock. Any hard clods or tablets will need to be crushed and powdered on a flat rock, using another rock for a hammer. Large impurities can be separated from the powder with a fine screen, like that used on a screen door. Then add water a little at a time to the powder to get the right consistency for clay. Of course, you can also liquefy the powder and use the wet processing technique to separate any impurities.

Adding Temper

Here I am kneading in coarse sand from the beach near the clay deposit to temper the clay, so it will be less prone to cracking during drying, firing and use.

Once you have worked to find and purify a source of clay, you may be surprised to learn that the next step is to put a bunch of junk back in. But the problem is that pure clay shrinks a lot as it dries. Perhaps you've seen a dried up mud puddle where the surface has cracked and even peeled back a little bit. Well, that's the drying clay at work, and you do not want your pottery to turn out that way, so you need to temper the clay with other ingredients to reduce shrinking and cracking.

In some ways clay has a lot in common with cement and concrete. Cement powder is extremely fine like clay, and if you mixed cement powder with water, then it would tend to shrink and crack as it cured. But cement can be made very strong by mixing it with sand and gravel to make a composite material we call concrete. The sand and gravel will not shrink, and the particles interlock with each other just like interlocking your fingers on both hands, so it is hard to crack them apart. Besides the sand and gravel, you can also add little string-like fibers to concrete for greater strength. Tempering your clay with sand or fibers will similarly reduce problems with shrinkage and cracking.

Fine sand might seem like the logical choice, to produce clay that is nice and smooth to work. But coarse sand will interlock better to make pottery that is less prone to cracking. This is important when working with wild clays, because each type of clay has it's own qualities, and most are not as reliable as store-bought clay. When you make a pot with coarse sand in it, you will be able to see the chunks in the walls of the finished product. It may not be the most refined pottery the world has ever seen, but if it resists cracking during drying, firing, and use, then that is the part that really counts. I learned this trick from Bart Blankenship (author of *Earth Knack: Stone-Age Skills for the 21st Century*) on a two-week canoe expedition down the Green River in southern Utah. We collected the coarse sand from an anthill, where the ants hauled it up one piece at a time from their underground tunnels.

One concern when adding temper is that some types of sand will expand and contract more than others, as a pot is heated and cooled during cooking. Some types of sand could also have water bound up inside that will tend to explode out during firing, ruining your pots. You just have to try what you have on hand and see what happens.

A substitute for sand is to use ground-up pottery shards, called "grog". Clay that has been fired already is more stable, so you can grind up any broken pieces and mix them with your new clay. You can also use ground-up eggshells or seashells, but it is better to incinerate them, apparently to shrink and stabilize the particles, before mixing with your clay.

Finally, you can also add organic fibers to help bind the clay together during drying. Cattail fluff and thistle down have long fibers that are difficult to work in, but the length really helps to tie everything together. A more common source of fiber is dried animal poop: from cows, deer, elk, and moose—pretty much anything that has been eating plants and breaking down the fibers. Just grind up the cow patties or deer droppings and mix it in with your clay. The fibers are used only during the drying phase. They will completely incinerate during the firing process, so you won't have to think about having all that crap flavoring your soup when you eventually cook in the pot!

At present I like using coarse sand for temper more than fibers, since the fibers burn out, making the finished pottery less dense. Air pockets are left behind where the fibers were, insulating the pottery so that it is more difficult to cook in. I think the pottery is also more frail and prone to breaking. Nevertheless, I'm sure Native Americans used manure in their pots, many of which have lasted a 1,000 years or more already.

The difference may be in the quality of the clay more than in the temper. The Natives of this area did not have a pottery tradition, and if they did, they may have used coarse sand as temper to make up for the marginal quality of the clay. You may need to experiment with all different kinds of temper—and different combinations of temper—in your local clay deposits to see what works best for you.

Keep in mind that every clay deposit has it's own characteristics. Some clays may be workable just as they are without adding any temper. Other clay deposits may be lousy no matter how good your tempering job is. Two different types of clay that are both difficult to work with may be improved just by mixing them together.

The amount of temper needed may be surprising—often up to one-third by volume of the clay. An easy way to measure a third is to flatten a ball of clay, then cut out a pie-shaped slice one-third the size of the whole, and replace it with an equal amount of temper. My process is a bit more haphazard; I just knead the temper in a little at a time until it looks and feels right.

Also note that clay improves with age, becoming more workable, if you mix it up and let it sit in a bucket or bag. And don't throw out your clay if you find it covered with mold. It too helps improve the workability of the clay.

Wedging the Clay

Wedging is the process of kneading the clay for an extended period before you make something with it. Wedging helps to drive air pockets out of the clay, distributes the moisture more equally, and theoretically helps to align the flat particles or "platelets" with each other so that the clay will be stronger.

My wedging technique is simply to slam a ball of clay down on a rock or board again and again, turning it each time so that it stays in one semi-round lump as I work. I do the wedging while working the temper in, so I tear apart the ball and stick it into the sand, then put it back together and wedge it for awhile, and repeat the process over and over again until I've got enough temper mixed in. I'll wedge it for a few more minutes after that, but more gently, until all the cracks are worked out and I have a nice round ball. Tossing it firmly from hand to hand also helps to shape it as a ball. When the wedging is complete, then it is time to actually make something with your clay.

Push your thumb into the middle to start the hole.

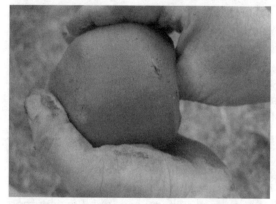

Slowly spin the pot while gently pinching the edges.

Three fingers are in, but it is time to patch cracks.

Smooth and flatten the rim when it gets too thin.

Making Pinch Pots

To make a pinch pot, start with a round ball of clay about the size of a baseball. It should be moist enough that you can push your thumb in without seriously cracking the ball, but not so damp that the walls will sag as the pot gets bigger. Push your thumb in carefully, and smooth out any small cracks as they form.

Then start spinning the ball slowly on your thumb, gently pinching the walls thinner and continuing to smooth the outside. Pull your thumb out and work your index and middle fingers into the hole, continuing to spin, pinch and smooth as you go. Besides pinching with the fingertips, you can push out from the inside while reinforcing the outside with your palm. Soon you will be able to squeeze three fingers into the hole, but be sure to stop frequently to patch any cracks.

Cracks can be smoothed over with the back of a fingernail, gently smearing clay across the wounded area. But if the crack is deeper, such that it comes right back to the surface after patching, then simply drag a sharp stick across it, dragging fresh clay more deeply through the gap. Periodically stop to smooth and flatten the rim, since it is most prone to thinning and cracking.

The thickest walls of the pot are usually down near the bottom. It takes a little effort to push that part out, but go slow and firmly cradle the bottom of the pot in your other palm as you spin and push, so that you do not push a hole right through the wall. Ideally, the walls of the entire pot should be uniformly 1/4 to 3/8 inch in thickness when you are finished.

Smooth over the walls inside and out when you are done. Of course you can imprint a pattern on the outside if you choose. It is also helpful to **paddle the clay** a bit after it stiffens up. I like to use the back of a spoon or a flattened stick. Paddle the outside walls gently to tamp the clay together. Paddling helps to drive together any subsurface cracks and increases the density of the walls.

Cracks appear on the outside as pressure is applied to thin the walls from inside. Use the back of a fingernail to smooth shallow cracks, or use a pointed stick when you need to dig into a deeper crack.

Carefully mold a flat disc of clay into a small bowl.

Flatten and wet the rim then add the first coil.

Pull the cloth to lift the bowl and smooth the joints.

Support the outside while working on the inside.

Making Coil Pots

A pot with a rounded bottom is inherently stronger than one with a flat bottom. That's not a problem when making a pinch-pot because you start out with a round ball, and the bottom remains rounded as you make the pot. The biggest challenge is that you cannot set the pot down on it's bottom, or the walls will slump and crack apart—unless you put the pot in a matching bowl to give it support. The bowl is also the secret to doing coil pottery.

Coil pottery starts with a shallow bowl covered by a thin cloth to keep the clay from sticking to it. Just make a flat disc of clay about the size of the bowl and gently press it into place inside the bowl. If you don't have a bowl, then you can place the cloth in a hole in the ground but you will have to bend over more to work on it. Next, dip your fingers in water and smooth over the inside, but try not to get the clay too wet. Then flatten and wet the rim, and you are ready to start adding coils.

It is easy to roll out a thin coil on a flat surface like a table, but in more primitive circumstances you may have to roll it vertically in the air. I use something similar to the floating handdrill technique, rolling a thin coil out below my hands and waddling my way upwards until I've rolled out all of the clay. It is helpful to do this step over your lap, since the coils frequently break and fall. Try to make the coil long enough to complete a layer around the pot in one run, but it is also okay if you have to fill in with short pieces.

With the first coil is in place, stop and carefully smooth over the joints both inside and outside of the pot. You can pull the cloth to raise the side of the clay bowl up enough to smooth the joints, and work your way around the pot like that.

Note that with commercial clays you can get away without fully welding the coils together, but with most wild clays you should take no chances. Blend the layers together fully or risk having them crack apart later. When the first coil is completely worked together with the base, then add the next layer. Coils can be laid in place to the outside of the previous layer (a longer coil) to make the pot wider, or placed to the inside of the previous layer (a shorter coil) to make the pot more narrow. Always support the outside of the pot with your palm and fingers while you are applying pressure to smooth the joints from the inside. You will also need to support the inside with your fingers when working the outside.

Back when I was just doing pinch pots, I wondered how the ancient potters of the desert southwest could have ever made such exquisite ceramic pots without a potter's wheel. There was such a gulf between my work and theirs that I couldn't imagine a person ever developing the skills to do such incredible work. But most of those beautiful pots were made just like this, starting with a clay disc in a bowl and working up coil by coil. Although my work remains crude compared to theirs, I could for the first time get a sense that—with a lot of practice—a person could learn to make pots as remarkable as those we see in museums today.

In the picture here, notice that I am supporting the inside with my fingers, while blending the outside of the joint with the back of a fingernail. A pot can be made about as big and wide as you want just by adding coils towards the outside of the rim each time, but here I have already begun to taper the top in a little bit.

The coils I use are relatively small. I've read of other authors making coils an inch thick, then flattening them to make a ribbon-like coil, which should enable you to build the walls at least twice as fast as I am. There is always something new to try!

Note that you may be able to add several layers before going back to weld the joints together. This will depend in part on the quality of the clay, as well as the weather, so that the coils don't dry out too much before you get back to them. With most wild clays it seems to work best to blend each joint in before going on to the next one.

When the clay has set up enough so that you can lift it out of the bowl, then stop and smooth over the bottom. There are probably a few cracks there from pressing the initial disc into the rounded bowl. But don't ever set the pot down on its rounded bottom while moist, or the walls could sag and crack. When you are done working over the bottom, just set it back on the cloth in the bowl for support.

In the other two photos I am adding a coil to the outside of the previous layer to make a nice rim, then welding the joints together with the back of my fingernail. With these simple techniques you can make a pot as big and elaborate as you want. But start small to practice your skills and to test the quality of the clay.

Another method you can try is to **mold a pot** into shape entirely inside or outside of an existing bowl. For example, you can place a cloth or a layer of leaves inside a bowl, then press flat slabs of clay into it to match the shape. Just be sure to use a bowl with outward sloping sides, so that you can lift the new bowl out of the mold. The same process can be done using the outside of an upside-down bowl as the mold. For lack of a bowl, you could always use a hole in the ground lined with leaves or cloth, or mold the bowl over the end of a rounded log. Always use some kind of liner to keep the clay from sticking to the mold.

Drying Pottery

No matter which method you use to make your pot, it will have to be thoroughly dried before it is fired. Otherwise the moisture in the clay will expand and explode. Since clay shrinks as it dries, the drying must be done slowly and uniformly to avoid cracking. At home I like to put my pots in the cellar for a day or two before moving them into the house. You can also put them in the cool shade of a tree and use a light covering of leaves to help trap in moisture. More rapid drying is possible with high-quality clay and carefully monitored conditions, but there is greater risk. In the desert southwest, Native American potters have dried some pots in as little as four hours before firing them. That would be an exciting challenge—to make a pot, fire it and cook in it—all in the same day!

Coils can be blended in with the back of your nail.

Lift the pot out of the bowl to smooth the outside.

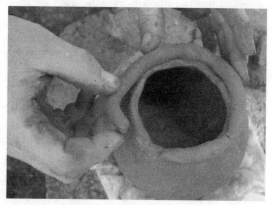

A longer coil is added to the top to widen the rim.

Blend the coil in with the back of a fingernail.

Firing Time

An un-fired pot will dissolve when wetted. To use the pot you need to fire or "sinter" it to bind all the separate particles into a single structure. Sintering begins at 660^{a}F, but you need to boost the temperature up to a minimum of 1112^{a}F to successfully fire the pot. At this temperature the pot will begin to glow red in the fire. At 1300^{a}F the pot will glow a dull red, indicating that sintering is complete. At 1470^{a}F the pot begins to "vitrify" or become glass-like, as the minerals melt into one another. When the temperature reaches 1600^a the pots glow a bright cherry red. Higher temperatures help to fuse the minerals together, making the pottery denser and less porous, but it is impractical to reach such temperatures in a campfire.

To start with, you will need to drive atmospheric moisture out of the pottery. Just as there is moisture in the air around you, there is also moisture in the walls of a "dry" pot. You have to drive the water molecules out of the pottery without heating it so much that they explode out. My preferred method is to put them in the oven with the door open (we cook on a wood stove). After a while I close the oven door to boost the temperature. An hour later I transfer the very warm pots into our masonry fireplace and quickly start a roaring blaze. The pots are placed away from the cold air supply and up on pieces of wood, rock or brick, so they will not be insulated from the heat by the ashes. It is easy to achieve a dull red glow, but you have to make sure that the entire pot reaches that temperature, and not just the most visible part. I've also fired pots to a cherry red glow, but I realized then that I was close to warping the metal door on our fireplace. I won't try that again!

Firing pots in a campfire is similar, but it requires more attention. First, place the pots up on rocks or sticks, so they are not resting on the cool ground. Then start a ring of fire around the outside to slowly warm the pots and drive out the moisture. Gradually move the fire closer to the pots over a two-hour period until all moisture is driven out of the pots. Then build a small bonfire fire up over the pots and fire them for one to two hours. Avoid wind and rain, either of which can be fatal to your pots.

If there is lots of air around the pottery then the iron content will oxidize or rust, giving the pots a reddish color. However, if the pots are covered with manure or sawdust to choke off the air supply then they will absorb soot and smoke, turning a deep black color. Often you will get a mix of shades on a single pot.

When the pots are completely fired, allow the fire to die down, and try to keep the pots protected in an insulating layer of coals and ashes. It is best to allow the pots to cool down naturally until you can handle them, but it is possible to speed up the process when necessary by dragging the coals back a bit.

When the pots are finally cool, lift them up and tap the outside with a fingernail. A glass-like ring indicates that firing was successful. Note that working with wild clay guarantees some failures. So be sure to make lots of pots with many types of clay and different tempering strategies to increase your odds of success. The more you experiment the more successes you will have.

The "dry" pots are surrounded by a ring of fire to drive out atmospheric moisture.

The fire is moved in over the pots and built up into a bonfire.

The 3 pots of wild clay fired great. The 4th pot of "better" clay broke and the 5th disintingrated.

A collection of pots I have made and fired. The three in the foreground are from the firing above.

Place three small stones in the fire pit to hold the pot up to apply heat to the bottom.

A lidded pot is much more energy-efficient. Oatmeal is cooking in the left pot to better seal it.

Use both hands to lift the pot. Green plants make a good potholder.

Two sticks held together make a good utensil to eat with. They can be disposed of in the fire.

Cooking in Clay Pots

It is a thrill to be able to cook in pots you have made with your bare hands from the raw materials of the earth. But along with the exhilaration of using the pots comes a certain degree of trepidation—what if they all break? At some point you will have to make a leap of faith and bravely put your pots to the test, so here are a few tips to reduce the chances of breakage.

First, avoid thermal shock to the pots. The greatest risk is when the vessels are empty. Especially avoid pouring hot water into a cold pot, or vice-versa, filling a hot pot with cold water.

Once the pot is full then there is less danger of cracking it, even if you put a pot of ice water right on a hot fire. The reason is because the water wicks out through the walls of the pot and keeps the vessel cooled to the temperature inside. Yes, it would be better to warm the pot more slowly, but is not always practical to do so—especially when camping in Montana in the middle of the winter. But let me point out that you need to fill the pot all the way to the top with water or else the walls above the water line will rapidly heat up and crack while the water below is still cold.

For greater efficiency it is helpful to place three small stones in the fire pit to hold the pot up enough to apply heat to the bottom. Scrape the fire away from the stones so you can carefully set the pot in place without burning your hands and possibly dropping the pot. Then rake the coals back around the pot and add fuel to gradually build up the fire around the pot.

Since the walls are thicker but less dense than a metal pot—and therefore more insulated— you will find that it takes longer to bring water to a boil. Some wild clays make especially light and airy pots that can be a real challenge to heat up. You just have to apply a little more fuel. A lid to trap in the heat will greatly accelerate the cooking process.

Add water frequently, since some cooks away and a lot more wicks out through the walls. Avoid dumping a lot of cold water in at once. Cooking oatmeal in a clay pot will seal it very quickly. Keep a stir stick handy to keep your food from boiling over or sticking and burning to the walls.

When your meal is done, simply scrape the fire away from the pot and use two hands with gloves or a bandana, or bark potholder to pick it up. Since most pots are made with rounded bottoms for greater strength, it is helpful to scoop out a small depression in the soil before setting them down.

Be sure to clean out the pot after you eat. Otherwise, the moisture will wick out of the leftovers, causing the food to stick to the walls of the pot. Support the outside walls of the pot with your hand when you are scrubbing and pushing outward from inside.

When you are ready to move camp then scrub the outside of you pot clean with sand before packing it away.

Sometimes the most challenging part is to get from one camp to another without breaking your pots. Stuff them with something firm but soft on the inside and pad them well on the outside. I've always used my pack for a backrest or even a seat, which is a bad idea with pottery inside!

I eat my ashcake with the rice on it and drink some water, too. Eating this simple meal takes me back to another book I wrote, *Direct Pointing to Real Wealth*. In that book I wrote about how hunter-gatherer societies typically expended less time working than we do here in America. That idea sometimes surprises people who think that hunter-gatherer peoples must have worked all the time just to stay alive. Actually, *hunter-gatherer societies were among the most leisured cultures in the world.*

The reason for their leisure is not because they were more efficient than modern societies. The hunter-gatherer lifestyle is highly inefficient and working people typically harvested only two to three calories of food energy for each calorie of body energy expended. By contrast, American wheat farmers typically harvest 300 or more calories for each calorie of body energy expended. Hunter-gatherer societies had more leisure because they produced their food supply but little else.

In America we work to pay for many things besides food, and food typically takes up a smaller portion of our budgets than other expenses such as shelter. But even with food we pay an exorbitant price that people in other cultures do not pay. We especially dispose of a lot of money for processing. For example, people require about 2,500 calories per day. If one were to live on one-calorie diet sodas they would have to spend $1,250 per day, at 50¢ per can, just to meet their caloric requirement. In America we make those kinds of purchases every day and wonder why we are broke.

When I hear of people in America who claim to be poverty stricken, I do not know whether to cry or to laugh, especially when they are earning twenty thousand dollars or more per year. People in third-world countries often have annual incomes of under a thousand

Freshly fired pots on a camping trip. Here we are warming cones from the limber pine to extract pine nuts like those shown in the bowl.

dollars. Relatively speaking, they would be "millionaires" if they suddenly made twenty thousand dollars, and they could do just about whatever they wanted. Renee and I understood that principle of relativity and incorporated it as part of our strategy for financial success. We maintained a sort of a third-world lifestyle while we put most of our incomes into building our home. We earned $10,000 to $12,000 per year for each of our first four years, but at the end of that time period we had a net worth that would measure well over the $40,000 we earned. We do not make much money, but many people, even here in America, would say that we are extraordinarily wealthy.

A crow lands in an aspen tree overhead. It looks once around and flies away. I take a moment to listen to the water in the stream and the birds singing in the trees.

I load rice on another ashcake. My sudden movement startles the mouse that lives in my shelter. It was out foraging again but ran away when I moved. I eat and watch, and soon it reappears. It looks at me, but does not seem to be too concerned as long as I stay still. It scurries about, taking care of its mouse life, and I see it from time to time by my pack or between the rocks. I bite into my rice and ashcake as I watch my little friend.

Seeing the mouse stimulates many thoughts for me. It is possible that while my lunch is food for my stomach, the mouse is food for thought.

I remember reading an educational and entertaining book, *The Sacred Cow and the Abominable Pig*, where author Marvin Harris explores the mysteries behind how cultures develop **beliefs about foods** and why some cultures favor particular foods while others are repulsed by them. The answer to many such mysteries, according to Harris, lies in basic economics.

The word "economics" in anthropology does not necessarily mean "money", but rather it means "practical"; when a particular choice is economical it means that it is worth investing time and labor into it. Many varied factors make a food economical for a culture to consume, and Harris claims that cultural beliefs about which foods are "good" or "bad" to eat evolve around those economic factors. One factor is the straightforward caloric balance—

Mice and the Hantavirus

We used to eat mice all the time on our camping trips. We caught them in our deadfall traps. That was before hantavirus hit the news. A hantavirus "outbreak" in 1993 killed 32 people in the United States, including two people in Montana. Hantavirus is an unusual sort of disease, particularly because it is not new. As one Montana Health Department official said, hantavirus appears to have been here all along, and we are only now giving it recognition as a disease. Scientists were previously aware of the virus, but not of this particular, very deadly strain of it. It is now known that millions of rodents, mostly deer mice, carry the virus.

It has been discovered that as many as one-in-ten deer mice in the state of Montana carry the hantavirus. So it amazes me that I am still alive after hearing about the virus. All my life I have been around mouse-infested buildings, particularly sheds, chicken houses and old buildings. Hantavirus is a threat as an airborne virus, found mostly in mouse droppings and urine. In the chicken house at my grandmother's place there were hundreds of deer mice. All my life I have been in such places, sweeping, shoveling, raking, and otherwise stirring up the air. Today I find myself terrified of such places and when I go into them I wonder if my life expectancy has suddenly been shortened to two to six weeks, the incubation time for the disease. The disease has a sixty percent fatality rate.

This is one of those instances that makes me think of wave-particle duality (from Chapter 2: Mind), where reality is created by our perception of it. As far as I know, no one died from the hantavirus until that outbreak in the southwest that killed a number of people in a short time. As soon as the virus was identified and publicized, people immediately started dropping dead from it all over the country.

I thought this "coincidence" was rather disturbing, and I tried to eliminate the idea of the hantavirus from my mind to keep it from becoming part of my reality too. But I eventually conceded that it was to late. The box was opened, and we as a culture perceived that the cat was dead. Hantavirus as a deadly disease is here to stay.

It is unclear whether or not people died from hantavirus in the past. Some cases may have been misdiagnosed before the disease was recognized. Even today we know relatively little about hantavirus. If it is has been around us all along then perhaps most people have a natural immunity to it. In any case, here are the accepted facts:

The Facts: Hantavirus is spread from rodent-to-rodent or rodent-to-person by inhaling airborne particles of rodent urine, droppings, or saliva. It can also be spread through biting or by handling the blood, nesting materials, or droppings. Mice do not appear to be affected by the virus, and neither cats nor dogs are known to have ever spread the disease to a person. Nor can people spread the disease to each other. Once in the body, it stays in the body.

Initial symptoms typically appear between two and three weeks after infection. The symptoms may appear flu-like, including the chills, muscle and body aches, headaches, coughing, nausea, a fever, vomiting or diarrhea, and feeling tired. These symptoms may persist for a few hours or several days before the disease progresses. Hantavirus is a respiratory disease, and the virus grows in the capillary cells of the lungs. It produces tiny holes in the cells, and the liquid plasma of the blood stream fills the lungs with fluid. The immune system attacks the virus and damages the capillary cells containing the virus. The infected person can die in as little as 24 hours after the lungs begin filling with fluid. The disease is difficult to treat once finally diagnosed, because the antiviral drugs do not have time to work before the lungs are severely damaged.

Fortunately, the virus is easily killed on contact with conventional household cleaners, like Lysol or bleach. It is suggested that you spray dead mice or other rodent-exposed materials before handling them. You should avoid dry sweeping or vacuuming any mouse-infested areas. It is better to wet clean, using a disinfectant. You can wear a respirator with a HEPA filter on it when working in rodent infested areas. I use a regular dust mask and spray it down with a household cleaner before putting it on. Then I walk into the area, and spray cleaner all over the air, and onto any noticeable accumulations of droppings or nesting materials.

It is impractical to avoid all contact with rodents when engaged in primitive living, especially because it is nearly impossible to mouse-proof a primitive shelter. Mice will be inside of most shelters within a day or two of construction. The best actions to take are to 1) keep a clean shelter, 2) change the bedding materials frequently, and 3) move often.

Finally, realize that you still have a better chance of being killed by lighting than by hantavirus. We get pretty excited by some intangible disease that kills 32 people in one year. Yet, we think nothing about getting in a car, even when we know that more than 30,000 people die in cars in this country every year. Already we have learned to coexist with the plague, tularemia, rabies, and scores of other diseases that we can catch in contact with wild animals. Just be aware of the facts and know what to do and what to look for. Really, it would not bother me to continue trapping, skinning (carefully), and eating mice, except that there is not much meat on them anyway.

what is the nutritional value of the food relative to the calories it takes to produce or harvest it? Other factors shaping food beliefs are the known positive or negative environmental consequences or restraints of producing those foods.

In India, for example, the dominant Hindu religion forbids killing or consuming cattle. This was not always so. Indian people regularly consumed beef up until a few centuries B.C. at which time the rising population created more and more need for cropland, since crops can produce more calories and protein per acre than livestock. Stock needed to be kept for plowing fields, producing milk, and producing dung for fuel. Over the centuries beef consumption dropped until only the wealthy priests consumed it. The disparity between rich and poor opened a niche for the religion of cow protection, which flourished among the peasants and eventually became the dominant religion.

Similarly, Jews and Moslems who do not believe in eating pork today have ancestors who did domesticate and consume pork until economics made it impractical to raise pigs. That was at a time when the Middle East was largely forested and supported the rich foods and resources necessary for pork production. Deforestation, desertification, and competition with human crops made it impractical to raise pigs, and pork subsequently became "bad to eat" among religions of the area.

Harris continues in his book with similar explanations for why differing groups of people either favor or disdain meats such as horses, dogs, cats, rats, insects, and people. In the case of rodents, insects, and other creepy crawlies, many people believe that they are bad to eat because they are filthy and are not fit to consume. Harris contends just the opposite reasoning; he says that the reason these creatures are "filthy" is because they are economically "bad" to eat, meaning that we have more worthwhile sources of protein, so we scorn the uneconomical ones.

In the business of primitive skills most practicing abos adopt the "anthropological approach" to food and set aside cultured beliefs about what is "good" or "bad" to eat. After all, food is food. As long as it tastes good and is not poisonous then it is edible. Right?.

Given peoples' prejudices about certain foods, one can be sure that food culture always makes for a lively topic of discussion. Therefore, whenever we want to spice up a conversation, we just tell people, "We eat mice."

My friend peers out of the shelter with shining, beady black eyes. "It is okay," I whisper in my mind, "I'm not going to eat you." I finish my rice and put the rest of my ashcakes away for the trail. My mouse friend disappeared into the shelter. It is time for me to be along my way as well.

◊　◊◊◊　◊

Plants

The afternoon sun radiates warmth down across the mountains. I extinguish my cooking fire then follow the course of the water as it flows downstream from my campsite. Thick stands of short river birch, willows, and dogwoods grow in profusion under the canopy of quaken aspen, making navigation nearly impossible. I wander through the brush, climbing over piles of dead vegetation, squeezing through a tight stand of willows, crawling under fallen aspens. I cross a small stream on a log and step through the tangled vegetation on the other bank.

A species of violet thrives in some of the shady areas where other vegetation is sparse. It has large heart-shaped leaves up to three or more inches across. It makes a good salad plant, but you have to check them carefully, as they appear similar to the arnica, which is a powerful medicinal plant. I pick a couple violet leaves to enjoy on my walk.

I had the opportunity to learn to identify most of the plants I know while in junior high and high school. I spent most of my weekends and summers with Grandma Josie. We went walking every day and each time I would collect a couple new plant specimens to bring home. I spent hours studying the plants and **cross-referencing** them through about ten different books. This enabled me to check for accuracy with the different photos in each book. If I could not identify a plant through my books then I brought it to the herbarium at Montana State University in Bozeman for positive identification.

The glacier lily.

Once I had a name I studied the uses of the plant in every book I had until I knew fairly well. On our walks, Grandma and I would quiz each other on plant names and uses. In our efforts to fool each other we would point out specific plants that were tricky to identify. We pointed out plants that were growing in odd habitats, or immature plants, dead stalks, and even parts of plants. With constant drilling I learned the plants so that I will never forget them. I learned to pick up a leaf, seed, or twig on the ground and trace it to its parent plant. I learned to identify many plants from the time they were a half-inch tall in the spring until they were dead, leafless stalks in the fall and winter.

Attention to details is important when learning plants. Too often people try to learn plants while towering over them and they never get a good look at what they are studying. Plants have tremendous variations, and while most plants within a species have an average appearance, there are always extremes that at first glance look nothing at all like the plant they are.

Many years ago my brother asked me to teach him plants and to drill him on their names. So I taught him some plants and then quizzed him as we walked. I liked to pick out the extremes of each plant species to throw him off. In one case I picked out an easy plant and asked him what it was. "Dandelion." he answered. "Good," I said, "now what is this one?" I pointed to a much different plant two feet away. He struggled to answer for a while and finally gave up. The plant was also a dandelion.

There are good reasons to study plants very carefully. The most important reason is to get a **positive identification** on every plant you pick. The extremes of one species of plant can look much like another species, increasing the possibility of confusing poisonous and edible species. Beyond that, it is helpful to know plants in all stages of growth so that you can use them at all times of the year. Most guidebooks will help you identify plants when they are blooming. It is up to you to track them through the seasons and learn them in that way. As you proceed you will find that the more plants you know the easier it is to learn new ones.

In the past there were limited ways to learn plant identification. You could take a college course in botany and learn to use a botanical key, or you could learn plants from pictures or from people you meet. Unfortunately, the language and the process of a botanical key is stifling and tedious. With a key you may spend more time learning about and studying the key than learning and studying actual plants. Matching plants to pictures in books may be less intimidating, but there is a greater chance of making a critical error in identification. Either approach requires a phenomenal commitment of time and effort to develop competency.

Few adults have the luxury of time that I had as a teenager to spend hours every day studying plants. The shear enormity of the subject can seem so overwhelming that many people do not even begin. Fortunately there is an easier way to learn about plants now.

Initially I studied plants one-at-a-time. There are hundreds of thousands of species of plants in the world, and I approached them one-by-one, as if each one had nothing to do with any others. It seemed that all plants were completely different, with no rhyme or reason as to what they were or what they could be used for. It seemed like there should be some rationale to the plant world, but I did not find it in my library of books.

Then we hosted a medicinal herb class through our school. Robyn, an herbalist, identified plants for the group and explained the uses of each. I thought I "knew" most of the plants we found, but Robyn used an approach I had never seen before. On this walk we found many plants from the Rose family. She told us that most members of the Rose family were astringent, and that an astringent tightens tissues and closes off secretions. An astringent herb, she said, would help close a wound, draw down inflamed tissues, dry up digestive secretions (an aid for diarrhea), and about twenty other things. In a few short words and phrases she explained what an astringent does and gave us the uses of virtually every member of this one family. She went on to summarize several other families of plants in a similar way. She cracked open a door to a whole new way of looking at plants.

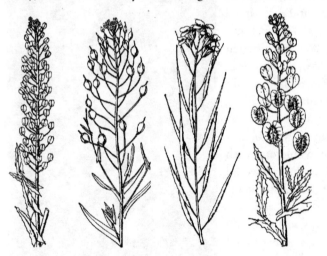

Each of these is a different but related plant. You do not necessarily need to know the specific names of each of them to be able to know their uses. All of these plants have a similar pattern and all belong to the Mustard Family. They have a somewhat similar odor and flavor, and similar chemistry.

Now, some of my books listed the family names of the plants, but never suggested how that information could be useful. I realized that while I knew many plants by name, I never really stopped to look at any of them! This may sound alarming and contradictory, but it is surprisingly easy to match a plant to a picture without studying it to count the flower parts or notice how they are positioned in relation to each other. For example, I could easily recognize a sunflower or a leaf from a sunflower, but I never stopped to look at the flower parts, or even to notice how the leaves were positioned in relation to one another.

I was totally dismayed that I had been studying plants for all those years, and no book ever mentioned that there were patterns or any kind of logic to the plant world. In short, this one class totally changed everything I ever knew about plants. From there I had to relearn every plant I already knew in a whole new way. I set out to study the patterns in plants, learning to identify the plants and their uses together as groups and families. Eventually this research turned into a book, *Botany in a Day: Thomas J. Elpel's Herbal Field Guide to Plant Families*. The text is now used as a manual at herbal and wilderness schools across the country, and it has been picked up by quite a few universities as well.

Botany in a Day is not meant to be used by itself, but it makes other plant books much easier to use and cuts years off the task of learning about plants and their uses. In the book I highlighted the patterns of plant families common across North America. As you learn these patterns you will notice similar characteristics between the plants of your area and the plants in different regions and even different continents. I still recommend that you **purchase a multiple number of plant books**, so you can cross-reference between them to make sure you accurately identify all the plants you work with. Ideally, you want a mix of books, some with photographs, some with drawings, and definitely one botanical key. You might be surprised at how different one plant can appear in a variety of books. And you might be surprised at how similar many other unrelated plants may appear. Always use the Latin name to cross-reference between books, since common names can vary from one book to another. Latin names are seldom altered, so you can use them to be sure you are still reading about the same plant in each book.

About Common and Latin Names: The Latin names of plants may seem intimidating at first, but do not fear them, they are true allies in learning plants. A plant normally has only one Latin name, while it may have dozens of common names. Also, a common name may be used for several different and totally unrelated plants. For instance, there are several plants called "pigweed", and without the Latin name you can never know for sure exactly which plant you are talking about.

You do not need to memorize every Latin name; you only need to refer to them when you want to communicate about the plant to another person, or if you want to research that plant in other books. I have included many common names in this book, and I would encourage you to write in any other common names that you like better. In fact, you can make up your own common names for the plants, if it helps you to remember them. I do!

As long as you can remember the common name then you can return to it in the book and look up the Latin name to cross-reference with other sources. The Latin names are standardized all over the world, so you will see exactly the same terms used by people in China, Kenya, Vietnam, or Sweden. Latin was chosen for this purpose because it is a "dead" language. No group of people still speaks the language, so it is not evolving and changing—thus the names should always stay the same. You may be surprised by how many of the names you memorize just as a result of looking them up in the indexes of other books.

Every plant has a unique name in Latin, and the name is always in two parts. For example, "sweet cicely" a local plant with a potent anise-like flavor, is called *Osmorhiza occidentalis*. The first name is the genus name (plural: genera), and it is always capitalized. The second part is the species name, and it is always lower-case. Both are always italicized.

These two-part Latin names are much like the system of first and last names we use to describe each other. For example, I belong to the genus Elpel, and my species name is Thomas. Other "species" of the Elpel genus include: Cherie, Nick, Alan, Marc, and Jeanne. The species names are meaningless on their own, because many people have the same names around the world. But the names Cherie Elpel or Nick Elpel are quite unique.

In a similar way, there are five different species of sweet cicely just in Montana. These are very closely related plants, so they all have the same genus name, *Osmorhiza*; only their species names are different. Fortunately you do not have to write out Osmorhiza for each species. You can abbreviate the genus name after the first time you have used it. For instance, the other species of Osmorhiza in Montana are *O. longistylis*, *O. chilensis*, *O. purpurea*, and *O. depauperata*. If you want to talk about the whole group at once then you just write out "*Osmorhiza spp.*". This abbreviation means "species plural".

◊   ◊◊◊   ◊

I eat the large lettuce-like leaves of the violets and walk on my way. I walk downstream until I stand at the edge of a field. Gophers play and frolic in the field and let out a shrill "chirp" at my approach. They are really ground squirrels, but people here call them "gophers".

A patch of glacier lilies graces the bank of the creek here at the edge of the field, among the grasses and under the aspens. A month ago their blossoms carpeted the land, but now only the seedpods and wide leaves remain. Many acres of these lilies grow in this area of the Tobacco Root Mountains. The bulb-like root is called a corm and it is especially sweet and crisp, a true delicacy. They average about an inch long and less than a quarter-inch in diameter, although the bigger ones can be the size of a small thumb. Those are prizes.

Glacier lily roots are buried about six inches into the soil. It would be discouraging to try digging out a quantity with a pocket knife, but there is a simple tool called a digging stick which makes the job much easier.

The Digging Stick

The digging stick is little more than a piece of wood with a sharp point, but it is surprising how much you can do with it. The digging stick can be used for small jobs like unearthing roots or bigger jobs like making a pit shelter. The digging stick can even be used for major undertakings. The Hohokam people, who inhabited Arizona and Mexico a thousand years ago, dug extensive irrigation systems with digging sticks. Individual canals were up to fifteen feet wide and ten miles long.

You can make a digging stick out of almost **any solid piece of wood**, but hardwoods are definitely better. In Southwest Montana the best native woods are **chokecherry**, **serviceberry** and **hawthorn**. I like a digging stick that is 16 to 24 inches long and 1 to 1 1/2 inches in diameter. I often carry a digging stick in my belt when I am out, or I make one on the spot as I need it. Digging sticks can be much larger. Agricultural peoples used sticks that were four to six feet long. These sticks were often selected to utilize an existing branch as a natural foothold. Then they could be used much like an ordinary shovel.

The digging stick is used as a lever to pry dirt and roots out of the ground, so the leverage can break the **tip** if it is not beveled correctly. Beveling the tip from two sides is instinctive, but it weakens the wood. Instead of beveling the tip from two sides, bevel it from one side only. The one-sided bevel makes a sharp tip, and it leaves the circular growth

Using a digging stick to harvest lily roots.

rings intact on the unbeveled side. When using the stick as a lever, make sure the unbeveled side of the tip is the side going into the force. The force against the stick compresses the circular growth rings and strengthens the tip. If the stick is used the other way then the force can pull apart the rings and split the stick.

The digging stick is handled differently for different tasks. To dig up a root, place the stick beside the plant. Put pressure downward on the stick and work it back and forth to leverage it into the ground. You can also pick up another stick or a rock, and pound the digging stick into the ground. Work the stick in under the root and lift the root out. If there are more roots nearby then work the stick in beside them and leverage them towards the hole left by the first root. The soil gives way into the existing hole and makes digging easier.

In moist soils a digging stick can work better than a shovel for harvesting roots. A shovel digs up a large clod that has to be broken apart to retrieve the root. But a digging stick brings up just the root with very little dirt. Digging sticks have advantages over shovels in other ways as well. They are free, and they are lightweight to carry.

The digging stick is handled differently for fire pits and other excavation work. Kneel down and hold the stick with one hand at the top and the other hand a few inches up from the tip. Jab the stick into the ground and pull it towards you to rip out chunks of sod. Scoop loose material out of the pit with your hands.

The digging stick has one other use. It can be used as a "throwing stick" or "rabbitstick" for killing small game. It can be hard to hit a target with just a rock, since the rock must be thrown very accurately. But a throwing stick cuts a swath through the air that is as long as the stick itself. This increases your chances of hitting your target.

Using a bone as a hammer to pound a digging stick into dry soil.

The digging stick is a very useful and versatile tool. Slip one in your belt next time you are out. It is hard telling what uses you will dig up for it.

◊　◊◊◊　◊

I select a stand of large glacier lilies and push the digging stick into the ground beside one. I work the stick back and forth, pushing it deeper into the ground. I work it deep into the soil then use it like a lever to lift out plant and sod alike.

I find one nice corm and dig the next closest lily. The soil moves more easily as I leverage it into the first hole. I continue working in this fashion, digging each closest lily until I have a nice handful. I replace the sod to let my garden grow again, then wash my bounty in the stream and nibble along my way. I savor the sweet, crisp roots and enjoy a couple leaves as well. The glacier lilies provide food for thought and my thoughts are about food.

Thinking back, it seems that learning to identify plants was easy. But learning to find truly **edible plants** was much more difficult. As a beginner in the primitive skills I read that "nature was like a banquet", and "all you had to do was eat", so I anticipated that I should be able to set up camp anywhere I wanted, and I would always find a well-balanced meal right there.

I was quite discouraged on my camping trips when I always went hungry. I learned virtually every plant of any significance across southwestern Montana, and I knew hundreds of edible species, but could never seem to find any to eat on my camping trips. Sure there were lots of salad plants, but it is difficult to live on just greens!

A digging stick with a branch for a foot peg can make digging easier.

I realize that many other practicing primitives have had similar experiences with trying to find wild plant foods to eat, and I would like to share some insights that helped me break through the barriers and find success at nature's banquet.

At first I looked for excuses. For instance, historically the native peoples used this area only seasonally, and no group was known to have lived here full time. Bands of Shoshone from Idaho and Wyoming visited the area in the summer, primarily for hunting. Other native peoples, including the Nez Perce, Blackfeet, and Flathead were seen in the area, but did not occupy Southwest Montana on a regular basis. It seemed that my area had too few edibles for

Nature is like a banquet, except that the table is very long, and you have to be in the right place at the right time.

even the native peoples! This helped me to justify my failure to find harvestable foods. I grew envious of other parts of the country that had seemingly inexhaustible food supplies, like acorns or wild plums or big camas bulbs. I told myself that the Indians ate corn and beans and squash and potatoes, and provided over half of our modern food crops, all of which could not survive in the wild any more, because of breeding. I further decided that most of our wild plants were forage for the big game animals that dominate this landscape.

Now that has changed. In a moment of analytical insight I realized that I had not fully tried to use edible plants, and that my excuses were true, but irrelevant. I realized that it is true that the plants of my area are primarily forage for big game animals, but that "primarily" does not mean "exclusively". I acknowledged that, sure, many Indians of the New World ate foods like corn, beans, and squash, but that, wild or domestic, those crops never existed in my area anyway. I understood finally that primitive peoples used this area only seasonally because that is the nature of a hunter-gatherer lifestyle—to walk from one meal to the next as each comes into season. I realized that nature really is like a banquet, and that only the buffet table was a little longer than I expected. In fact, it was many miles longer than I expected. I was always at the table, just not at the right parts of the table at the right times!

I already knew every plant of any significance in my entire mountain range, and indeed, across all of southwestern Montana. I was not going to find some new plant with a big starchy root like a potato, or some tree with a nut like an acorn. The native peoples were using this area at least seasonally, and that that was far more than I was. I knew every plant they did, plus additional species introduced from Europe. I had not yet found anything to eat, but suddenly understood that I was very close to using the resources of my area as efficiently as any primitive peoples who ever lived here. Good or bad, that got me excited about edible plants again for the first time in years.

I realized I needed to concentrate my efforts on the few key species that could really support a person, and to plan my camping trips to coincide with the harvest times for each of those resources. So I made a mental list of the key plants in the area that seemed like they might be worthwhile to work with.

To make my list, I eliminated all the non-edible plants, and all the "edible" plants that are useful only as tea. I also eliminated all salad greens and potherbs, which are edible, but which could not sustain a person. Wild greens are very important, and many are very delicious, but they do not provide caloric sustenance. *You are encouraged to learn more about wild salad and potherb plants through the many other excellent edible plants books on the market, including Botany in a Day.* I further eliminated all the "starvation foods" because I was not interested in starving. And I eliminated any plants which experience had shown me were unpalatable, because I knew I would not be motivated to harvest something that did not taste good.

The root of the pond lily (Nuphar spp.) is listed in many books as edible, but our species is dangerously medicinal.

I also eliminated those plants that were edible, but too rare to be harvested, and those which were edible, but definitely not worth the expense of energy. In order to survive on a particular food source you have to be able to harvest more calories than you expend. You have to harvest enough calories to replace those spent, and to allow you to build a shelter and meet all your other needs. Many "edible" wild plants require so much work to harvest them that you could starve to death even if you ate all day long every day. Other roots could sustain you very easily, but only if you have a good system for harvesting them.

I kept on my mental list the plants that were abundant, tasted okay, and had nutritious properties. Mostly that included roots, seeds, fruits and nuts, but also a few greens that are noted for exceptional nutritional properties. I also kept on the list some fruits, such as the wild strawberry and the dwarf huckleberry (*Vaccinium scoparium*), which are not economical to harvest (one cup per hour of effort), but which are still worthwhile to collect for their exceptional flavor.

Many of the potentially sustainable wild foods on my list turned out to be species that grew only in the fertile, warm valley bottoms, around the farms and towns. This is no coincidence, since that is also where the native peoples camped. It is only us modern abos that expect to eke out a living perched on top of a mountain! If you want to be as successful as the natives were at finding food resources, then you have to follow in their footsteps. I used to camp only in the mountains behind my home, but now I frequently venture out along the fringes of the farmlands.

My range currently extends in about a thirty-mile radius in every direction from our home. That is about as far as I can reasonably go by foot on my regular camping trips, and still walk back home. You can make a pretty good guess as to where I will be camping according to what is in season.

I was not going to find some over-looked species of wild potatoes or acorns. I knew every plant of any significance for hundreds of miles around me. I had to learn to harvest the plants I already knew.

108

I enter a small meadow rich with roses, sweet cicely and musk thistles. All **thistles** are edible, if they have not been sprayed with herbicide, but the big musk thistles (*Carduus nutans*) are certainly the tastiest. It is one of my favorite snacks, and there is a technique to peeling the stalk while avoiding the stickers. Thistles are only good when the stalks are still fleshy; as summer progresses the stalks become woody and inedible.

I carefully grasp the tip of a budding flower and bend the stalk over to see how much of the plant is still succulent and where it has already become a woody stalk. With one quick slice of my sheath knife I cut through the stalk taking only the top succulent part. I do not cut all the way through the stalk, but rather, I leave the "rind" intact on one side and let the thistle top hang down from that rind. I carefully grab the thistle top and pull it gently away from the parent stalk. This action peels the rind off the side of the stem that is still attached to the main stalk. The peeled side of the stem provides one safe, stickerless place for my fingers. The rest of the process is like peeling a banana. I start at the cut and peel the spiny rind off on each side of the stem. I walk on my way, savoring the almost "domestic" taste of the thistle.

True hunter-gatherer cultures were much more nomadic than I am, and they regularly traveled hundreds of miles from one food source to another. They lived full-time as nomads and had no homes to return to, so they kept walking forward. Today, in my recreational camping, I have both advantages and disadvantages compared to what the native peoples experienced.

One advantage I have is that as an individual I can take advantage of much smaller crops that would not have sustained a larger group of people. A crop that is big enough to sustain me for two weeks would only feed a band of fourteen people for one day—hardly worth stopping for. Another difference between my experience and theirs is that they had to find food. For them it was a matter of survival. For me it is recreation and education. They had to harvest food no matter what the crops were like, while I can plan my camping trips to coincide with the peak of each crop, and take advantage of the best nature's banquet has to offer.

On the other hand, the native peoples had an advantage in covering so much more ground, because they encountered many excellent crops that do not occur in my territory. Serviceberries (*Amelanchier spp.*) are one of my favorite wild foods, but the nearest good patch I have found is in a subdivision 60 miles away, out of my camping range. Hawthorn berries (*Crataegus spp.*) and huckleberries (*Vaccinium spp.*) also grow abundantly near that area. The delicious blue camas (*Camassia quamash*) first appears about 100 miles in another direction, and sego lilies (*Calochortus spp.*) are also 80 miles away. Wild plums (*Prunus americana*), wild grapes (*Vitis spp.*), and "Indian turnips" (*Psoralea esculenta*) are 200 miles away. It is not practical for me to harvest any of these foods on my camping trips, but I do gather them when modern life happens to bring me in the right area at the right time.

Next, I conducted timed studies of many of the wild foods on my list. I brought a watch along on my camping trips and clocked how much of each resource I could harvest per hour. For the first time I had a procedure for determining whether or not I was wasting my effort with any given food resource, and for the first time I found a relative abundance of wild foods in my area.

One thing I learned during my timed studies is that surprisingly few people have the patience to spend even one hour harvesting a resource, much less the two to three hours per day that was typical of most primitive peoples. Harvesting wild foods can be remarkably tedious for us modern abos, since we come from such a fast-paced culture. Nevertheless, I recommend the experience for everyone at least once, to find out what it is really like to earn a living as a "hunter-gatherer".

One hour's work harvesting glacier lily roots.

I also discovered that many of the wild foods in my area are genuinely stunted (typically 1/3 the size) compared to the same plants in other regions, especially the root crops like salsify (*Tragopogon spp.*), yampah (*Perideridia gairdneri*), and glacier lilies (*Erythronium grandiflorum*). The smaller roots in my area are apparently an effect of the grainy soils of decomposing granite; the soil dries out as soon as the rain stops. Working with these anemic plants has enabled me to hone both my skills and my patience, so that other areas seem comparatively lush and abundant.

Perhaps the most important lesson I learned is the value of having a quality experience. I have noticed that wild foods taste much better if I harvest and eat them because I am excited and want the variation in my diet, than when I force myself into a situation where I must find food whether I feel like it or not. Also I have learned to appreciate gourmet cooking. A sautéed dish of roots, greens, mushrooms, and some kind of meat is much more enticing than just a pot of boiled roots. Quality experiences will always bring you eagerly back for more, and therefore I recommend bringing whatever you need to maintain that quality. A few basic foods like rice and flour and cooking oil can make the difference between a good trip and a bad one. I also like to bring a gold pan for stir-frying, sautéing, and for winnowing wild grains. These kinds of adaptations are not technically primitive, but they keep me returning, and that's what it is all about!

I hear a vehicle coming up the road. I decide to move along. With the glacier lily roots and thistle stalk in hand I start back towards the brush. At the edge of the meadow along the fringe of brush, I stop to look back. The vehicle is a jeep. It stops on the hillside road, up above the field. Two people get out. They have guns.

I disappear into the brush. I walk a ways, then crawl through some tight spots, where I discover a very small nook, a meadow that is only twenty-some feet across and about forty long. Small granite boulders stick up as lumps two and three feet high. There are several thistle plants and a patch of stinging nettles.

The "sting" from the stinging nettles (*Urtica dioica*) is caused by formic acid injected by the hollow hairs under the leaves. For obvious reasons you are wise to pick nettles with gloves or a shirtsleeve. However, you can also pick them carefully by the stem with your bare hands, as long as you are careful to avoid touching the underside of the leaves. Most of the time you won't get stung this way. Nettle stings are not too potent anyway, but you can treat them with a little mud or an astringent plant. I usually just dip the irritated part in cold water for a moment.

Remarkably, stinging nettles can be eaten raw if you first crush them thoroughly to destroy the needles. Most people just boil the young greens for a highly nutritious potherb. I like to dry the whole plants, then strip and powder the leaves for a food additive and stew thickener. It is especially nice to take nettle powder along on winter camping trips when other greens are scarce.

I do not choose to depend on wild edible plants, but I use them to supplement my diet of basic camping foods. I have probably planted more edibles than I have harvested. I have tried to play a sort of "Johnny Appleseed" to increase the diversification of edible and utilitarian plants here in the Tobacco Roots. I can't say I've had a lot of success, but I routinely bring in seeds or live plants and try to place them in their proper habitat throughout the immediate watershed. I especially hope to establish useable populations of cattails, camas bulbs, sunflowers, hawthorn berries, and a variety of other more minor crops as well. If you try this in your area make certain you do not introduce any known noxious weeds, and in particular do not introduce any plants that are totally foreign to your environment, or they may become noxious weeds.

This "wild gardening" that I do is nothing new to me. I have been casting out seeds and trying unorthodox experiments since I was old enough to wield a shovel. I transplanted wild plants to our home, and I cast the seeds of domesticated plants into wild fields—all for the sake of experimentation. My experiments yielded little in the way of food, but I always harvested some morsel of knowledge. I instinctively knew that traditional gardening/farming made no sense at all. Traditional methods of farming creates monocrops of plants with vast open, barren ground between the plants. I never bought into that idea, nor the idea that you have to wage an endless battle against weeds and pests to grow a crop.

The blue camas (Camassia quamash) is native to Montana , but doesn't grow in my local area. I hope to get this wonderful edible plant established in the appropriate habitat near home.

110

Thus I was delighted as a teenager to discover the Japanese farmer, Masanobu Fukuoka, and his methods of "natural" farming. **Natural farming** is different from both organic farming and traditional scientific farming. Organic farming and scientific farming add complexities to farming, whereas natural farming takes them away. For example, in organic farming the farmer commonly delivers nutrients to the plants through various witches' brews of organic compost. In scientific farming the farmer applies the nutrients through petrochemical concoctions. But in natural farming the farmer uses the ecosystem to recycle nutrients so that he does not have to do all that work himself.

Death camas (Zygadenus spp.) has a similar bulb and leaves to blue camas, but the flowers are smaller and white. Photo by Gene Ward.

With Fukuoka's method of natural farming the ecosystem does most of the work for him, beyond casting the seed and harvesting the crops. Because of this, Fukuoka describes his techniques as the "no plowing, no fertilizing, no weeding, no pesticides, do-nothing method". What he does do, in my words, is to tilt succession in the ecosystem to favor his crops. Basically, weeds take over cultivated land such as gardens, not because they are aggressive or intend to do malice, but because disturbed soils are their ideal habitat. Desirable plants can spread like weeds too—if you create the ideal habitat for them. Fukuoka learned to manage the ecosystem of his fields to favor his rice and barley crops, his garden vegetables, and his orchard. I am studying ways to tilt our own local ecosystem in favor of the crops that are appropriate for the area.

I hear the occasional "pop" of the guns from the field. The ground squirrels wriggle in spasms and become still. A woodpecker hammers away at an aspen tree back behind me.

A slight breeze rustles the quaken aspen leaves and gently sways the top-heavy timothy grass back and forth. I listen to the gun shots from the field below. The sound of gun fire always makes me uncomfortable and a little nervous. There are roads on both sides of the small field where they are shooting. The two people are on the one road and when they aim at the "gophers" they are shooting towards the other road. I have walked on that other road in plain sight before, making sure I was well seen, but the gopher hunters never once stopped shooting at targets in my direction to let me pass.

On one other trip to this camp I was at my shelter when I heard shots from a high-powered rifle. I stepped out in the open to see what was going on and there were people shooting from the road. They were shooting at a coyote about a hundred yards from me.

At last, the sound of gunshots ceases. I hear two car doors slam. Next I hear the sound of the engine. They back down the hill, turn around, and drive away. I do not mind guns during general hunting season in the fall. I expect people to be out with guns at that time, and I avoid going into the brush until the season is over. But in the summer one never knows when or where someone will appear with a gun or what they will be shooting at. I often hear people say they were shooting at some noise in the brush, and that concerns me, because it could be me.

I have developed an aversion to guns, even though I myself once engaged in the gopher slaughter. But even though I have an extreme dislike for guns, I also recognize that to outlaw guns and hunting, as some animal rights activists groups would do, would trigger the greatest environmental catastrophe of all time, due to animal overpopulation. At one time there were predators to keep the populations of grazing animals in check, but they are gone now. The big predators became extinct with the arrival of primitive peoples on this continent many thousands of years ago. The remaining predators became either wholly or locally extinct with the arrival of western civilization in the last two hundred years. Humankind now has little choice but to fill the roll of the predator. It is a genuine concern that every year the anti-hunting movement grows a stronger political arm.

I stand up and start walking and pick the blossom from a sweet cicely plant. I crush it up, breath in the strong licorice-like smell, and chew a little bit of it for the flavor.

Thinking about it, I suppose it is kind of neat that animal rights activists and so many other people are becoming more sensitive to other beings in the world. I even have to agree with animal rights activists that the wholesale slaughter of animals every year is hard to stomach. At least the attitude many people have about killing is offensive. To kill for the fun and the pleasure of killing is to me, sick.

The taste of the sweet cicely is almost overpowering. I pause a moment to imagine how it must feel to be the sweet cicely. I imagine what it would be like to be the blossom torn from the plant, and I try to sense what it must be like being crushed and eaten....

My thoughts make me think that animal rights activists are well intentioned, but blind when they desire to stop killing all animals. And when they choose to become vegetarians to avoid killing, then I think they are as insensitive to plants as the pleasure hunters are to animals.

The delicious licorice-like sweet cicely (Osmorhiza occidentalis).

Plants are sensitive beings too, and scientific research using galvanometers, or lie detectors, attached to plants has indicated that they may have a form of "extrasensory perception". According to Peter Tompkins and Christopher Bird in their classic book *The Secret Life of Plants*, plants seem to be able to read the emotional intent of people or other plants. Tests have shown that plants have a strong emotional reaction when people think about maiming them, and plants will often "pass out" in a stressful situation. Other tests have shown that by magnifying the physical movements of plants it can be seen that they go into death spasms when killed, much as animals do. Even the carrot and cabbage experience traumatic death spasms when killed, such as when scalded in boiling water. Other tests have indicated that these characteristics occur not just in the whole plant, but in individual cells as well.

At least animals have the decency to die when we kill them, but a vegetable, like a head of lettuce ripped from its roots, sits there day after day in our refrigerators, waiting for the possible chance of finding nutrients and water to keep it alive. Then this live vegetable lands on our plates, and dies cell by cell as it is shredded between our teeth, and the few cells that make it past our teeth only go on to be dissolved alive in the gastric acid of our stomachs.

When people stop eating meat to avoid killing I think they are blind. It is easy to see animals bleed and suffer, and we can associate with that because they are in many ways like ourselves. But the vegetables we eat experience something too; it is only that our blindness and our arrogance keeps us from understanding these rich living beings.

We cannot avoid killing. We must take the lives of plants and/or animals in order to sustain our own lives. Instead we should choose to kill in a more respectful way; we should kill only out of need, and we should appreciate the lives that are given up so that we may go on.

I savor the taste of the sweet cicely and speak thanks to it in my heart. I walk onward.

There are many different species of wild onions (Allium spp.). All of them smell like onions and all are edible.

◊   ◊◊◊   ◊

Worthwhile Plant Food Resources

In every state there are several thousand species of plants. As out-lined in the illustration, only a few of those plants are extremely poisonous. Many other plants are "poisonous", but not all that dangerous. The vast majority of plants are neither edible nor poisonous, just not very palatable or digestible. Out of what is left, there are hundreds of edible plants, but most are useful only as greens. There are relatively few plants with starches, oils, sugars, or protein to provide real sustenance, and many of those are impractical to harvest. In a book of this nature the plants section must necessarily be limited, in order to allow room for all other aspects of primitive living. Therefore, I have presented only the most worthwhile of the edible plants that I have first-hand experience with. This text is unique in its presentation, since many related plants are lumped together in the descriptions. I think you will recognize the advantages to this kind of a presentation. Nevertheless, you are encouraged to cross-reference this material with other sources for the most accurate identification and uses of these plants. It is especially helpful to research the dangerous poisonous plants first, so you can watch out for them in the field.

Very Poisonous Plants: There are only a handful of very poisonous plants. Those are plants that have a high probability of killing you if you ingest them, and you should learn about these plants as soon as possible. These include water hemlock (*Cicuta*), hemlock (*Conium*), death camas (*Zygadenus*), and monkshood (*Aconitum*).

Mildly Poisonous Plants: There are many plants which that poisonous properties, but would not endanger a normal adult in moderate amounts. Some of these plants could make you quite sick, depending on how much you consumed, but you would have to work at it a little bit to kill yourself with them.

Plants that are not poisonous, but not usually food except as tea: There are many plants which are not poisonous, but which do not quite qualify as food for human beings. For example, you would not eat such things as sagebrush, willows, trees or sedge grasses.

Salads and Potherbs: Many of our edible plants make excellent salads or boiled greens ("potherbs"). These greens are a good garnish to a meal, but do not make a meal in themselves. Salads and potherbs are usually rich in vitamins and minerals, but lack carbohydrates, fats, or protein.

Fruits and berries: Fruits and berries are very intermittent across the landscape. You might have to walk a hundred miles or more to find a good crop, but that one crop may provide more fruit than you could possibly use. Berries are not usually a complete meal in themselves, but they always make the primitive experience seem a little more "worthwhile".

Starchy Roots: Most plant roots are woody, but a few species store carbohydrates through the winter in the form of starch in their roots. The plants use these nutrients to start growing in the spring. Plants with starchy roots are most useful from fall until early spring.

Seeds/Nuts: There are a tremendous number of edible seeds, including most grasses. Seeds are a valuable source of carbohydrates, oils, and sometimes protein. However, many edible seeds are impractical to harvest, and most seed crops have very short seasons. Seeds usually fall to the ground within one or two weeks of maturing, so you have to be in exactly the right place at the right time to take advantage of them. Nuts are even better sources of nutrition, but uncommon in the north, except for pine nuts.

Edible, Medicinal, and Poisonous Plants

Plants which are not poisonous, but which are not usually food, except as tea.

Poisonous Plants

Edible Plants

Mildly Poisonous Plants
Very Poisonous Plants

Salad/Potherbs
Berries/Fruits
Starchy Roots
Seeds/Nuts

Medicinal Plants

—Edible Lichens—

Lichens are a symbiotic association between algae and fungus. The algae is a layer of single-celled plants just below a gelatinized layer of fungal hyphae. The algae captures nutrients that land on its surface and provides energy through photosynthesis, while the fungus absorbs moisture and provides a protective structure for the algae. The varied and often bright colors of the lichens come from acid crystals that are used to etch holes in rock or wood. Thread-like anchors are inserted into those holes. Most of the so-called "mosses" found in trees are actually lichens. The true mosses are distinctively green like other plants. There are many edible and poisonous lichens. The only one I have eaten so far is the easy-to-identify black tree lichen.

Black Tree Lichen (*Alectoria spp.*)

The black tree lichen is common in damp western forests. It is the dark, stringy "moss" than hangs from the branches of trees. Montana Indians washed and soaked the lichen, then cooked it for one to two days in a steam pit. The cooked lichen was eaten or dried and powdered and used as a mush or thickener later. It is reported that Flathead Indian families ate 25 pounds of the lichen each year. In the right habitat there is no limit to the amount of this resource you could harvest. Black tree lichens can also be cooked on the stove. Several hours of simmering are required to reduce the stringy mass to a gelatinous black goo. My experience with the tree lichen is limited, but early experiments suggest that the black goo would be especially useful as a substitute for gluten to help hold together crumbly, wild flour breads.

—Syrup—

All members of the Maple Family have a sweet sap that can be harvested for syrup, although some species are more productive than others. Birch trees also have a history of use in syrup production. Maples and birches are found throughout the northern latitudes, with the greatest concentrations in the eastern states. **Maples and Birches** are common in the city. It would be feasible to harvest maple syrup with primitive equipment, but I've always used with modern implements. It is a good activity for kids.

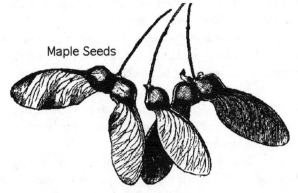

Maple Seeds

I put 2 taps in my neighbor's box elder maple in mid March and collected 6 gallons of sap in 3 weeks. This boiled down to 1.5 cups of thick, rich syrup—a real treat. The sap "runs" in the trees on warm days from January to May, depending on where you are located. To collect the sap simply drill a hole 1 inch in diameter and 3 inches long into the trunk of the tree, about 2 feet above the ground, and on the South side. I use a short length of 3/4" PVC pipe for a spout. The hole should be drilled in at a slight upward angle, and the spout tapped only part way in. A notch can be made into the top of the PVC pipe to hold the wire handle of a bucket, or you can use sheetrock screws to attach the bucket or its handle to the tree trunk. A large tree (16+ inches in diameter) can have more than one tap. The sap is mostly water. It is boiled down to remove at least 30 parts of water to get 1 part pure maple syrup. Birch sap is much more watery, so you may have to boil away 50-60 parts water to get 1 part syrup.

The wild maples and birches of my area are more like bushes than trees, with a maximum trunk diameter of three or four inches. For trees this small we found the best method is to drill a 1/4" hole an inch into the tree, at an angle. Make two slashes in the bark, forming a "V" down to the hole. (Do not slash all the way around the tree— that will kill it.) Pound a stick into the hole, and the sap will run out and drip off the end of the stick. I take along a battery-powered drill and use a sheetrock screw to attach a plastic bucket below the spigot. In our area the sap flows from March to May. The small trees only produce a pint of sap per day, and the syrup content seemed low. It took me a month to get a pint of syrup from 8 trees. It was not particularly economical, but it sure was good. We monitored the trees for negative impacts, but they survived just fine.

In most primitive circumstances you would probably be better off to drink the sap straight, rather than consuming time and fuel to boil it down for syrup. The sap tastes like water with just a little sweetener in it. It is excellent if heated for tea. The inner bark of the birches and maples are also edible, but I have yet to work with them.

—Starchy Roots—

The Cattail Family

The cattail is probably one of the most recognized wild plants in North America. It can be found in many swamps with its long, slender, flat leaves, and a seed head that looks like a hot dog on a stick. The seed head starts developing early in the season. At first it looks like two hot dogs on a stick. The top portion is comprised of thousands of minute male flowers. It produces pollen for about two weeks early in the summer. Cattails are cross-pollinated by the wind. This upper hot-dog-on-a-stick withers away through the summer and eventually drops off. The female part of the stalk is also comprised of thousands of minute flowers, each producing a single seed. The seeds are almost microscopic in size; they are carried away in the wind by the fluffy cattail down when the seed heads are broken apart.

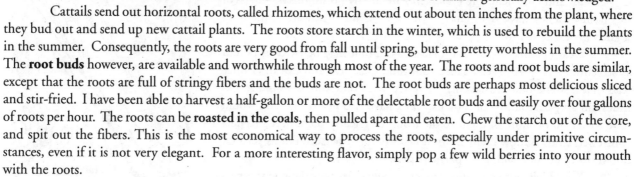

Cattails (*Typha spp.*)

Almost any good boy scout knows the cattail, and how to harvest food from it at any time of the year—at least, that is what I always heard. For years I was rather embarrassed that I knew so little about the cattail, especially considering that it is my profession to know such things. Now that I have finally taken the time to do methodical studies of the cattail I know there is more to it than is generally acknowledged.

Cattails send out horizontal roots, called rhizomes, which extend out about ten inches from the plant, where they bud out and send up new cattail plants. The roots store starch in the winter, which is used to rebuild the plants in the summer. Consequently, the roots are very good from fall until spring, but are pretty worthless in the summer. The **root buds** however, are available and worthwhile through most of the year. The roots and root buds are similar, except that the roots are full of stringy fibers and the buds are not. The root buds are perhaps most delicious sliced and stir-fried. I have been able to harvest a half-gallon or more of the delectable root buds and easily over four gallons of roots per hour. The roots can be **roasted in the coals**, then pulled apart and eaten. Chew the starch out of the core, and spit out the fibers. This is the most economical way to process the roots, especially under primitive circumstances, even if it is not very elegant. For a more interesting flavor, simply pop a few wild berries into your mouth with the roots.

A more refined product can be obtained by separating the starch out for use as flour. There are two common ways of doing this. The **wet method** involves shredding and mashing the roots in water, then allowing the starch to settle to the bottom, and pouring off the water. The advantage to this method is that the roots can be processed

One hour of harvesting cattail roots can yield quite a pile of roots and "root buds".

immediately, assuming you have a pot to work in. However, this method misses a significant amount of starch that is difficult to separate from the fibers. Also, even after settling over night, there is still a lot of fine starch suspended in the water that is lost when the water is poured off. This method requires at least an hour of labor per cup of flour. Other types of dry flour can be added to soak up the moisture if you want to bake with it right away. Under semi-primitive conditions I have processed cattail roots in a shallow gold pan. I saved the water, after settling out the starch, and used that water to cook my hot amaranth cereal. The cereal took over an hour to cook, so I kept adding more starch water. This thickened into a whitish "milk-like" substance, a nice compliment to the otherwise seedy cereal.

The **dry method** for obtaining flour involves pounding the starch out of the dry roots. Drying the roots whole can take a week or more, but you can speed up the process considerably by separating out just the starchy core. The outer layer is a spongy foam-like casing that contains no starch. Split open the root, and you can pull out just the core. Use the side of a knife to scrape the residual starch off the outer-layer. The starchy mass will dry within a few hours. Then pound the starch out between two rocks. The flour can be used on its own, except that it contains no gluten to hold it all together. It works best mixed with an equal amount of wheat flour. I was able to obtain a cup of flour per hour of processing effort this way. You might do considerably better however, since the cattails in my area seem smaller on average than in other regions of the country.

Cattail **pollen** can also be used as a source of flour. Shake the flower stalks over a can or basket, or in a bag to catch the pollen. The season is very short and easy to miss if you are not around the cattails every day. Also you need a couple calm days for the pollen to accumulate on the flower heads before you harvest; even a slight breeze will shake all the pollen loose into the water. In our area the pollen season runs from the end of June to mid July. The pollen is often mixed with other sources of flour. Optionally, the entire male flower head can also be stripped off by hand and used as meal.

The **green flower heads** are also edible, at about the same time as the pollen. They can be steamed or boiled and eaten just like "corn on the cob". These are quite delicious. The tender young shoots are edible early in the spring. Later in the summer you can pull apart the main stalks to find tender new leaves forming inside the base.

The Lily Family

If you find a plant with parallel veins in the leaves and flowers with parts in multiples of three, chances are you have a member of the Lily family. Extreme caution is advised with members of the Lily Family. Death camas (*Zygadenus*) and false hellebore (*Veratrum*) are highly poisonous members of this family. They have tight clusters of cream-colored flowers, sometimes slightly greenish-yellow.

Death Camas contains a toxic alkaloid that may be twice as potent as strychnine. Ingestion can cause vomiting, diarrhea, and death. I once read that a single bulb mistakenly harvested with blue camas would sometimes kill an entire family of Indians. Yet I have also heard that you would have to eat 50 or more of them to die from it. Clearly there needs to be a controlled study of how many bulbs it takes to kill a person, but as yet I do not know of anyone willing to participate in the study!

False Hellebore contains dangerous alkaloids that depress the nervous system, resulting in a slower heart rate and lower blood pressure.

Death Camas!

Onion, Garlic, Chives, Leeks (*Allium spp.*)

There are many species of wild onions, found in habitats ranging from swampy soils to dry deserts, with colors varying from white to red to purple. The rule is: if it looks like an onion and smells like an onion, then it is an onion! Always smell the plant if you are in doubt. Be especially careful if you have already crushed and smelled one onion; you might only be smelling your hands the next time. Wild onions are not much of a food on their own, but they make a great addition to almost any wilderness meal. They are best fresh or fresh cooked, since they do not reconstitute well once dried.

Wild Onion

I recently found a patch of several hundred thousand wild onions with white and red blossoms. I returned a few weeks later to camp nearby, but when I went to harvest the onions I was unable to locate even one. All traces of the vegetation above ground were completely gone, and random sampling of the soil failed to produce any bulbs. Now I want to return to that site when the onions are in bloom so I can spend some time observing how they could so completely vanish. My best guess is that the ground squirrels ate them all.

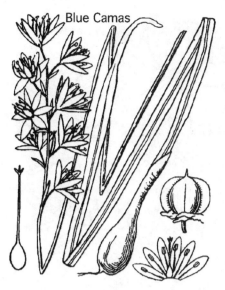
Blue Camas

Blue Camas (*Camassia spp.*)

Blue camas looks similar to death camas (*Zygadenus spp.*) before it blooms. Make sure you have the right camas. One wrong bulb in the bunch can spell disaster. Blue camas should only be gathered when in blossom. Its blue flowers easily distinguish it from death camas. Also see the picture a few pages back.

Blue camas bulbs are starchy and tasteless, varying from marble to golf-ball size and larger. I have found them growing in clumps along the creeks of south-central Idaho where you could reach down and yank up a whole meal. More often the plants grow individually along intermittent creeks or in damp meadows. Camas was a major food source for the Native Americans. It is always a thrill to me to find some. It does not grow in my area, but there are some small pockets of habitat that may support them once introduced. Raw camas is not readily digestible. Longer cooking converts the starches into more digestible forms. Native Americans often cooked them in a steam pit.

Brodiaea (*Triteleia/Brodiaea*)

Brodiaea has bell-shaped blue flowers. The cooked bulb is edible and delicious; it has a buttery texture and flavor similar to the yellow bell. The plants in my area are small and rare, but it is very common in some parts of the Great Basin Desert. I had the opportunity to dig up several cups of larger roots on an expedition in eastern Oregon... a real treat.

Sego Lily (*Calochortus spp.*)

The sego lily is rare in my area, but in some parts of the arid west can be found in abundance. The bulb is delicious roasted or boiled, similar in texture and flavor to camas.

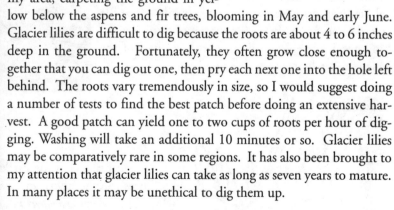
Sego Lily

Glacier Lily, Adder's Tongue, Dog-tooth Violet (*Erythronium spp.*)

Glacier lily roots are crisp and sweet. There are acres and acres of them in my area, carpeting the ground in yellow below the aspens and fir trees, blooming in May and early June. Glacier lilies are difficult to dig because the roots are about 4 to 6 inches deep in the ground. Fortunately, they often grow close enough together that you can dig out one, then pry each next one into the hole left behind. The roots vary tremendously in size, so I would suggest doing a number of tests to find the best patch before doing an extensive harvest. A good patch can yield one to two cups of roots per hour of digging. Washing will take an additional 10 minutes or so. Glacier lilies may be comparatively rare in some regions. It has also been brought to my attention that glacier lilies can take as long as seven years to mature. In many places it may be unethical to dig them up.

Glacier lily roots grow deep into the ground.

Yellowbell (*Fritillaria spp.*)

The yellowbell often grows in tough sod, but is otherwise shallow and relatively easy to dig. The roots are small, and somewhat difficult to clean, but exceptionally delicious. An hour of harvesting can be expected to yield a cup or less of the roots, which will require another 15 minutes or so of washing. The whole plant is edible, either raw or cooked. Yellowbells seldom grow in enough abundance to justify collecting a significant quantity of them. The leopard lily is even more rare.

The Parsley Family

Water Hemlock!

Plants in the Parsley Family have a flower/seed head that looks like an "umbrella" with many "spokes" coming from a central point. In botany this is called a "compound umbel" because there is a smaller "umbrella" at the end of each of those spokes. Extreme caution is advised with the Parsley Family. Water hemlock (*Cicuta spp.*) and poison hemlock (*Conium spp.*) both belong to this family. Water hemlock is the deadliest plant in North America, and people die from it nearly every year thinking they have found some kind of wild carrot. I recommend that you use my book *Botany in a Day* to master the patterns of the Parsley family before you start working with any individual species.

The Parsley Family includes mostly medicinal and spicy plants, including anise (*Pimpinella*), celery (*Apium*), chervil (*Anthriscus*), coriander (*Coriandrum*), caraway (*Carum*), dill (*Anethum*), fennel (*Foeniculum*), and parsley (*Petroselinum*). There are also a number of edible roots in the family including the carrot (*Daucus*) and parsnip (*Pastinaca*).

Yampah (*Perideridia gairdneri*)

Yampa is widespread throughout the Rocky Mountains. The roots are one of my favorite wild edibles. They are okay raw, but absolutely delicious cooked. Using a simple digging stick in dry soil I dug 1 cup of roots in one hour. The grainy soil there did not hold moisture very long. In better soils the roots can be three times as large, indicating it may be possible to dig up to 3 cups of roots per hour of work. I also like to eat small quantities of the seeds.

Biscuit Root (*Lomatium & Cymopterus spp.*)

Biscuit roots vary from a few inches to a few feet tall, with fern-like leaves of many different shapes and patterns. Some species could easily be mistaken for poisonous members of the family. All biscuit roots have starchy taproots of various sizes, but some are edible while others are highly medicinal. The medicinal biscuit roots have a strong smell, while the edible ones do not. In the Pryor Mountains of south-central Montana I was able to dig up nearly a quart of the delicious starchy roots in about an hour.

A harvest of bistort roots.

Bistort

The Buckwheat Family

Most plants of the Buckwheat Family have swollen nodes or joints, like "knees" on the stems, and usually triangular seeds. Domesticated plants include buckwheat (*Fagopyrum*), rhubarb (*Rheum*), and sorrel (*Rumex*).

Bistort (*Polygonum bistortes*)

There are many species of *Polygonum*, but as far as I know, bistort is the only one with a starchy, edible root. It is common throughout the Rocky Mountains. The raw roots are quite astringent, so they will really make your mouth pucker. But the cooked roots are delicious, with a nut-like taste. I can collect approximately 1 cup of roots per hour with a digging stick. The seeds are also edible. I sometimes snack on the whole flowers.

118

The Purslane Family

The Purslane Family consists of mostly small plants with succulent vegetation, usually growing in areas of intense sunlight. The purslane plant (*Portulaca spp.*) does not have starchy roots, but it is notable because the leaves and stems are surprisingly high in fats and carbohydrates. They can be eaten raw or cooked. The dried plants would make a good soup thickener. Purslane is rare in the north, except as a garden weed.

One hour of digging for spring beauty roots yields a modest, but delicious meal.

Spring Beauty
(*Claytonia spp.*)

Spring Beauty

The spring beauty grows in the mountains, blooming just a few weeks after the snow goes off. The white blossoms have five petals, but only two sepals, an easy way to identify the plant. The small potato-like roots are edible raw, but gourmet when cooked. In local patches I can harvest about 1 cup of roots per hour of digging. Washing the roots takes another ten minutes. The spring beauty was a favored crop of Montana Natives, and I suspect the roots are significantly bigger in some parts of the state.

Some authors suggest peeling the dark skin off, but I find that to be unnecessary. Eating the cooked spring beauty is like eating a new red potato with lots of butter on it. It is simply unbeatable. The greens are also edible and delicious raw or cooked.

Bitterroot (*Lewisia spp.*)

The bitterroot is the state flower of Montana. It is not protected by law, but be careful not to over-harvest it. The foothills behind our home have small colonies of bitterroots, usually a dozen or so plants—not enough to justify harvesting any. However, I discovered a patch of thousands of plants about 35 miles from my home. I collected over a gallon of the whole plants in a one-hour harvest in May. Trimming away the vegetation left approximately 1.5 quarts of roots. Peeling off the bitter bark took another eight hours! The peeled roots cook up nicely in a stew. They are starchy, gelatinous, and filling. However, it is important to remove all of the red bark. Even a little bit will make the whole stew bitter beyond edibility.

Bitterroot has a well-known history as one of Montana's premier native food crops, so I figured I must be missing some critical detail in my processing techniques. I've since heard that the Flathead Indians have a Bitterroot harvest every spring. They test the roots in mid April to see when the bark slips easily, then organize a harvest day for everyone who wants to be part of it. As with many wild plants, precise timing is the critical factor. You have to get the roots at exactly the right time to be able to process them efficiently.

The bitterroot is easy to dig, but removing the bitter root bark is extremely time consuming unless picked at exactly the right time.

The Aster/Sunflower Family

A sunflower looks like a simple flower, but it is really a composite of hundreds of smaller flowers, and every seed is produced by a single flower within the larger head. The burdock and dandelion also have composite flower heads made up of many small flowers, although they are otherwise quite different in appearance from a sunflower.

Burdock (*Arctium spp.*)

Burdock is often mistaken for "wild rhubarb" because of its big leaves. But the stems are never red, and the older plant produces a tall flower stalk with Velcro-like burs. Burdock is a biennial with an edible taproot. The first year it produces basal leaves and stores starch in the root. The second year it uses the starch to send up a flower stalk, set seed, and die. The root is edible during the first year, especially in June and July, and later becomes woody. It has been cultivated for food in Europe and Japan. With a primitive digging stick I dug up a quart of roots in one hour. Washing added no more than ten minutes. I cannot eat too many of the roots plain, but they are good as a side dish to a meal. The big leaves are ideal for covering a steam pit to keep dirt out of the food.

Forty min. of digging yields a decent harvest of burdock roots.

Dandelions (*Taraxacum officinale*)

Dandelions may be the most recognized plant on earth. They certainly grow everywhere, from lawns to high mountain meadows. Although there are native dandelions, the most common species is *T. officinale*, an import from the Old World. All dandelions are edible, though palatability may vary from region to region.

The cleaned, chopped and boiled roots make a pretty decent meal, and it seems to be one of the more efficient root crops to gather for a meal. The roots are rich in inulin polysaccharides, which have a tendency to sweeten the longer they are cooked. I will have to do a timed study on one of my camping trips.

Mostly I like to harvest dandelion roots out of the lawn at home for use as a coffee substitute. The roots should be washed, dried, and then slow roasted in the oven until they are dark in color and rich in aroma, but not burned. Then the roasted roots can be ground into powder in a grinder as shown here, or on a stone metate. I really enjoy the dandyroot flavor, but the main reason I drink it is to promote healthy liver function. When constipated, the dandyroot drink helps to get my system moving again. Dandelions are not necessarily laxative, but stimulating the liver facilitates better digestion as well as better health overall, so that I can better fight off the colds the kids bring home from school. I also like to eat dandelion greens. At home I frequently add a few leaves to my salads or pile them on thick on a hamburger, veggieburger or egg sandwich.

Dandelions consist of many small flowers in a single head.

Donny is grinding dry-roasted roots for a coffee substitute.

—Fruits—

The Rose Family

The Rose Family includes an astonishing number of our domestic fruits such as the strawberry (*Frageria*) apple (*Malus*), pear (*Pyrus*), quince (*Cydonia*), loquat (*Eriobotrya*), blackberries and raspberries (*Rubus*), plus cherries, plums, apricots, peaches, nectarines, and almonds (*Prunus*). There are numerous wild fruits in this family too, some of which are covered in this section.

Almost all plants in the Rose Family have oval, serrated leaves. Some species have simple leaves, while others are made up of smaller "leaflets" grouped together. The leaves always alternate along the main stem of the plant.

Many species from the Rose Family mature a fruit with the five sepals still attached to the end, as shown here with the wild rose. If you find a bush with oval, serrated leaves, and a berry with five sepals still attached to the end, then it is most likely a member of this family.

Raspberries, strawberries, and cherries have different fruit types, but also belong to the Rose Family.

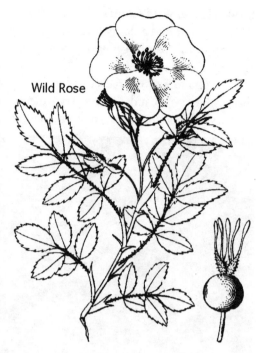

Wild Rose

One hour of picking strawberries yields about one cup of fruit.

Wild Strawberry (*Frageria spp.*)

If you can identify a domestic strawberry then you can identify a wild one too! Strawberries are often the first ripe fruit in the mountains, and the plants continue to produce through the summer.

The strawberry is one of the most delectable treats of the west, although not always the most economical food source. Usually I gather only about a cup of strawberries per hour of picking, but on rare occasions I have found patches where I could pick nearly a quart per hour. Resisting the temptation to eat them is the hardest part! Strawberries in the eastern states may be nearly tasteless.

Raspberry, Blackberry, Salmon Berry, Thimble Berry (*Rubus spp.*)

The *Rubus* genus of the Rose Family includes aggregate berries of several colors—red, black, purple, and yellow-orange, usually ripe in August and September. Various species of this group are found across most of the northern latitudes, and all of them produce edible fruits.

Blackberries are especially abundant along the Pacific Coast from California to British Columbia. They are by far the most prolific producers of this group and the most economical to harvest. Where blackberries grow in abundance they are often treated more as a weed than as a delectable berry crop. I try to stuff my face with as many as I can when I am in blackberry country.

Salmon berries are common in the Pacific Northwest, from Washington north to Alaska. Red raspberries are more common inland, throughout the Rocky Mountains. In a good patch I've been able to pick a quart of berries per hour. Thimble berries have a palm-like leaf and few fruits. They are really delicious, but there are seldom enough fruits ripe in one place and one time to bother collecting them, so I just eat them straight off the bush. The young stalks of any species can be peeled and eaten for a semi-sweet spring treat.

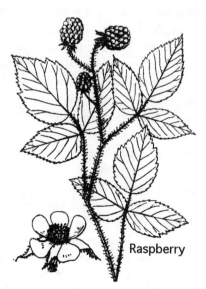

Raspberry

Chokecherry, Wild Cherry (*Prunus spp.*)

If you find a fleshy fruit with a "seam" down one side and a stony pit in the middle, it is almost certainly a member of the Prunus genus of the Rose Family, usually a wild cherry or plum. Chokecherries are the only species of this group in my area.

Grandma Josie picked at least five gallons of chokecherries every year. She boiled the juice out and made chokecherry syrup and chokecherry wine. I loved the syrup on our pancakes and I tried the wine a few times too. For survival food, however, chokecherries seemed useless, because we discarded the pulp and kept only the juice.

Mashing chokecherries on a metate stone.

But then a Crow Indian woman named Alma Snell showed me the native way of processing the fruits. She learned the old ways of her people from her grandmother who was the subject of a 1932 book by Frank B. Linderman titled *Pretty-shield: Medicine Woman of the Crows*. Alma later wrote her own book of memoirs called *Grandmother's Grandchild*, an English translation of a Crow word to signify a child raised by their grandmother and the special bond between them. I can relate to that.

Anyway, you put the fresh cherries on a metate stone and mash them up, pits and all, then dry them. The nut inside the pit has an almond-like aroma. This is no coincidence, since the almond is closely related. The combined cherry-almond aroma is wonderfully intoxicating to work with when you mash them on a rock. Like most members of this genus, cherry pits contain a form of cyanide, but the compound is ery unstable and easily destroyed by mild heat and oxygen. Mashing and drying the chokecherries renders them safe to eat. Alma Snell mixed chocolate with her mashed chokecherries to make delicious cherry chocolates.

The pit shells are crunchy, but not nearly as much a problem as you might imagine. I cook up the fresh mash and use it as a filling in "chokecherry ashcake turnovers" and the dried mash I use as trail mix. In timed studies I handpicked up to 1 gallon of cherries per hour, which takes another 40 minutes to mash with a rock. Nutrition-wise you get both the fruit and the almond-like nut, so it is a power-packed wild food.

Wild Plum (*Prunus spp.*)

Like chokecherries, the plum is a member of the *Prunus* genus, with a distinctive "seam" down one side of the fruit and a stony pit in the middle. Wild plums are prevalent across the northern latitudes where there is abundant soil moisture and long growing seasons. In some locations the semi-wild plums planted by homesteaders have naturalized across the countryside. I am most familiar with the wild plums of eastern Montana.

Compared to other wild fruits, picking wild plums is like going to the supermarket. Given a good crop, you can easily pick more plums than you can use. The plums are delicious raw and sweeter after a frost. Mashing and drying them sweetens them even more, and the natural sugars visibly crystallize in the flesh. I have not yet tried processing the nuts inside (see chokecherries).

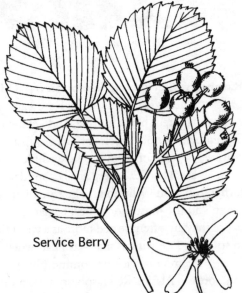

Service Berry

Service Berry (*Amelanchier spp.*)

Service berries have oval-shaped serrated leaves and pulpy purple berries with the star-like sepals still attached. Many wild berries are all juice, but service berries are both juicy and fleshy. They are one of my favorite berries, and I can eat a quart of them on site. I have to travel sixty miles to get to the nearest worthwhile patch, but in favorable conditions I can harvest 2 to 4 quarts per hour of effort. Service berries are easy to dry and store, an excellent trail food.

Hawthorn

Hawthorn (*Crataegus spp.*)

All species of hawthorn produce edible berries, black, purple, red, or yellow, and all of them are crammed full of big, hard seeds. The blue-black or purple ones are the most pulpy and delicious, whereas the red ones are more seedy and astringent. Hawthorns produce in abundance and are well worth harvesting. They are easy to dry. Hawthorn berry tea is one of my favorites.

Rose Hips (*Rosa spp.*)

The nicest thing about rose "hips" is that the red fruits stay on the bushes for most of the winter. I grew up eating them and drinking rose hip tea. The rose hip is famous for it's vitamin C content. It has a thin, fleshy skin, but that skin contains loads of vitamin C. The seeds are also very nutritious and contain a great deal of vitamin E. The most abundant species produce dry hips chock full of hairy seeds, but other species produce slightly fleshy rose hips which are really a treat.

Rose hips are quite addictive, and I can eat them all day when I am out walking. I thought the rose hip might make a decent cereal if the whole fruit were ground into a powder. Unfortunately it was not too exciting, and I concluded that the best way to eat rose hips is one at a time while walking. They also make an excellent tea. In a timed study one hour of picking yielded 3 quarts of rosehips.

Mountain Ash (*Sorbus spp.*)

The mountain ash grows sporadically through the Pacific Northwest, all the way to Alaska. It is often planted domestically here in southwest Montana. The yellow-orange berries are mealy, and initially very astringent, but much sweeter after a frost. The dense clusters of berries make harvesting really easy.

Cotoneaster (*Cotoneaster spp.*)

The cotoneaster is native to Russia, but planted domestically in northern cities across North America. I include it here because it is helpful to practice recognizing Rose Family fruits while in the city. Look for a hedgerow with small, oval leaves and pulpy, purple berries with the five sepals still attached. The edible fruits stay on the bushes through most of the winter, a good snack when you are on an "expedition" across town.

The Gooseberry Family

The gooseberry family includes only one genus of plants, *Ribes*, consisting of both gooseberries and currants. All species of currants and gooseberries are edible, although a few are extremely rank in odor and flavor. All gooseberries and currants have a palm-shaped leaf, although each has its own unique form. The semi-translucent berries usually have visible lines running from stem to the tip.

Gooseberries are sour at first, but become quickly addictive. I think they are one of the better berries for cooking, especially when you do not have any sugar. Many wild berries taste flat when cooked and require sugar to sharpen the taste, but gooseberries retain their flavor. Still, a little bit of sweetener really classes them up. Currants, especially the common translucent-orange "squaw currants" are not nearly so flavorful as gooseberries. They are best fresh or dried rather than cooked.

In my studies I've been able to pick a quart of berries per hour on good bushes. With the aid of stick and a tarp to beat the bushes I can collect 3 or more quarts per hour. Most of the berries sink in water, so it is easy to separate out the debris with a bucket and a hose.

Gooseberry/
Currant

Surprisingly, you can often find gooseberry bushes in the midst of winter still covered with half-dried berries. They are even more delicious then.

The Blueberry Family

Members of the Blueberry Family have a distinctive indentation in the end of the berry, either star-shaped or circular, where the five tiny sepals can still be seen. The leaves always alternate along the stem of the plants. All berry producing members of this family produce edible fruits, although most species of *Arctostaphylos* are astringent, due to the high tannic acid content.

Blueberry, Huckleberry, Cranberry, Bilberry, Lignonberry (*Vacciniu spp.*)

Various members of this group are common in the mountains across the northern latitudes and all produce delicious edible berries. But some are larger and more economical to harvest than others. In the Tobacco Root Mountains behind my house there are very few purple huckleberries, but lots of the small, red "wortle berries" which I call "dwarf huckleberries". These are just as tasty as the others, but much more tedious to pick. A one-hour study of handpicking produced one cup of berries. That was an exercise in both patience and abstinence! The use of a comb to strip the berries from the plants speeds up the harvesting a little, but takes some leaves with it. Fortunately, the leaves are also edible and healthy for you. We like to take the kids and go camping in other mountain ranges around the state with larger species of huckleberries that grow bigger fruits. The berries are packed with valuable anti-oxidant flavonoids, so the more you stuff you face, the healthier you will be!

One hour's harvest of dwarf huckleberries.

Blueberry/Huckleberry

Kinikinnick, Bearberry, Manzanita (*Arctostaphylos spp.*)

You might be surprised at first that the lowly kinikinnick or bearberry would belong to the same group as the robust manzanita bushes, but if you look close you will see they are large and small versions of the same kind of plant. Bearberry is abundant in the arid forests of the northern Rockies. The most common species has dry, tasteless, mealy fruits. Nevertheless, they are worth sampling when you find them. One species of bearberry has delicious, sweet berries, but it is rare. Manzanita berries are also dry and mealy, and somewhat astringent tasting.

The Honeysuckle Family

The plants of the Honeysuckle Family are mostly bushes with opposite leaves and usually pithy or hollow stems. The fruit is a fleshy berry. The remains of the sepals can be seen attached to the fruit. One characteristic found in several, but not all of the members of this family, is that the flowers and berries appear in pairs. Even the large bunches of the elderberry often consist of many individual pairs of berries.

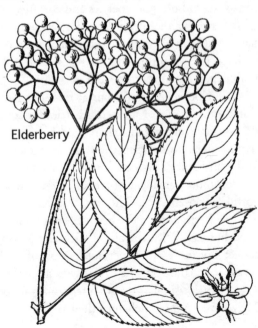

Elderberry

Elderberry (*Sambucus spp.*)

Elderberries are easy to gather in abundance. The blue or black varieties are edible. The flowers can be batter-fried. The light-blue berries are the sweetest. I like the dried berries as a trail food. The nearly black elderberries in my area are barely edible straight off the plant—but can be made palatable with sweetener. Note that the red-berried species have **toxic** berries, leaves, and stems.

The Oleaster Family

The Oleaster Faily consists of shrubs and small trees, with or without thorns. The presence of silvery hairs on the leaves gives the bushes a grayish appearance. The fruits are silver or red-orange berries.

Russian Olive, Oleaster, Silverberry (*Elaeagnus spp.*)

The Russian olive is an introduced tree. It is especially tolerant of drought and alkaline soil. It is cultivated in many areas, but often naturalized in the countryside. The silvery fruits are astringent, but edible. They can be dried and powered, and are used in bread in Arabia. Our native silverberry also produces an edible fruit.

Buffaloberry, Soopollalie, Soapberry (*Shepherdia spp.*)

Buffalo berries are found throughout the northern plains on grasslands where the ground is dry and the growing season is long, but the water table is within a few feet of the surface. The berries are sporadic, but usually abundant when you find any at all.

The fresh berries really pucker up your mouth when they first ripen in July. A hard freeze helps sweeten the berries. On a good bush I can hand-pick a quart or more of berries per hour. I've also used a stick to beat the half-dried berries onto a tarp in March. Twenty minutes of

Buffalo berries can be found clinging to the branches through the winter.

beating yielded more than a quart of berries, but it was difficult to separate the thorns and twigs. Processing would no doubt be easier in the summer when the moist berries would sink to the bottom of a bucket of water, like gooseberries.

The soopollalie or soapberry grows in northern forests. The underside of the leaves are silvery with a sprinkle of cinnamon-colored dots. The fresh berries are real face-squeezers, but better after a frost. The berries contain a large amount of saponin, and can be whipped to a froth and mixed with sugar to make "Indian Ice Cream".

The Grape Family

If you can recognize a grape, then you can identify the members of the Grape Family with their climbing vines and tendrils, plus the distinctive clusters of berries. The palmate or "palm like" leaves are alternate, forming opposite from the tendrils and flowers.

Wild Grapes (*Vitis spp.*)

Wild grapes are found over many parts of the country where soil moisture is persistent, and the growing season is long, usually near creeks or rivers. In Montana wild grapes are found in the eastern part of the state. Grapes are edible and delicious. Sometimes in winter you can find raisins still hanging from the vines. Some species of wild grape have slightly fuzzy berries.

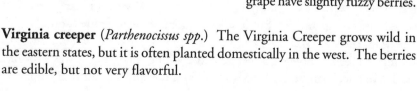

Wild Grapes

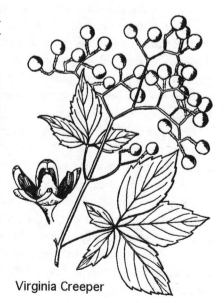

Virginia Creeper

Virginia creeper (*Parthenocissus spp.*) The Virginia Creeper grows wild in the eastern states, but it is often planted domestically in the west. The berries are edible, but not very flavorful.

—Seeds—

The Plantain Family

The Plantain Faily is a group of small plants with deep, straight veins in the leaves, and small greenish flowers on a short stalk. The seeds form in small capsules along the flower stalk. The common plantain is the easiest to recognize. Once you know it then the narrow-leafed plantains will be easy to identify too.

Plantain (*Plantago spp.*)

Plantain seeds are highly mucilaginous so they swell up like slimy, translucent fish eggs when cooked, but they are quite nutritious and worthwhile, if you can find them in abundance. I seldom find plantain in any great abundance, except for in lawns. I did a one hour seed study in Grandma Josie's yard. I stripped the standing seed stalks with two fingers, catching the seed capsules in my hand, and collecting them in a bag. One hour of picking yielded 1.5 quarts of rough material. I spent 20 minutes winnowing out the chaff for a final yield of 1.75 cups. A better way to harvest them might be to cut and collect the whole stalks, then to rub them between the palms to loosen the seeds. Then winnow out the chaff. The leaves are delicious batter fried.

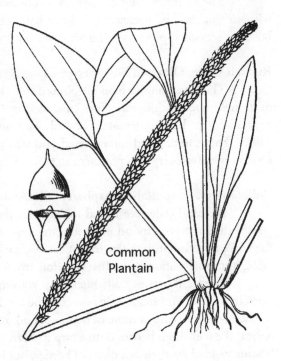

Common Plantain

The Aster/Sunflower Family

A sunflower looks like a simple flower, but it is really a composite of hundreds of smaller flowers, and every seed is produced by a single flower within the larger head.

Sunflower (*Helianthus annuus*)

Wild sunflowers inhabit disturbed soils. They often grow about fifty sunflower heads per plant, each loaded with little seeds. Early botanists brought this sunflower back to Europe and then to Russia, where it was convinced to develop a single big head with large seeds like the ones we buy at the store today.

Wild sunflowers are just as edible as the domestic varieties and very rich in oil and protein, but the seeds are much smaller. Nevertheless, when you find one sunflower you are likely to find quite a few, so this is potentially a very good food source. The challenging part is to process the seeds efficiently.

Ideally you want to harvest sunflower seeds when the heads have dried enough to release the seeds. The problem is that the seeds drop before you can get there to harvest them. Look at a mostly dry sunflower head and you will see that some of the seeds are stuck in place while others have already fallen. In a big enough patch you could beat the loosest seeds out of the heads into a basket, gathering only a few seeds per head until you had enough. Smaller patches have an abundance of seeds, but not enough loose ones to harvest with a beater.

pistil (female)

stamens (male)

petals

pappus (sepals)

ovary (seed)

Each seed is produced by a single tiny flower within the flowerhead.

I've tried working with both green and dried heads and have yet to find an efficient way to extract the seeds. My preferred method is to cut the green heads after the petals have fallen. I rub the flower parts off and peel away the green bracts around the head. Then I rub the seeds out into my goldpan and winnow out the trash. The flower heads are very resinous, so it is important to clean out most of the debris. The process works, but the yield is only about half a cup per hour of processing. I've also tried rubbing seeds out of the cut and dried flowerheads with my fingers or on a rock, with similar yields. I'm sure there is some secret to harvest these seeds in mass quantities, but it will take some time to figure it out.

After removing the seeds from the head, there are still the shells to contend with, and they are too small to crack open one-at-a-time. I've tried grinding the seeds whole on a metate and cooking them, but it was a lot like eating wood chips, so my preferred method is to chew handfulls of seeds whole and raw and spit out the pulp.

The Grass Family

All of our cereal grains belong to the Grass Family, including wheat (*Triticum*), rice (*Oryza*), wild rice (*Zizania*), corn (*Zea*), oats (*Avena*), barley (*Hordeum*), millet (*Echinochloa*), and rye (*Secale*). The seeds of virtually all other grasses are also considered edible—if they are not infected with the ergot fungus. A notable exception is rye grass (*Lolium*), which is used as a sedative and vasodilator. It is considered poisonous in excess.

Although most grass seeds are edible, they are not all necessarily economical. Some seeds are too small, or otherwise difficult to process into a useable product. Very small seeds can be difficult to digest. They can be too small to grind on a metate, and too small to swell and turn to mush when cooked as a hot cereal. The best grasses to work with are those with big seeds, much heavier than the surrounding chaff. This makes it easier to blow the chaff away, while keeping the seeds.

There are three main techniques of harvesting cereal grains with crude implements. One method is to simply strip the whole seed heads by hand, collecting the material in a container. Another method of harvesting is to beat the seed heads with a stick, while catching the seeds in a pan or tarp. The third method is to cut the whole stalks, place them on a tarp, and then beat the seeds out. The plants can be dried on the tarp to make the seeds drop easier.

The next step in the process is to break the seeds free from the chaff. Rubbing the rough material between the palms is sufficient for most grains. Some seeds, however, are encased in a husk that is impossible to rub free of the grain. These seeds are ground up husk and all, for a high-fiber cereal. Also, a few grass seeds can be parched and then rubbed to remove the husk. Grasses that are hairy or sharp should be avoided, as they could cause irritation or injury to the throat.

Winnowing is the next step, to remove the chaff once it is broken free of the seeds. Winnowing is a little like gold panning, where you catch the weighty metal and wash the lighter debris away. In fact, I recommend using a gold pan for this process. Swirling the pan, and occasionally tossing the grain lightly in the air, brings the light chaff to the surface, so it can be blown away.

Another commonly used method is to toss the rubbed material in the air, such that the seeds will fall straight down on a tarp, and a light breeze will carry the chaff away beyond the tarp. I have not had good results with this method, so I prefer the gold-pan/blowing technique, where I can precisely control the flow of wind. In either case you will not be able to completely clean out the chaff. There is always some left. That is okay. It is good roughage for the digestive system.

Rye Grass
(Lolium)

About the Ergot Fungus

Be sure to inspect the seeds of all grasses for the presence of ergot fungus (*Claviceps purpurea or C. paspali*). Ergot consumes the grass seeds, forming a black or purplish powder. Ergot can stimulate uterine contractions and cause abortions. A derivative of ergot is used as a medicine for migraine and cluster headaches. Ergot is also a source of LSD.

Ergot contamination in cereal grains can be extremely dangerous. *C. paspali* effects the nervous system, causing trembling, staggering and paranoia. The witch hunts of Salem, Massachusetts in the 1600's are believed to have been a result of ergot contamination in stored grains. Many people were burned at the stake by the Puritans running around on LSD. *C. pupurea*, on the other hand, restricts the blood flow to the extremities, slowly killing the flesh on the fingers, toes, and ears, with long-term consumption. Gangrene bacteria, similar to botulism, rots away the dead tissues, often forming a foul gas. A religious order was formed to deal with this disease; the medics torched the rotting flesh off the victims and prayed they lived. They group adopted St. Anthony as their patron saint, and the disease came to be known as St. Anthony's Fire. In 1916 Federal Government regulations restricted the use or ergot-infested grain to .3% of weight for making flour. This virtually ended the disease of ergotism in this country.

Harvested grains without ergot can be cooked whole as a hot cereal, or ground into flour and used for bread or mush. Cooking them whole may reduce the labor involved, but the grains must be cooked almost to mush or they will pass through your system undigested. The very small seeds may not ever soften enough to become digestible. Another alternative is to sprout the seeds. This makes the material digestible, although it also converts much of the starch and oil content into proteins. Some wild grasses that have a known history of use as cereal grains include wheatgrass (*Agropyron*), Bentgrass (*Agrostis*), Sloughgrass (*Beckmannia*), Bromegrass (*Bromus*), Deschampsia, Crabgrass (*Digitaria*), Barnyard Grass and Millet (*Echinochloa*), Wild Rye (*Elymus*), Fescue (*Festuca*), Mannagrass (*Glyceria*), Barley and Foxtail Barley (*Hordeum*), Rice Grass (*Oryzopsis*), Switch Grass (*Panicum*), Bluegrass (*Poa*), Bristlegrass or Foxtail (*Setaria*), and Wild Rice (*Zizania*). Note that only one or two species from each of the genera above are likely to be worthwhile candidates for harvesting. My experience with harvesting seeds has been limited to the following:

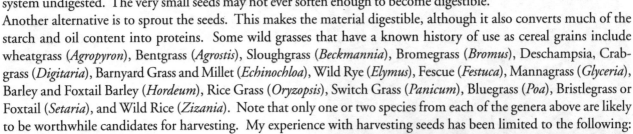

Timothy Grass (*Phleum spp.*)

Timothy grass is not native, but it is so prolific in the wilds that you would never know it is new here. Strip the seeds off by hand, or collect the whole stalks and rub or beat the seeds out. Timothy grass seeds are easy to winnow, and really a quite beautiful grain. I hand-stripped the seeds for my studies and came up with about 1 quart of rough yield. Twenty minutes of winnowing work left me with a little over a cup of pure seed. The seeds can be boiled and eaten as a hot cereal.

Reed Canary Grass (*Phalaris spp.*)

The reed canary grass grows tall along many rivers (different from the true reed grass). In a one-

I put the seed heads on a tarp and beat the seeds out with a stick.

hour study I cut a whole garbage bag full of seed heads. I brought them home and spread them on a tarp to dry then beat the seeds out with a stick for about 15 minutes. After separating the stems out I had about two gallons of seed and chaff. Another forty minutes of careful winnowing gave a final yield of about three quarts of good grass seed.

Grasses can also be eaten as **greens**, except that you only swallow the juice and spit the fiber out. Chewing on the tender grasses, and particularly the immature seed heads, is an excellent way to get a healthful and sustaining dose of vitamins and minerals. Just graze on the tender grasses as you walk through the woods. Please note, however, that a few grasses produce cyanide compounds as they *wilt*. This may be an evolutionary strategy to ward off foraging animals when the plants are already stressed from heat or drought.

The Amaranth Family

The amaranths or pigweeds are widespread in the northern latitudes. The plants are annual weeds with alternate leaves and typically red stems. If you have ever weeded a garden then you have probably met a member of this group. Just watch for the weedy plants with red stems that develop poky seed clusters around the upright stalks. Rub the seed cluster between your palms and blow away the chaff and you will see the shiny black seeds, often with red and pale seeds mixed in.

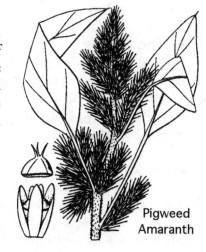

Pigweed Amaranth

Pigweed, Amaranth (*Amaranthus spp.*)

A species of *Amaranthus* was once grown extensively as a crop by the Aztec Indians of Mexico. It has been making a comeback in recent years, and you can now buy amaranth seed or products made with the flour at most health food stores. Our wild amaranths are most often found in weedy lots and farm fields. They are just as good as the commercial variety.

Amaranths are prickly, so it is impractical to try hand-stripping them. I cut the whole plants and place them on a tarp, then beat the seeds out with a stick. The plants have to be dried before they release all their seeds. An hour of picking, fifteen minutes of beating, and a half hour of winnowing yields close to a gallon of the seeds at the peak of the season.

Amaranth seeds can be boiled into a nutritious hot cereal. The seeds are small and hard enough to be difficult to digest, so cook them for at least an hour to make them swell and split. Parching or sprouting the seeds prior to cooking may make the final product easier to digest. The seeds can be parched by placing a gold pan on the coals and stirring the seeds.

The Goosefoot Family

The Goosefoot Family is a large group of plants that includes beets, chard, and spinach. Many, but not all of the wild species have edible leaves and seeds. But the most worthwhile members of this family certainly belong to the Goosefoot genus. The Latin "Chenopodium" also means goosefoot; the name comes from the shape of the leaves.

Goosefoot

Goosefoot, Lamb's Quarters, Strawberry Goosefoot (*Chenopodium spp.*)

Archaeologists have discovered that the Paleo Indians were consuming large quantities of goosefoot seeds in southwest Montana 9,400 years ago. The Indians used the slimleaf goosefoot, which has an incredibly bitter seed. I finally threw out my harvest of slimleaf goosefoot seeds; it was just too over-powering for me.

The common goosefoot, or "lamb's quarters" is naturalized here from Europe and commonly found in gardens. Goosefoot is edible as a salad or potherb. It is rich in calcium and vitamin A. The seeds are easy to gather and highly nutritious.

Most seed crops need to be winnowed to separate the seeds from the chaff because the chaff is indigestible cellulose. Not so with the goosefoot. The plant is quite edible and delicious, and the chaff that comes off with the seeds is just dried plant—extra nutrition for you. You can rub the seeds between your palms to separate the chaff if you want to winnow it out for a more refined product, but is not necessary. One hour of hand-stripping the seeds from the dead stalks in September yielded slightly over a gallon of unprocessed seeds.

Another Chenopodium, sometimes called strawberry goosefoot, is unique from the other species because it develops a bright red berry around its seeds. They are bland and uninteresting compared to other berries, but easy to gather and highly nutritious, like getting a fruit and a grain together. I gathered 3 1/2 quarts of berries in one hour.

Chenopodium ambrosioides grows frther south. It is important to mention because it is a known anthlementic, containing an oil used to kill intestinal parasites. The plant is edible, but excessive use of the seeds could be poisonous.

—Nuts—

The Pine Family

The Pine Family includes fir and balsam fir (*Abies*), larch or tamarack (*Larix*), spruce (*Picea*), Douglas fir (*Pseudotsuga*), the hemlock tree (*Tsuga*), and of course, the pines (*Pinus*). The pines have 2-5 needles in clusters. The larch has 15-40 needles in whorls. All other members of the family have solitary needles. All members of the family produce edible nuts or seeds, but only a few of the pines are readily processable. I have also harvested a limited quantity of Douglas fir seeds.

The Pines (*Pinus spp.*)

Many people are familiar with the pinion pine nut from the southwest as a gourmet food, but the nuts from other pines are equally delicious and nutritious! All pine nuts are edible, but many species are impractical to harvest. The whitebark (*P. albicaulis*) and limber pines (*P. flexillis*) have a known history of use. The nuts from these trees are only about half the size of the pinion nuts, but there are still dozens of nuts in a single cone, and dozens or hundreds of cones on a single tree, and thousands of trees! Other pines around the country have certainly been used as well, you just have to get out and try the different trees to find which ones are most practical to harvest.

Lash a short stick to the end of a longer stick to make a hook then use the hook to pull cones down from the trees. The cones may need to be dried more

Cracking pine nuts with the gentle touch of a stone.

to open them up; this can be done by placing them in a warm, sunny spot, or by placing them in a pit that has been warmed with a fire. Be sure to scrape out all the hot coals before placing the cones in the pit.

In the foothills we've been able to gather the green cones of the **limber pine** as early as July. The cones can be opened with the aid of heat from the fire, and pulled apart by hand. It is a pitchy, messy job, but highly nutritious. I have not yet figured out what happens to the nuts later in the season, but they sure vanish.

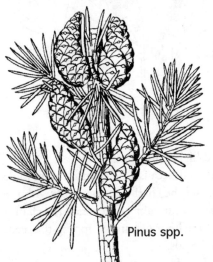

Pinus spp.

The **whitebark pine** grows high in the mountains, mostly above 8,000' elevation here in southwest Montana. The green or dried cones can be harvested throughout September and into October, but the size of the crop varies tremendously from year to year. In a good year you will find lots of pine nuts and lots of bears. The ground is littered with bear piles, each containing the remains of hundreds of pine nuts.

Sometimes you can find squirrel caches with a little searching, usually in hollow logs or tucked in rock crevasses. One good squirrel cache can provide a couple dozen cones and enough pine nuts for one to two hearty meals. Cones from squirrel caches are usually more ripe and open, and sometimes a little rotted, but the nuts are often still good inside. These cones are easy to peel apart to release the seeds. Any stubborn cones can be warmed by the fire to make them open up. I like to collect a few cones and pick out the nuts while I walk, giving me pure pine nut power to get over the mountains.

Pine nuts are good raw, but gourmet when roasted. I roast the nuts in my gold pan over the fire, stirring constantly. Roasting makes the shells more brittle. The thicker shells of the pinion nuts can be gently cracked with a stone after roasting and winnowed out. The shells of the whitebark pine are thinner, however, and the cracking/winnowing process is less fruitful. I've been able to remove a significant portion of the shells, but far from all of them. Nevertheless, the thin shells are readily edible and add good roughage to the diet, so I usually eat them whole, just like the bears. Pine nuts are undoubtedly the richest wild food I've ever eaten.

—Mushrooms—

I learned just a handful of mushrooms as a child. On walks with Grandma Josie, we mostly collected and studied wildflowers, but she would never pass up fresh meadow mushrooms (*Agaricus campestris*) when we found them. Once or twice each year we collected and ate fairy ring mushrooms (*Marasmius oreades*) from the lawn. We also collected the inky cap or shaggy mane (*Coprinus spp.*), which usually dissolved into black ink in a bag in the refrigerator before we ever got around to eating them. Sometimes we ate the western giant puffball (*Calvatia booniana*). Grandma once used the spore mass from a dried puffball to promote clotting on a horse's wound. Her favorite was the morel mushroom (*Morchella esculenta*), and she loved to go morel hunting in the spring, but I usually missed that adventure since I was in school. We occasionally ate tree mushrooms, also known as oyster mushrooms (*Pleurotus ostreatus*), which could be found growing on dead cottonwood trees about the same time the morels were popping up in the soil below. I've learned a few more edible mushrooms since then, and it is always a delight to find them and add them to a meal, either at home or on the trail. A few mushrooms like morels and king boletes are so good that I often plan my camping trips around the mushrooms, to try and be in the right place at the right time for some gourmet eating.

The inky cap usually grows in manure. These two sprouted on the edge of a cow pie.

From a survival standpoint you will often hear that mushrooms are mostly water. While that is true, what is leftover is mostly protein, and mushrooms often grow in such abundance that you could easily eat a lot of them. Mushrooms are also rich in B vitamins and several minerals, including potassium, phosphorus, sodium, iron and calcium. I just like to harvest mushrooms because they taste so incredibly good. Well, some of them any way.

Like plants, most mushrooms are harmless and some are definitely edible, but you only need to ingest one highly poisonous one to kill you. Therefore, positive identification is essential before you sample any wild mushroom. There are a dozen or more highly edible, easily recognizable mushrooms that occur over large parts of North America. For most practical purposes, that is all you will ever need to become a gourmet chef. Included here are some of my favorites. Be sure to use a dedicated mushroom guide for more thorough identification.

Tree mushrooms grow in great abundance on dead cottonwood trees.

Tree Mushrooms (*Pleurotus ostreatus*)

Tree mushrooms are usually the very first mushrooms out in the spring here in the northern latitudes. They are most often found growing on the wood of dead cottonwood trees, but sometimes on willows, alders and oaks. There are several varieties that look somewhat different, but all are light-colored shelf-like fungi (white, light gray or lightly tanned) with white gills.

Tree mushroom season starts before the morel mushrooms and usually out-lives the morel season. We don't normally go hunting for tree mushrooms. Instead we go looking for the more elusive morel mushrooms, but always come home with a few tree mushrooms as well. The less morels we find, the more tree mushrooms we harvest as our consolation prize. In other words, they are a good mushroom, just not as good as morels. The young mushrooms are best. Later they become tough and rubbery. I like to chop the mushrooms into small pieces and fry them in oil, or better yet, stir-fry a blend of tree mushrooms, greens and meat.

Morel Mushrooms (*Morchella esculenta*)

Morel mushrooms live in the soil and help to decay organic matter. They look a lot like a sponge. In mid-May on a warm day after a good rain, that is the time to go hunting morel mushrooms among the cottonwood groves that follow the rivers here in southwestern Montana. Unfortunately, we are often short of either rain or warmth in May, so sometimes I do more hunting than gathering. The season starts earlier in warmer parts of the country. One thing I've learned about morels is that it is difficult to predict where they will pop up each year. A rich patch often yields nothing the following year. Morels also grow among aspens or in conifer forests, especially after a fire. Thousands of mushroom pickers flood into Montana to pick morels the first spring after a big forest fire.

The elusive morel mushroom.

Morels were always Grandma Josie's favorite mushroom. It was kind of a family obsession for a long time, and my aunts and uncles and great aunts and Grandma all went morel hunting together. Grandma soaked the morels in salt water to scare out the bugs then simply sliced and fried them in a little oil and served them as a delicious side dish to any meal. I like to camp among the cottonwoods early in spring just to take advantage of this great wild food.

Giant puffballs are easy to find!

Giant Puffball (*Calvatia booniana*)

Puffball mushrooms have no gills or noticeable stems. A young puffball is solid white inside, but it turns yellow and then olive-brown as it ages, eventually turning into a mass of brown powdery spores. They are most often found in mid summer among sagebrush rangelands before the soil moisture dries up.

I always like to find dried puffballs and squeeze out a puff of brown "smoke". Grandma Josie once used the dried powder to help stop the bleeding on a wounded horse.

The giant puffball mushroom is truly amazing, especially because it can grow so incredibly large. I often find puffballs larger than a basketball, and I've heard of some locally weighing more than 80 lbs. Of course they are only good when they are small. It is not my favorite mushroom, but it is often very abundant, and I like to cut it up into my stews when I am camping.

King Bolete (*Boletus edulis*)

My friend Jack Fee introduced me to the king bolete on an expedition, and my life has never been the same since! The king is often very abundant in moist soil under spruce trees in mid summer. The one pictured here has a very small top, which matures into a large cap that looks just like a hamburger bun. Instead of gills it has thousands of little yellow tubes beneath the cap, called "polypores". A king bolete can grow to twelve inches across, but they are always full of worms by then. The younger ones are definitely better, although I don't mind eating worms now and then.

To prepare the mushrooms you can cut away the polypores, slice the mushroom, and fry it. It has a wonderful, meaty taste. The polypores are also edible, but cook up kind of slimy, so it is better to trim them off. I once found king boletes sprouting up everywhere at a reunion for Renee's side of the family. I cooked up a large mess for anyone brave enough to try wild mushrooms. Nobody died (although some expected to), and the treat actually went over quite well.

A delicious king bolete. My favorite!

ANIMALS

The mid-afternoon sun is gradually descending across the sky. A small creek gurgles its way down a gully, spilling over the rocks and through the mosses, rolling and frolicking in the hands of gravity. Brook saxifrage and arrowleaf groundsel perch quietly along the waters edge, seeming to listen to the music. A chickadee calls from the trees. Upstream a buck mule deer is grazing. It stops and looks around.

I still my movements and watch him for a few minutes. He lowers his head to graze and I move into a stalk. The pine needles are dry and crunchy, and I lightly prance from rock to rock. I step in cattle tracks where the needles are already packed down, making it possible to stalk quietly. I keep a loose and fluid motion, moving in quick spurts as the buck deer grazes. I move short distances and then stand motionless. The buck grazes then lifts his head and surveys the forest. He returns to his grazing and slowly moves through the trees. I follow him in short, quiet prances and then stand motionless according to his pattern of grazing and watching.

Deer see in black and white and use unfocused, **peripheral vision** to scan the landscape for movements that may indicate danger. A person needs very little camouflage to stalk them. Dull colored plaid clothes or fringe help to break up the silhouette of the human form, and by keeping the arms close to the body a person can easily pass as tree trunk or fence post. Deer do not notice that some posts get closer and closer every time they look up. As the deer graze, their eyes are focused on the ground in front of them and one can make quiet a bit of movement without them noticing.

The buck moves slowly, but it is still a challenge for me to keep up with him. I take my time to patiently stalk, and I wait for the safe moments to move. The buck walks down to and then crosses the small but loudly gurgling creek. I know that his big, furry ears collect only the loud music of the water as he crosses the creek; I take advantage of the moment to move more quickly and carelessly, knowing that my own noises will not be heard. The buck meanders away from the stream and I resume my quiet, careful, patient stalking, slowly getting ever closer.

It is all right to make some **noise** in stalking. Noise arises all over in the woods and it does not alarm the animals unless it becomes an audible pattern of footfalls. I create a certain amount of noise, even when careful, but by stopping and starting frequently I avoid creating a definite pattern.

The buck moves behind some trees and passes around the bend of the hill, out of sight. I move quickly to catch up while I have the opportunity. I follow a trail just slightly higher than that of the animal. My trail crosses the top of a boulder protruding from the hill. From there I look out through the forest to see the buck deer. He is gone. Somehow he must have heard me, smelled me, or something. He must have bounded quickly away. My stalk is over and I step out to the edge of the boulder to find a seat, to think about what went wrong.

My abrupt movement towards the edge of the rock creates a flurry of motion. The deer had lain down at the base of the rock a few feet below me, and now he leaped to his feet and sprinted out fifty feet away, then turned back look at me. I sit on the granite boulder and watch him. He watches me. He cautiously walks back and forth looking at me. He takes a few quick bites and nervously jerks his head up again and watches me. He moves away and then comes back. His antlers are beautiful and velvet. He watches me and I watch him. We spend ten minutes together, existing with a tenuous trust between us. At last both of my legs fall asleep from sitting motionless on the rock. I must move. I wish to the deer that he will go away so I do not have to scare him. Moments later he moves away, still grazing and still watching me, and he disappears around the hill.

Sneak Stalking and Trust Stalking

Most of the time when I stalk I start out with "**sneak stalking**". After I have been detected I switch to "**trust stalking**". Trust stalking is a technique where you do not try to hide from the animal you are stalking. You let the animal know you are there. You show that you are non-threatening. In trust stalking you do not want to be so motionless that the animal becomes suspicious, nor do you want to move so much that you scare it.

I learned about trust stalking while in high school from a psychologist/outdoorsman named Fred Donaldson. He did much of his work with captive wolves and coyotes. The caretaker of the animals had a very "dominant" relationship with them, but Donaldson took the time to build trust with them as an "equal". He spent a great deal of time outside the pens just being there before moving inside. With time he was able to play with them as if he was one of them. He also used the technique with deer and elk and at least once he spent an afternoon in a meadow building trust with a bear.

Donaldson spoke of two zones of trust with the animals. There is a certain level of trust required to get "in range" and another level of trust required to have "an experience" with the animal. In a place like Yellowstone National Park the animals are used to having people nearby, so it is easy to close the first gap, but more difficult to build trust to close the second gap. The opposite is true outside of the park. It is difficult to get within range of the animals, but once there it is easier to build trust and have a close encounter.

I went trust stalking with Donaldson once in Yellowstone Park. On the first encounter a bull elk grazed up right in front of him, stopped and scratched behind it's ear with a hoof, then grazed on-ward. I was fifteen or twenty feet behind him. It was clearly a very different experience than that of a tourist getting close to an animal.

Since then I have continued trust stalking, mostly after I my attempts at "sneak stalking" have been foiled. I stand still at first then gradually add motions, so I do not startle the animal (usually deer). I start with blinking, then add slight head twists, then more head twists, and slight body twists, eventually moving my arms and legs, but always in a slow, relaxed motion. After a period of time I can I take a step or two, then stop again to look around. The animal you are stalking will decide how close it lets you get to it, depending on how much it trusts you and how much it wants the relationship. I do not stare, but usually act somewhat impartial and neutral to the situation. It is a real gift when an animal trusts you enough to come towards you. One of my most memorable stalking experiences was not with deer, but with wild turkeys, as I wrote in my journal:

In trust stalking you let the animal know you are there. I often graze on the grass and bushes, to show that I am completely non-threatening.

"A band of seven turkeys foraged through a small stand of cottonwoods, bobbing their heads up and down as they walked and crossed an open field to a thicket of willows. I put my pack down and took off my boots, then stalked quietly around the far side of the willows. I heard their gentle cackling back and forth, stalked closer, then stood still. The turkeys came single file out of the ditch, through the brush, and appeared fifteen feet from me. One stopped to look at me for a moment and then the whole band continued on its way to the next thicket of buffalo berries.

"I knew nothing about stalking turkeys. How difficult to stalk were they? Did they favor sight, sound, or smell? Did they see in color or black and white? I followed the band past the thicket, but they kept on moving. I saw a small porcupine in the open field, slowly yet determinedly going somewhere. The turkeys entered another section of the irrigation ditch on a direct course toward the porcupine. I wanted to see the encounter, to get a sense of how these animals would react to each other, but the moment was hidden from view as I used the cover of bushes to conceal my movement. The porcupine must have been surrounded by the turkeys for a moment, but apparently they had little interest in each other.

"The turkeys were fast movers. I stopped to watch the porcupine. I've often encountered them in the middle of fields, sometimes in day and sometimes at night, never quite sure what they were doing out there. I stood a few feet away and watched as this one steadily grazed the first short, green grasses of spring. I feared that I had lost the turkeys, but soon enough

they reappeared from a stand of willows and again marched across the open field toward another thicket. I stepped away from the porcupine and my ankle popped, alerting my bristly friend. I stood still. The porcupine rose up on its hind legs peering out with its dim senses, detected nothing, and returned to grazing. I tip-toed away to follow the turkeys.

"I followed the birds for hours. They darted quickly across the open fields back into the thickets, and I quickly trotted after them each time they disappeared from sight. Gradually I discerned a pattern, that they always seemed to turn to the right, as we worked our way back around in one big circle. Finally I anticipated their next move and arrived right at the end of a berry thicket just as the birds appeared. They grazed to within ten feet of me, stopped to check me out and then went on about their business, pecking and walking away.

"I was seriously out of shape for stalking. My legs quivered constantly, and I was glad for the slight, but steady breeze. It is relatively easy to stalk when everything else is waving back and forth too. The turkeys moved on to yet another thicket and the race was on again. It was kind of like playing tag. I had to follow when they were not watching, anticipate their movements and arrive at the far side of a thicket before they did. Each time I got a little closer.

"It seemed that my stalking became sloppier and sloppier as the game progressed, yet I kept gaining more ground, getting ever closer to the birds. I started with sneak stalking, but it seemed that it had turned into trust stalking along the way. It was as if I stalked into their subconscious minds. I was there behind every bush, a little different in appearance from everything else they knew and always slightly quivering, but apparently harmless. By late afternoon I had almost become part of the band. I know they must have heard me or seen me walking along with them, but they did not seem to mind. They entered one thicket a short distance ahead of me and flushed out a whitetail deer, then looped back around, coming to within five feet of where I stood under a cottonwood tree."

I think trust stalking usually works best when you pretend you are grazing. You can graze standing up if there are bushes at your height. Otherwise it is often better to get down on all four's to graze. For the most part you should ignore the animal you are stalking. You can try grazing slowly towards it, but you risk breaking the trust that way. Watch them closely (without looking directly at them) and you will be able to tell if they think you are moving too fast for them.

On one occasion I trust stalked to within ten feet of a young adult bull moose. I was pretend grazing, but kept getting sucked into the act so that I was really grazing—and believe me cottonwood branches and buds taste awful!

When trust stalking, it is also good to send caring thoughts to the creature you are stalking. Renee describes trust stalking this way:

"When I see a cottontail and it sees me, we talk. I usually talk to the animal, but not out loud. I tell it I will not harm it, that I respect it, and most importantly, I radiate love toward the cottontail. It's not really necessary to transmit anything else than the basic love that you feel toward the animal. The communication takes place when I am able to radiate love from every part of me and the little animal sends trust or understanding or love back. When this happens the physical gap is crossed and the little cottontail and I are together with this world. The really neat thing is that you can trust stalk a person, even a stranger, in the same way."

For me, both sneak stalking and trust stalking become a sort of **meditation**. I usually start out quickly as I move toward an area where I want to stalk. As I approach a stalking site I gradually slow down. I move slower and slower and spend time standing still, observing, listening and tuning in with my senses. By the time I reach an area where I expect to see game I am spending more time standing still than moving. I hold my hands clasped together in front of me and maintain centered, balanced posture and walking. I feel my internal tempo slowing down with the pace of my movements and I feel very attuned to the land by the time I am in position to wait for the deer to come. I usually stalk in the early morning or late evening and pick a spot where deer are likely to pass through as they come out to graze or head back to their day beds.

I should emphasize that there is a potential risk in trust stalking wild animals. Moose, elk, bear, and yes, even deer could seriously injure or kill you if you broke trust with them up close. The risk is yours to take, but I encourage you to always err on the side of caution.

Stalking close to animals is also controversial. Many people believe it is just plain wrong to interfere with the animals' lives this way. I believe this kind of connection to the wild animals is essential however, because it increases our awareness of the animals and their needs, so we can become better advocates to protect their habitat.

◊　◊◊◊　◊

I wait until the velvet antlered buck disappears out of site. I stand up and work the circulation back into my legs. Then I start walking, and I think as I walk. For a long time it has been a dream of mine that one day I would bring my bow and arrows with me when I went out to stalk the deer. I built a powerful sinew-backed juniper bow and a set of arrows for the hunt. I only need to practice and learn to use them. I walk onward out of the tree line and back into a meadow of grass and sage.

A cow in the distance lets out a loud bellow. It stirs up the other stock, and several of them start a chorus of mooing. I strip a few leaves of sagebrush, crush them in my hand and savor the rich smell. The ground below the sage is covered by a mat of dry moss, waiting for the next rain so it can grow again. The grainy, sandy soil is exposed in places and the grass is thin and widely spaced around the sagebrush. Over the years I have learned to read the meaning of these spaces between the plants.

Lush spring growth masks the truth that the ground is mostly barren below.

I have said that you can learn a lot about the **ecosystem** through the process of learning by using. At the same time, there is much in nature that goes unnoticed unless someone helps us see it. For example, many well-intentioned people have misconceptions about how the environment works. You may hear people say that cattle are destroying the West, and that we need to remove all livestock from public lands. What they do not realize is that hoofed animals are a critical link in dryland ecosystems. The problem with cattle on public lands is not that they are there, but how they are managed. By mimicking the prehistoric patterns of grazing animals on western rangelands, it is possible to put *more* cattle on the land while greatly invigorating the native flora.

People often think of ecosystems in overly simplistic terms. For example, it is a commonsense but erroneous assumption that people and animals always degrade the vegetative environment, and that only rest repairs that damage. I am reminded of an informal study on the effects of livestock on a replanted conifer forest. By logic it was assumed that cattle would trample and kill the freshly planted trees, but to find out for sure the logging company agreed to a test with the rancher who owned the cattle. Cattle grazed a section of the replanted area and were fenced out of another section. By the end of the season, the cattle had indeed killed 20% of the newly planted trees, but in the spring another story emerged. The grass in the ungrazed plot provided cover for mice, which girdled and killed 80% of the trees planted there. Contrary to expectations, the trees were more likely to survive with the cattle than without them.

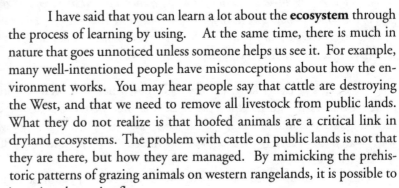

Returning to the present, the sagebrush, moss and soil, I start on my way. I remember now that all ecosystems lay somewhere on a scale between being **brittle** or **nonbrittle environments**. The distinction between one and the other is not so much a measure of the quantity of moisture received, but of how that moisture is distributed across time and geographic space. A region receiving 50 inches of moisture distributed evenly throughout the growing season would be very nonbrittle. However, an area receiving 50 inches of moisture—but all in one month—would be extremely brittle. Also, a region may have listed averages of annual precipitation, but in any given year the actual precipitation may be much higher or lower than the aver-

Desert soils without significant hoofed animal impact become light and puffy from repeated cycles of freezing and thawing. The wind blows right through the soil, robbing it of moisture before new seedlings can establish.

age, thus increasing the brittleness. In the Kalahari Desert of southern Africa, home to the !Kung people, the total amount of precipitation can vary as much as 500% from year to year. Even if the region receives its average annual precipitation, the moisture may still be unevenly distributed across local geographic space.

Brittleness is also determined by how the land reacts to stimuli such as fire, animal grazing, or no grazing. Brittle and non-brittle environments can react differently to these factors.

The area around Pony varies from mostly nonbrittle along streams and some north facing slopes to semi-brittle or brittle in the flat fields to mostly brittle on south facing slopes. Our summers are usually dry, but peppered with sporadic and unpredictable thunderstorms. There is about 17 inches of average annual precipitation in the town of Pony.

The south slopes receive as much moisture as the adjacent north slopes, but the south facing slopes dry out even in the middle of winter, while the north-facing slopes accumulate moisture in the snow pack. In the spring the snow melts and saturates the soil. Indirect sunlight slows down evaporation and allows the north slopes to retain moisture longer into the growing season. The moisture fuels both plant growth and biological decay.

With the leaves of sage in hand I walk, or wander and add to my bouquet of smells. I pick needles from the Douglas fir and clip the top from a horsemint plant. I savor the smells and rub the plants on my arms, neck, and face. The processes of the ecosystem fascinate me, and I often study these processes on my excursions and think about them as I walk.

It seems that the **plants**, **herbivores**, and **predators** of the earth all co-evolved in a way which was mutually beneficial. They evolved to maximize the total use of the flow of energy from the sun and the cycling of water and minerals. In brittle environments like the Great Plains, co-evolution has facilitated almost magical symbiotic relationships between plants, herbivores and predators.

The grasses developed their growing points low on their leaves to be protected from the grazing animals, and yet the grasses were dependent on the trampling hooves of the animals to break down the old dead stems and leaves so that light could reach the low growing points of the new growth. The hooves of the bison broke down the sagebrush and other plants to allow more grass to grow. The presence of wolves and other predators kept the bison in tight herds, focusing the impact of the hooves. The dead vegetation formed organic litter on the ground to help retain moisture for plant growth. Gradually the debris rotted and returned the nutrients to the soil for more growth.

Soils without hoofed **animal impact**, wild or domestic, can become inhospitable to plants in brittle environments. Raindrops strike the bare soil and pulverize the granules. Upon drying, the fine particles of silt, sand and clay form a hard surface crust, which restricts air, water and new seedlings. Another problem can be caused by the cycles of freezing and thawing, plus wetting and drying, which can cause the top inch or so of the soil to become so porous and fluffy that seeds dry out before they can germinate. The hooves of the bison broke up the crust and packed down the fluffy soil, improving its ability to supply water and minerals to the germinating seeds. Their

hooves and urine killed invading mosses and opened space for grass seedlings. The wolves and other predators kept the herds of bison focused and agitated. The effect of the predators caused the bison to trample and pound the earth as they stampeded away to other regions.

The **stampeding** bison left behind a swath of destruction and trampled vegetation and dung, all of which helped to retain moisture and enhance growth. The moving bison left the prairie to recover without further interference, allowing for lush and unrestrained growth. Thus, the flourishing grasses supported the bison, which supported the predators that herded the bison which ultimately encouraged the grasses to flourish.

Disruption of that natural symbiotic relationship causes a cascading deterioration in the environ-

Silently, the top soil that sustains us blows away. Here sand dunes form at the edge of an Idaho farm field.

ment. The elimination of the predator and the fencing of the brittle prairie led to changes in the movements of grazing stock. This change ultimately led to fewer grasses and deterioration of the land. Herds now spread out and graze over wide areas; they no longer trample down the brush and so the brush spreads. Herds no longer trample down the dead grasses and so the new grasses die at the base as light no longer reaches their growing points. Old vegetation stands for years as it slowly decomposes through oxidation and weathering. Nutrients are locked up in the old growth and are unavailable for the new growth. Succulent growing seedlings are eaten again and again as grazing stock returns to the same areas without giving the plants time to recover. The ground develops a hard cap without a large trampling herd to break it up. Seeds cannot grow through the capped surface. Bare patches develop between the plants. Weeds and grasshoppers thrive in the open patches. Moisture is lost as runoff. It runs off and causes floods, and because the water does not enter the water table, the springs dry up and then the creeks dry up when the rains stop. In very brittle environments the effects can be almost beyond imagination.

Much of the Sahara Desert once supported lush grasslands and flowing springs. The holy lands once supported Mediterranean forest, streams, and farmland. Greece, which is today known for being rocky and open was also once forested. In the American southwest the Anasazi Indians abandoned their established dwellings more than eight hundred years ago, apparently because deforestation and **desertification** caused by their society disrupted the landscape's ability to retain water, causing cycles of "floods and droughts". This apparently resulted in the subsequent collapse of their agriculture and their society. The area around Salt Lake City is dominated by sagebrush today, but was reported as having grass "belly high to a horse" before it was settled. All around the world the pace of desertification continues unabated. According to *Newsweek* magazine 40% of North America's cropland and rangelands have turned to desert. In a moderate place like Pony the desertification goes unnoticed by most, but already we have lost inches of soil off the hills due to poor grazing practices.

I pause for a moment along my way and bury my nose in a wild rose blossom. Then I eat the petals. There is not much substance to them, but just the same, it is kind of fun to eat flowers. A small patch of stonecrop grows nearby. It is a short, succulent plant with yellow flowers. It grows only a few inches tall, sparsely colonizing the bare, grainy soil where little else will grow. I pick a sample and eat that too.

From where I stand near the tree line, where the sage gives way to Douglas firs and lodgepole pines, I can see open patches on the distant hills, places that had been opened by clear-cut logging. These clear-cuts are more than just a place where trees have been cut down. They are symbols that speak of the never-ending controversies that surround land and resource management.

There are some who would say that we should not manage the ecosystem at all. To some people the idea of **managing the ecosystem** is blasphemous, like playing God. But truly, it is impossible to not manage the ecosystem. Every action we take, with or without planning, is a management decision. Even primitive hunter-gatherer societies "managed" the ecosystem, albeit usually without a plan, as they torched forests and grasslands to drive out game. In previous times the impact of that type of "management decision" could often be absorbed by ecosystem. Today, with six billion people in the world, everything we do has definite consequences in the environment. The fact that management has been carried out without plans or without informed plans is the reason that humankind has caused the defoliation, deforestation and desertification of more than half of the planet since preBiblical times.

Due to humanity's past ineptitudes at stewardship, the Center for Holistic Management in Albuquerque, New Mexico, was formed to help people to better manage natural resources. The **Holistic Management** process begins with a comprehensive three-part goal. The first part is a Quality of Life goal, where you define what you value in life, what is really important to you. Next is the Production goal where you describe in general terms what you want to produce to support your quality of life. The third part is a Landscape Description Goal where you first gain an understanding of how the ecosystem works and then you describe, as a goal, how the ecosystem must function to be able to support on a sustainable, indefinite basis, the level of production you need for maintaining your defined quality of life. You can then work towards the three-part goal by using an in-depth understanding of the ecosystem and the elements that shape it.

In most cases people use the Holistic Management process to manage for greater productivity, ultimately tightening plant cover and healing the land.   However, the goals process could theoretically require land that is managed for desertification and low productivity. Weeds, bare land, blowing sand and eroded gullies are—in a sense—just as natural as the lush grasslands or forest that could also potentially grow in the same location; it is simply a different level of succession.

For example, the Great Basin Desert of Utah, Nevada, and southern Idaho is dominated by sagebrush with open, barren ground in between the brush. By managing the land differently, using cows to mimic the movements of the plains bison, the Great Basin could literally be turned from gray to yellow. Grass could fill in the spaces between the sagebrush and herds of stock could dominate much of the desert, but this may not always be desirable. As it is, wild onions dominate much of the open space between the sagebrush. Wild onions thrive in poor conditions, and a management shift that favored grasses could lead to a significant decrease in the wild onions. If endless acres of wild onions were essential to your goals then you would continue to manage for desertification, erosion, and drought.

I developed a theory while in high school that the means towards improving our environment and boosting the economy were one and the same. I searched for ideas that passed my litmus test for being socially acceptable, financially attractive, and environmentally sound. Holistic Management passed my test the first time I heard of it. The Holistic Management process typically helps to heal the land while also increasing people's prosperity. Holistic Management is used mostly on ranches, and ranchers use it to increase the plant productivity on their land. This translates into much higher stock densities and hence a greater level of prosperity.

The Center for Holistic Management has been in existence only since the mid 1980's, but already holistic thought is expanding throughout the human ecosystem. There are a scattering of holistically operated ranches throughout the west. Some of the terminology from Holistic Management is showing up in Forest Service literature, and Holistic Management classes are being introduced at many universities.

The cows quiet down once again and I walk onward, carrying my bouquet of smells. Thoughts of hunting return to mind. Modern hunting is too easy.

People, even kids, can purchase some artillery and suddenly they become the "all powerful masters" of the woods. I remember in junior high and high-school listening to other kids tell their tales of glory about how they pulled a trigger and blew some creature or another to oblivion.

Primitive hunting is more humbling, and the time spent preparing for the hunt, making the equipment, and learning to use it encourages a more sensitive hunting ethic. Primitive hunting has a whole different mood and appeal than modern hunting. It is most often typified by the primitive bow and arrow.

To make a traditional bow, one would spend a great deal of time selecting the wood, seasoning it, and shaping it into its final form. One would start by selecting a bow stave, or several, from the best available local woods, such as serviceberry, chokecherry, maple, or juniper. Days or weeks might be spent searching for just the right piece. Next, the selected wood would be seasoned for a year or more in a cool place where it can dry slowly without splitting. At last, one would then make the bow, and if it is to be a well-done bow—complete with sinew backing—the process could be spread over several weeks. All in all, while this process helps to make a good bow, it is a long time to wait if you are hungry!

Primitive hunting techniques require that you hone your skills and awareness.

In the long run, if you have a serious interest in primitive archery you will likely want to research and make a good quality, long-lasting bow, perhaps through some of the books listed in the resource section in the back of this book. In the interim, while you are waiting for your good bow staves to season, you can make and use a "quickie bow". A quickie bow is simply a bow that does not take long to make. The method I use takes only a few hours spread out over three or four days, based on a technique developed by Jim Riggs of Oregon. In developing the method Jim once said that he had to "break all the rules" of traditional bow-making.

The Quickie Bow

Willow, or any other reasonably straight green wood can be used for quick bows. The wood is shaped fresh off the bush, and after being mounted on a rack to recurve the tips, it is baked in the direct sun for a few days to dry the wood. This sun baking often leaves the bow with scores of splits, or checks, running the entire length of the bow. But despite the appearance, these lengthwise splits seldom hurt the bow, and so the bow can be made and ready to use in only a few days.

The quickie bow could be useful in a survival type situation. But for most people, the primary usefulness of the quickie bow is as a medium to practice both bow-making and archery techniques while waiting for the really good bow stave to season. By practicing your bow-making and archery techniques with quick bows you will have a better idea of what you are doing when it comes time to cut into that special stave that is being seasoned to make a long-term bow.

You can use your body as a vice to hold the bow while you work on it.

To make a quickie bow, start by **selecting a bow stave** of green wood that is about three to four feet long, reasonably straight, free of major knots, and roughly an inch and a quarter in diameter at the handgrip, give or take a little bit. Check it from every direction and sight along it before you cut it. Check it completely because it is a shame to cut down a live branch or a tree only to find that it is not as good as you first thought. A branch with one curve over the length of the potential bow is okay; avoid those with more than one curve, and especially those with curves in differing directions. Use a saw or a knife to cut the stave and cut all the way through the wood. Do not cut part way through and attempt to break the rest off, as it will split the end of the bow stave.

No matter how straight your stave is it will still have a natural bow to it, meaning that it will bend more easily one way than another. You need to find and work with the natural bow of the wood. A stronger bow can be made by working against the natural bend, but bows made this way often twist around to bend the "right" way when a string is put on them. To **find the natural bend**, simply hold both ends of the stave and bow the middle with your knee. The bow will turn and settle into the proper position.

Next **mark the center** of the bow. Use a piece of string to measure the length. Fold the string in half to find the midpoint. Mark the center with a pencil line, charcoal, or by cutting into the bark at the sides of the bow.

As you **shape your bow** you will be removing material from the "belly side" only. The belly is the side that is towards you as you shoot; the side away from you is the "back" of the bow. Avoid cutting into the growth rings on the backside of the bow. If a growth ring is severed on the back the bow can flex unevenly to both sides of the cut, and therefore break it at that spot.

Shape the bow so that it **tapers evenly** from the center, including the handhold, all the way out the limbs. The bow should flex evenly across its entire length if you hold it with two hands and bend the center with your knee. If one section bends easier than the rest then you need to shave everything else to match it.

A drawknife is much easier to use than a standard knife and you can improvise by merely stabbing a sheath knife into a block of wood. The block of wood forms the second handle. The ideal tool to have for holding the bow while you work is a "shaving horse". It is a vice oper-

A shaving horse is a simple foot-operated vice that makes bow-working a snap.

ated by foot pressure. I consider the shaving horse a necessity for working finer bows, but for quickie bows you can get by using any of a dozen or more postures that enable you to serve as a human vice while still having your hands free to use the drawknife.

Work slowly, take your time, frequently **sight along the bow** to see that you are shaping it straight, and periodically flex it carefully and lightly to test it. For approximation, your finished bow will be half or less its original thickness at the handgrip, decreasing more as it tapers to the tips. Ultimately, it will depend on your sense of feel to determine when it bows just right. At any time in the process you can remove the bark, being careful to peel it off; avoid cutting into the back of the bow.

The next step, when you are satisfied with the feel of your bow, is to **recurve the tips** to give the bow greater power. This is easily done while the wood is green and supple. First tie the bow securely at its center, with the belly-side up, to a pole or two-by-four. Then wedge sticks under the limbs of each side to the point where you want the curve. Force the limbs down over these sticks and tie them securely in place. Do this carefully because the bow does not have much strength to bend in this direction. Lengthwise cracks are usually okay. Widthwise cracks are often fatal, but can be salvaged if the crack is only at the surface. Go ahead and let the bow dry on the rack. Put it in the sun and let it bake for a few days.

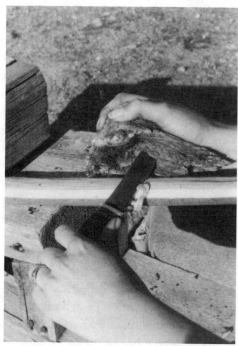

A sheath knife stabbed into a block of wood becomes a simple drawknife with two handles.

When the bow is thoroughly **dry**, remove it from the frame and it will hold the recurved position. If there is a horizontal crack across the bow shave it down beyond the crack, and shape the rest of the bow to match so the bow will once again flex evenly.

You are now ready to **notch** your bow and string your bow. I make the notches about one inch from both ends, and I cut a little ways into each side of the bow. Do not notch across the backside; this will weaken the bow.

For a **bowstring** you can use conventional nylon string, or you can make a cordage bowstring from plant fibers, sinew, or rawhide. My bowstrings are all rawhide, either braided or corded.

Tie the bowstring securely at one end of the bow and make a non-closing loop at the other end, which can be slipped on and off the bow at will. String your bow and test it carefully. Fine tune it as necessary until it feels balanced and ready to shoot. Then you need an arrow.

The green wood quick bow is tied securely to a stout pole, then blocks of wood are wedged under the limbs to recurve the bow.

◊   ◊ ◊ ◊   ◊

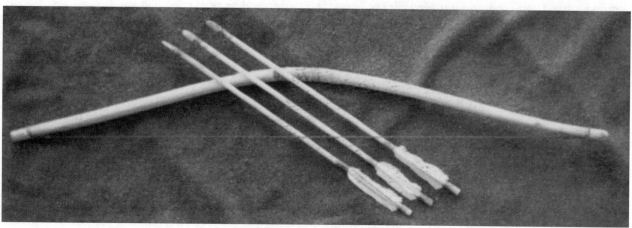

A finished quickie bow with arrows.

I walk, gradually winding my way in a big circle back towards camp. A squirrel sees me, scampers up a lodgepole pine and screams to the world of my presence. I cross through a barb wire fence and pass by an old mining claim and the remains of a cabin. A bottle lay shattered and spread out over the ground. It is, or was, an antique bottle and time has altered the chemistry of the glass turning it blue. I pick out the heavy bottle bottom, and with a rock I break away the protruding fragments that used to be the walls of the bottle. I grind down the sharp edges of the glass, leave the rock, and carry the bottle bottom with me. Later I will turn it into an arrow point.

Arrow points can be made from many materials, including stone, bone and metal. Southwest Montana has many quarries where native peoples mined for the flint or chert rocks that formed in sedimentary formations. These materials can be made into very durable arrow points. Obsidian, which is igneous natural glass, was also used widely in the area since there are sources in and around nearby Yellowstone Park. Bottle bottoms work equally well for arrow points, and the materials are more evenly spread throughout the ecosystem, both in urban and remote areas.

The process of making arrow points from flint, chert, obsidian, bottles, and other glassy stone is called "flintknapping". **Flintknapping** is a very popular form of art among those practicing primitive skills. I call it "art" because the primary objective for many flintknappers is to simply master the art of producing good quality points. Producing points for hunting may be one reason for people to practice knapping, but it is not the reason that drives many people to expend hundreds of hours mastering the techniques of producing fine-quality points. It is relatively easy to create a shard of glass or stone that can be used to kill. One can do this with minimal knowledge of flintknapping, just by breaking and shattering glassy rocks, and picking through the pieces. At the same time it is helpful to know some knapping techniques so that you have some control over the process. Then you can make the finished products uniform for mounting on arrows. There are many good publications and experts to learn flintknapping techniques from, and as you learn them it is important to ask yourself what your objectives are. I say this because there is a certain pressure at times that if you are going to get involved with flintknapping, then you have to learn to do it "right". There is nothing wrong with flintknapping for art; it is just wise to ask yourself what it is that you want from it.

Learning a skill from someone is largely a matter of copying what they do. Most flintknappers have extensive and heavy tool kits that sometimes weigh as much or more than the total amount of gear I have on this

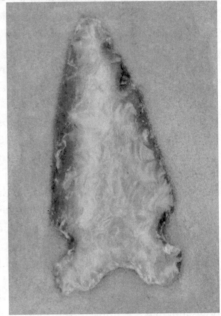

A glass bottle arrowhead.

trip. My own goal is to continue developing "scout-like" abilities, to be able to travel light, with a minimum of gear. A traditional flintknapping kit is just too much to carry. It is also unnecessary. One of the most satisfying and productive flintknapping sessions I have ever had involved the most minimal of tools. I sat in an old mining dump using a square nail wrapped in a leather pad for a knapping tool, and knapped away at the antique bottle bottoms scattered around in the dump. My friend, Jack Fee, who was with me at the time, used an old rubber boot sole for a pad on his hand. You really do not need a lot of fancy tools to do good work.

At present, the stone and glass points I make are mostly for practice. I save each of them for future use, and seldom mount them on my arrows. My reasoning is simple. Stone or glass points often break in the first couple shots. It is difficult to become an expert archer if you have to spend one or two hours or more doing repairs after every half-hour of shooting. For this reason, I use **bone points** on my arrows. They are more resilient than stone or glass. Bone points are also very easy to make. Even without and special tools or knowledge, you can make a quality bone point in only fifteen or twenty minutes.

For small game it is not necessary to have anything more than a sharpened shaft for a point, so one can do fine without stone, bone, or metal points. For big game, stone or metal points are the most effective, although stone points are not legal in some states. Stone can be even more effective at killing big game because the points often shatter inside the animal against its bones. When the animal moves it literally shreds itself to death as the fragments are jostled around. When I am ready for the deer hunt I will use either stone or steel points on my arrows. In the interim I use the bone points since they are weighted similarly to the stone points but do not shatter as easily.

Abrading a bone point.

Bone Arrowheads

I use deer or elk leg bones for my arrowheads, but other bones should work equally well. Try to select bone material that is approximately the thickness of the finished point to minimize your work. You can break out useable blanks to work with in a couple ways. One method is to simply crush a bone with a rock and see if there are useable splinters. A better way, using leg bones, is to first cut off the "knobs" at both ends of the bone and then split the bone with a knife. Use a knife that can take some abuse so you do not hurt your good knife. You may cut the knobs off the bone very easily with a saw, or almost as easily by merely abrading through the bone on the corner of a sharp rock. A big weighty rock works best for this step so you can lean into it as you abrade through the bone. With the knobs off, place your knife where you want to split it and whack the back of the knife with a heavy stick.

A bone fragment that is about the size of the finished point will suffice, but I prefer to break out long pieces so that I have a handle attached to the point as I make it. This helps me to avoid abrading my fingers as I grind the point into shape.

To shape an arrow point, start by **abrading** the bone flat. Do this on a rock with a grainy surface. Slightly grainy concrete like a sidewalk can be ideal for this. There are many naturally occurring rocks that have similar texture. Again, it works best to abrade on a rock that will not move while you lean into your work. Abrade the point flat and to the proper thickness. Abrade the tip to a point and grind the edges into a blade. Do not make it too sharp though, as the sharp points are more susceptible to damage in use. Next, use the corner of a sharp rock to abrade notches into the sides of the point. Then abrade a line across the bone surface, and snap the point off from the "handle". Last, just abrade the butt end at the break to smooth it out, and you have a ready point.

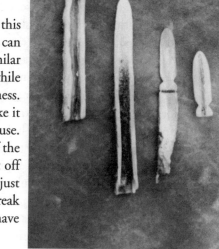

The steps in shaping a bone point.

◊   ◊◊◊   ◊

Robin Hood?

With bottle bottom in hand I take a few moments to explore the ruins of the old cabin. Several chipmunks live around the cabin, as they do around many abandoned man-made structures here. In the corner there are rusty stove parts, too far gone to be of use to anyone. I take a few moments to trust stalk with the chipmunks. One of them is harvesting something from the seemingly barren yellowish-orange soil of the mine site. I stand still and in a few minutes it comes within inches of my feet as though I do not exist. I feel a sense of warmth from the short encounter and when it leaves, I leave also, and continue with my thoughts on bows and arrows.

Like the quickie bow, good quality finished arrows can also be made from green wood in about three days. If one starts bows and arrows together then all can be ready to use at the same time.

143

Making Arrows

Arrows can be made from about any wood which is reasonably straight, at least 3/8 inch in **diameter** and preferably lightweight. Most of my arrows are willow, although they tend to warp out of shape easily. I have heard that other woods stay a little truer.

Left to right: steel, stone, bone points.

The arrows should be roughly half the **length** of the bow they are made for. I have two sets of arrows: 22 inch arrows for my shorter bows and 30 inch arrows for my long bow. To begin with, cut the shafts at least six inches or so longer than you need. Cut the shafts green and make about a dozen arrows at a time. It is okay if the wood is bowed as long as there are no sharp kinks in it.

Next **strip the bark off**. This is easily done using a knife held at a 90° angle to the wood. Place the shaft on your thigh, hold the blade still across the shaft, and pull the shaft towards you. It is a rapid means for peeling or shaving any small pieces of wood.

Peel the shafts, and then begin the **straightening** process. The green wood has moisture in it, which makes it more supple for this step. Heat the shaft, sight down it and firmly flex it with your hands to straighten it. I prefer to do this at home where I can evenly heat the arrows on top of our antique cookstove. Arrows can also be heated over the campfire if you are careful not to scorch the wood. According to Richard Jamison in *Primitive Outdoor Skills*, arrows can easily be straightened by rubbing them over a hot rock, which has been removed from the fire. Avoid flexing the arrows so far that you kink them. Kinks in the fibers are not repairable.

Straighten each arrow as best as you can, then set them aside. The wood will retain some moisture so the arrows will warp out of shape again. Straighten them once each day for three days. By the third day the arrows will be nearly dry, and they will retain their shape fairly well.

After the first round of straightening you can begin **sizing the arrows** to make them all of uniform diameter. To do this first drill a 3/8 or 5/16 inch hole through an antler, bone, or piece of wood. This serves as a sizing guide. Slide it onto the small end of the arrow to see how far it goes along the shaft. Shave the rest of the shaft until you can slide the sizer all the way up to within a quarter or half inch from the large end. This end is the "nock" where you hold the arrow against the string and pull it back. Having the wood flare out at this point makes it easy to hold onto the arrow as you draw the bow.

The sizing of the arrow shaft is a real critical step. The arrow must be flexible to perform properly. *A limber arrow functions like a spring.* Upon release the arrow flexes and stores energy, and then releases it in flight. An arrow that is too stiff is like launching a board; it is too stiff in flight.

Once the arrows are properly sized they can be sanded. **Sanding** the shafts makes them beautiful and sleek and it seems to help straighten them. Conventional sand paper can be used. Alternately, two blocks of sandstone can be used. Hold them together and pull the arrow back and forth through them to sand the shafts. This will wear a groove in the stones so that they fit the arrow more closely. When the stones gum up with wood take and rub them together for a fresh surface. I prefer to use "**sand leather**", which is like sand paper except that the sand is glued to leather instead of paper. Take cheap scraps of leather, pour a thin layer of hide glue on it, and cover it with fine sand. When the sand wears off simply add more glue and sand. Make a quantity of sand leather when you make it because the surface wears off quickly. The preparation of hide glue is covered later in this chapter.

By now, your shafts should look almost professional, as if you are making progress towards an actual product. The next step is to **notch** the smaller end of the shafts to receive a stone, bone, glass, wood, or steel point. A simple trick helps in making these notches quickly and cleanly. First, determine the finished length of your arrows and mark all of them at that point. Then draw an outline of the notch on the shaft as it will appear when finished. This serves as a guide so you can better visualize the notch you are working on. The outline will look like a mortise and tenon joint. You want to pull that "joint" apart, so that the notch, the "mortise" is clean and ready to receive the point. To do this, first cut across the shaft in the places shown in the photo to separate the wood fibers. Then, with the tip of your knife, make incisions along your lengthwise lines to help separate the wood at the joint. Flex the "tenon" piece, the scrap, back and forth in each direction to aid in breaking the bond. Then carefully snap it out. The notch can be touched up by carefully removing any remaining material with a blade or file. Practice this with scrap sticks until you are proficient at it.

When the shafts are straight, dry, sized, sanded, and notched you are ready to put the **points** on. There will be slight variations between the points and the notches so match them together for the best fits. You may have to abrade either the point or the shaft for a better fit. One at a time, dip the notched shaft and the point into warm hide glue then put them together. Dip fine sinew fibers in the glue and wrap these around the point to secure it to the shaft. There is no need to tie a knot; the sinew will shrink and dry hard around the point and shaft.

The next step is to **fletch** the arrows. I use peacock or chicken feathers for this. To cleanly and easily strip fletchings from the feathers first hold the quill in your teeth. Hold the tip of the feather with one hand and with the other start near the tip and carefully lift the vane away from the quill and work down the feather. With practice this will yield the vein attached to a thin strip of the quill, which will make a sleek fit against the shaft. On each arrow, use only fletchings that bow the same way. For example, to fletch one arrow use three feathers from one wing, and strip the same vane off each of those feathers.

That done, trim each fletching to an equal length, then cut the vane away from the quill strip for about 3/4 of an inch at each end of the fletching where the sinews will bind them to the shaft. Also trim the vane down on each so the arrows will cut through the air better. Now, moisten a sinew in your mouth while you arrange the fletchings to the desired positions on the arrow. Hold them in place at their forward end and wrap them tight with a sinew. Once you have the fletchings anchored where you want them, dip other sinews in hide glue and wrap these around the same area to securely fasten the base of the feather. Set it aside for the glue to firm up while you do the others.

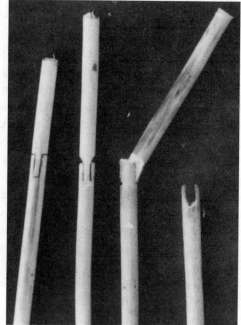

Notching the tip of the arrow to receive a point. Outline the notch with a pen for clarification. Cut into the shaft across the wood fibers. Next, with the tip of your knife, make incisions along the vertical lines to help separate the wood at the joint. Flex the the scrap piece back and forth in each direction to aid in breaking the bond. Then carefully snap it out.

When you return to your work, moisten a sinew in your mouth and this time wrap the tips in place on the shaft. Using a fine stick or toothpick, brush glue onto the length of the quill strip on each fletching to glue them on the shaft. The tips will stick out under the one sinew. Pull these to tighten the fletchings against the shaft. Wrap the tip end securely in place with sinews dipped in hide glue. Let your arrows dry.

Finally, make the **nock** in the tail of the arrow using either a file or a very sharp blade with careful hand, or saw a nock on the corner of a sharp rock. Align the nock with the fletchings so that, when released from the bow, two of the feathers will glide cleanly past the bow, and the third feather will be directly perpendicular from the bow. This way none of the feathers will catch on the bow when the arrow is released.

This done, you are ready to put your craftsmanship to practice. The English style of archery is to hold the bow vertical while using the tips of the index and middle fingers to pull the arrow back the cheek where it is sighted and released. The Native American style is different; the bow is held level or diagonally at chest or stomach level, and is drawn using the thumb and index finger. It is aimed and released by feel. Sometimes the arrow is held still and the bow is pushed forward to draw and release it.

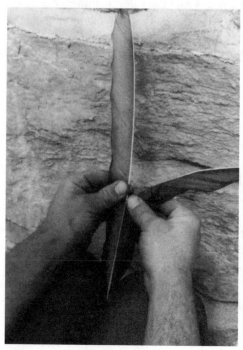

Splitting a feather.

◊   ◊◊◊   ◊

All About Hide Glue

Animal skins consist of a network of gluey collagen protein fibers. As a raw skin dries, the gluey fibers set up and the hide becomes stiff as a board, just like the dog chew toys sold at stores. To tan or soften a hide you have to counteract the glue by lubricating the fibers (with lecithin from brains—more on that in the next chapter), and by pulling the hide to keep the fibers moving so they cannot glue together. If you want to extract the glue from the hide then you simply simmer the hide to dissolve it.

A) Cut-up scraps of rawhide. B) Dried hide glue. C) Powdered hide glue.

I usually use scraps and trimmings left over from the hide-tanning process to make glue, but you do not have to go through all the work of scraping and stretching a hide if all you want is glue. You can effortlessly dehair a hide for making glue by leaving the hide in a creek or a bucket of non-chlorinated water for several days until the hair slips off easily with a push of your hands. Then you can simmer the hide for glue. Note that a smoked hide will not produce hide glue. Glue can also be made from animal tendons, hooves, cartilage, membranes, horns and antlers, and even fish skins, but I've only worked with hide scraps since I always seem to have a supply on hand.

I usually make hide glue in a coffee can on the wood stove. I put a large handful of hide scraps in a full can of water and cook it all day. It cooks down first into a thin, light brown glue and becomes thicker and darker the longer it boils. You can make the glue thicker by simmering the water away or by adding more hide scraps. Avoid boiling the glue pot, as that may weaken the glue. I'm sure I've boiled many batches and I've never had a problem with it, but for the best quality hide glue it might be best to keep the heat down low. The pieces of hide slowly dissolve in the hot water, but there are usually residual bits of hide to pull out or strain off later.

Hide glue is quite aromatic. It is not the kind of smell that most people will tolerate in the house. I don't mind the smell, but I cannot get away with it for more than two or three days before Renee wants to throw it and me out the door. Members of your household may be less tolerant, so plan on cooking your hide glue outside over a campfire, propane stove, or ideally a solar cooker that would keep it simmering while the sun is shining.

Hide glue is a lot like Elmer's glue except that it is dark and it is a lot stickier. Properly made hide glue is reportedly stronger than five-minute epoxy, and I believe it. If a sinew-backed bow breaks apart, the sinew-backing seldom peels off of the bow. More often, it is the wood that fails, and the leftover scraps remain firmly glued in place. (Fortunately, sinew-backed bows seldom break apart.)

Hide glue has to be used warm. The simmering process extracts both gelatin and glue from the hide so your pot of glue sets up like Jello™ when it cools to room temperature. (If you have ever wondered where Jello™ came from, well, now you know!) At the other end of the scale, glue that is too hot will cook the sinews or hide you want to use it on, so keep the glue warm as you work, but cool enough that you can keep your fingers in it.

You can keep hide glue indefinitely, but you must dry it, freeze it, or keep simmering it. A pot of hide glue will rot in a few days at room temperature, and it is nasty smelling stuff when it goes bad. To keep the glue from rotting, I leave the pot on the stove every day until I am sure I am done with it for a while. I add water to keep it from cooking dry on the stove. But I let it dry out when I want to store it.

To dry the glue I set the can up on a trivet to keep it from burning on the bottom. Then I let the water simmer away until the glue is really thick. Next, I pour the glue into a flat, flexible pan and let it completely dry out. Dry it over a good heat source so it will dry before it rots. Remove the glue by flexing the pan to break the chunks of dried glue out of it. These dry chunks of glue can be stored indefinitely. An alternate way to dry the glue is to let it jell, then cut it up into glue-flavored Jello™ cubes. Thread the cubes on a string and hang them up to dry. The dried glue is easy to carry on camping trips. To reconstitute the glue, simply crush it into powder with a hammerstone and dissolve it in a pot of hot water.

◊   ◊◊◊   ◊

Sinew Preparation

Sinews are fine thread-like fibers from tendons. You can use tendons from any animal, but I use tendons from deer and elk, which are very plentiful in the fall and winter during and immediately after hunting season.

There are thick, round tendons along each of the animal's legs, below the joints that lay persons might call the "knees". There are also thin, wide tendons, which can be found along both sides of the backbone, called "backstrap sinews". The round leg tendons require more work to process into sinew fibers, and the fibers are shorter, but they are readily available. To get a supply of leg tendons, I simply stop by the wild game processing plants in the fall and rummage through their "inedibles" barrels. The barrels usually contain all kinds of goodies, and I often come home with legs for tendons, heads for brains (for tanning), and sometimes I also find antelope hides for tanning. I prefer to pick up bigger legs, like elk and moose, since the tendons are longer, but I always come home with a stack of deer legs too.

Left to right: dried tendon, pounded tendon, separated fibers.

To remove the leg tendons, start by skinning the legs. You will find tendons on the front and back of each leg. Cut them loose at each end with a sharp knife. Some of the tendons will be pretty clean as is, but others will have a sheath around them that should be removed. The sheath looks and feels similar to the tendon, but it has cartilage that does not work well for sinew fibers. The sheath can be difficult to remove, but a pair or two of pliers makes the job easier. Use the pliers to peel back the sheath to unveil the tendon inside.

Backstrap sinews can be removed immediately after skinning an animal. There is a thin layer of fat and meat along the back bone over the backstrap meat. Peel back this layer and you will see a silvery band running along each side of the backbone. Slide a dull knife under these sinews, then tilt the blade up and scrape from underneath to remove the meat and fat, as pictured in the section on butchering later in this chapter. Work all along the length of the sinews, lifting and scraping them. Cut and remove the backstrap sinews when you have as much length as you can get; that should be about sixteen inches for a deer, and up to two feet for an elk.

Dry the back sinews or leg tendons in a warm place, but not in the sun. I usually dry them in the house near the wood stove. Once dry, the tendons are ready to process into individual sinew fibers. Processing backstrap sinews is easy. Simply use the thumb and index finger of each hand to hold the tendon at two points close together then twist the fibers around to separate them. Work the entire length of the backstraps this way.

Leg tendons require a bit more work, quite a bit more, in fact. Start by pounding the tendons with either a wood mallet or a very smooth stone on a wood surface such as a log or stump. Do not use a rough stone, because it will cut the fibers. Pound the tendons thoroughly, from one end to the other to loosen the fibers. Then pull them apart into individual fibers with your fingers. This step may take an hour or two per tendon. The fibers can be split down again and again, to finer and finer threads. I usually work them down until they feel "cottony", without hard spots in them. Once separated into individual fibers, the sinews are ready to use. The long, coarse backstrap sinews are excellent for sewing. I prefer to use the finer leg sinews for most other purposes, including attaching points and fletchings. I have also used leg sinews for sinew-backing my bows.

Sinew-backing a bow is the primitive equivalent of a fiberglass-reinforced wood bow. Like the fiberglass fibers, sinew fibers reinforce the wood to keep it from breaking and to increase it's power. I used over twenty leg tendons just to sinew-back my juniper long bow. Given the amount of time it takes to process each tendon, that was one big job. Many bowers use backstrap sinews for backing their bows and that should be a lot faster. (Quick bows do not need sinew-backing; save the resources and labor for making your long-term bow.) For many jobs, like attaching points and fletchings, the sinews may be used as is. Just moisten them in your mouth, then wrap them in place, and they will dry and shrink in place, without any knots. However, I prefer to dip them in hide glue, which helps them to stick in place even better.

◊　◊◊◊　◊

I stand at the edge of a meadow. The ground squirrels run about playfully in the short grass. One sees me and gives the shrill alarm. All at once there are a hundred of them standing straight up, looking at me. I walk towards them, and one at a time they pop down into their holes. Before me, an owl feather, light, soft, and wispy, lays on the ground. I pick it up and carry it with me. It has much to say.

I used to fletch some of my arrows with owl feathers, but not anymore. It is illegal to possess **predatory bird parts**, and in the eyes of the law I committed a crime at the moment I picked the owl feather from the ground. Actually, there are many aspects of primitive living that come into direct conflict with contemporary laws, especially in regards to wildlife. Some primitive hunting and fishing techniques, such as deadfall traps and fish traps are illegal in many states. In all states there are designated seasons specifying when you can and cannot hunt game animals and when you can and cannot fish the streams. Also, in many states it is illegal to pick up road killed game. It is a federal offense in all states to even possess predatory bird parts, such as hawk, eagle, or owl feathers. Local law enforcement will often cordially ignore many primitive skills activities that are not legal—but not the possession of predatory bird parts.

It is helpful to realize that **laws** usually have a positive intention behind them. Laws may seem a little arcane at times, such as when you find a dead bird and you cannot put its feathers to good use on your arrows. Nevertheless, there is a positive intention behind the law. That intention is to prevent people from killing and selling predatory birds. For the most part the law works.

It is unfortunate that this law also punishes those of us whose intentions are pure and positive. My own beliefs regarding this issue have changed over the years. As I said, I once used owl feathers on my arrows; these were from road kills. But I discontinued using them because I always had to think twice about whom I showed them to. I also once found a bald eagle feather, which was so majestic that I was inspired to paint a picture of it. While my painting hung on my wall, the eagle feather that inspired it landed in the bottom of a drawer and eventually disappeared.

People develop a justifiable paranoia over possessing bird parts. At many of the black powder and primitive rendezvous that I have been to there were rumors that the "Feds" were going to make a "sweep" through camp. Ultimately, I came to the conclusion that just as a matter of convenience it is better not to use predatory bird parts in the first place. I no longer do.

Law enforcement is sometimes a little more lenient with issues such as primitive hunting and fishing techniques than with bird parts. The laws that exist for hunting and fishing do so for good reasons. Fish traps were outlawed to prevent people from blocking a creek with a cage and cleaning out the whole stream. The people who enforce those laws usually recognize the positive intentions behind those laws, and they will often judge your circumstances accordingly. Some abos and schools have been told openly and directly that they will be just fine using their primitive techniques as long as they hold valid licenses and keep within daily limits. This is, of course, the exception rather than the rule.

It is harder to understand the positive intention behind the laws that forbid using **road killed game animals**. I suspect the purpose of the law is to prevent people from hunting in the summer and claiming that they picked up their deer alongside the road. One thing for certain is that it is hard to leave a freezer full of fresh meat on the side of the road to rot. In some states you can apply for a special permit for picking up road kills. In most states I suspect that the law enforcement would simply rather not witness you loading up a deer along the road. If they do witness the incident then they will likely ask you to put it back or they may follow through with the laws because they have to.

Personally, I have grown more and more sickened about the carnage and waste along our highways. On average there is a deer killed every day within thirty miles of our home. We never see most of the kills, however, because the highway department clears the roads every day or so and drags the deer carcasses off out-of-sight to rot. At the same time, even in this era of affluence, about 20% of Montana children remain undernourished, living in households where there isn't enough money to buy quality food. How can we justify letting this resource go to waste when there are so many people in need?

Besides being abundantly available, road killed game is also exceptionally high quality meat, organically grown and lean on fats. This is an important point when you can no longer trust the meat sold in the stores, with all the hormones and antibiotics that are pumped into farm animals. After being raised on venison, I still prefer the taste of it to any domestic meats.

Butchering a Road Kill Deer

In the past I always imagined perfecting my archery skills so that one day I could go out and take a deer by my own hands. But then I see how many animals are slaughtered on the road and left to rot, and it is hard to imagine going out and killing even one more. If I ever do go hunting for deer then it may not be for me, but for my kids who are growing up and want to learn hunting skills. In the meantime, my kids find it amusing that their dad would break the law by picking up roadkill game.

I point out that laws are not perfect. There are usually positive intentions for them, but reasonable behaviors often become illegal under blanket policies. This may be an alarming statement to some, but I'm certain I've never met a person who has obeyed all laws all of the time. It would be nearly impossible to avoid breaking the law, even if you wanted to, since there have been more laws written than anyone person could ever know. I also expect my kids to break some of my own rules, since parents also tend to issue blanket policies that sometimes outlaw reasonable behaviors. And my kids have convinced me more than once that they were being reasonable when I was not. I want to raise good and moral kids, not automatons that would obey every law regardless of whether it was right or wrong.

In the long run, I plan to promote legislation to create a reasonable permit system for picking up roadkill game in Montana. This permit system should pay for itself, rather than robbing funds from other Fish, Wildlife & Parks programs. One idea I had is to set a license fee of $1,000 to cover administrative costs, which would also limit the program to those individuals or organizations that have a serious and sustained interest. Applicants might include private individuals, non-profit organizations that provide food to the hungry, as well as schools for biology classes, and zoos or wildlife sanctuaries to feed wolves, bears and other carnivorous captives. Qualified applicants would be issued special permit stickers for their vehicles, and they would purchase salvage tags for something like $25 each to carry with them on the road. Each animal taken would have to be immediately tagged and photographed on site, with the permit numbers visible. Photos would be e-mailed to Fish, Wildlife & Parks to show which tags have been filled and where they were taken. Yes, there is a bit of red tape involved, but the upfront costs and photographic record would help prevent problems with poachers who might abuse a more simple system, hunting deer out of season and claiming they just picked up roadkill.

I know that a law was passed in Oregon to allow Native Americans to pick up roadkill game, in compensation for hunting rights lost to us newcomers on this continent, so that would be another viable option. The important thing is that the carnage of our roads should be put to good use before we go out and kill even more living beings.

As with a lot of the skills I have learned, it was Grandma Josie who got me started picking up road killed deer. She could never stand to see the animals go to waste either. Mostly, she just liked to have good bones and meat scraps to feed her dogs, but of course we always put the choicest meats in the freezer for us. Neither of us knew the "right way" to gut and butcher a deer, but we muddled through it the best we could. Cutting and wrapping the meat was easy, since Grandma had a life-time of experience of doing that for hunters in the family. I've butchered enough road kills since then to become quite comfortable and proficient at the process, and I know enough about battered meat and bloated carcasses to provide guidance where other texts on hunting and butchering might leave off.

As for the deer shown in the pictures to follow, it was not a road kill per se, but a "fence kill" I picked up on an out-of-state trip. It was a young buck, less than one year old. Sometimes when deer jump a fence they stick a back leg in between the top two wires. On the way down their leg twists the wires together much like you might do with a stick. In one case I saw where a deer jumped the fence at such a rate of speed that it left it's entire back leg in the fence, right up to the hip joint. I don't know what happened to the rest of the deer.

Anyway, this particular deer was stuck in the fence, with three legs on the ground and its back leg sticking straight up in the air. I don't know how long it had been standing there like that, since it was almost out of sight from the road. I hoped that I could just untwist the fence wires and let it go, but on closer inspection the leg was completely broken off and held together only by the tendon. Killing it seemed like the only reasonable course of action, so I slit its throat with my knife then cut the tendon to let it drop to the ground. At that point I had a freshly dead deer at my feet, and there is no way I could just walk off and let it rot. So into the car it went. I butchered it in the mountains and packed the meat into the cooler for the trip home.

The important point is that whatever you do in primitive living I ask you to respect the positive intentions of the laws. If your methods conflict with the written law then use your skills quietly and do not come to me if you do get in legal hot water. Please be a respectful and cooperative representative of the wilderness.

Gutting the Deer

The first step in processing a deer is to remove the innards. Most people would call this "field dressing", and it is done immediately after the kill. First they cut the throat and allow the animal to bleed out a bit; then they slice it open all the way to the anus and remove the insides. It isn't really field dressing when I do it, because the animal has usually been dead on the road from one to several hours before I find it, and I certainly don't take time to gut it there. I find something to wrap the carcass in without getting blood stains all over the car, then haul it wherever I can to process it. I don't bother to bleed the carcass, as the blood has usually congealed by then anyway.

Now I would recommend that for your first one or two deer that you pick up only the freshest, cleanest kills, so you don't gross yourself out any more than necessary. Otherwise, as the carcass sits there for a while, the bacteria in the gut continue digesting the animal's last meal, releasing gas as a by-product. But the dead animal cannot fart the gas out of its system, so it blows up like a balloon. The more bloated it is the more likely you are to encounter some serious out-gassing during transportation or butchering.

So you need to gut the animal quickly to prevent bloating, and also to cool the carcass to prevent spoiling the meat. But let me also say that I once picked up a fresh kill late at night and didn't bother gutting it until morning. Yes, it was bloated and seriously gassy by then, and the gas forced its way into the surrounding meat (I know this sounds really gross), but I think it actually improved the flavor and texture of the meat. Granted, I am used to working with dead things, so I am not easily grossed out!

Also keep in mind that spoilage happens much faster in hot weather, so you can expect greater success finding fresh road kills in cool weather. Then you don't have to arrive immediately on the scene of the kill to get good meat. In cool weather you will also have more time to run around with the carcass in the back of your car while you cancel your other plans for the day and set up for butchering. Indeed the greatest obstacle to using road kill is that you have to seize the opportunity when it presents itself, and that usually happens when you are in a rush to get to some important appointment.

To start with, slice from the anus all the way up to the throat. Then go back and cut through the thin layer of fat and meat on the belly to expose the guts, always being careful to avoid rupturing anything inside. The more bloated the carcass the more careful you will have to be. In the second photo you can see that the stomach is slightly bloated and the pressure is forcing the stomach out as I work.

To remove the intestines without spilling the contents, it is helpful to cut through the pelvic bone. This is easily done where the two haves are sutured together. You will feel a ridge of bone with your fingers. Just put your knife blade right on the ridge and use a wooden mallet or stick to tap the knife through. Cutting through the bone on either side would be much more difficult.

Cut from the anus up to the throat, being careful to avoid rupturing the intestines.

The deer is slightly bloated already, so the stomach is pushing its way out as I work.

Use a wooden mallet to tap the knife to split through the ridge on the pelvic bone.

Here the pelvic bone has been cut open so that it is easy to pull out the intestines.

Next cut through the breastbone to open up the chest cavity. You may be able to force the knife through with a strong arm, otherwise just use a wooden mallet on the back of your knife. You will also need to cut across the throat to release the esophagus, if you haven't done that already. Then just grab the esophagus and pull the innards out towards the rear end. In the pictures here I have the deer on a slight incline with the head up, so that the guts are already slumping down with gravity.

Just below the heart and lungs is a thin membrane called the diaphragm. You will need to cut through that layer when you get to it. Then you can continue rolling the whole mass of innards back and out of the body. Take some care at the tail end to avoid squeezing pellets out the anus, but it is no big deal if you do. Even if everything goes wrong and you somehow rupture the stomach, intestines and/or bladder, well you can still wash it up nice and clean, so don't sweat it. Some people tie off the end of the intestine to avoid accidentally squeezing out any pellets, but that is hardly necessary. One thing you will find for sure is that everyone has their own system for gutting, skinning and butchering, but all paths lead to approximately the same end.

I like to save and cook the heart and liver and kidneys, though I usually wait until I am the only one home before cooking a dish like that. I have also eaten the lungs of small creatures, but never tried deer lungs, although they would be edible.

Among the literature on primitive skills you can find ways to use pretty much every part of the deer. For instance, you could clean out the intestines to use as a wrapping for sausage. The bladder could be made into a water bag, and you could cook with hot rocks in the stomach. The bones can be used to make many different types of tools, and the tendons are great for sinew fibers. You can make decorative bags from the lower legs or "hocks" and of course you can tan the hide. The hooves can be removed for rattles or decorations, and any small bones that do not become tools can be turned into jewelry.

Sometimes it is implied in the literature that you should use every part of the deer this way, and you would be dishonoring its life if you didn't. While I think it would be an exciting project to try and use everything once—especially after killing a deer with a bow you made yourself—it would be highly impractical to use everything *every time*. It is a big enough job just to gut, skin and butcher a deer in a day, or part of a day, to get the meat in the freezer, or on a drying rack if you are making jerky. I also flesh the hide and set it out to dry, but that is quite enough for one day. It could take a couple of weeks of work to literally use everything (assuming you already know how) and you probably don't have that kind of time. I sure don't. I throw the scraps to the dog, and she is more than happy to help. If I want parts off of the legs or head later, then I just run down to the butcher during hunting season and get as many as I want. Keep in mind that we are working with road killed animals here, and you are doing a great honor to the deer's life by using it at all. So don't let anyone play a guilt trip on you if you give half the deer to your dog.

Cutting the breast bone may also require a wooden mallet on the back of the knife, but not this time.

With the carcass completely open, you can start at the esophagus and pull everything out.

Here are the heart and lungs. I have the deer on a slight incline, so the innards spill down and out.

Here the gut pile is on the ground and I am lifting the end of the intestine out of the pelvis.

Skinning Your Deer

Many people like to age a deer carcass after gutting it. They hang it up and prop open the chest cavity and pelvis to allow air circulation, then leave it hanging for a couple days up to a couple weeks, depending on the weather. Flies may be attracted to the carcass in warm weather to lay their eggs, so it has to be tightly wrapped in a sheet for protection. In cold weather you risk freezing the hide onto the animal. Aging the carcass this way may help to tenderize the meat, but it is hardly necessary. I think it is best to finish the job when you start it and get the meat into the freezer as soon as possible.

I still remember as a kid when a hunter gave Grandma Josie a deer and it froze solid while it was aging. Grandma and my aunts had to bring the carcass into the house and set it on the kitchen table to skin it. They could peel the skin back just a little at a time, then they had to aim a hair dryer under the skin to loosen the next little bit. That turned into a very long and tedious skinning job!

While it is possible to skin flat on the ground, I find it a lot easier to do it in the air. Hanging the deer up also helps to keep the meat out of the dirt. Some people like to hang a deer by the back legs, but I prefer to hang it by the neck, as shown in photo A. The hide just seems to come off easier that way. In this case I used some scrap baling twine to tie it up to a tree branch. A come-a-long is helpful for hoisting

Peeling the skin off.

heavier animals. In photo A I have also cut around the circumference of the neck and I am using my knife to free the hide above the front shoulders.

Remove the lower legs either before or after hanging the deer. Just flex the legs back and forth to find the joint, then cut through it with your knife. Photos B and C show me cutting through the joint on a front leg. The joint is a bit more complicated on the back legs, but cut through as far as you can, then break it apart over your knee, as shown in photo D.

Next use your knife to split the skin open along the inside of the legs, as shown in photo E. Now you are basically done with your knife, so set it aside. Avoid using the knife to separate the hide from the meat, or you risk cutting into the skin and making it less valuable for tanning. Most holes in a finished piece of buckskin come from the skinning process and those holes are completely unnecessary. After the initial cuts have been made, the rest of the skinning job is a lot like peeling a big, fuzzy banana. Just grab the hide and start peeling it down, as shown in photo F. You will need to lean into it with your body weight in some places, but you may be amazed at how quickly and cleanly you can skin a deer this way. I usually cut the tail off, but this time the hide peeled right off the tail, as shown in photo G.

There will be a thin layer of meat left on the hide when you are done, as you can see in photo H, but don't worry over it. It is a thin layer of muscle tissue, which the animal uses to twitch its hide to scare away the flies. It is not really useful for table meat, and it is a real treat for the dog when you flesh it off the hide during the tanning process. (You should flesh the hide right away and either freeze or dry it until you are ready to tan it. Read more about that in the next chapter.)

When the skin is off, then you are ready for the butchering. I usually set the hide aside and flesh it after the meat is in the freezer, but in this case I laid it out flat to hold the meat while I did the processing.

The peeled hide has a thin layer of meat on it, but no knife scars.

Butchering Basics

Butchering is the process of cutting up the carcass into pieces small enough to fit in your frying pan and in the freezer. As with any skill, there are a zillion ways to do it, and even I don't do it the same way every time. The process shown here is substantially different than what a professional butcher would do with power saws. This is a style of butchering that works when the only tool you have is a knife. The objective is to package the meat cuts as various steaks, roasts, boiling bones and stew meat for the freezer. The process would be a bit different if you were doing the job primitively with the intent to dry or smoke the meat. While I would like to process a deer that way sometime, it is simply more practical to butcher the meat for the freezer.

Pull the front quarters out and cut through at the shoulder joint. The knife goes right through.

To get started take and pull the front leg out and cut through at the shoulder joint. This is the easiest cut and the knife goes right through. Then place the front quarter on a cutting surface and cut it apart at the joints. The bottom section has tough meat that is good for a use as a "boiling bone", but not much else. The next section up is more tender, but still lacking in meat, so that also makes a good boiling bone. The third section is the shoulder. It makes a good roast, although this one was a little small.

Cut the front quarter apart at the joints to get two "boiling bones" and a "shoulder roast".

Sometimes we buy freezer wrap to wrap up the meat, but it is hardly necessary. If you save your bread bags and other plastic bags, then you will probably always have more bags on hand than you could ever use. Just be sure to place the print side out, since there may be toxic heavy metals in the ink. I like to double bag each portion and close the bags with a twist tie. I write on the bags with a permanent marker, or sometimes stick labels on them. Each portion is given an appropriate label such as "V-Shoulder Roast". The "V" stands for venison. Some people like to date their meat cuts so they know how long it has been in the freezer, but we always go through it so fast that there is hardly a need to date it. When the front quarters are cut up, then you are ready for the hind quarters.

Remove the hind quarters at the ball joints. Flex the limb back and forth to guide you.

The hind quarters are cut off the carcass much as the front quarters were, but the ball joint is a bit more difficult to find in all the meat. Cut close to the pelvis and flex the limb back and forth as you go to guide you. Then move the meat to your cutting board and cut it at the joint. The lower piece makes another good boiling bone. The big hunk that is left over makes great steaks. Butchers usually leave the bone in place and cut across it with an electric saw to make round steaks. You can do the same thing at home if you have a meat saw with a sharp blade. Although the round steaks are really beautiful, I think it is too much trouble by hand, so I prefer to trim out the bone before cutting the steaks.

You can feel the bone through the meat. It is closer to one side than the other, so cut through from the shallow side and carefully trim around the bone to leave all the meat behind. Once the bone is removed then you can go back and cut the meat into nice rump steaks. Try to cut across the muscles rather than with them. Optionally, you could leave the bone in place and have a nice big rump roast. You will develop your own preferences and patterns as you gain experience.

Cut the hind quarter apart at the joint. The smaller piece makes another good "boiling bone".

After the four quarters have been processed and put away, it is time to start working over the ribs and backbone. This is also the time to separate out the backstrap sinews, if you plan to save them. The backstrap sinews form a thin, wide band along both sides of the backbone. These sinews are longer and easier to separate into individual threads than leg sinews, so they are really nice to have for projects. But, realistically, the only way to get backstrap sinews is to harvest them yourself, since professional butchers usually cut the ribs off of each side of the backbone, then saw through the vertebrae to make t-bone steaks.

The rest of the hind quarter is great for rump steaks, but you have to remove the bone first.

To save the backstrap sinews you need to peel back a thin layer of fat and meat along the backbone to expose the wide silvery bands. You may use a knife to cut in under the sinews, but then you should switch to the back of your knife or a stick to lift the fibers and to scrape them clean. It is easiest to clean the sinew while still on the animal this way. Work all along the length of the sinews, lifting and scraping them. Then pull on the fibers to get the upper end out, where the sinews are hidden under thicker muscles. Finally, cut the sinews off at the bottom where they start to form a round bundle, and lay them out in a warm but shady place to dry. (Read more about sinew-processing a few pages back.)

With the bone removed it is easy to cut the meat into steaks.

At this point you can still cut up the ribs and t-bone steaks if you have a sharp meat saw. Even a dull meat saw will cut through the ribs, and I often save them on larger, meatier animals. But the only tool I used on this project was a knife, so I just cut all the meat off and left the bones behind.

First I lifted the backstrap meat out from along both sides of the backbone. This is the most tender meat on the whole body, which would otherwise be turned into t-bone steaks. It peels easily away from the vertebrae with minimal need for a knife.

On the cutting board the long, skinny backstraps make for some pretty small steaks, but you can improve the size of the steaks by cutting them twice as thick. Next, cut these thick steaks in half, but stop before cutting all the way through, and let the two halves lay down flat so that they are connected in the middle to make a "butterfly steak", as shown on the following page.

After processing the backstraps I went back and peeled off the thin layer of meat covering the ribcage. Normally this layer would be left on the ribs, but in this knife-only method it was easier to strip it off and dice it into small pieces of "stew meat".

Keep in mind that with road kill there is typically a lot of impact damage, usually to one leg and one side of the ribcage. The worst pieces with all the broken bits of bone are best given to the dog. The meat that is simply bruised or "bloodshot" is still good eating, no matter what it looks like. I thought it was especially nice working on this "fence kill" since there was no damage to the meat.

On a similar topic, note that stressing an animal during hunting (with lots of running) increases the lactic acid in the muscles, which can accelerate spoilage, but it does not otherwise hurt the meat. Of course, that wouldn't be a concern with road kill anyway.

Lift the backstrap sinews out and scrape the meat off with a dull knife or a stick.

Pull or cut the backstrap meat from along the vertebrae. This is the choicest meat on the animal.

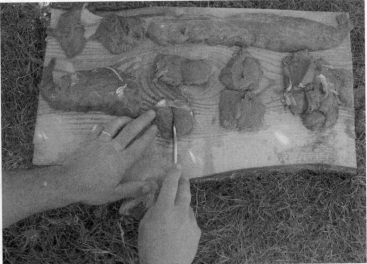

Cut the backstraps into double-thick steaks, then cut the steaks again, but not all the way through. The two halves make a "butterfly steak".

Sometimes I cut through the joints between the vertebrae to make "neck roasts" or at the other end to make a "pelvic roast", but in this case I just stripped off the meat as well as I could and left the bones for the magpies to pick over.

After cutting the carcass down from the tree I also removed the tongue, as it is very edible. To do this, first cut the cheeks open between the jaws so you can open the mouth up wider. Then you can reach in with a knife to get to the back of the tongue.

Wash, package and label all of your good meat and put it into the freezer as soon as possible. If you think your freezer is too small, then you might be surprised to see what a little pile of meat comes from one whole deer. Chances are you can fit it all into even a small freezer with room to spare. Then you and your family will be able to enjoy many very tasty and very healthy meals over the weeks and months to come, and you will have the satisfaction of knowing that you put a roadside carcass to good use.

◊   ◊◊◊   ◊

I stripped a thin layer of meat off the ribs and cut it up as stew meat, leaving behind just the bones.

Slice the cheeks open between the jaws. Then you can reach the back of the tongue with your knife to cut out this additional piece of meat.

156

I walk to the opposite end of the field and throw the owl feather into the air. It floats to the ground. A rock invites me to sit and watch the ground squirrels playing in the meadow. I do.

I pick the flower stalk of a lupine, admire its purple blossoms, and bury my nose in it. Two ground squirrels chase each other across the field, running round and round each other. When it comes to catching ground squirrels and other game, I often feel as if I go round and round too. Primitive hunting can be a very humbling experience that way. It is much different than hunting with a gun where all you do is aim and pull the trigger. In primitive hunting you have to study your prey and outwit it. Unfortunately, it is I who is the one most often out-witted!

Although I am very comfortable with my bow-making skills, I've never put in the hours to develop any real proficiency with using them, and I rarely bring one along on my camping trips. Hunting remains my weakest skill area. Most of the time I just do the best hunting I can with sticks and rocks. When I am successful in the hunt it is not usually due to any great skill on my part, but because the animal pretty much laid down at my feet and gave me every opportunity to kill it.

Porcupines are about my speed for hunting. The nice thing is that when you find one you can stand there ten feet away from it and devise a battle plan without scaring it away. You can even talk out loud if you have a partner, to discuss how you are going to kill it. Then go make your weapons and come back for the kill. But don't be fooled into thinking porcupines are slow. They can move amazingly fast as soon as they realize their quills will not protect them from you.

The weapon of choice for hunting porcupines is a simple **spear**, a sturdy stick with a sharp point. Ideally, you want to spear it through the belly and hit the heart, but that is kind of hard to do, since they protect their undersides. But you can spear hard through the ribs first and pin it to the ground, then come in with a second spear from underneath. If it breaks away and runs, then make sure you can block it from heading towards any thick brush where you won't be able to find it. Porcupines won't charge and attack you, but they may run blindly in your direction, so be nimble to make sure you don't get hit with a tail full of quills.

Once I killed a **muskrat** with a very blunt spear. The muskrat hid underwater next to the stream bank. I picked up the closest long stick and thrust it at the muskrat, pinning it against the bank until it drowned.

A lucky shot with a rock stunned this rabbit long enough for me to run forward and tackle it.

I have also taken **cottontail rabbits** with **throwing sticks** and **rocks**. Sometimes I bring along a nice throwing stick I made, but more often I just pick up ready-made sticks on site. The sticks cut a wider swath through the air than a stone, so you have a greater chance of hitting your target. Cottontails usually aid in the hunt by sitting perfectly still in the open, pretending they are invisible. But just when I think my aim is good enough to get a rabbit whenever I want one, I find that I cannot seem to hit them at all!

I have tried many times to hit **pigeons** in flight with sticks and rocks, but so far I've only been successful once. However, the young pigeons, called "squab", are much more delicious anyway. Ideally, you want to find the pigeons when they have grown to full size, but are not quite flying yet. I grab them from their nests below bridges or in abandoned buildings.

Of course I have also thrown many sticks at tree squirrels, but with minimal success. One time I climbed a tree and smoked a squirrel out of a woodpecker hole, then clubbed it as it came out.

But more than any other animal, I have hunted the ground squirrels. I have hunted with sticks and rocks, bows and arrows, spears, snares, deadfall traps, tin can traps, commercial rat traps, and by any other method I can think of. It seems that I can always catch one or two ground squirrels here and there, but never enough to achieve true sustainability. My greatest successes have been with the aid of deadfall traps.

I killed this pigeon with the throwing stick. The nest with the two good eggs were found afterwards.

Deadfall Traps

The trap I have used the most is called the **Paiute deadfall trap**. It was used extensively by the Paiute Indians of the Great Basin Desert for trapping small game, often very small game, like mice. The trap works well for mice and we used it extensively in the various programs for adolescents that we have worked for. We usually used a raisin or ashcake dough for bait.

The trigger system for the Paiute deadfall consists of several pieces, including the post, the lever, the string and toggle, and the baitstick. The trap is set so that all of these pieces are in a delicate balance, and they are held together under tension from the weight of the rock. The trap and rock in the photo are about the ideal size for ground squirrels; use the picture as a model for building your own traps. Make the traps quite a bit smaller for mice.

The Paiute trap works well for mice, but is less predictable for catching ground squirrels because the ground squirrels often spring the traps without going in. I think they may stand up to look the trap over, and in doing so they put their feet on the protruding lever and cause the trap to fall. Another disadvantage to the Paiute-style deadfall is that each part of the trap supports the weight of the rock, thus requiring some stout trap parts and making it more difficult to set the trap with a "hair trigger".

A Paiute deadfall trap.

A different deadfall trap that solves those problems is the **springpole deadfall trap**. It was invented by John McPherson of Kansas (author of *Primitive Wilderness Living & Survival Skills*). The advantage to this trap is that the trigger and springpole can be set first, then the stick supporting the rock is set up afterwards, as shown in the photo. This way the trigger does not support the weight of the rock, and you do not have to support the rock while setting the delicate trigger. Also, this way you do not have to worry about the rock falling on your hand while you are setting it. The main disadvantage to this system is that when it is sprung the bait is flung out of the trap where it can be consumed, whether or not you caught anything. With the Paiute deadfall trap the bait is usually safe under the rock when the trap is sprung, so you can reuse it.

◊   ◊◊◊   ◊

The day is quickly slipping away, and I want to move to another camp before dark. I get up from my granite seat and leave the lupine blossom on the rock. My motion causes alarm in the field and all the ground squirrels stand up to watch me leave. I bow to them and exit. As I walk back towards camp I remember some of the fun times that we have had eating mice.

Because they are small, mice can be roasted and eaten whole, without skinning them. The fur is burned off in the fire, and the bones are very small and fragile so it is easy to chew them up. But I always skinned my mice because the furs make nice finger puppets. One mouse fur is just right to fit over one finger. They are very cute.

A skinned mouse may be added to a stew or roasted on a stick. Renee's co-instructor on one course in Idaho prepared mouse marinated in beef bouillon and watercress. Renee said it was the best mouse she ever ate. And no, there is not much meat on a mouse. (Be sure to read the section on "Hantavirus" earlier in the book.)

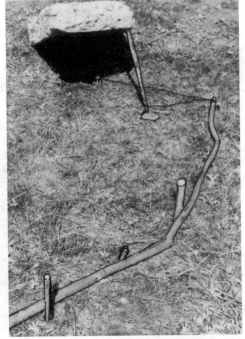

A springpole deadfall trap.

◊   ◊◊◊   ◊

CLOTHING

The sun is steadily reaching for the western horizon. I squint towards the light and put my hands up to shelter my eyes to see better. A red tail hawk glides overhead and cries out with a piercing shriek, as if to let us ground-dwellers know that he is king of these skies. I follow it across the sky until it disappears beyond the trees. It is still afternoon, but already the sun almost sits on the nearby mountain peaks. I need to pack and leave now to get to my other camp by dark.

I return to my shelter and pack my gear in my canvas-sack backpack. My leftover ashcakes smell good, so I bite into one and set aside two for the trail. I put on my braintanned buckskin shirt for protection because I feel a slight sunburn on my back. The skins are soft as chamois cloth. I pause a moment to run my fingers through the fringe of my shirt and to think.

Braintanning a hide is a very unique and magical process. The name "braintanning" refers to the tanning agent, brains, which are used to soften the hides. Brain matter contains an oil called **lecithin**, which lubricates the fibers of a hide and enables you to stretch the hide until it is soft. There are many, many different methods for braintanning, and almost every tanner develops his or her own unique process, so when you hear about the tanning process from another tanner it will likely sound much different from the process I describe here.

All braintanning processes, to my knowledge, are variations of either the dry-scrape method or the wet-scrape method, referring to the process used to remove the hair. In the **dry-scrape** method the fresh hide is stretched and tied in a rack and allowed to dry. Then the hair, epidermis and membrane layers are removed with a razor sharp scraper. The epidermis is a thin layer on the surface of the hide. "Dermis" means skin, and "epi" means above, so the epidermis is literally the layer above the skin. The membrane is a thin tissue layer on the inside of a hide.

In the **wet-scrape** method, which I use, the hide is soaked for a few days to loosen the hair. Then it is draped over a fleshing board and the hair, epidermis, and membrane are removed with a wet-scrape tool, typically a steel blade like a drawknife, but not sharp enough to cut into the hide. There are advantages and disadvantages to both the wet-scrape and the dry-scrape methods. People often prefer which ever method they learn first. I learned to tan hides with a wet-scrape method from my cousin, Melvin Beattie, who has since produced a video on braintanning called "*Tanning Spirit*". I have made only minor variations in the process he originally taught me. Also, the process I describe here applies only to hides you are tanning with the hair off. The process for tanning pelts or hides with the hair on is quite different.

My daughter Felicia shows her buckskin dress.

Braintanned Buckskin

To begin the braintanning process you will need a hide. I recommend that you tan an antelope or deer hide before trying something big like an elk. Tanning is a lot of work, and you would be wise to learn with smaller, easier hides before tackling the bigger ones.

It is easy to find hides during the hunting season. I pull a half-dozen deer and antelope hides out of the dumpster every fall, and I only check there about once a week. The rest of the hides I get just seem to land on my doorstep. This will happen to you too, as the word gets out that you tan hides. People will bring you every kind of dead animal imaginable. Of course you can also get hides by doing your own hunting, or by picking up road kill on the highway. If you do, then the first step in the tanning process is the skinning. Be sure to read more about how to skin and butcher a deer in the previous chapter. Once you have obtained a hide then you can move to the next step, which is fleshing the hide.

Fleshing: Fleshing is the process where the big chunks of fat, meat and membrane are scraped off the hide. Drape the hide over a rounded board and use a two-handled, dull blade to scrape the hide clean. The tool should be dull, so that you could not possibly slice into the hide—either yours or the animal's. I use a planer blade from a sawmill for my work. A section of leaf spring from an automobile can also work real well. For simple handles, just slide a six-inch piece of tight fitting radiator hose on each end of the tool. I use a portable booth, as shown for fleshing and dehairing hides. The rounded board has a notch at the top end, which fits snugly against a peg in the booth. The hide is draped over the board with one part pinched between the notch and the peg to hold it in position. The scraping tool is then used to scrape the meat off the hide. This step takes 5-20 minutes for a deer hide. When the hide is clean then you can continue the tanning process or you can store the hide until you have time to work it.

Storing: To prepare a hide for storage, simply lay it out flat to dry. Be sure all parts of the hide are exposed to air, and be sure there are no folds. Folded areas do not dry out so they rot. When the hide is dry then simply stow it away some place where it will stay dry. That is all there is to it; you do not need any salt or other special treatments. The hide will be in good shape when you are ready to tan it—regardless of whether that is next month, next year, or in the next decade. If you cannot flesh the meat off of the hide right away then roll it up and put it in the freezer until you can.

Sometimes you will be given hides that are dried, but were never fleshed. That is not desirable, but it is okay. I make sure the hides are thoroughly dry and then I add them to my stack. Mice will chew on the dried meat, but they rarely hurt the hide itself. Also, the larvae of the "carpet beetle" may infest the hide, but they do not seem to hurt it. (They do ruin furs if they get into them.) The real problem with unfleshed hides is that they are slimy to work with later. One of the four hides we worked with during a hide-tanning class was not fleshed before it was dried. The hide became a magnet for flies once it was resoaked. Hundreds of flies swarmed around the unfleshed hide, while they were not interested in the other hides. But slime and flies aside, the hide still became a beautiful piece of buckskin.

Again, drying and storing is not necessary if you are ready to immediately start the tanning process. But it is nice to know that you have the option of storing the hide if you are not ready to work it yet.

Soaking: Soaking is the next step in the tanning process. The hide is soaked in water to loosen the hair so it can be taken off in the following step, which is dehairing. A hide is typically soaked in water for about 2-4 days. Bacterial action gradually eats away at the hair folicles, loosening the hair. You must not soak the hide in chlorinated city water. Chlorine kills the bacteria, and it also bleaches essential oils from the hide.

Creek water, well water, or spring water can be used to soak a hide. We have a spring, so I set the stiff, dry hides under the sprinkler until they are flexible enough to shove into a five-gallon bucket of water. It is more difficult to soak your deer or antelope hide in a big barrel or in a creek, than in a bucket. Deer, antelope, and elk hair is hollow, so the hide will try to float to the top of the water despite your efforts to weight it down with rocks. A five gallon bucket works well because the hide fills the entire bucket so it is saturated, and yet there is no standing pool of water for the hide to float in.

In hot weather the soaking process will be very short, but in cold weather it can take a long time. Warmth encourages bacterial growth, and cold slows it down. The bacterial action produces an odor, which can take some getting used to. Perhaps it is a little like cow manure: the smell can be offensive if it is new to you, but when you become used to it then it can seem almost pleasant. With hide tanning, however, the odor can be diminished considerably by changing the water once or twice a day. This flushes out the smelly water, but does not seem to flush the bacteria out of the hide and hair. The hide has soaked long enough when you can pull small clumps of hair from the neck area, which is always the most stubborn part of the hide. Then you are ready for the next step, and that is "dehairing".

Dehairing: Dehairing is the process of scraping off the hair and the epidermis layer. The epidermis prevents the lecithin in the brains from entering the dermal layer, and it inhibits you from stretching the dermal layers during the softening process. The epidermis layer must come off for the brain-tanning procedure to work. This is important, so let me say it again: the epidermis layer *must* come off for the tanning process to work. *All of the epidermis must come off* for the braintan process to work. Got it?

To dehair a hide, first drape it over a fleshing/dehairing board as discussed with the fleshing process, except this time put the hair side up so you can work on it. The hair comes off easiest if you scrape with it, rather than against it. So start as close to the top end of the hide (the neck) as you can and scrape down from there. Later, to dehair the neck, you have to turn the hide around and scrape back against the hair. Use a knife to trim off any odd, tattered ends of the hide, typically at the ends of the legs.

Be sure and scrape the epidermis layer off as you scrape the hair. The hair will usually come off quite readily, so you may be tempted to scrape all the hair off before scraping off the epidermis. Don't. The epidermis layer looks similar to the dermis layer, so if you leave an area of epidermis on the hide then it can be difficult to tell where it is. Scrape a small area of hair away; then scrape and rescrape the epidermis layer until nothing more comes off. Really lean into it and scrape as firmly as you can. The hide can take quite a lot. If the board and the scraping tool are free of blemishes then it is basically impossible to cut into the dermis layer. Ripping is another matter, and you should work more carefully in thin areas of the hide and work carefully around any holes. Any deep knife cuts on the inside of the hide also have the potential to rip open. Scraping the hair and epidermis layer off the hide usually takes between 1 and 3 hours for a deer hide. It should feel like work.

Refleshing: When you have taken the hair and epidermis layer off the hide then flip the hide over on the board and reflesh the other side. The first fleshing was just a quick pass over the hide to scrape off the big stuff; you could not do much more than that with the thick padding of hair on the other side. But with the hair off, you can now scrape the daylights out of the flesh side.

There is a thin membrane on the flesh side of the hide, often referred to as the "hypodermis" layer. "Hypo" means under, so "hypodermis" literally means "under the skin", as in a "hypodermic needle". The hypodermis, like the epidermis, inhibits brain matter from penetrating into the dermis layer, so it must be scraped off. Again, if your tools are free of blemishes then you cannot cut into the hide, but do be careful to avoid ripping weak areas. The hypodermis does come off easier than the epidermis, except that it does not ever quite run out. There are always little bits of membrane on the hide. Scrape it as good as you can. A lot will come off the first time you scrape an area. When it is hard to scrape any more off then it is good enough. This step typically takes 30 minutes to 1 hour to complete for a deer hide. It should also feel like work.

Storing: At any point during the tanning process you can dry out the hide and store it until you have an opportunity to work it again. Then just soak it up when you are ready to continue the process. Optionally, you could store the hide in your freezer if

Dehairing a hide.

Close-up of fleshing/dehairing board.

161

Wringing moisture out of a hide.

you have extra space. The next step, when you are ready for it, is prestretching.

Prestretching: Prestretching the hide is the process of opening up the fibers of the hide so the brains will penetrate more easily in the next step. As I wrote previously, brains contain an oil, lecithin, which is used in the softening process to lubricate the fibers of the hide. However, oil is thicker than water, so it does not penetrate the hide as readily. Therefore, the hide must be opened up to receive the brain matter. Prestretching the hide includes several steps, and the process begins with wringing the hide.

-**wringing:** Wringing the hide takes some of the moisture out of it and makes the successive steps quicker. First, wring the hide with your hands and squeegee out as much moisture as you can to make the hide less slippery. Now, wring the hide as shown in the photo, using one stationary stick (in this case the stick is part of the framework that will become a thatched hut), and a shorter stick that you can use to twist the hide up tight. I lay the hide out so that the neck area of the hide is wrapped around one stick and the tail is wrapped around the other stick. At each end the hide is brought around the stick and laid back on itself. These ends will be rolled tight into the middle as you wring the hide, so they should not come undone. Be sure to wring the hide with the hair side out and the flesh side in. The animal sweats from the inside to the outside when it is alive, so moisture moves more easily from the inside to the outside when you wring the hide too.

Preferably when you set up a wringer you should make it such that you are reaching slightly down to it instead of upward. This way water from the hide will not drain down the length of your arm—which can be a little disconcerting on a cold day.

Twist the hide up as tight as you can. It is virtually impossible to rip a deer hide this way, but do be more careful with antelope hides. Twist the hide up tight, then hold it and let it drip. Let it drip for a few minutes then twist it a little more. Again let it drip, then dry off the remaining moisture with a towel. Unravel the hide, and stretch it out some. Offset it from its previous position in the wringer, and wring it again. Each wringing should take 10-15 minutes.

Unravel the hide after a second, thorough wringing. The hide should be small, somewhat translucent, and it should be bunched together in tight wrinkles. The next step is beaming.

-**beaming:** Beaming the hide stretches out the wrinkles in the skin and redistributes the remaining moisture. The beamer is simply a board (or beam) such as a 2 x 4 sticking straight up, with the top end tapering to a blunted point. The beamer in the photo has a metal edge imbedded in the top, but that is not necessary.

To use the beamer, pull the hide slowly and firmly across the edge or across a rounded corner. The beamer stretches small areas of the skin very intensely; other steps in the stretching process work bigger areas of the hide, but with less intensity. Work over the whole hide, bringing each part once over the beamer. Hold the hide up to the light to see which areas you have worked over and which areas still have wrinkles. Beaming the hide should take about 20 minutes.

-**pulling:** This step involves pulling the hide like a big sheet of taffy. This process stretches and opens the fibers across the entire hide. The most effective way to do this is for two or more people to work together. If you are working as a pair, then stand across from each other and grip opposite ends of the hide. Both of you should lean back at the same time to stretch the hide. Then come forward, rotate the hide a few

Beaming a hide.

inches and lean back again. Rotate the hide each time so that you are always stretching the fibers from a new angle. Three people can work together in the same way, with all three people leaning back at once. The most effective way to pull the hide is to have four people working in pairs. The hide is pulled lengthwise between two people, then cross-wise between the other two people as shown in the photo; then the hide is rotated slightly and the process continued. It is very effective. With bigger hides there is room for even more people. In fact, you may have seen photos of large groups of natives playing "trampoline" where they bounced a child around on a hide. That is how they stretched the hide.

If you are working alone then there are a couple methods you can use to pull the hide. One way is to find a clean spot and stand on one end of the skin while you pull up on the other end. Pull it once then rotate it and pull it again, etc. An easier way to do the same action is to hang the hide from hooks in the ceiling and pull down. To do this, first pick up 6 small, steel rings at the hardware store and attach about 8 inches of heavy cord to each ring. Then wrap one marble or small stone into the hide at each leg and one at each of the two sides. Use the cord attached to the rings to tie around each of the marbles. Fix at least 3 heavy duty hooks into an overhead beam; place one in the center and the others about 2 to 3 feet out from center. More hooks can be added

Beaming should be done slowly and firmly.

at each side; then you can work with any size hide on the same set of hooks. To stretch the hide just start pulling down at one point on the hide, then move your hands a few inches and pull down again. Rotate your hands around so that you pull on the three open sides of the hide. Pull down on the hide, and pull across it. Then rotate the hide so it is hanging from a different side and repeat the process.

Whether you are working alone or as a group, there are a couple tips you should remember. First, you do not need to pull the hide with your arm strength. This will only wear you out. Just hold onto the hide and lean back with your body weight. Develop a rhythm as you work. Lean back, then step forward, regrip, and lean back.

When you grip the edge of the hide it is instinctive to bunch your hand into a fist and dig your fingernails in so that the hide comes across your knuckles. This is a good way to blister your knuckles quickly. Teach yourself to grip the hide with the palms of your hands and the pads on your fingers.

During the prestretching you should pull the hide for at least 30 minutes to 1 hour, but more is better. I alternate back and forth between pulling the hide and working it around the rope.

-roping: In this step the hide is pulled back and forth around a rope or cable. The friction warms the hide slightly and the pulling stretches it. For years I used a rough-textured rope 1/2 to 3/4 inch in diameter and secured it from floor level up to an overhead beam. A rope has to be tied securely, otherwise it rolls up in the hide as you work. A steel cable, 1/8 to 3/8 inch in diameter works even better, and that is what I use now. You can attach it loosely between two points, because it does not roll up in the hide.

Pull the hide back and forth around the rope. You do not need to pull the hide hard. Do not work against yourself. Pull with one hand, ease up with the other, and work into a rhythm. You should be continuously repositioning your grip on the hide as you go, so that you work all parts of the hide around the rope. I usually alternate so that I work the hide around the rope for 10 or 15 minutes at a time, and then I pull it again for 15 or 20 minutes.

In his excellent book *Deerskins into Buckskins*, author Matt Richards outlines a process where the hide is soaked in a solution of wood ashes or lime prior to dehairing to break down mucous in the

Pulling a hide.

163

hide. Removing the mucous this way allows the brains to penetrate easier, and reduces the need for so much prestretching effort.

Other tanners in recent years have adopted a pre-smoking process, where the hide is smoked before it is brained. The softening process is made easier and more reliable this way. The technique works best for dry-scraped hides, which come out of the rack nice and flat. Wet-scraped hides need to be thoroughly pre-stretched, then tacked out flat to dry. The dried hide should be white and papery but flexible for the smoke to penetrate.

A new process I am exploring to "effortlessly" prestretch the hides is to freeze-dry them outside on cold winter nights. The water molecules inside the hide expand and stretch the hide from the inside, at the molecular level. Freeze-drying may take several nights, depending on the thickness of the hide and the humidity in the air. The hide may be left out during the day if the weather is cloudy and cold, but do not let the sun shine on it, or the ice melts and the hide tightens up as it dries. I put the hide in a plastic bag in a cool place then hang it out again the next night.

This freeze-drying process even makes it possible to tan hides with the epidermis on, for more water-resistant clothing. This is a whole new method of tanning that I am still developing.

Braining: There is an old saying that every animal has enough brains to tan its own hide. That may or may not be true, but it really does not matter. Brains are easy to come by, and everyone I know always uses more than enough for the job just to be sure. About one pound of brains is good for a deer hide; you can use less for an antelope and more for an elk. Any type of animal brains will work, and there are many ways to get them. You can collect heads of deer, antelope, elk or cow from local slaughter houses. Then you can either saw or ax the skull open to scoop the brains out. Check your hands over carefully to make sure you do not have any cuts or scratches, and be very careful you do not get scraped by a fragment of bone while digging the brains out. Raw brains can easily penetrate a cut and give you a nasty bacterial infection. Another way to remove the brain, according to my neighbor, who was once a federal meat inspector, is to stick a pressure hose into the hole at the back of the skull where the spinal cord comes out. The pressure hose will force the brain to pop right back out that hole, "in about 3 seconds", he said. Another way to get brains is to let someone else do it for you. You can order brains by the case through most grocery stores, and the cost is usually just a little over a dollar a pound.

The first thing you need to do to prepare the brains is to mash them up. I recommend doing this at least once by hand, just for the experience. There is really nothing wrong with squeezing brains through your fingers. Most of us have just been thoroughly cultured to "wig out" over it. Actually, brains make your own skin soft too, and they feel almost soapy when you work with them.

Another way to prepare the brains is to pull out the aboriginal blender and puree them. Liquefy the brains until they look like a strawberry milk shake.

Next, cook the brains. This has absolutely no effect on the brains or the tanning process; the brains work either raw or cooked. The purpose of cooking them is for your own protection. If you have a cut or a deep scratch on your hands then the raw brains can get into that and give you a nasty bacterial infection. You can get the same infection when handling the meat, but the brains penetrate into very small cuts. It is hard to treat a bacterial infection at home, and you will usually need a doctor's prescription for antibiotics, so check you hands carefully before you handle raw brains, and cook the brains just to be safe. Add some water to them and boil thoroughly.

Pour the cooked brains into a bucket and add water. If you dried the hide after the prestretch process then add a full gallon of water; if there is still moisture in the hide then add less water. The water temperature should be warm. Warm water thins the oil in the brain matter so it penetrates the hide easier; hot water will cook the hide and turn it to rags. When the temperature is right then work the hide down into the water. A prestretched hide should soak up the brain mixture very quickly, even if the hide was completely dry. Leave the hide in the brains for an hour or two then restretch the hide.

Restretching: Restretching the hide is the same process as prestretching it; it just helps the brains to penetrate deeper into the hide. This time however, place a bucket under the hide when you wring it to catch the brain matter as is drips from the hide. Sometimes you may not need to restretch the hide, and occasionally you may need to restretch it a number of times. There is really no good way to tell for sure, but a prestretch and a restretch will usually do the job. When I show people my hide-tanning equipment I usually refer to it as my "tanning gym". You may be able to sense that by now; there is a lot of physical work in tanning a hide.

Sewing: You can stitch up the bullet or knife holes in the hide during any one of the stretching processes. Just stitch them up while there is still ample moisture in the hide. Use a "glover's needle" (available at leather supply stores) and some heavy thread; I use nylon. Dental floss or artificial sinew (waxed nylon thread) also work great.

Put the stitches on the flesh side of the hide. Holes caused by knife scores have a very definite direction to them. Look at the direction of the slice, and stitch it back together in that direction. It is okay if the hide puckers a little when you sew it; it will stretch out flat later. I use a back-and-forth stitch on my hides, but most any good stitch will work.

Final Stretching: The final stretching is the same process as the prestretching and the restretching, except this time you do not stop pulling the hide and working it around the rope or cable until the hide is completely dry. The magic of braintanning lies in this final stretching. One moment you will be working with a wet, slimy hide, the next you will have some areas of soft chamois-like leather. Gradually the entire hide will transform so that it is soft as velvet, and the color will change from many hues to a solid sheet of white, as if it were bleached. The final stretching, from beginning to end, should take 2 to 4 hours in good, warm conditions. If the weather is too hot then the hide may dry and stiffen before you can adequately work it. If it is cold where you are working then you could be stretching it most of a day to dry it.

Sewing the holes closed for tanning.

Some stiffness will likely appear in the hide as it dries. The most stubborn areas are the neck, the hind flanks and the backbone. Pay special attention to these areas and work them around the rope a lot to keep them loose.

At this point, if everything went right, you should have a very soft piece of beautiful, white braintan buckskin—something you can be very proud of. Hides do not always turn our right the first time. Occasionally, you will have to rebrain and restretch the hide. You can do this as many times as it takes to get it right.

Working Big Hides: I don't have enough arm strength to properly work larger hides like elk when they are still damp and heavy. So I often lace them up in a rack and set the rack down flat, yet propped up on some cinder blocks or logs. Then I use it like a **trampoline** to let my body weight do all the stretching work.

My son Donny and I worked together to stretch this elk hide in the rack. We look like we are working really hard, don't we?

To lace up the hide, just make small slits all the way around the perimeter with a knife. Then lay the hide down inside the rack and start lacing from the top and bottom of the hide first, and then the sides. I use scrap pieces of baling twine for the job, since there is plenty of it here in hay country.

Do not use short laces and lots of knots, because the lacings need to be adjusted constantly. Instead, use a long lace and one knot to start, then run the lacing through the holes and around the frame again and again as you go around the hide. If you run out of lacing, just tie on another piece on and keep going until you reach a corner of the rack, before you tie off to the rack.

When the hide is nice and tight, then you can step in the middle and start stretching. The hide can take a lot in the center, where your weight is evenly distributed across the entire hide. Kids can easily bounce up and down without hurting anything. But be careful around the edges near the laces, as too much weight will rip the holes out where the lacings go through. I usually stand near the middle and put one foot out by the edge, rocking forward with as much of my weight as I think it can take. Work around all the edges this way and walk back and forth all over the middle too. You will find that the hide is loose and baggy after about a minute of stretching. So stretch it a little more, then go back and tighten the lacing around the perimeter. You will have to tighten the laces many times during the stretching process.

Avoid working in really hot weather, as the hide may dry out too fast while you are adjusting the laces. It is actually preferable to work hides in the rack during winter to take advantage of the freezing weather. I rack the hide up and stretch it a few times, retightening the laces each time, then walk away and let the hide freeze. Water in the hide expands as it freezes and stretches the hide on the molecular level. The hide will also slowly dry when it is frozen, but much more evenly than in warm weather.

Later in the day, or the following morning, I go back and work the hide some more, stretching it trampoline-style and again tightening the laces. If there is still a lot of moisture in the hide then I repeat the freeze cycle and stretch it again later on, until the hide feels nearly dry, but still has enough moisture to work it around. Then I take the hide out of the rack and bring it inside our warm house to finish pulling and roping it by hand. Don't trim off the edge with all the lacing holes until you are sure the hide will soften the way you want it to, since there is always a chance you will need to rebrain and restretch the hide.

Smoking: White buckskin was often used for making ceremonial dress clothing. But it was not used for regular wear because it turns back to rawhide if it gets wet. So for practicality, you will usually want to smoke your hides. Smoking preserves the tan. Then the hide can get wet and it will remain soft when it dries.

Hides are essentially a network of gluey collagen fibers. When a hide dries out as rawhide, the shrinking and hardening is caused by the glues setting up in the hide. In the tanning process you use the lecithin from brain matter as an oil to lubricate the fibers of the hide. Then you keep the hide moving through the entire tanning process to prevent the fibers of the hide from binding together. Rawhide or unsmoked tanned hides can be boiled to make hide glue, but a hide changes when it is smoked.

The chemistry of smoking a hide has long been a mystery, but new information has become available in recent years, thanks especially to the work of Steven Edholm and Tamara Wilder in their encyclopedia-like book, *The Ancient Art of Braintanning*. In a nutshell, the formaldehyde and other aldehydes in the smoke create a strong chemical bond with the collagen fibers, filling the spaces that water normally binds to. A smoked hide can still hold a lot of water like a sponge, but it does not chemically bond to the hide. The hide retains its loft when wet, and does not become slimy like an unsmoked hide. For more details on the chemistry of braining and smoking a hide, plus other great tanning tips, be sure to read Steven and Tamara's book.

Smoking a hide.

Anyway, to prepare a hide for smoking, first fold it in half along the backbone. Start at the neck and stitch around the perimeter where the two halves meet. You can use a needle and thread or a common household stapler. Clothespins also work. Matt Richards, in *Deerskins into Buckskins* simply uses a bead of glue around the perimeter. I hand-stitched my first fifty or so hides at about an hour apiece before I learned about using a stapler from a hide tanner in Washington state. The job takes only a few minutes with a stapler. Stitch, staple, pin, or glue the two halves together, but leave an opening at the bottom, or tail of the hide that is big enough to fit over a stove pipe. Make a "skirt" from old Levi's or other cloth, and stitch this to the opening in the hide. This puts some distance between the hide and the stove to protect the skin from getting scorched.

For the sake of being authentic, you can smoke the hide over a fire pit in the ground. However, it is harder to control the airflow to the burning materials in the pit. Ideally you want the materials to smolder and smoke profusely, ready to burst into flame, but held just short of that threshold. You can reach that precise level of incomplete combustion more easily with a stove, especially an airtight stove, than you can over a fire pit.

The hide is hung from a tripod and the skirt is placed over the stovepipe or fire pit for smoking. A hide can be smoked by hanging it in a smokehouse or something similar, but it takes much longer since the smoke passes by the hide, instead of being forced through it. It can take several days to smoke a hide in a smokehouse, but only 10-45 minutes per side when the hide is stitched together and the smoke is forced through it.

You can use just about anything for smoking materials. Most people use dry, rotten, punky wood. Cottonwood produces a bright, almost orange colored hide. Aspen produces a dirty brownish-yellow. Rotten pine turns the hide a dark brown and slightly grayish, but do not use pitch, which can turn the hide black. Chokecherry wood produces a rich yellowish-brown. I use whatever I can lay my hands on first, which includes dry grass (bright yellow) and sagewort (brown and slightly gray), but most often I just use bales of straw.

To use rotten woods, first start a good fire and establish a bed of coals; then put the punky wood on the coals to smother the flame so it just smokes. Dry grass is much more flammable, so you have to be careful. I stuff a small stove with as much grass as I can. I put so much grass in there that there is no room for it to burst into flame when I light it, so it just smokes profusely. This produces smoke so dense that you can see the yellow color right in the smoke. If the grass is damp then I start a fire first and build up a bed of hot coals before stuffing the grass in.

If you are using a fire pit then stake the skirt down around the pit. If you are smoking it with a stove then hang the skirt over the stovepipe. I staple the skirt together right around the stovepipe to get a good seal. Make sure that the smoke can get to all parts of the hide. If any section is folded over then prop that area open so the smoke can get there. My cousin attaches fishhooks from the hide to the tripod to hold those areas open. I slide small twigs in through the seams or through a hole and prop the hide apart with those.

Stay close to the hide through the smoking process. If the grass or wood punk flares up then you need to smother it or pull the hide off immediately so you do not cook your hard work. Also, periodically peek in through a hole in the hide or pull apart a couple stitches so you can see how the color is coming. Put a wad of crumpled newspaper in the hole to keep the smoke in, and just pull it out for a peek now and then. When one side seems well smoked then turn the hide inside out and smoke the other side. Smoke both sides of the hide thoroughly, then take it down and pull out the stitches or staples. Roll it up and put it in some safe place outside of the house for a few days for the smoke to set up. After the smoke has set up for a few days then you can hang the hide up to air out some of the smoke smell, or you can start cutting and sewing. In any case, keep it out of the house for a while. The smoke is very strong, and it can make you sick if it is in your home with you.

Notes: Sometimes a hide will not tan out soft the first time through, and you will have to rebrain it. I have found that you can save quite a bit of work if you smoke the hide prior to rebraining it. The smoke will penetrate any semi-soft areas and deactivate the glue there. Then you have less work to do when you retan the hide. In fact, there is hardly any work to do at all—just an occasional stretching, and quite a bit of hands-off drying. Just for the sake of experimentation I have also tanned a hide using just smoke, no brains. It works, but the hide has to be stretched open for the smoke to penetrate, and it is hard to stretch the hide without the brain matter in it. I ended up stretching and smoking the hide four times to get it soft, and even then it did not have the loft of braintan buckskin until I later brained it and worked it one more time.

◊ ◊◊◊ ◊

Two mountain bikers careen down the road near my camp, hollering back and forth as they ride. I cannot see them, but I can hear them and it wakes me from my reverie. I shoulder my pack, take a bite of ashcake and start out for my shelter at Hollowtop Lake. On my way I cross the creek and stop long enough to loosen my cup from my belt for a drink. I drink my fill, wash my face, and continue on my way. My feet are on the trail and my mind returns to buckskin, and how to sew with it.

I used to do my sewing the hard way. I would use the sharp leather punch on my Swiss Army Knife to poke a hole through each layer of hide. Then I would run a standard needle and thread through the holes. But braintan buckskin is unique stuff. It seems like the punch holes almost "heal" themselves and disappear faster than a person can put a needle back through them. This can be frustrating because a standard needle cannot penetrate buckskin without a hole. Later, my cousin Mel showed me some techniques that changed my sewing forever. He learned them while rigging parachutes in the Navy. But first, lets start with the basics.

A buckskin bag. Notice how the welts were used to add decoration.

167

Sewing Buckskin

The first step in working with buckskin is to decide what to make, and that may depend on what kind of hides you have. You need to have the right thickness of skin and the right number of skins for the job. To make moccasins for example, you need either an elk hide or a thick deer hide. Or to make a full-sleeved shirt you will need a minimum of three deer hides, and possibly as many as six. Once you have tanned the right material then you need to think carefully about how you use it; braintanning is hard work so you do not want to wreck a good hide. More than that, buckskin garments can last for many years, so you want to make something that is worth keeping around.

Patterns: The first thing you will notice when you lay a piece of buckskin out flat is that it doesn't lay out flat. The buckskin process starts from a three-dimensional animal so the end product does not conform too well as a two dimensional plane. If a hide does lay flat then it is only a temporary illusion; it will warp back out of shape later on through everyday wear. These special effects of buckskin can present somewhat of a challenge to the novice seamster or seamstress. Perhaps someday genetic scientists will make stone-age life easier by creating a breed of two-dimensional deer.

In the meantime, no matter how careful you are, you will still run into a variety of problems from the stretchiness of the skin and its tendency to revert to a three-dimensional form. While you are working you will find that two pieces of buckskin cut to the same length rarely are the same length, and if they are then they will rarely remain that way as you stitch them together. Once you get through those hurdles then the end product will ultimately stretch out of shape anyway.

In his classic book *Blue Mountain Buckskin* author Jim Riggs suggests some ways to minimize the problems with stretchy buckskin. For example, be sure to cut each piece of any paired patterns, such as mittens, sleeves, or moccasins, from the same direction in the hide. Hides especially tend to shrink along the length of the backbone and stretch outward towards the sides, so cut your patterns in the same direction, and avoid cutting patterns diagonally across the leather because they will stretch in multiple directions and twist. Also, be sure and make shirts and pants a little large so they will fit after they stretch and shrink.

I often spend days working on a pattern and cutting out the pieces. For example, to make a shirt, I start first by daydreaming and sketching. Then I find an old shirt that fits loosely and which is pieced together similarly to what I envision in my new shirt, and I cut it apart at the seams. I use the shirt as a basic pattern for proportions and draw a new pattern on paper, usually adding an inch or two in every direction. Then I crease the paper sleeves and fit them against the pattern for the main body to be sure the sleeves will come out of the shirt at a natural angle, instead of arching upward. When I am satisfied with that then I put the paper pieces on my body and tape them together to find out if the pattern has at least ballpark accuracy. Later I spend a few hours deliberating over which pieces should be cut from which hides. I work carefully as I trace the flat patterns on the not-so-flat hides to minimize the distortions, and I cut them out with a pair of standard sewing scissors. Next, I attach the pieces together with single stitches at all the critical points and try it on. I trim the pieces if necessary, and I continually try the garment on and trim off little bits here and there, as needed, all the way through the sewing process.

Sewing: There are a number of ways to sew buckskin. The simplest way is to punch holes through at intervals of every few inches along the seams and tie knots at each spot with buckskin lace. In this method you leave several inches of extra hide around the pattern so you can cut fringe out of the excess material. The fringe and lace hangs down together and helps block breezes from blowing through the open spaces between the knots. Alternately, you can use a buckskin lace as thread and just make big stitches in and out every inch or so along the seams.

My clothes used to be tied together they way I first described, but I changed that after Renee and I got home from our walk across Montana in 1988. The fringe swept the ticks off the bushes along the way, and

A glover's needle, leather ring and rubber finger makes it easy to stitch through three layers of buckskin.

without tight seams they just crawled right inside my clothes. I found fifteen ticks crawling on me in a single day during the peak of tick season. Now I stitch all the seams tightly together with nylon thread, using the method my cousin learned in the Navy.

The most important sewing aid is a **glover's needle.** A standard needle is round, and it cannot penetrate buckskin no matter how sharp it is. But a glover's needle has a razor-sharp triangular tip. With a glover's needle you can easily push straight through three thicknesses of average buckskin with no awl and no pliers. Two other essential items include a **leather "ring"** to put over your middle finger and a **"rubber finger"** to put over your index finger. Use the leather finger to push the needle through the leather as shown in the picture, and pull the needle out the other side with

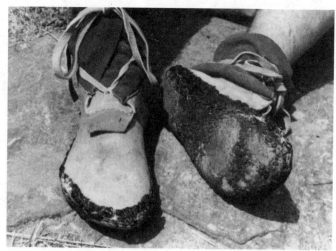
Custom brain-tan moccasins with painted on soles.

your thumb and rubber index finger. The rubber finger makes it easier to grip the needle. The finger I use is recycled from a rubber work glove. For thread I use a heavy nylon material, about the thickness of stout fish line. The nylon thread and glover's needles can be purchased at leather supply stores. With this sewing kit you can stitch a garment very quickly, and it is relaxing too; I have sometimes stitched away eight hours and more without tiring of it.

In this sewing process the patterns are always cut to size and any fringe or other ornamentation, if desired, is added as an additional piece called a welt. In the photo I am sewing together two pieces of buckskin, the front and back of a shirt. The third piece of buckskin shown sandwiched between the others is the welt. The welt covers up the threads in the seam; this protects the thread from wear and tear, and it keeps them out of sight. The welt can be done in a variety of ways for ornamentation. The most common style of welt is fringe. Cut your patterns out to exact size; then attach the scraps from the edges of the hide back in as welts. For fringe the welt can be made of scrappy material. The uneven edge will not show once it has been cut into fringe.

In addition to being beautiful, fringe has a variety of positive attributes. The main advantage to wearing fringe is that it helps break up your outline so that you look a little less like a human when you are stalking game. Fringe also provides you with a seemingly endless supply of string for all those times when you need to tie something up. There are theories that the fringe helps to wick water away from a shirt so that the moisture can drip off the tips of the fringe, but I think the extra material only sponges up more water.

Do carefully consider where you put fringe on your clothes. Avoid putting fringe where it will hang down and interfere with your bodily functions when "nature calls". Also avoid having long fringe on your sleeves where it will drag across your plate on those occasions where you wearing your skins to the dinner table.

For a different style of welt other than fringe, first stitch in a wide piece of buckskin; then trim it off flush, so that the end product becomes just a slim stripe right up the seam. It can be quite attractive. Alternately, an inch-wide welt can look nice on some bags, and I have put scalloped welts into some of the clothing I have made for Renee. I also sometimes use a fancy welt of cream or red satin cloth. I crease it, iron the crease, and stitch it in with the creased edge out. It adds a classy touch. As you stitch the seams together, be sure to keep checking the lengths of the pieces because one side will often stretch out longer than the other as you work. Bunch the longer side up a little at a time to use up the extra length. This is called "puckering".

Caring for Buckskin: Buckskins are easy to care for. The smoke serves as a built-in deodorant, so you do not have to wash your clothes very often. When you do, simply put them in the washing machine with cold water and some soap made from animal fats. For decades Ivory Snow was advertised as "99 & 44/100% pure", but it isn't any more. Last time I looked it was a chemical detergent. White King is still made with animal fats, but it contains whiteners too. The whiteners really cleaned up some years-old stains on my shirt, but then I had to smoke it again to give it color. Hang your skins up to dry when you pull them out of the wash. I usually stretch them around just a little to keep them really soft, and I would suggest making one last stretch lengthwise before you dry them. Pants and shirts tend to shrink lengthwise, so it is best to stretch them out in that direction before drying them.

◊　◊◊◊　◊

My moccasin has come untied. I stop and put my foot up on a rock to retie it. This time I put in a double knot to make sure it stays. My mind returns to the present for a moment, and I take time to tune into my environment.

The immediate area is a mix of aspens and Douglas fir. A few showy white thimbleberry blossoms peek out around the lush green vegetation beneath the canopy of trees. It will be quite awhile yet before the raspberry-like fruits come on. I will be watching them. I run my hand over the large leaves. They are shaped similar to maples leaves, but bigger. These leaves are often six inches or more across. Around here that seems like jungle growth. These lush plants seem almost out of place here in Montana. Most vegetation has smaller, more stout leaves for protection against the extremes of the climate and the jaws of grazing animals.

A sudden breeze brings a refreshing gust of cool air. It will soon be night and cool. I notice the distinctive scars on the aspens where deer and elk have stopped to rub the velvet off their antlers. I continue on my way, conscious of just how comfortable my footwear really is.

In addition to my moccasins I am also wearing some Teva-style sandals. These are made out of old tires, as I mentioned in an earlier chapter. I wear my moccasins inside these sandals. Granted, shoes made from tires may not initially seem like the most primitive technology in the stone-age sense, but they are definitely practical.

You see, I'm hard on shoes, and it's not uncommon for me to go through half a dozen or more pairs of commercial shoes each year. I maintain an active lifestyle, hiking, playing, camping, and working. Water wears out a shoe quicker than anything else. A few trips in and out of the creeks, puddles, and swamps, and they just come unglued.

If I do not happen to dissolve my shoes in water then I wear out the soles on gravel. It has always amazed

Moccasins with tire sandals are an unbeatable combination.

me that tire companies can manufacture a tire and warranty the tread for some 50,000 miles, yet I can wear out the sole on any ordinary shoe in less than a year. How come we cannot buy a shoe with a 50,000 mile warranty?

I have never been satisfied with conventional shoes, and it's not just because I wear them out so easily. Mostly it is because I do a lot of camping, and ordinary shoes have many drawbacks for this type of lifestyle. For one thing, I tend to rot my feet out each summer. Shoes are like incubators, holding in the dirt and sweat at warm temperatures, culturing all kinds of fungus and bacteria. Walking through a little bit of water once or twice a day just compounds the problem, making it nearly impossible to dry out the shoes. My feet even rot when I take care of them, washing and drying my crusty socks each day.

While I am at it, I have other complaints too. You see, I like getting close to nature, by participating in nature, instead of merely camping in it. I like to touch nature, and I feel so removed in a pair of ordinary shoes.

I go barefoot as much as I can, but like most people, I have tender feet—because I don't go bare foot all the time. Moccasins are ideal for camping, at least to a point. I can really feel the earth through them, and it has a profound psychological effect on me, making me feel so much more in tune with my surroundings. The trouble with moccasins is they wear out—fast. It takes me about eight hours of physical labor to tan a deer hide, several more hours to stitch a pair of moccasins, and one or two days of hiking to wear the first hole in them. The holes always start at the toughest points on your foot, so they are not initially a problem. You can get several more days of hiking in before you have to stitch in a new sole. Still, that is not a very long time at all. I have heard that some Native Americans carried multiple pairs of moccasins on journeys and spent each evening around the campfire fixing them. I read in one account where a party of Indians and westerners were climbing a gravely mountain and had to put on a new pair of moccasins every three hours!

I may practice primitive camping, but I also have to face the modern realities of the clock. My camping trips are short and full. I always have a lot of things I want to do while I am out. Fixing my moccasins every day is not one of them.

To solve that problem, I have tried over the years many marriages between buckskin and rubber to make lasting soles on my moccasins. The "paint-on" sole, a mixture of ground up tires and Barge Cement glue, does not work all that well. It helps, but even that wears through quite quickly under harsh conditions, and the rubber coating makes it difficult to dry out the leather of the moccasins. Besides, they are not very patchable once a hole gets started.

I have also tried working with the "crepe soles", a thick sheet of rubber cement that you can buy, cut and glue to the bottoms of shoes. The problem I had with those is that my feet no longer stayed in the right place on my moccasins. I slid off the back edge of the sole.

After these constant problems with shoes, I was ecstatic to learn of something that actually did work. My friend Jack Fee and I were preparing to go out on a three week expedition in the mountains. He made a new backpack for the trip, and I made some new moccasins. The best idea I had yet to try for protecting the soles was a mixture of pine pitch, charcoal and dried manure. I figured I could easily dope a little fresh material on the soles each night at camp to keep them from wearing out. I thought I was on to something, and the finished sole even looked good. Unfortunately, I wore completely through the pitch in two short city blocks during a test run. I was out of a plan before we even began our expedition.

Jack then told me a story about Indians from Mexico came to the United States and won foot races in sandals cut from tires. I've been interested in using tire soles before, but it seemed like I would have to glue or stitch the tire to the moccasins. I had reason to doubt that it would work. I also once had a pair of tire sandals, made in Mexico, where the leather lacing was nailed to the tire soles. Those came apart within a couple of days.

Jack had never seen the tire sandals that were reportedly used by the Mexican Indians, but decided to see what he could do anyway. I was quite impressed with the final product, a sort of Teva-style sandal.

I was most impressed with the fact that there was no glue, and no stitching or strapping on the bottom of the sole where they would be exposed to the ground. Instead he cut the sole with some side tabs out of the tire as one contiguous piece. The first model was crude in appearance, but amazingly comfortable. I too made a pair for the expedition.

The field tests of our sandals were quite exciting. The tire sandal and moccasin combination meant we had "modular" shoes. We wore both the moccasins and the soles when hiking, and then just one or the other around camp. We could use just the moccasins for stalking, or just the tires for walking in water. We climbed 10,000 foot peaks twice and really put on the miles. I did not wear socks, and never washed my moccasins, but my feet were in healthy condition for the duration of the trip—a first for me.

We did find that we would get blisters if we wore just the tires for any significant hiking, but we seemed to have no problems when the tires were worn in combination with moccasins, or with a couple pairs of heavy socks. I was amazed at how comfortable these sandals were, particularly because I once wore conventional hiking boots on a 500 mile walk across Montana, with severe blistering for the first 250 miles of the trip. Our new type of footwear gave me a freedom and comfort I had been searching for for a decade.

After 50,000 miles on a truck, there is still tread to spare!

Our prototype sandals were crude, but effective. Since then, I have developed the idea some more, into the tire sandals shown in these pictures. The most significant modification was the addition of the tab at the very back of the shoes. That tab is not always necessary, except in water. Without it your feet slide forward off the front of the soles when the tires are wet. That back tab holds your foot securely in place. I also added the rubber buckles and did away with the rope and buckskin ties of our early models.

Also, for our prototypes we just traced around a pair of conventional Tevas onto a tire, and started from there. I have since developed a system for creating a pattern to match your own foot. Plan on spending most of an entire day making your first pair. You will get faster as you make more.

Tire Sandal
Pattern

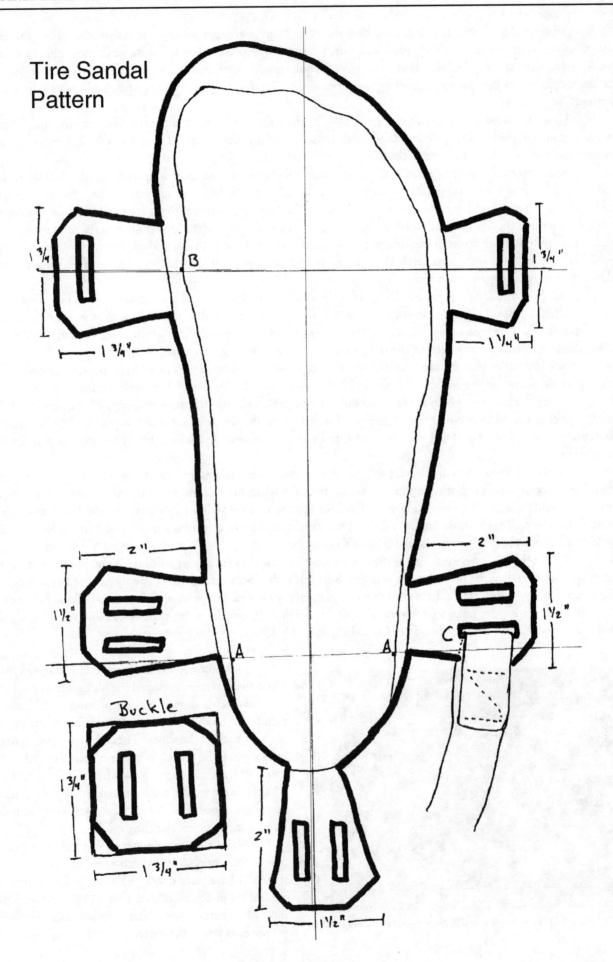

B

A   A   C

Buckle

Tire Sandals

First, place either foot in the center of a large piece of paper, at least an 8 1/2 x 14. Trace around your foot, being careful at all times to keep the pencil straight up and down. Next make a mark on each side directly down from the point on your ankles (A) (see pattern). Also make a mark at the point along the inside of your foot, directly back from your big toe (B).

Remove your foot from the pattern. Now sketch a bigger outline around the tracing of your foot. Add about 3/8 inch for the toes and sides, but not to the back. Then use a ruler and bisect the pattern lengthwise, extending the line three inches past the heel. This serves as a guide to help you sketch the rear tab accurately. Now connect the marks you made by your ankles (A), extending a line three inches beyond each side of the pattern. The tabs will be sketched in front of this line. Also draw a line for the front tabs, extending from the single mark (B) across the pattern, perpendicular to the line that bisects the foot lengthwise.

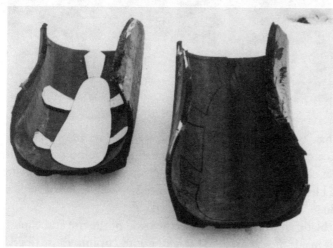

Tracing the pattern onto the inside of a tire.

The positioning of the tabs is quite variable, and you can choose to move them forward or back, or at angles to one another, and all usually work, although the arrangement I have suggested may work more consistently. Problems usually arise with the front set of tabs. If positioned at angles across the pattern they can twist and dig into your foot. If the tabs are moved forward or back then the edges can dig into that point (B) on the inside of your foot. That point is more pronounced on some people's feet than on others.

Now sketch in the five tabs, as shown on the pattern. These tabs are sized width-wise for 3/4 inch wide strapping, and should be made according to the approximate dimensions I've written in on the pattern, regardless of how big or small the foot. If anything, you might make some adjustments length-wise, adjusting for particularly large or small feet. Finally, sketch in the holes that you will cut out to thread the strapping through. This just helps you remember to cut them the right direction when you get to that stage. Cut the pattern out, and it can be used for both sandals, assuming your feet are fairly similar to one another.

As for tires, I recommend truck tires, rather than car tires. The "corner" of any tire, where the sidewalls and tread come together, is always much thicker than the rest. You can work with that thickness in the tabs of the shoes, but not in the sole itself. Pickup tires are wide enough to work with, and you can make about three pair of shoes from one tire.

Most importantly, always use tires that do not have steel cables running through them. All tires have some kind of fibrous reinforcement in them, typically nylon or rayon threads. Most of the newer tires also have a layer of steel cables, which is not workable at all. Still, there are a few billion of the older tires around without steel cables, so you should not have to look too far to find some. Just look on the sidewalls of the tire and it will be printed there how many plies of nylon, rayon, or steel are imbedded in the rubber.

We used simple utility knives to cut out our first sandals. This way you can trace around the pattern on the outside of the tire and start cutting. However, it is very laborious and not much fun. It is hard work, and you could easily slip and cut yourself with the utility knife. Along the way I have discovered that it is much easier and more enjoyable to cut tires using sharp wood chisels or a bandsaw. I have also heard it is easier to cut rubber under water.

Chiseling out a pair of sandals.

To do the chisel or bandsaw method you must first remove a section of tire. This allows you to run the piece through the bandsaw, or to put it on a wooden block where you can chisel from the inside out. A circular saw works well for cutting tires except that it creates a lot of blue-black smoke and binds frequently. Cut out a piece that is at least a half inch longer than your pattern, and save as much of the sidewalls as you reasonably can. These are useful later for making the buckles. Do not try cutting through the inner edge of the tire, which has an imbedded steel band to fit the tire snug against the rim.

Now trace the pattern on the inside of the tire, being certain that the pattern is centered and straight on the tire. Even a slight 1/2 inch angle along the length of a shoe can cause problems when you wear it.

I would suggest making only one sandal at a time and completing it. Finish the one and try it on; you might think of some modifications to improve the next one. Few of my pairs of sandals are exactly identical, as I usually find some new idea to try on that second one.

Simple but stylish.

The next step, after cutting out the sandal, is to thin the four side tabs. The tabs are usually cut from that "corner" on the tire, where there is a thick lump of tread. These are easiest to thin on a bandsaw. You can also do a crude but adequate job by cutting the lump down with some careful chiseling or with a sharp knife. Thin down as close as you can to the nylon/rayon plies, without actually cutting any of them. This step is not easy by any method I have found, and I typically leave 1/8 to 1/4 inch of rubber covering the plies, for a total thickness of up to half an inch. That is still thick, but workable.

Now, to make the tabs flex upward, take a razor blade and slice straight into the tread of the tire at the joint where the tab attaches. Slice in all the way until the plies inside are exposed. Be careful not to cut into those fibers.

Chisel out each of the eyelets, where the strapping will be threaded through. For this I use a 1 inch chisel and a 1/4 inch chisel. Be careful to not cut too close to the edge. If you break out the side of a tab, then you will probably have to start all over. Also cut a set of buckles from the sidewalls of the tire. These are easy to make.

For strapping, I use nylon harness strapping, available at farm and ranch supply stores. 3/4 inch wide strapping works well with the one inch slots. Cut the pieces extra long. You can trim them off after you thread them

through. Use a match and melt the end of the nylon strap to secure the threads. To do the back strap, thread through the hole marked point (C) on the pattern and stitch an inch or so of the strap back on itself. Thread around through the other eyelets, through the buckle, through the other hole on the first tab, and once again through the buckle. (My sandals are done differently in the photos.) The front strap should be threaded through the buckle, through both eyelets, and back through the buckle again. This system is a little hard to adjust, but once set, I can slip my foot in and out without having to tighten or loosen them.

The finished shoes should be comfortable to wear, although you may need to do some fine-tuning to get them right. For any serious hiking you should wear a couple heavy pairs of socks or moccasins, or bring

A pair of sandals I made for Renee.

along some moleskin. As for making moccasins, I learned how from my cousin Mel. He learned it from Reginald and Gladys Laubin's book, *The Indian Tipi*, published by the University of Oklahoma Press. It is a common book, and may be in your hometown library.

◊   ◊◊◊   ◊

I walk onward, enjoying the feel of my footwear and the aroma of the Doug fir trees. I listen to the bubbling of the water in the stream, tune into the slight quaking of the aspen leaves. The sky is clear. The air is warm. The shade is nice. I touch a fir tree as I pass by, running my fingers across the rough texture of the bark. A squirrel chatters at me, unseen in the canopy of trees. I pick a strawberry leaf to nibble on and pause to feel the fuzzy, woolly leaves of a mullein plant.

The mullein is an introduced plant from Europe. It is a very useful plant in primitive living, but it is also displacing native species in certain habitats. I realize that the European invasion of the Americas is still going on. The battle that our European ancestors started against the Native Americans still tragically continues against the native plants. Exotic species continue to infiltrate new grounds, rewriting the ecosystem across every field and meadow and mountain. These invaders can be kept in balance with careful and intensive ecosystem management, but for better or worse, they are here to stay. Already the species landscape we see today is radically different than in the past, and it continues to change in dramatic yet subtle ways, totally different from what it was, but only noticed by the trained eye.

Like my feet, my thoughts carry me forward, and the woolly leaf of the mullein reminds me of another useful import from Europe, wool. Humankind has been making and using products from wool for twelve thousand years or more, but mostly in the old worlds of Asia and Europe. There is little documentation of the use of wool in the Americas prior to the arrival of European sheep. Native Americans must have made some use of wool from the buffalo, but I have yet to read about it.

Wool is strong; an individual fiber can be flexed some 20,000 times without breaking while other materials such as silk break after about 1,800 flexes and rayon breaks with about 75 flexes. Wool is also very warm. Air trapped between the fibers gives it insulating value, and the fact that few of the fibers come in contact with your skin helps minimize the amount of heat conducted away through the material. Wool is also warm because it can absorb as much as thirty percent of its weight in water without feeling wet. In soaking up moisture wool fibers even release heat, 27 calories worth per gram of fiber.

In primitive living today, wool is a resource that has replaced many original resources that are no longer practical. Instead of having buffalo robes or rabbitskin blankets, we usually carry wool blankets. Instead of wearing fur clothing at the risk of being shot, we often wear woolen clothing.

Wool is most commonly used in the form of manufactured wool blankets. These are used principally for bedrolls. They are also sometimes cut and sewn to make "**capotes**", a bathrobe-style outfit with a hood. Blanket capotes are a luxurious kind of camp accessory, both aesthetic and comfortable. But they are ungainly for use on the trail.

A more practical style of blanket coat for trail camping is the **blanket poncho**. It is very easy to make. Take an inexpensive wool blanket and cut a single width-wise slit right in the middle of it. Put it over your head and wrap a belt around yourself and the blanket to hold it snug against your body. For all its simplicity it is surprisingly beautiful and it serves the dual purpose of a coat by day and a blanket by night, an important consideration when you are packing lightweight for the trail.

Another way wool can be used is through the simple and magical process of making **felt**. I first learned about felting at Rabbitstick Rendezvous, a primitive skills gathering in Rexburg, Idaho. Felt is made when wool fibers are agitated under heat and moisture. The fibers are covered with thousands of tiny scales, as many as 2,000 per inch of fiber. In the felting process the fibers become entangled with one another and the scales lock together making a strong and durable product that will not unravel. The scales are also what makes wool seem scratchy to some people.

A blanket poncho worn with a hooded sweatshirt to protect the neck and head.

Felting with Wool

To make felt, first you need wool, and there are many sources for wool around the world besides sheep. Angora goats and angora rabbits produce wool, as do llamas, yaks and some camels. The American bison—like the wild sheep our modern stock were bred from—grow a thick, woolly coat in the winter and shed it in thick clumps in the spring. The wool can be found hanging in the sagebrush or lying on the grass.

Sheep wool is the easiest material for most people to locate. You may be able to buy cleaned and carded wool at a local craft shop, or they may be able to direct you to someone who raises sheep locally and sells the raw fleeces. A raw fleece is wool that has not been cleaned or carded and is still full of straw, dirt, and oily lanolin. There are probably hundreds of different breeds of sheep in the world, and the wool on each of them is unique. Some work extremely well for felting and others do not. When buying wool, try to find someone who is knowledgeable about felting and ask what type of wool they recommend.

Carding the wool.

If you buy raw wool, the next step in the process is to wash the wool. This can be done by placing the wool in nylon bags in the **washing** machine. Palmolive liquid dish soap is the best cleanser to use since it has a near neutral pH and will not harm the wool. I use Ivory liquid soap and it works fine. Wash the wool with hot water and then use the spin cycle several times to spin the wool dry. Do not use the agitation (wash) cycle on the washing machine because it will cause the fibers to felt together. In the interest of simplifying the felting process for primitive living I have found that the wool can be used dirty and it will wash clean later, during the felting process.

The next step with raw wool is **carding** it to separate the fibers. The primitive method, for lack of carding brushes is to simply pull the wool apart to spread and fluff the fibers. The more conventional way is to use a set of carding brushes. Place a small amount of wool on one brush and repeatedly pull the brushes across each other. Decide what you want to make and then card a very big pile of wool for the project.

The finished blanket.

Laying out the wool for a felt baby blanket.

Agitating the fibers together by foot.

As a rule of thumb, the amount of carded wool you need is always greater than the amount you have carded!

Your first felting project should be something very simple like a **potholder**. To make a potholder use a square or round kitchen pan for a form. Place thin layers of carded wool in the pan with the fibers of each layer running crossways to the fibers below. Add layers until you have a pile of fluff six inches or more in height.

Then pour warm or hot water with soap (i.e.: dish soap) over the wool and pat the fibers down into the pan and the water. The purpose of the soap is to **lubricate the fibers** so they slide together more easily. With unwashed wool the soap also helps to clean out the dirt and lanolin. To simplify the process for primitive living, I have tried felting without soap and found that it works, but not as quickly or as well.

Anyway, if you are going to add a **colored design**, now is the time to do it. You can make a design by felting dyed or naturally colored wool right into your project. Simply place the colored fibers on in the desired pattern and spread a thin layer of white wool over the pattern to help bind it in. The design must be added before you start the felting process. During felting the fibers will lock together and you will not be able to add more material.

Felt products shrink a lot in the process so be sure to start over-size!

To turn your warm water, soap, and wool into felt begin by working the material with your fingers, doing what is called "**pony prancing**". Use all your fingers to prance and poke the wool to work the fibers together. Be careful to only use downward motions. Sideways motions will push the material around and alter your design. Flip the piece over from time to time and work both sides. As the felting begins and the fibers start locking together, you can give it more abuse. Work it vigorously and shape the edges and pick it up and work it between your hands. Keep the water warm or hot, preferably hot. The heat helps the felting process. A project like a potholder will take about an hour and shrink an inch or more on the sides. When it is felted properly then let it dry and it is ready to use. You can wet it again and continue felting it tighter at anytime if you so choose.

More advanced projects such as the **mittens** in the photos are made without seams by shaping the product around a **resist**, typically a plastic pattern. The process is somewhat different from a simple potholder.

For a pair of mittens make a resist by tracing around your hand. Cut the pattern out of a piece of heavy plastic. Place a layer of carded wool in a pan, wet it down and place the resist on it. Wrap the wet wool over the top of the resist and add another layer. Place the fibers on top, wet them down, turn the whole thing over, and wrap the fibers around that side. Keep alternating like this until you have built up half a dozen or more layers of wool.

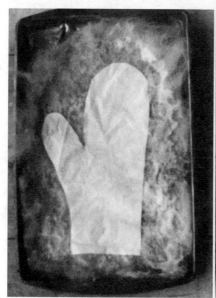

A plastic resist is used to make an open space inside the felt for your hand.

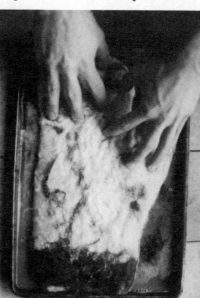

"Pony prancing" starts the felting process by interlocking the fibers.

The finished mittens are warm, beautiful and seamless.

The wool will spread out somewhat and the mitten will look huge. That is okay. Next add colored wool for a design and begin working it into felt. Work it for most of an hour until it the fibers are locking together. Cut open the end (where you put your hand in) and pull out the resist. Wear the mitten as you continue felting it and it will shape specifically to whichever hand you are wearing it on. Wear it on the one hand and work it with the other. With the mitten still on your hand, work it over a hard surface to really compact the fibers. A washboard is usually used for this step, and a glass washboard works best. However, for lack of a washboard I used the front of the refrigerator for making the mittens. I really leaned into it and polished the refrigerator till it shined. The compaction on the wool quickly shrank the mittens down two inches in both length and width, and they would have been too small if I continued working them.

When you finish your mittens or other project, hang them up to dry. You will have a very beautiful, warm, durable, and valuable product that you can be proud of.

◊   ◊◊◊   ◊

I follow a trail through the forest. It is an animal trail along a lively stream. It is one of two outlets from Hollowtop Lake. Here the forest is thicker, darker and cooler. The ground beside the trail is green with moss. From the edge of the stream I pick a few leaves of brook saxifrage and I nibble on them as I walk. The day is growing old. I hasten my way towards camp.

Sunset

The sun is setting. It is now behind the mountain peaks, and it will soon leave only darkness. But for now it is still light and the sky above is many shades of blue. To the east it is dark blue, and grayish, but not intense. Overhead the sky is light blue and pale. To the south it is more gray than blue. North of me the sky is calm and clear, light blue. And to the west, along the ridge of the peaks, the sky is still and almost white in the evening sun.

I am near my camp now, and I stop to take a break and stretch. I fill my copper cup with water from the stream and kick back for a bit, using my pack for a backrest. I have traveled many miles with this pack.

Canvas sack backpack.

It is a **backpack** made from two canvas sacks, antique cement sacks, which I have sewn together for strength. Two wide strips of leather sewn to the canvas serve as shoulder straps. I place the bulk of my gear inside the canvas bag and then close it with a drawstring at the top. I make up my blankets into a long roll, which I wrap over the pack in a horseshoe shape. I secure it in place with four leather straps that are sewn to the pack. I tie my buckskins on top where I can easily get to them. Sometimes I carry my journal and water bottle in a smaller possibles bag, which balances on top of my pack, behind my neck and shoulders.

It has been a good and comfortable pack system, and I have traveled far with it. It is much better than the rawhide pack with a wooden frame I once carried. I made the rawhide pack specifically for our trip when Renee and I walked across Montana. I had limited experience with other packs before that trip, so I did not know that my rawhide version was more uncomfortable than a pack should be. It was almost a year after our walk when I made the canvas sack pack and realized what comfort was. Thinking back, it was no wonder I lagged behind Renee from one end of the state to the other!

Besides the rawhide pack and my canvas sack pack, I have also put on many miles with a **bedroll pack**, where all the gear is rolled up in a wool blanket, then tied in a bundle to make kind of a soft backpack. The bedroll pack requires about ten feet of cord and roughly an equal amount of strap, like seat-belt webbing or some other type of material, to serve as shoulder straps, as you will see on the following pages. I first learned the bedroll pack as a student on my 26-day expedition with Boulder Outdoor Survival School. Later we used the same type of pack on expeditions with troubled teenagers in Idaho and Utah.

More recently I have become a fan of **Roycroft-style pack frames**, which are made from three sticks lashed together as a triangle. The gear is lashed onto the pack frame, as are the shoulder straps. However, the type I use isn't a true Roycroft pack, because I like to lash a couple extra cross pieces onto the pack to better attach the straps and gear.

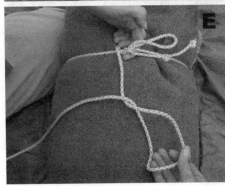

The Bedroll Pack

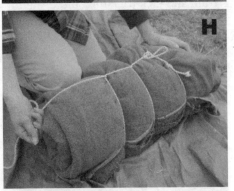

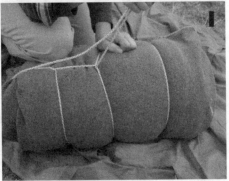

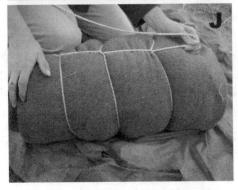

To make a bedroll pack, start by laying your blanket out flat, usually on a poncho. Place you gear on the blanket, except for the things you need to use during the day. Your gear should be neatly laid out in about the middle third of the blanket and close to the edge. This done, flip the other thirds of the blanket over the middle third and your gear (A). Start at the end where your gear is and roll the blanket up like a sleeping bag. Roll it as tight as you can (B).

Next, take a ten-foot long length of cord. Tie a small loop at one end. Wrap the cord around the width of the pack about one third of its length and run the end of the cord through the loop. Pull the end back towards itself to cinch the cord down around the pack (C). Tie a knot at the loop such that you create a second small loop. (D). Now give the tail a twist to make another loop (E) and put it over the smaller loop and pull it tight (F & G). Repeat that knot one time (E, F & G).

Then run the cord down the pack and around it as if you were wrapping a present. In other words, wrap around the width of the pack and come back to catch the cord you are holding. Pull the cord lengthwise again to cinch the cord around the pack. No knot is needed at that point. Repeat that step once (H).

Now turn the pack over and continue with the cord around the pack lengthwise, wrapping once around the three cords in the back. Be sure to keep it tight (I & J).

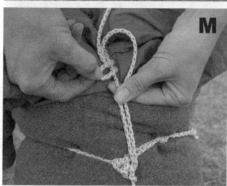

Bring the cord all the way around the pack to the starting point and run it through the loop again (K). Now fold up the poncho and other loose clothes and place them on this top end of the pack (L). Cinch it very tight and tie a knot (M & N). (This is the same knot as shown in D-E-F-G)

Now use ten feet of nylon strap and run both ends under the widthwise cord with one end on each side of the knot. Pull the ends back through at the midpoint and cinch it down (O). The strapping should be secured around the knot to form the top of the shoulder straps.

Pull the ends of each strap under the bottom widthwise cord and leave the strapping loose. This forms the shoulder straps (P). Put the pack on like a backpack and hold on to the loose straps. Pull these around your waist and tie them in front of you with the pack in a comfortable position. This completes the bedroll pack (Q & R).

A variation of the bedroll pack is to tie the cording the same, but secure the strapping to two points to make a single strap. Put the strap on over your shoulder or neck and shoulder and the pack will ride under your arm.

Another simple type of bedroll is the "horseshoe" pack. Lay your gear in a line along one side of your blanket. Make your blanket into a long roll with you gear inside. Tie cordage around it in several points to hold it together. Bring the ends of the blanket together to form a "horseshoe" shape and tie these together. Put it on over your head and shoulder so that the open end of the horseshoe is by your side and the other end is by your head. It is a comfortable pack since the load rides evenly in front and behind you.

◊   ◊◊◊   ◊

Pack Frames

Pack frames are easy to make and they are a very comfortable way to carry your gear on a primitive wilderness expedition. A pack frame is also faster to pack and unpack, and it can be made from all wild materials.

A very simple pack frame can be made with just three sticks lashed together to make a triangle. The straps and gear are attached to the triangle. The softest part of your gear is placed against your back and partly squeezed through the frame to provide padding. I prefer the style shown here, with a crosspiece at the top to attach the shoulder straps to, and another crosspiece halfway down to keep the gear from pushing through too much. These cross pieces also make it easier to lash the gear in place, although the pack frame definitely takes longer to make this way.

To make a pack frame, start by cutting some straight and sturdy sticks. For this project I used willow. The two vertical pieces should be about the distance from your armpit to fingertips. The bottom piece should measure from elbow to fingertip. The other crosspieces can be a little shorter (A).

Completely build the triangle before adding on the crosspieces. Use the tip of your knife to score the sticks where you want the notch (B). Slide the knife underneath the willows to score the backside. Then carefully cut the notches on all three points of the triangle until the pieces fit snugly together (C). Good notches with marginal cordage will hold together better than bad notches with good cordage.

When the joints are nice and tight the next step is to lash them together. For this pack I made dogbane cordage and used a square lashing (D). I often use rawhide for the lashings, especially for the wilderness survival expeditions we lead through our school. Everyone makes a pack frame on the first day to carry their gear. When the triangle is completely lashed together then you can go back and score and notch the cross pieces, and lash them in place as well (E).

At this point, the frame is complete, but you still need backpack straps. My primary pack has felt straps I cut from a failed blanket I tried to make. I moved the blanket from one workspace to another before the fibers were interlocked and created some holes which I was never able to felt back together. So I cut the good parts of the blanket into pack straps, and to my amazement they have held up for hundreds of miles.

We've also used nylon straps, seatbelt webbing, and buckskin for shoulder straps, and in one case we salvaged shoulder straps from a broken aluminum pack frame. But my favorite straps are the all-primitive ones, such as the ones shown here made from cattail cordage. I simply cut the long, mature cattail leaves in the fall when they were starting to yellow, and twisted them together to make some very thick cordage (F). You would be surprised how much cattail cordage it takes to make a set of shoulder straps. I had about twelve feet for this project, and that was just barely enough. The big knots especially consume a lot of material. In the mountains where there are no cattails, it would be possible to make pack straps from the inner bark of a pine tree. Just be sure to harvest it in a very out-of-the-way spot where other people won't see the scarred tree.

To attach the straps to the pack at the top, simply fold the cord at the middle and push the two ends through above the upper crosspiece. The fold in the middle of the cord makes a natural loop when brought back under the crosspiece, so run the two ends through the loop to secure the straps in place (G). Then tie the straps off at the bottom corners, such that the straps are long enough for the pack to fit you comfortably (H).

Optionally, you can simply wrap around the bottom corners of the pack and tie the cord around your waist for a waist band. But I prefer straps that are just tied off at the pack. Notice that the crosspieces are placed on the side of the pack frame away from your back.

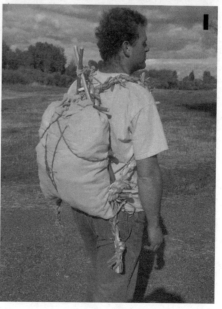

To complete the pack you still need some cordage to tie your gear in place. I prefer buckskin lacing cut from scraps of my braintanned hides. However, any natural or synthetic cordage will work. In our classes we usually use plastic baling twine, simply because it is very abundant here. But by itself, the twine tends to come unravel, which makes it really hard to tie and untie knots down the road. So I like to cord two pieces of twine together to make a more durable and somewhat primitive cord, even if it is made from plastic twine. The cord should be attached to the middle of the bottom crosspiece of the pack in the same manner the shoulder straps were attached at the top. That leaves you with two free ends to lash your gear onto the pack frame (H). With the aid of the upper crosspieces it is really easy to tie your gear securely in place so it won't come undone just as you are wading across a creek. I seldom bring a blanket on these outings anymore, so I often bring a canvas bag to put my gear in, but you could also just wrap everything up inside an extra shirt or poncho. Be sure to place the softest gear against your back.

◊   ◊◊◊   ◊

I slip my pack on and walk upstream to the lake. It is evening and the fish are jumping in the water. Otherwise it is very still and very peaceful. This is a high mountain lake, about 8,500 feet in elevation, but not quite above timberline. There is something special about this place. It is so clean, so pure, so wild and untouched. "Is this

what all the world was like before we changed everything?" I wonder to myself. It is hard to imagine that a place like this could ever be defiled with roads and development. No one would let it happen.

Then it hits me. Just out of sight beyond the ridge there is an exploratory gold mine and more roads. I saw that road when it was first bulldozed up the mountain in about 1985. We were on a family picnic up Potosi canyon. I told my mom I could walk back to Grandma Josie's house, and off I went. Of course I had never done that before, and I had no maps, but it seemed simple enough. I just had to go up the road, hop over the mountain and walk down to town.

It didn't take long for me to realize my goof. I was hiking deeper into the mountains when I should have been going the other way. But for some reason I

Hollowtop Lake

just couldn't turn around. I was drawn up the mountain and shocked by what I saw. It was like someone went for a Sunday drive in their bulldozer, cutting a road to the top of the mountain, as if they only wanted to see what was on the other side. I hiked all the way to the top, crossed the saddle and walked down the South Boulder drainage until I reached the little town of Mammoth well after dark. I called Mom and she kindly made the hour-long drive around the mountains to bring me home. Back then none of us knew anything about mining or mine regulations and mine politics. And the road was way out there, out of sight and mostly out of mind. Besides, it didn't seem like my business anyway. I assumed that there were people in charge of watching over the forest.

We were soon embroiled in the more menacing problem of the Chicago Mining Company and their Pony Gold Mill above town. We were forced to learn more than we ever wanted to know about mining, and the issue consumed all our energy. It is only now, years after the Chicago Mining Company went belly-up and crumbled, that the mining activity on top of the mountain has finally popped back onto the radar screen. That original road stopped just below the mountain pass at one mine, but it was extended in 1989 all the way up and over the 9,400 foot pass to the Nicholson Mine so the mine operators could do some test drilling for gold.

In the Environmental Assessment issued by the Forest Service, a wildlife biologist expressed concerns about the mountain goat population that inhabits the peaks. He recommended that no roads should be built to the saddle,

The road to the Nicholson Mine crosses a 9,400 foot pass in an inventoried roadless area, completely bisecting the proposed Middle Mountain Wilderness Area.

and that any roads built nearby should be reclaimed that year to avoid disrupting the mountain goat patterns. The Forest Service permitted the project anyway, but at least they required the mine operators to build their road, drill their test holes, and completely reclaim the site within a 90-day period. The site is only accessible for about that many days each year. The rest of the time it is packed with snow. Unfortunately, the permit was issued for 1989 and the road is still open and active all these years later!

The mine isn't a big one. There are just a couple of guys poking around for gold on top of the world. It took them thirteen years to complete the test drilling they were given ninety days to do. It is such a small operation that it wouldn't really make a dent of difference if it was down in the foothills like so many of the other mines.

But the roads have significantly altered the fragile alpine habitat. Part of the road was built before it was even permitted, and it wasn't built to proper specifications. Like I said, it was as if someone went for a Sunday drive in a bulldozer! The road was corrected by building it in the right place, but the reclaimed roads were vegetated with non-native species. What was once an island of native biodiversity is now adulterated with foreign plants.

I find myself staring toward the Nicholson Mine, as if I could see through the ridge of granite that hides it. I follow the ridgeline with my eyes and remember what it is like to be up there where the vegetation is sparse and rarely more than a few inches tall. From on top you can look out at all the jagged peaks of the Tobacco Root Mountains. Many of them have no vegetation at all.

When I am up there I really feel like I am on the edge of the planet, scraping against the vast emptiness of space. It is both beautiful and hostile, and I rarely get to spend much time there before the threat of wind, lightning and rain sends me running back down for cover.

This entire end of the mountain range was once proposed for wilderness designation. It was included as the Middle Mountain Wilderness Area in a bill passed by Congress. President Ronald Reagan was reportedly prepared to sign the bill into law, but he was encouraged to veto it by Montana's Republican Senator Conrad Burns. The Middle Mountain Wilderness Area was again included in a bill that passed the U.S. House in 1995.

I supported wilderness designation, mostly because it seemed to be the chic environmental thing to do at the time. But I was ambivalent about the need, because to my way of thinking wilderness is everywhere and we are part of it. Why draw a line on the map and label one side as wilderness and the other as sacrificial? We should treat all land equally and utilize the resources of this wilderness we live in, but do it in a truly conscientious and sustainable manner. It seemed a shame to lock up a lot of perfectly good timber and other resources with no option of using them. At least that was my ideology. Then I awoke to reality.

I've seen too many roaded mountain sides and too many invasive plants using the roads as highways into the pristine backcountry. I have seen the way our public agencies bend over backward for anyone that wants to go for a Sunday drive with their bulldozer across the mountains. A special place like Hollowtop Lake has little or no real protection. "How long," I wonder, " will it be before there is a road up this side of the mountain too?"

The Middle Mountain Wilderness would encompass mostly mountain peaks and mountain lakes. On a map the proposed wilderness looks like many fingers, because there are roads following most of the creeks high up into the mountains, and roads cannot be included in a wilderness area. One of the key problems with the Nicholson Mine is that the roads were built in an inventoried roadless area. The roads completely bi-sect the proposed wilderness area and jeopardize the possibility of future designation. The Forest Service should be protecting the forest, but they have spent thousands of hours of time facilitating work at the Nicholson Mine, all of it at taxpayer expense.

The agency personnel who issued the original 90 day permit for the Nicholson were transferred elsewhere and the mine was permitted again and again and again until 2002, when they finally finished drilling and applied for a new permit for yet another road. I joined a Forest Service tour of the project area along with other concerned individuals. But the mine operator invited twenty of his buddies to join the tour and they all stood there on top of the mountain and told us how mining is good for wildlife. The District Ranger for the Forest seemed to agree and suggested that the project had no significant impact. The Forest geologist just laughed when my neighbor pointed out the irretrievable loss of resources. He acted like it was the most ridiculous thing he ever heard. Neither of them believed us when we pointed out that the original permit required reclamation within 90 days. We had to show them the Forest Service Environmental Assessment to prove it, not that they really cared anyway.

For lack of good management, I now realize, we desperately need wilderness designation to protect what we have left before it is all gone. I have vowed to do everything I can to make that happen.

I stop to clear my mind. While the Nicholson Mine is an important issue, I do not need to dwell on it here at the lake. I love the beauty of this place and for a moment I stare down into the placid waters. From the depths awakens an old but pleasant memory.

I was camped here some time ago, and I was exploring the lake shore one quiet evening. Two people emerged on the opposite shore of the lake; one of them was fishing and the other pulled out a flute. I chose a granite seat beside the lake and listened as the flutist's notes flowed out across the still water. There was harmony that evening. I will never forget it.

A fish breaks the placid surface of the lake just in front of me. It finds its mark and disappears again into the depths, leaving only ripples on the water. I walk to my campsite and unload my pack in the shelter. This is the shelter I built between two boulders. It is not hidden, but it is off the beaten path so I do not think too many people see it. It has not changed much since I came last summer. I pull out my flint and steel and kindle a fire then fill up my cooking can with water from a nearby stream and set it on the fire. It quickly comes to a boil, and I add some fir needles to it for tea. I dig out my journal, and a pen, and sit back to reflect on the day and to think about what the day means to me.

Primitive living is a great metaphor for me, and I love to walk the metaphor. It is always a thrill to put on my pack and leave the contemporary world behind. Out on these camping trips I am able to clear my mind and get in touch with the natural world. I get a fresh perspective on my life in the modern world and return home with new ideas and new energy. But make no mistake about it—I certainly don't live this way all the time.

I spend the majority of my time in the contemporary world, and much of it in front of a computer running our business or writing books and editing videos. Together, Renee and I have built a house we love and we have four wonderful kids, plus a bunch of horses, chickens, cats and a dog. We even have our favorite TV shows. Our lives are very much rooted in the modern world, and I feel I can make a difference by being part of the modern world—far more than I ever could by walking away from it all.

But no matter what I am doing, primitive living is always there in the back of my mind, as I daydream about the next grand adventure I want to go on. In the same way that primitive living allows me to reflect on contemporary life, I have the chance to reflect on primitive living while going about my daily life at home. It gives me the time to think back on what I have learned and experienced, what I believe in, and what I am into primitive living for.

For example, when I first started learning these skills the available literature seemed to imply that you should go out with nothing and work your way up from there. I lived on those books and followed them like gospel. I went on many, many camping trips with little more than a flint & steel kit or a bowdrill set. I made bad shelters and ate little or no food. I was constantly cold and hungry and miserable. I'm not sure why any body would keep doing these skills if they had half as many lousy camping experiences as I did! It is hard to learn new skills when your physically wasted, and it took me years to convince myself that it really was okay to bring food or other luxuries on a camping trip. When I decided to focus on having a quality experience, then I started learning the skills I always wanted to know.

Now, with the passage of time and experience, I find that there are other things I also like to do besides work for my subsistence. I like to explore, to watch animals, to write in my journal, and to do many other things. While it is still rewarding and exciting to develop my primitive skills abilities, there are other activities that are equally rewarding and exciting.

My tea is hot. I put away my journal and my pen. With a red handkerchief I pull the can off the fire and pour my copper cup full. I set it aside to cool. Then I sit back to think about what it is that I am seeking.

Primitive living, as I wrote in the second chapter, is in many ways like a metaphor where we role-play certain personas, such as the archaeologist, the medicine man, the musician, or the survivor of Armageddon. When I imagine various roles in primitive living, there is one persona that appeals to me more than any other. That is the persona of the scout.

I have always been drawn towards the idea of being able to move lightly, freely, almost invisibly through nature—to be like the breeze—present, but invisible. The persona of the scout—and I am referring to the Indian scouts of another era—is symbolic of that desire. It is distinctly different from the personas that appeal to me at other times, such as when I teach. Many of the roles I play are directed towards helping other people and helping the earth. But the persona of the scout is very personal to me; it is something I seek distinctly for myself. It is my dream to be able to move and live as the scout, to travel unhindered, hopping, skipping, and gliding through the wilderness.

The scouts of another era typically traveled with little or no gear. They were the masters of primitive living and they almost literally lived by their bare hands. But as I suggested along the way, there are trade-offs. For me, taking less gear means I can travel farther and dance on the way but it also means I have to spend more of my time providing for my sustenance. It is important to me to travel light like the scout, and at the same time, I want to have enjoyable experiences that make me want to return again and again. I want to travel light and I also want to spend much of my time playing, exploring, or writing in my journal.

Thus I seek to **balance** what I take and what I bring so that I can have both the lightest load and the most free time. In many ways the approach I am leaning towards in defining my future in primitive living is similar to the planning approach used in Holistic Management that I wrote about in chapter eight. First, I have defined that I am seeking a quality of experience in that "I want to enjoy my time in primitive living". That is much like the *quality of life* goal used in the holistic process. Second, I have defined in general terms what I want to do, that is "to achieve a scout level of ability in the ecosystem". This is comparable to the *production goal* used in the holistic process where people define what they want to do to provide their living from the land.

Currently, I am in the stage of brainstorming and assessing a description of what I need to help me achieve those goals for quality of experience and what I want to do. I sift through different technologies and ideas for primitive living and select the ones that bring me closer to my desired goals. The skills and ideas that pass my criteria begin to form a description of what I need to know and do to achieve the scout ability I am seeking. It is similar to the *description goal* in resource management of how the ecosystem must function to meet the other goals, except it is instead a description of the capabilities and knowledge I need to meet the other two goals.

The first two goals, to have a quality of experience and to become a scout, set the criteria, and the description goal is the fulfillment of that criteria. As I sort through ideas, the ones that meet the criteria set by the first two goals becomes part of the description. For example, there are many ways to go about cooking. A scout with no gear has the options of cooking on a stick over the flames, or cooking in a steam pit under the fire. These are good cooking methods up until one wants to boil a liquid. For me, to have an enjoyable quality of experience I like to have the convenience of cooking in a container. For containers I have a variety of choices including coal burned bowls, pottery, pieces of hide or stomach suspended from a tripod or hanging into a hole in the ground, or modern implements. To meet the criteria of the scout, so I can travel lightweight, I often use a tin can and/or a gold pan. This gear allows me to enjoy a quality experience, and it adds only negligible weight to my pack.

Of course there are difficulties in finding the ideas and technologies to meet my specified criteria. Most primitive skills literature and archaeological records are oriented towards bulky material culture like baskets, pottery, or weaponry. By the time you make these, plus your bowdrill set, your shelter, and your tanned hides—well, you need a pickup truck to move to your next campsite! That does not fit my personal criteria for becoming a scout. Therefore, on my own, I am gradually developing many of the techniques I need to meet my criteria. The pit shelter is one such development designed to allow me to travel lightly like the scout, while at the same time allowing me the quality of comfort.

As I look for ideas or develop my own, I certainly lean towards the primitive skills that give me the satisfaction of saying, "I did it myself". For example, I find greater satisfaction in finding a bottle bottom and making an arrowhead from it, as opposed to being dependent on obsidian trucked in from elsewhere or being similarly dependent on a commercially manufactured steel arrowhead. At the same time, I do not limit myself to only primitive choices. In sorting for the resources to meet my criteria, I use a process somewhat similar to that used in Holistic Management. From the Stone Age to the Space Age I pick and choose through the various technologies for the resources that best help me to reach my combined goals

I pick and choose between all technologies from the stone age to the space age and select those that best fit all of my goals.

As an example, the Swiss Army knife is a tool that meets my criteria for being lightweight, and it enables a more enjoyable experience. One can do a lot with stone tools, but stone has its limitations in size, weight, and capabilities. One time I participated in a semi-advanced survival trip where it was decided that we would bring implements such as knives, but we would not use them the first day. We built a shelter in the rain and then attempted to make working bowdrill sets with damp materials and stone tools. We worked hard all the way up until it was almost too dark to work. We were nearly prepared to shiver together all night in the shelter, but I asked if anyone would mind if I used my knife on my set. No body objected, so I quickly fine-tuned my set and easily started a fire. I was just beginning to shape my ideas about having an enjoyable quality of experience, and that event impacted me significantly.

The Equipment Checklist

At first glance you might be surprised at the extensive equipment list I have compiled. I write about bringing "little or nothing", yet this list may initially appear as a "lot of something". Allow me to clarify.

This is a list of *choices*. Each time I go out I pick through the list and select the items that are appropriate for the trip I am taking. Every time and place is different, and a person will always have unique goals for each trip. Consider, is it summer or is it winter? Is this an over-night trip, or a month long trip? Is there going to be one stationary camp, or is camp going to be in a new place each day? Goals can vary tremendously from one camping trip to another, and thus so can the equipment utilized along the way. The following list will give you an idea of some of the choices I make, and should help give you some insights on what to bring for your own unique camping trips.

This list is divided into several sections, the first being for very warm summer weather, while the other sections are added for other times of the year.

Ultra Light Summer List: This first list is specifically put together for camping trips during extremely warm weather where I plan to be on the move every day, traveling, exploring, and going through lots of water. It is for those times and places where I can be adequately warm throughout the daytime hours with just shorts and a T-shirt. For these trips I choose gear that will not be damaged by water and plan to take only what I can cram into and onto a regular fanny pack.

For clothing I bring my homemade **tire sandals** and **moccasins**, plus a **T-shirt**, **shorts**, and **belt**. For fire starting I sometimes make a simple **handdrill** set, but also carry a **bic lighter** in case the handdrill set gets soaked. I make shelters as I go, but I also bring along some type of **tarp**, **poncho**, or plastic **garbage bag** for wet weather emergencies.

To do my cooking, I bring a lightweight **stainless steel or tin can**, and I pick up new twigs at each meal for **chopsticks**. My food consists of **rice**, **flour**, and **trail mix**, plus an assortment of previously gathered **primitive foods**. These are all tightly wrapped in plastic bags for weatherproofing. I do some kind of additional foraging virtually every time I go out. I seldom carry water on these trips, but just drink what ever I find.

Additionally, I bring a **handkerchief,** which serves the multiple purposes of *potholder, washcloth,* and *snot rag.* I bring a film canister full of **baking soda** for use in *leavening my bread, as toothpaste, with water for a stomachache,* or *treating bee stings.* I also bring a **Swiss army knife**, a **comb**, and a **toothbrush**.

I always peruse the rest of my lists to consider additional options.

Medium Weight Summer List: This list is for camping trips in cooler summer weather. I bring everything from my Ultra Light list, except the fanny pack, which I replace with a bigger, homemade **canvas backpack** or **pack frame**. This list is light enough to still allow me to travel freely, but I bring along gear that I do not want to drag through the water with me.

For additional clothing I bring **jeans**, a **flannel** or **buckskin shirt**, a **hooded sweatshirt**, and a **pair of socks**. I do not need the socks with my moccasins or tire sandals, but instead use them as "sleeping socks" worn only at night to keep my feet warm.

For fire-starting implements I still bring the **bic lighter** for emergencies, but also bring my **flint & steel fire kit** and frequently my **bowdrill set**. I bring a **canteen** or **water bottle**, but only fill it up when I will be away from the water for any length of time.

I bring an additional cooking implement in the form of a **gold pan**, which I use for stir-frying and sautéing. I sometimes use it as a shovel too. Sometimes I bring a **spoon**, instead of making chopsticks along the way. I add to my food supply with **vegetable oil** and **brown sugar** for doing some more stylish cooking. The oil is for frying food, and the sugar is usually for wild berry "ashcake" pies.

Climbing Hollowtop Peak.

Spring/Fall List: For cooler weather, typical of spring and fall, I start using several additional pieces of equipment. One thing I sometimes bring is **plastic bags** to put on over my socks inside my shoes. This way I can continue wearing my tennis shoes or tire shoes even in cold, wet weather. The bags do not last long, but they slow down the movement of moisture around my feet. This keeps my feet reasonably warm even when my shoes are soaking wet. I also bring **warm gloves** for these times of year, and frequently a **wool blanket**, which has a slit cut in the middle for use as a coat. I have a **belt** that wraps around the blanket coat to hold it close to my body.

Winter List: For winter camping I once traded in my denim jeans for good **wool pants**, but now I just bring a pair of **sweat pants** to wear over the jeans. The space between the jeans and the sweats can be stuffed with grass for extra insulation. I also bring felted **wool mittens**, a **wool scarf**, **wool hat** and **sorrel boots** or my own **felt boots**. Despite my "roughing-it" type of camping style, I am really a fair-weather camper, and I only go out during the many sunny and warm spells we get here in the winter. I am not very interested in snow, so I often put on my tennis shoes and hike out across the farm fields of the Gallatin Valley, which are bare and dry during much of the winter.

Optional Gear and Luxuries: These are additional items I pick through each time, selecting whatever is appropriate for the trip I am taking. I frequently bring a **watch** for doing timed plant studies. I collect various roots and seeds and use the watch to see how much can be harvested per hour. Since I don't wear a watch at home, it sometimes seems really weird to carry one on a camping trip!

I like to bring minimal **first aid supplies**, at least Band-Aids, when I go alone. But I always bring a complete kit when traveling as a group. Other items I choose from include: a **sun hat, mirror, small flashlight, camera, fishing license, maps, big knife, books, paper** and **pens**.

I never liked flashlights because the batteries didn't last long enough to justify using them. But the newer, more efficient LED lights seem to go forever on just one battery.

Other Food Items: The most useful foods I bring along are the **trail mix, flour, rice, oil** and **brown sugar**. Between these and the many **wild foods** of our area, I can concoct some pretty exciting meals and deserts. Other lightweight foods I frequently bring include: **lentils** or **beans** (sometimes plain, sometimes instant, refried bean flakes), **bouillon, ramen noodles, potato flakes, hot cereals,** and **powdered milk**.

This is the sum total of all the gear I take on my various camping trips throughout the year. Depending on my goals and the length of my expeditions, I carry anywhere from about eight pounds up to almost thirty pounds of gear with me on the trail. The bulk of the weight is usually food, both "contemporary" foods that I have bought and "primitive" foods that I have harvested. The next heaviest item is usually the extra clothing, the shirts, sweatshirts, and pants, etc., that have to be carried through the hot days for use during the much cooler evenings and mornings.

Deciding what to bring on your own camping trips is a matter of considering your goals. What do you want to do? Where do you want to go? I would suggest that you always maintain a flexibility to consider all ideas, new and old. Assess what needs you have to be able to fulfill your goals in primitive living. Brainstorm ways to meet those needs, and test your ideas. To meet my own needs, I am continuously doing short, weekend-style camping trips so I can prove or disprove new ideas. Each time I make new changes in what I take and what I make, adapting to meet my own personal goals.

I encourage you to always pack for the best quality of experience you can have. Everyone has their own creature comforts they really need, and some items you will always want, even if they are heavy. Others may provide you with a greater quality of experience just by leaving them behind so you can move along more freely. You set the goals and shape the experience. The only rule of the game is, "You want it, you carry it."

◊　◊◊◊　◊

A pinecone drops from the tree near my camp. The squirrel scrambles down the tree, bounces easily across the ground and climbs another tree. Gradually my view of the land is becoming dimmer. The sun is setting.

A few thin, yet puffy clouds still grace the sky to the west. They are soft and yellow in color with a tinge of orange along the fluffy edges. Another part of the sky is pale red, somewhat pinkish. The sunset is calm, setting peacefully after the intensity of the day. The colors fade slowly. The clouds become a light orange with some red, and there is a subtle splash of lavender. These colors in turn yield to deeper blues.

My view of the landscape is shrinking, slowly closing in on my encampment. Gradually the reds and yellows fade completely. The glow from my fire reflects from the boulders of my shelter and the surrounding trees. The flickering of the fire seems to make shadows dance among the trees. Up above the first stars are showing.

With time, my fire burns down to glowing embers. Darkness surrounds my camp, except for the glimmer of stars in the sky. I snuggle into my blankets for the night. Just beyond my shelter I hear the quiet steps of deer passing by on the trail.

◊   ◊◊◊   ◊

Afterword
THE ART OF NOTHING

Westerners who first met the Shoshonean bands of Indians in the Great Basin Desert typically described them as being "wretched and lazy". Many observers remarked that they lived in a total wasteland and yet seemed to do nothing to improve their situation. They built no houses or villages; they had few tools or possessions, almost no art, and they stored little food. It seemed that all they did was sit around and do nothing.

The Shoshone were true hunter-gatherers. They spent their lives walking from one food source to another. The reason they did not build houses was because houses were useless to them in their nomadic lifestyle. Everything they owned they carried on their backs from place to place. They did not manufacture a lot of tools or possessions or art, because it would have been a burden to carry.

We often expect that such primitive cultures as the Shoshone must have worked all the time just to stay alive, but in actuality these were usually very leisured peoples. Anthropological studies in different parts of the world indicate that nomadic hunter-gatherer societies typically worked only two or three hours per day for their subsistence. Like the deer and other creatures of the wild, hunter-gatherer peoples have nothing more to do than to wander and eat.

The Shoshone had a lot of time on their hands only because they produced almost no material culture. They were not being lazy; they were just being economical. Sitting around doing nothing for hours on end helped to conserve precious calories of energy, so they would not have to harvest so many calories each day to feed themselves.

A true hunter-gatherer!

Today many of us westerners find ourselves fascinated with these simple cultures, and a few of us really dive into it to reproduce or recreate the primitive lifestyle. In our typical western zeal we get right into it and produce, produce, produce. We work ambitiously to learn each primitive craft, and we produce all kinds of primitive clothing, tools, containers, art, and just plain stuff. True hunter-gatherer cultures carried all their possessions on their backs, but us modern primitives soon find that we need a pickup truck just to move camp! In our effort to recreate the primitive lifestyle we find that we have ironically missed our mark completely—that we have made many primitive things, but that we have not begun to grasp the true nature of a primitive culture. To truly grasp that essence requires that we let go, and begin to understand the *art of doing nothing*.

Understanding the art of nothing is a somewhat challenging concept for us westerners. When we go on a "primitive" camping trip, we take our western preconceptions with us. We find a level spot in a meadow to build our shelter, and if a site is not level then we make it so. Then we gather materials and start from scratch, building the walls and roof of a shelter. We do what we are accustomed to; we build a frame house on a surveyed plot in the meadow. Then we gather materials and shingle our shelter, regardless of whether or not there is a cloud in the sky, or whether or not it has rained at all in a month.

Part of the reason we act this way stems from our cultural upbringing. Another part of it is simply because it is easier for those of us who are instructors to teach something rather than to teach nothing. It is much easier to teach how to make something than to teach how not to need to make anything. The do-something approach to primitive skills is to make everything you need, while the do-nothing method is to find everything.

For example, the do-nothing method of shelter is to find shelter, rather than to build it. Two hours spent searching for a partial shelter that can be improved upon can easily save you two hours of hard-working construction time, and you will usually get a better shelter this way. More so, the do-nothing method of shelter is to look first at the incoming weather, and to build only what is needed. If it is not going to rain then you may be able to do-nothing to rainproof your shelter. Then perhaps you will only need to put your efforts into a shelter that will keep you warm, instead of both warm and dry.

There are many things, both small and large, that a person can do, or not do, to better the art of doing nothing. This can be as simple as cupping one's hands to drink from the stream instead of making and carrying a cup, to breaking sticks to find a sharpened point, rather than using a knife to methodically carve out a digging stick. Hand carved wooden spoons and forks are do-something utensils that you have to manufacture, carry, and worse—you have to clean them. But chopsticks (twigs) are do-nothing utensils that do not need to be manufactured or carried, and you can toss them in the fire when you are done.

Henry David Thoreau wrote of having a rock for a paperweight at his cabin by Walden pond. He threw it out when he discovered he had to dust it. This is the very essence of a do-nothing attitude.

The do-nothing approach to primitive skills is something that you do. Doing nothing is a way of saving time and energy, so that you can finish your daily work more effectively. One thing that I have found through the years of experimental research into primitive skills is that there is rarely enough hours in a day to complete all of a day's tasks. It is difficult to go out and build a shelter, make a working bowdrill set, set traps, dig roots, make bowls and spoons, and cook dinner. Hunter-gatherer societies succeeded in working only two to three hours per day, yet in our efforts to reproduce their lifestyle we end up working all day.

Doing nothing is an approach to research; it is a way of thinking and doing. For instance, I do a lot of timed studies of various primitive skills: i.e.: how long does it take to construct a particular shelter? How much of a particular food resource can I harvest per hour? Can I increase the harvest using different gathering techniques? One thing I have noted is that it is only marginally economical to manufacture common primitive deadfall traps. It is time intensive; it adds weight to carry, and the traps often have short life spans. The do-nothing alternative is to use whatever is at hand, to pick up sticks and assemble them into a trap, without even using a knife. Preliminary tests of this "no-method" have produced results equal to conventional, carved and manufactured traps, but with a much smaller investment of time.

Primitive hunter-gatherer type cultures were very good at doing nothing. Exactly how well they did this is difficult to determine, however, because doing nothing leaves nothing behind for the archaeological record. Every time we find an artifact we have documentation of something they did; yet the most important part of their skills may have been what they did not, and there is no way to discover what that was by studying what they did.

At home in the wilderness...

Nevertheless, what you will discover for yourself, as you learn the art of doing nothing is that you are much more at home in the wilderness. No longer will you be so dependent on a lot of tools and gadgets; no longer will you need to shape the elements of nature to fit our western definitions. You will find you need less and less, until one day you find you need nothing at all. Then you will have the time on your hands so that you can choose to do nothing, or even to go do something.

BIBLIOGRAPHY

_____. "1995 World-wide Gold Consumption." Down to Earth. The Montana Environmental Information Center. Volume XXIV. No. 3. August 1998. Page 2.

_____. Shelter Shelter Publications. Bolinas, California. 1973. Reprinted by Random House.

Baker, Dean. "*Giardia!*" National Wildlife. August/September 1985. Pg. 21.

Blankenship, Bart & Robin. Earthknack. Gibbs Smith Publisher: Layton, UT. 1996.

Brown, Tom Jr. The Search. Berkley Books. New York, NY. March 1983.

Callahan, Errett, "*The Medicine Bow Indian Wickiups*". Bulletin of Primitive Technology. Vol. 1, No. 5. Spring 1993. Pg. 74.

Campbell, Paul D. Survival Skills of Native California. Gibbs Smith Publisher. Layton, UT. 1999.

Conniff, Richard. "*RAP: on the fast track in Ecuador's tropical forests*". Smithsonian. June, 1991. Pg. 38-39.

Duke, James A. Handbook of Edible Weeds. CRC Press: Boca Raton, Ann Arbor, London, Tokyo. 1992.

Edholm, Steven & Tamara Wilder. Wet-Scrape Braintanned Bucskin. Paleotechnic: Boonville, CA. 1997.

Fukuoka, Masanobu. The Natural Way of Farming. Japan Publications, Inc. Tokyo & New York. 1985.

Gibby, Evard H. How To Make Primitive Pottery. Eagle's View Publishing: Liberty, UT. 1994.

Graves, Richard. Bushcraft. Warner Books: New York, NY. March 1978.

Greater Yellowstone Coalition. An Environmental Profile of the Greater Yellowstone Ecosystem. GYC: Bozeman, MT. 1991.

Haines, Joan. "*Hantavirus is here to stay*". Bozeman Daily Chronicle. January 4, 1994. Pg. 7.

Hall, Alan. The Wild Food Trailguide. Holt, Rinehart, & Winston: New York. 1973, 1976.

Hamm, Jim. Bows & Arrows of the Native Americans. Bois d'Arc Press: Azle, Texas. 1989.

Harrington, H.D. Edible Native Plants of the Rocky Mountains. University of New Mexico Press. 1967.

Hart, Jeff. Montana: Native Plantsand Early Peoples. Montana Historical Society Press: Helena, MT. 1976, 1992.

Harris, Marvin. The Sacred Cow and the Abominable Pig, Simon & Schuster, Inc. New York, NY. 1985.

Hyde, Nina. "*Wool: Fabric of History.*" National Geographic. May 1988. Pgs. 552-591.

Jackson, Wes. New Roots for Agriculture. University of Nebraska Press: Lincoln, Nebraska. 1985.

Jamison, Richard Primitive Outdoor Skills. Horizon Publishers: Bountiful, UT. 1985.

Jamison, Richard & Linda. Woodsmoke: Collected Writings on Ancient Skills. Horizon Publishers: Bountiful, UT. 1994.

Jerome. John L Fourteen Thousand Feet: A History of the Naming and Early Ascents of the High Colorado Peaks, Published by the Colorado Mountain Club, 1931.

Johnson, Phillip. "*Learning the Language of a Stream*", National Wildlife, Vol. 24. August-Sept. 1986. Pgs. 30-35.

Keegan, Barry. "*Fast, Survival Bow Drill Strings*". Wilderness Way. Volume 4, Issue 2. Pages 34-48.

Kingsbury, Lawrence A. "*Shoshoneans used to Occupy Area*" Southwest Montana Tourism 1986, pg. C5.

Klein, Robyn, "*Attacking Heart Problems*", The Montana Pioneer, September 1994.

Kochanski, Mors. Bush Craft. Lone Pine Publishing: Redmond, WA. Expanded Edition. 1998. Pgs. 12-28.

Laubin, Reginald & Gladys. The Indian Tipi: Its History, Construction, and Use, University of Oklahoma Press, Norman, Oklahoma. 1957, 1984.

Lee, Richard B. The Dobe !Kung, Holt, Rinehart and Winston, Inc. 1979.

Lust. John, N.D., D.B.M. The Herb Book. Bantam Books: New York. 1974. 16th printing: 1983.

Moore, Michael. Medicinal Plants of the Desert and Canyon West. Museum of NM Press: Sante Fe, NM 1989.

Moulton, Gary E., editor. The Journals of the Lewis and Clark Expedition. Vol. 5 July 28-November 1 1805. Lincoln and London: University of Nebraska Press, 1988.

MT Dept. of Health and Environmental Sciences, "Giardia", Pg. 3.

Nyerges, Christopher. "Purifying Water." Survival Advisory. March 1982. Page 35.

Rabkin, Richard, M.D. "The Indian Rope Trick: The Cultural Creation of Reality." Whole Earth Review, Sausalito, CA. Summer 1987. Pgs. 63-65.

Richards, Matt. Deerskins into Buckskins. Backcountry Publishing. 1997. Pgs 15-19.

Riggs, Jim. Blue Mountain Buckskin. Jim Riggs. Second Edition. 1982.

Rocky Mountain Institute. *"Practical Home Energy Savings."* <u>Newletter</u>, Vol. 7, No. 1, Spring 1991. Pg. 12.

Rocky Mountain Institute. *"RMI's Approach to Market Ju-Jitsu."* <u>Newsletter</u>, Vol. 8, No. 3, Fall/Winter 1992.

Rohr, Dixon. *"Too Much, Too Fast."* <u>Newsweek</u>, June 1, 1992. Pg. 34.

Savory, Allan. <u>Holistic Resource Management</u>. Island Press: Covelo, CA. 1988.

Sturtevant, Dr. E. Lewis. <u>Sturtevant's Edible Plants of the World</u>. Dover Publications:New York. 1972.

Tompkins, Peter & Christopher Bird. <u>The Secret Life of Plants</u>. Harper & Row Publishers. 1973.

Waldman, Carl. <u>Atlas of the North American Indian</u>. Facts on File Publications: New York, NY. 1985.

Wheat, Margaret M. <u>Survival Arts of the Primitive Paiutes</u>. University of Nevada Press. Reno, NV. 1967.

Webster, Guy. *"Crawdads colonize the West's waterways."* <u>High Country News</u>. June 19, 2000. Pg. 3

Wescott, David (Edited by) <u>Primitive Technology: A book of Earth Skills</u>. From the Society of Primitive Technology. Gibbs Smith Publisher. Layton, UT. 1999.

Wescott, David (Edited by) <u>Primitive Technology II: Ancestral Skills</u>. From the Society of Primitive Technology. Gibbs Smith Publisher. Layton, UT. 2001.

Willer, James, Ed.D. *"Primitive Fishing: A Wonderful Workshop."* <u>Bulletin of Primitive Technology</u>. Fall 2001. No. 22. Pages 90-91.

Winters, Kathy, *"Hantavirus: What is it and what can be done about it?"* <u>MONTGUIDE</u>. Montana State University Extension Service phamplet MT 9404.

Index

—Botany in a Day—

Thomas J. Elpel's Herbal Field Guide to Plant Families

Botany in a Day is changing the way people learn about plants! Tom's book has gained a nationwide audience almost exclusively by word-of-mouth. It is now used as a text and recommended by herbal and wilderness schools, individuals and universities across North America.

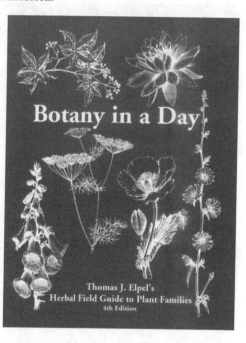

Too often people try to learn plants one-at-a-time, without rhyme or reason. But now you can cut years off the process of learning about plants and their uses. Learn how related plants have similar features for identification. Discover how they often have similar properties and similar uses. Instead of presenting individual plants, *Botany in a Day* unveils the patterns of identification and uses among related plants, giving you simple tools to rapidly unlock the mysteries of the new species you encounter throughout the continent. Tom's book takes you beyond the details towards a greater understanding of the patterns among plants. You will discover that you can learn plants by the dozens—just by looking for patterns.

Most plant books cover only one or two hundred species. *Botany in a Day* includes more than 100 plant families and over 700 genera—applicable to many thousands of species. Understand the magic of patterns among plants, and the world will never look the same again! Exquisitely illustrated with some of the best plant drawings of a century ago.

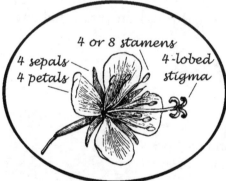

A typical flower of the
Evening Primrose Family

"Botany in a Day truly has the potential to become one of the most useful botany and herbal primers ever written."

—Peter Gail, Ph.D.
Goosefoot Acres Center for Resourceful Living. Cleveland, OH

"Botany in a Day has my highest recommendation for anyone beginner or expert interested in plants. Herbalists, naturalists, gardeners, and especially those involved in teaching outdoor and survival skills will wonder how they ever managed without this superb book."

—Susun S. Weed, Director
Wise Woman Center. Woodstock, NY

"Botany in a Day is exactly what I needed for my botany classes. It goes beyond what is available in the standard field key, providing a wealth of information on individual families. Now my students are able to key local flora confidently, knowing they have reached the correct family by referring to Botany in a Day's detailed descriptions and pictures. They can become truly acquainted with the family's characteristics, constituents, medicinal uses, and patterns. I personally love all the stories about the edible plants, which describe in delicious detail how long it takes to collect and prepare each one."

—Garima Fairfax
Rocky Mountain Center for Botanical Studies. Boulder, CO

HOPS Press - 12 Quartz Street - Pony, MT 59747-0697 - USA

—Living Homes—

Thomas J. Elpel's Field Guide to Integrated Design & Construction

The house of your Dreams does not have to be expensive. The key is all in the planning. How much a house costs, how it looks, how comfortable it is, how energy-efficient it

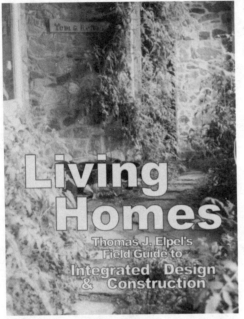

is—all these things occur on paper before you pick up even one tool. A little extra time in the planning process can save you tens of thousands of dollars in construction and maintenance. That is time well spent!

Living Homes takes you through the planning process to design an energy and resource efficient home that won't break the bank. Then, from the footings on up to the roof, author Thomas J. Elpel guides you through the nuts and bolts of construction for slipform stone masonry, tilt-up stone walls, log home construction, building with strawbales, making your own "terra tile" floors, windows & doors, solar water systems, masonry heaters, framing, plumbing, greywater, septic systems, swamp filters, painting and more! Living Homes includes an incredible 300+ photos and drawings.

Everything but the cover is **printed with soy ink on 100% post-consumer recycled paper, bleached without chlorine.** $1 from every book sold is donated to the *Institute for Solar Living* to support their work promoting sustainable living through inspirational environmental education.

—The Art of Slipform Stone Masonry—
Video Companion to *Living Homes*

Want to build a stone house? It's easier than you might think! *The Art of Slipform Stone Masonry* brings to life the nuts-and-bolts of the slipforming process featured in Tom's book *Living Homes*. In slipforming, forms on both sides of a wall serve as a guide for the stonework. The forms are filled with stone and concrete, then "slipped" up the walls to form the subsequent levels. Slipforming makes stonework easy even for the novice.

In this video, Tom builds an insulated workshop of stone, demonstrating the building process from site excavation right through to putting the roof on and finishing the inside. The video is designed as a companion to *Living Homes*. The principles of design and construction are out-lined in the book, enabling the reader to create dwellings customized to their own unique situations. In this video you will see just one application of those principles, but in vivid detail from start to finish. With both the book and the video you too will be able to design and build your own dream home. *The Art of Slipform Stone Masonry* is recorded on **certified quality recycled VHS tapes** for an environmentally friendly video!

Order on-line via our website at: www.hollowtop.com or call us at 406-685-3222.

—Direct Pointing to Real Wealth—
Thomas J. Elpel's Field Guide to Money

All living organisms consume energy, modify resources from the environment and produce waste. That is an inescapable fact of life. But in nature all material wastes are recycled as inputs to other living organisms. The only true waste is diffuse, low-grade heat.

In order to create a truly sustainable economy we must mimic the ecosystem so that the waste of every household and business becomes resource inputs to other enterprises, and the only waste produced is diffuse, low-grade heat from renewable resources like solar.

In *Direct Pointing to Real Wealth* author Thomas J. Elpel demonstrates that it is inevitable that we will create an ecologically sustainable economy. Tom turns conventional thinking on its head and out-lines steps you can take to increase your prosperity right now while closing the loop on waste and speeding the transition to a greener world.

Direct Pointing to Real Wealth is an enlightened look at the nature of money. Discover how the economy is like an ecosystem and how money is a token we use to represent calories of energy in the ecosystem. Tom's unique approach to money takes you beyond the numbers game to a direct examination of the laws of physics, biology, and economics. These laws are the same today as in the Stone Age, when people worked only a few hours per day and had much more leisure time than we do now.

Whether you are raising a family or running a business, Tom's book gives you a fresh new look at economics, ecology and how to achieve your Dreams. Break through perceived limitations to discover a world of prosperity and abundance!

"You have been a tremendous inspiration to us. Your books (<u>Participating in Nature</u> and <u>Direct Pointing to Real Wealth</u>) positively took ideas that had been running around in my head for years and tied them together for the foundation of my thinking. Without your books and ideas, I would still be trying to fit all my ideas and philosophies into one big picture. You've helped me get all those thoughts into goals, realistic goals, and I thank you."

—John Y. Wausau, Wisconsin

"For 24 years I have been helping to re-design perceptions and organizations, and I must say that your book is the absolute best economics teaching tool I have come across and believe me I have researched and experienced much."

—Peggy Z.
Progressive Input

Prosperity on an income of less than $15,000 a year? Tom and Renee Elpel prove that anyone can still live the American Dream— to own a quality home

HOPS Press - 12 Quartz Street - Pony, MT 59747-0697 - USA

The Art of Nothing Wilderness Survival Video Series
Video companions to *Participating in Nature*

Have you ever dreamed of being able to walk out into the woods to survive with nothing but the clothes you have on? You are not alone. In a society that is very disconnected from the natural world, many individuals find themselves wondering about what lies beyond the pavement. We know that our ancestors lived by their bare hands and wits alone, but how did they do it? How would you do it? What would it be like to be so connected with the natural world that you could just leave everything behind and walk away into the woods? It is easier than you might expect.

You might think you would need to take a lot of classes and learn a gazillion skills to survive, however, the real secret is in knowing how not to need very many skills at all. But, you won't get just a laboratory-style skills demonstration in these videos. Instead, Thomas J. Elpel and his special guests take you camping in the real world and connect the dots, demonstrating how each of these skills are applied together to meet your basic needs of shelter, fire, water, and plant and animal foods. Also included in the videos are wild mushrooms and unique tools and cooking techniques, plus great scenery and wildlife footage, so you really get a multi-dimensional sense of the skills and the place.

Each video takes place in a different setting in a different season, with Thomas J. Elpel and his guests demonstrating completely different skills to meet their basic needs. The *Art of Nothing Wilderness Survival Videos* are recorded on **certified quality recycled VHS tapes** for an environmentally friendly product!

Volume One: Three Days at the River—with nothing but our bare hands

No knife. No matches. No food, sleeping bags or other gear. Join Thomas J. Elpel and 13 year-old daughter Felicia for this extraordinary primitive camping experience in southwest Montana. In the cottonwoods along the Jefferson River they demonstrate all the skills required to meet their basic needs, starting with nothing but their bare hands. Skills include:

Shelter: Grass sleeping bag on hot ground.
Fire: The cottonwood root bowdrill set.
Water: Boiling water in found bottles and cans for purification.
Edible Plants: Cattail Roots, stinging nettles, rose hips, mustard greens and milkweed shoots.
Fungi: The edible tree mushroom.
Meat: Porcupine--killing, skinning, butchering.
Cooking: Shishkebabs and hot rock stir-fry.
Tools: Discoidal stone knives and digging sticks.
May 2002. 91 Minutes.

Volume Two: Mountain Meadows—camping with almost nothing but the dog

With little more than stone knives and the dog, Thomas J. Elpel and cousin Melvin Beattie venture into the Rocky Mountains to survive with whatever they can find and improvise from their surroundings. Among the wildflowers, wildlife and scenic meadows of southwestern Montana, they demonstrate all the skills needed to meet their basic needs, including:

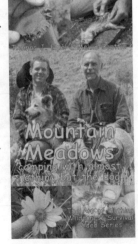

Shelter: A debris shelter with hot rocks.
Fire: The mullein on sage handdrill set.
Water: Purifying water with Aerobic Oxygen.
Edible Plants: Sweet cicely, wild sunflower, dwarf huckleberry, musk thistle stems and "artichokes", brook saxifrage, rose petals.
Meat: Ground squirrels--killing, skinning, butchering.
Cooking: Cooking on an upright rock slab.
Tools: Glass-knapped knives & the jo stick.
July 2002. 90 Minutes. **Look for these and more videos on our website!**

Order on-line via our website at: <u>www.hollowtop.com</u> *or call us at 406-685-3222.*